PUBLICATIONS

OF THE

NAVY RECORDS SOCIETY

VOL. 143

LETTERS AND PAPERS OF
PROFESSOR SIR JOHN KNOX LAUGHTON,
1830–1915

The NAVY RECORDS SOCIETY was established in 1893 for the purpose of printing unpublished manuscripts and rare works of naval interest. The Society is open to all who are interested in naval history, and any person wishing to become a member should apply to the Hon. Secretary, Department of War Studies, King's College London, Strand, London WC2R 2LS. The annual subscription is £30, which entitles the member to receive one free copy of each work issued by the Society in that year, and to buy earlier issues at much reduced prices.

———————————

SUBSCRIPTIONS and orders for back volumes should be sent to the Membership Secretary, 5 Goodwood Close, Midhurst, West Sussex GU29 9JG.

———————————

THE COUNCIL OF THE NAVY RECORDS SOCIETY wish it to be clearly understood that they are not answerable for any opinions and observations which may appear in the Society's publications. For these the editors of the several works are entirely responsible.

Frontispiece: Sir John Knox Laughton, 1830–1915, as Professor of Modern History, King's College, London. Reproduced with permission of King's College Archive.

LETTERS AND PAPERS OF PROFESSOR SIR JOHN KNOX LAUGHTON, 1830–1915

Edited by

ANDREW LAMBERT M.A., Ph.D., F.R.Hist.S.

PUBLISHED BY ASHGATE
FOR THE NAVY RECORDS SOCIETY
2002

Published by
Ashgate Publishing Limited
Gower House
Croft Road
Aldershot
Hants GU11 3HR
England

Ashgate Publishing Company
131 Main Street
Burlington, Vermont 05401-5600 USA

Ashgate website: http://www.ashgate.com

British Library Cataloguing in Publication Data

Laughton, John Knox, 1830–1915
  Letters and papers of Professor Sir John Knox Laughton,
  1830–1915. – (Publications of the Navy Records Society;
  no. 143)
  1. Laughton, John Knox, 1830–1915   2. Great Britain. Royal Navy – History
  3. Naval historians – Great Britain – Correspondence   4. Great Britain – History,
  Naval – 19th century   5. Great Britain – History, Naval – 20th century
  I. Title   II. Lambert, Andrew D.   III. Navy Records Society
  941'.081'092

Library of Congress Cataloging-in-Publication Data

Laughton, John Knox, 1830–1915.
    Letters and papers of Professor Sir John Knox Laughton, 1830–1915 / edited by
    Andrew D. Lambert.
        p. cm. -- (Navy Records Society publications)
    Includes bibliographical references.
    ISBN 0-7546-0822-0 (alk. paper)
        1. Laughton, John Knox, 1830–1915 – Correspondence. 2. Great Britain –
    History, Naval – Historiography. 3. Naval historians – Great Britain –
    Correspondence. 4. History, teachers – Great Britain – Correspondence.
    5. Historians – Great Britain – Correspondence.
    I. Lambert, Andrew D. II. Title. III. Publications of the Navy Records Society.

    DA70 .A1 2002
    [DA3.L38]
    941.08'092–dc21

                                                                        2001053583

ISBN 0 7546 0822 0

Printed on acid-free paper

Typeset in Times by Manton Typesetters, Louth, Lincolnshire and printed in Great Britain by MPG Books Ltd, Bodmin, Cornwall.

This volume is dedicated to the memory of Bryan Maclean Ranft (1917–2001), Professor of Naval History at the Royal Naval College, and at King's College London. A scholar, gentleman and friend.

CONTENTS

PREFACE

This volume of correspondence and related materials is drawn from a wide variety of sources. It reflects the broad range of Laughton's interests, and the width of his correspondence. The main body of surviving Laughton MSS was deposited at the National Maritime Museum, Greenwich, England in 1979, by his grandson. They remained uncatalogued and unsorted as MS79/067 until 2001. They are now catalogued under the call mark LGH, divided into 57 separate files, and contained in nine boxes, under which system they have been referred to in this volume. Folio numbers have been added to individual items where appropriate.

The collection originally comprised six boxes, one of which was occupied by the subject of flags – a subject that I have not addressed in this volume. Another contained letters from Mahan, all of which have been reproduced here. The other four contained what can only have been a sample of Laughton's incoming correspondence, together with draft lecture notes and other memoranda. There is also a separate collection consisting of Laughton's notebooks, filed under his name in the existing MS catalogue. These were deposited in the 1950s by his son Leonard Carr Laughton, who had used them extensively. No material from this source has been used here.

In addition to the Laughton archive a wide range of related collections have supplied letters. At Greenwich the files of Cyprian A.G. Bridge, William Laird Clowes, Julian S. Corbett, Reginald N. Custance, Geoffrey T. P. Hornby, Gerard H.U. Noel, Herbert W. Richmond and Charles Napier Robinson all yielded important material. In addition the archive of the Navy Records Society is held on deposit at the Museum. The early minute books contain much information on the nature of Laughton's work, a few pieces of correspondence and memoranda.

Laughton's service record and correspondence as a Lecturer at the Royal Naval College is contained in the Admiralty collection at the Public Record Office, Kew. The archive of King's College, London contains a Laughton file which relates to his appointment in 1885, together with other correspondence relating to his work at the College. The Naval Historical Branch, Whitehall, has a collection of his pamphlets, which were bound by his friend the Admiralty Librarian W.G.

Perrin in 1916. At King's College, Cambridge, the Oscar Browning and College MS provided important additional material. The Bodleian Library, Oxford, holds the Sidney Lee MSS (including material belonging to Leslie Stephen) which explained Laughton's role with the *Dictionary of National Biography*. The University of London Paleography Room at Senate House holds the papers of the distinguished historians Sir John Seeley and Albert Frederick Pollard. In the British Library, Manuscript Division, the Althorp MSS, in particular the papers of the 5th Earl Spencer, were of particular importance. At the Royal Geographical Society, London the Society archives, and minute books, together with the papers and manuscript journals of Sir Clements Markham were of interest.

Further afield important Laughton material was drawn from the library of the Royal Military College, Kingston, Ontario, which holds Laughton's personal bound collection of his articles, in three volumes. The Library of Congress, Washington DC, holds the papers of Alfred Thayer Mahan and Stephen Bleecker Luce. Additional Luce material was provided by the library of the United States Naval War College, through the assistance of Professor John Hattendorf.

All items printed here are identified by individual call marks, in accordance with Society practice. Where material has been drawn from collections other than the Laughton papers at the National Maritime Museum (LGH), the source and precise location have been identified.

The selection of letters and papers for this volume has been guided by a desire to reveal Laughton's intellectual life; what little is known of his private life is contained in my 1998 biography *The Foundations of Naval History*. All material has been produced in full, with the minimum of editorial intervention consistent with clarity. Where any excisions have been made they are indicated by an ellipsis , . . . , or [*brief details*] for longer passages. Where words in the original have proved impossible to read they have been marked [. . .]; where they remain uncertain they have been represented as [Naval?]. Editorial material has been restricted to footnotes. As many of these footnotes concern the titles of Laughton's published works these have been given in short form, with the full citation being provided in Appendix 3. Citations for other works are given in full the first time they are used.

ACKNOWLEDGEMENTS

I would like to take this opportunity to express my gratitude to all those who have helped this project reach fruition. At the National Maritime Museum Alan Giddings and Clive Powell proved indefatigable in responding to my queries, ensured the material was always to hand, and gave me the benefit of their expertise on the other collections. From his active retirement the late David Proctor recalled the arrival of the Laughton MSS at Greenwich back in 1979. At King's College, London, Patricia Methven shared her unrivalled knowledge of the College Archives; as did Andrew Tatham at the Royal Geographical Society. All of the record repositories I consulted provided the level and quality of support one has come to expect but should never take for granted.

My study of Laughton was fundamentally affected by the support of three scholars. My debt to them is larger than can be repaid in this format. The late Bryan Ranft once again encouraged my work, and provided invaluable advice on the three interlocking areas where his career overlapped with that of Sir John; this volume is dedicated to him. Don Schurman not only provided the starting point for this work, but gave me the benefit of his views and experience over the years. John Hattendorf contributed much from the perspective of the United States Naval War College, most notably on the careers of Stephen Luce and Alfred Mahan.

King's College provided financial support for a vital research visit to the United States, while my colleagues and students were kind enough to tolerate my interest. My student Robert Mullins, while researching his Ph.D. thesis on Anglo-American naval policy decisions in 1889 provided insights of considerable value.

In the final stage, that of converting the manuscript into a final published text, I had the inestimable benefit of support and guidance from the Society's General Editor, my friend and colleague Dr Roger Morriss. While the results bear witness to his efforts, and the exemplary standards he sets, any remaining omissions, errors and oversights are, as ever, entirely the responsibility of the editor.

Andrew Lambert
Kew
St George's Day 2001

LIST OF ABBREVIATIONS

BL	British Library
Bod	Bodleian Library, Oxford
C-in-C	Commander-in-Chief
DNB	*Dictionary of National Biography*
EHR	*English Historical Review*
FO	Foreign Office
HMS	Her Majesty's Ship (1837–1901); His Majesty's Ship (1901–52)
JKL	John Knox Laughton
JRUSI	*Journal of the Royal United Services Institute*
KCC	King's College, Cambridge
KCL	King's College, London
LoC	Library of Congress
NMM	National Maritime Museum
NRS	Navy Records Society
PRO	Public Record Office
RGS	Royal Geographical Society
RN	Royal Navy
RNC	Royal Naval College, at Greenwich from 1873
RO	[Public] Record Office: Laughton's abbreviation
RUL	Reading University Library
RUSI	Royal United Services Institute
SRG	Samuel Rawson Gardiner
UoL	University of London
USN	United States Navy
USNIP	*United States Naval Institute Proceedings*
USNWC	United States Naval War College

INTRODUCTION

From the dawn of historical writing naval history has been caught between the twin attractions of contemporary relevance, to serve modern navies, and the scholarly detachment of academic study. Between 1875 and 1915 Professor Sir John Knox Laughton spanned this divide to create the modern study of naval history, ensuring that it had an educational role in British Universities and Naval Colleges, as well as a central place in the development of naval tactics, doctrine and strategic thought.

John Knox Laughton was born on St George's Day, 23 April, 1830, in the major seaport of Liverpool. His father, once a privateer commander, had prospered as a wine merchant. Having benefited from an excellent school education, Laughton entered Caius College, Cambridge in 1848. Here he sat the Maths Tripos, a formidable examination demanding hard work and accuracy under sustained pressure, spread over eight days. Cambridge provided the defining experience of Laughton's life. The University gave him a service ethic that precluded any thought of returning to the commercial bustle of Liverpool, while the Maths Tripos taught him the value of sustained application, and speed of execution; how to master basic principles and to assemble evidence with real skill. That he graduated in 1852 with a Wrangler's degree (equivalent to a first class) is testimony to the power and endurance of his intellect. He would not know intellectual ease again until after the outbreak of the First World War, when failing eyesight and advanced age finally deprived him of the power to work.

Laughton entered the Royal Navy as an Instructor in 1853, and served afloat in the Baltic Campaigns of 1854 and 1855. He attracted attention for his outstanding pedagogic skills, and his courage under fire during the Second China War (1856–58). The midshipmen in his gunroom, perhaps the most brilliant collection ever assembled, included A.K. Wilson, Edward Seymour, Michael Culme-Seymour, Harry Rawson, William Kennedy and George King-Hall. All would reflect on the benefit they had acquired from their Instructor. In 1860 he met the then Lieutenant Cyprian Bridge, who became his closest friend, and greatest collaborator.

1

Considered one of the finest Instructors in the Service, Laughton was selected to come ashore in 1866 and teach at the Royal Naval College, Portsmouth. In this stimulating environment, working with the future leaders of the service, including the officers of HMS *Excellent* (the gunnery training ship), he devoted his efforts to examining the major contemporary issues. As a professional scientist and educator, he sought the underlying principles of the subjects he studied, and developed a sophisticated methodology to search for them. He began by writing important textbooks on oceanography and hydrographic surveying, but his major interest lay in the development of a modern naval doctrine to meet the altered conditions of the 1860s and an almost continuous technological revolution. While the introduction of iron armour and steam propulsion had persuaded the majority of commentators that the experience of the past was no longer relevant, Laughton recognised that this was wrong. He was the first to demonstrate the vital role of the past, accurately understood, as the basis for the development of contemporary naval thought and its underlying principles. As a key member of a short-lived, but impressive, naval intellectual movement of the early 1870s, Laughton responded to the clearly expressed needs of the officers he worked alongside. This period of work culminated in his *Essay on Naval Tactics*, published at Portsmouth in 1873. It was an exceptional, indeed epochal, contribution to contemporary debate in that it emphasised the role of history in the development of modern tactical thinking.

In 1873, the Naval College moved into the old Hospital complex at Greenwich, opening a new phase in Laughton's career. Now he had access to the wider audiences of London, and he exploited the opportunity, quickly becoming the College's official academic spokesman at the United Services Institution. It was here in 1874 that he delivered the Royal United Services Institution Lecture 'The Scientific Study of Naval History', which established history as the basis for doctrine development, secured a place for the subject in the Naval College curriculum, and encouraged further study. Like contemporary professional historians, Laughton considered the true value of history lay in the present and future. The methodology he had used to develop theories of atmospheric and oceanic circulation in the 1860s were applied with equal determination to naval history. Finding the existing published record episodic and lacking in scholarly rigour, he devoted his life to creating an accurate understanding of the past as the foundation for naval thought.

This volume does not contain any material from before 1875, a period that is covered in detail in my biography of Laughton, *The*

Foundations of Naval History.[1] In that period Laughton's ideas were widely circulated by leading journals, public and college lectures and, most effectively, in the *Edinburgh Review* to which he contributed more than 60 notices in 40 years. A powerful critic of alarmist polemics, partisan politics and inadequate history, his unsigned pieces made a major contribution to the intellectual life of the age. In them he developed his strategic thought and methodological ideas while exercising a majestic oversight of all work that touched on his interests. The audience for his lectures, articles and books included the entire officer corps of the Royal Navy, army officers, defence analysts and major American thinkers such as Admiral Stephen Luce and Captain Alfred T. Mahan. Laughton's work was critical to Admiral Luce's campaign to establish the US Naval War College in 1886, and the task he set Mahan. Both American officers were lifelong friends, and their correspondence provides a key insight into the naval intellectual world of the late nineteenth century. Laughton and Mahan worked together for two decades to advance the cause of naval education, strategic thought and history. They did so from a position of mutual respect; for Mahan always acknowledged Laughton to be 'the' historian, while Laughton deferred to his American friend as the pre-eminent analyst and strategic thinker of the age. The legacy of their relationship – the development of academically credible naval history as a vital element in naval education and strategic thought – remains central to the aims and methods of naval history to this day.

Reduced from the Naval College in 1885, Laughton secured the appointment of Professor of Modern History at King's College London, in succession to his close friend and academic exemplar Samuel Rawson Gardiner. Here he made a significant contribution to the professionalisation of English history. At the same time he wrote more than 900 lives for the *Dictionary of National Biography* – virtually the entire naval component. This work placed naval history before the widest audience, demonstrating that its leading figures were men of national importance.

As the most eminent naval intellectual, spanning the service and academic communities, Laughton exploited the popular navalism of the early 1890s. He took the lead in the foundation of the Navy Records Society in 1893 to publish edited archival material. The core membership, almost all of whom were personal friends, comprised naval and military officers, statesmen, journalists, and professional and amateur

---

[1] A. Lambert, *The Foundations of Naval History. John Knox Laughton, The Royal Navy and the Historical Profession* (Chatham Publishing, London, 1998).

historians. The Society operated as an unofficial historical section for the Naval Intelligence Department, then headed by his lifelong friend and co-founder of the Records Society, Admiral Sir Cyprian Bridge. The principal role of the Society was to provide the edited materials from which the service could develop doctrine and strategy. This connection continued through Laughton's personal relationship with successive Directors, from the prickly Reginald Custance to the urbane Prince Louis of Battenberg – an institutional link that saw almost all Directors and Deputy Directors on the Council of the Record Society. From the outset, the publishing programme of the Society was dominated by the needs of the service as interpreted by the Naval Intelligence Department, and it undoubtedly contributed a vital element to pre-war naval thinking. At the same time, Laughton's insistence that the work be conducted according to the best academic practice secured the support of his fellow professionals for this vital national task.

Through the Records Society, Laughton recruited a number of important scholars to work on the naval past. The most notable among them, Sir Julian Corbett, would continue his work, and deepen the process of creating a historically based national strategy. Another notable recruit was Captain Herbert Richmond, who combined historical scholarship, always with contemporary relevance, with a career in the higher reaches of naval policy and education.

Such was Laughton's standing in the naval world by 1895 that when he asked Captain Lord Charles Beresford[1] to check an old flag at Chatham, where he was Captain Superintendent of the Steam Reserve, the noble lord was anxious to help.

> Please command me if any, any time I can be of the least use to you, in helping with your most grateful and national work. All that you are doing deserves the unbounded gratitude and sympathy of our people. I wish your books were placed in all schools and the pupils made to study them, so as to instruct and let our people see how we happened at all to become a *nation*, very few know. The very best of good luck attend your efforts.
>
> PS As I live at Ham, I will do myself the pleasure of running over to see you, some day on my bicycle, when I can get home.[2]

---

[1]Lord Charles Beresford (1846–1919) Admiral and later 1st Baron Beresford. Leading naval reformer of the 1880s and 1890s; fell out with John Fisher in 1905–6, and from then on a severe critic of his reform programme.
G. Bennett, '*Charlie B*' (London 1968), pp. 191–5.
[2]Beresford to JKL 14.9.1895: LGH/54.

Suitably inspired, Beresford would write a popular life of Nelson two years later.[1]

By 1900 Laughton was universally recognised as a leading academic historian, and the principal exponent of his own branch of the modern discipline. Fellow historians, from Samuel Rawson Gardiner and Lord Acton to Charles Firth and Alfred Pollard, endorsed, supported and published his work. Laughton exploited his status. Recognising that his work would have to be continued on a more formal basis, he devoted the last decade of his life to the establishment of a department of naval history at King's College, within the new federal University of London. He hoped to educate naval historians in order that they might contribute to developments in the doctrine of the expanding Edwardian service. This project was widely supported, and led to the creation of a post in Imperial History at King's. But the department did not materialise, and the textbook Laughton was writing was incomplete at his death. Despite the efforts of Corbett, Richmond, Pollard and others, nothing came of the project, and to this day there is only one full-time post in a British University devoted to the study of naval history.

After his death in 1915 Laughton was largely neglected. Professor Schurman's excellent chapter in *The Education of a Navy: The Development of British Naval Thought 1867–1914* of 1965 was the first work to give Sir John due credit. Arthur J. Marder's 1940 study of the late-Victorian Navy ignored him, while recent work on the development of strategic thought has minimised his role, despite recognising that he laid the foundations for Mahan and Corbett in the 1870s. Ignorance of the central figure in the intellectual life of the service between 1870 to 1910 may account for the widespread belief that the Royal Navy was a colonial gunboat force unable to comprehend strategy and the operational level of war. My 1998 biography *'The Foundations of Naval History': Sir John Laughton, the Royal Navy and the Historical Profession* (Chatham Publishing) attempted to analyse his career. Much of that book was concerned with his astonishing published output, a critical element in the long-term development of the service mind. In a career that spanned the Crimean War and the First World War, Laughton advanced the use of naval history as a fundamental intellectual resource available to two great navies, inspired other strategic writers to follow his thinking, and at the end of his long life came close to rounding off his career by establishing naval history at the heart of the historical profession.

This volume focuses on the root of these achievements. This is the first time the Records Society has produced an edition of material

---

[1]*Nelson and his Times* (London 1897), written with H.W. Wilson (Bennett, p. 173).

dealing with an academic career, but it follows the usual pattern of 'naval' volumes in that it is concerned to show how the individual operated in his profession, to follow the stages of his career, to link him with patrons, friends and colleagues, to consider how he exerted influence and recruited followers, and assess how far he succeeded in the tasks he attempted. The correspondence printed in this volume sheds light on all these aspects of Laughton's professional life. He used it to develop his own understanding, to keep in contact with those at a distance, and advance his work. For a man who achieved so much through personal contact the letter was a key instrument. It is noteworthy that he corresponded far more with Mahan, who was an ocean away, than with Corbett, whom he met regularly in London and with whom he had a much closer working relationship. In consequence the reader should always be aware of the degree to which Laughton, ever a busy man, conducted his business by 'net-working' with those around him. This volume contains a representative selection of the surviving letters, but it cannot be representative of his wider human contacts. In addition the volume includes a few lecture notes and draft chapters from his last, incomplete, book. These give a flavour of his lectures, notably his critical role in creating 'Imperial' history to provide a proper context for naval history in London University. They reveal his hopes and ambitions at the end of an uncommonly long active career.

Ultimately this volume is an attempt to understand how Laughton thought and functioned. It stresses the contemporary influences at work, along with the professional and personal links that gave his effort direction and form. By placing Laughton at the heart of naval thought, it is possible to see how the civilians and the serving officers collaborated, why Mahan's books were so successful, and, critically, how the intellectual developments of the era influenced the Royal Navy. It is a contribution to the study of the Royal Navy, of the English historical profession and of the role of history in the creation of strategic thought.

'THE SCIENTIFIC STUDY OF NAVAL HISTORY', 1875–85

Laughton's archive does not contain any professional correspondence dating from before 1875, and the few private letters add nothing to our understanding of this period of his life. Laughton was a profoundly practical, systematic man. He does not appear to have done anything without a reason, and on that basis his actions have been treated as conscious, unless there is good evidence to the contrary. He began to retain incoming correspondence on a systematic basis in 1875, and this appears to reflect both his new found status as a leading authority on service education, meteorology, tactics and naval history, and the fact that the preserved correspondence was directly related to his writing and teaching.

Having moved to the new Royal Naval College at Greenwich in February 1873, Laughton quickly acquired a reputation as a public speaker. He became the unofficial College spokesman on academic subjects at the Royal United Services Institution (RUSI), where he was invariably supported by the first President of the College, Rear Admiral Sir Astley Cooper Key (1873–76).[1] His lecture on the need for a modern study of naval history, as the basis for tactical thought, doctrine, leadership and higher education, 'The Scientific Study of Naval History' given in 1874,[2] encouraged him to press the College authorities to fund a lecture programme. Although they were unwilling to meet his ambitious plans [4], he was able to provide a small annual lecture course. This course was the first formal, systematic attempt to use history as the basis for naval education. The range of his interests is revealed in his correspondence: searching for archival evidence [5]; discussing ancient galley warfare with an American naval officer and an Eton house master [7–10]; addressing the state of the contemporary Royal Navy, and particularly naval education, with Cyprian Bridge [6, 17]; investigating recent naval campaigns with William White and a Danish Naval Constructor [11–14]; joining the Council of the Royal Geographical Society [16]; and begin-

---

[1] Admiral Sir Astley Cooper Key (1821–88): Captain of HMS *Excellent* 1863–66, 1st Sea Lord 1879–85; see P.H. Colomb, *Memoirs of Sir A. Cooper Key* (London, 1898).
[2] *Journal of the Royal United Services Institute (JRUSI)*, **XVIII** (1874), pp. 508–27.

ning work on the *Dictionary of National Biography* [19–20]. In addition, Laughton found time to serve as President of the Meteorological Society in 1882, and secured for it the title of Royal.[1]

In 1875 Laughton began to correspond with Stephen B. Luce, a Captain, later Admiral, in the United States Navy [1–3].[2] The two men had met at the Royal United Services Institution in September 1870, and shared a wide range of 'naval' interests, ranging from sailors' songs and navigation to the role of history in the development of naval tactics and doctrine. Luce was a profoundly practical man, who devoted his immense energies to improving the training and education of American seamen and officers. His enduring legacies to his service, the United States Naval Institute and the United States Naval War College, reflected his appreciation of British practice, and the latter in particular was heavily influenced by Laughton's work. Through Luce, Laughton would influence the intellectual development of the United States Navy and its most famous officer.

Laughton's published work in this phase of his career was dominated by essays and reviews. In both formats he relied on his impressive historical knowledge, powerful logic and clarity of thought to analyse secondary literature and develop a coherent narrative that could be used to educate naval officers and inform the literate classes. The latter were addressed through his regular contribution to the *Edinburgh Review*. He had been introduced to this journal by his oldest friend, Cyprian Bridge, and he quickly became a regular contributor. His relationship with the editor, Henry Reeve, was so close that he was commissioned to write Reeve's biography.[3]

Laughton and Bridge were concerned by the increasingly 'theoretical' emphasis of junior officer education, Bridge being particularly outspoken on the subject [6]. Laughton's College lecture course, as with his earlier courses on meteorology and surveying, was published in a combination of mainstream and service journals, to make it available to a wider audience. The object was the advancement of education, rather than of knowledge. He attempted to strip away the layers of romantic fiction that had accumulated over most significant events in British naval history, with the intention of revealing the foundations of the subject so that it could be used to guide the work of the contemporary service. This phase

---

[1]His work in this field is noted in *Foundations*, but without access to the Society's archives his role remains uncertain. I have not attempted to follow this aspect of his career in this volume.

[2]Rear Admiral Stephen Bleecker Luce, USN (1827–1917).

[3]J.K. Laughton, *Memoirs of the Life and Correspondence of Henry Reeve* (London, 1898).

culminated in the publication of two teaching texts, *Letters and Des-patches of Horatio, Viscount Nelson* (1886) and *Studies in Naval History* (1887). The first of these had been developed with the College president, Admiral Sir Geoffrey Thomas Phipps Hornby, to give naval officers access to an outstanding example of intellectual development explicit in Nelson's career; the second reprinted the principal lectures of his college series. They completed the second phase of his work as a naval historian.

By the early 1880s, Laughton recognised that the only certain foundations of naval history were the primary sources housed in the Public Record Office. Here his close relationship with Admiral Key, now the First Sea Lord (1879–85), enabled him to gain general access to pre-1793 materials. He then worked to open the naval archives to all scholars, though the cut-off period never advanced beyond 1815 in his lifetime. Just as this work was reaching fruition, with work in hand for a new, Admiralty-endorsed history of the Royal Navy, which he had linked to the project to compile a *Dictionary of National Biography* [19], Laughton was removed from the College as part of an economy drive. At almost the same time his wife died, leaving him with four children of school age. He soon remarried, and the new family ultimately expanded to include five more children. Never a wealthy man – a reflection of his service ethic, commitment to the navy and his family – Laughton had to supplement his income. Consequently he did not simply retire in 1885, at the age of 55. He would continue to work for another thirty years, advancing the study of naval history to new and higher levels.

1. *Laughton to Captain Stephen Luce, USN*

RNC Greenwich, 9 July 1875

Dear Sir,
The order to Flag Officers & commanders to expect & enforce the claim emblematic of the Sovereignty of the Seas was cancelled by the Instructions which were officially issued on 1st Jan. 1807, but were signed 25th Jan. 1806: the delay being due to some details of accounts which had not received the sanction of the King in Council.

There was no Gazette, Royal Proclamation or published order in Council renouncing the claim; in the correspondence relative to the Treaty of Amiens our Government absolutely refused to relinquish it: (see Ross's Correspondence of Cornwallis vol. III p.430)[1] and a case of its being demanded occurred so late as August 1806.

---

[1] C. Ross (ed.), *The Correspondence of Marquis Cornwallis* (3 vols, London, 1859).

It thus was abolished merely by the issue of the new Instructions, in 1807; and the tradition in our service has always been that it was felt that a claim which was simply a nuisance, of no meaning in time of war & embarrassing in time of peace might be then honourably & gracefully given up. At the same time it is quite possible that the omission had been previously determined on. The Instructions of 1806–7 are more than twice the size of the previous edition of 1790, & the revision had been going on during 1805 & a great part of 1804. But on this point there is no evidence, & the actual fact is that the order remained in force till 1st Jan. 1807.

I have forwarded a paper partly on this subject, which I wrote only last year, & which may have some interest for you.[1] I have been on leave, or I would have acknowledged your letter sooner.

2.   *S. Luce to Laughton*

U.S. Navy Yard Boston Mass., Equipment Office, 26 July 1875

Dear Sir,

I have the honor to acknowledge the receipt of your kind favor of the 9th inst. and beg to express my thanks for it and for the paper on 'The Scientific Study of Naval History'.[2]

I note particularly what you say in regard to naval tactics, and agree with you fully in your views. In a very limited and unpretending way I have recently contributed two or three articles to an Encyclopaedia now in course of publication in New York, and one is on the subject of naval tactics, in which I had endeavoured to trace its history from the time it first grew into an art to the present. Limited as to space and time I fear it did not do justice to the subject, but such as it is I should be glad to send you a copy, merely to prove the truth of much what you have so well expressed on the subject.[3]

With regard to what you say on the general question of seamen, I forward herewith a paper read by me before our Naval Association in

---

[1]J.K. Laughton, 'The Sovereignty of the Sea', *The Fortnightly Review*, **V** (August, 1866), pp. 718–33.

[2]J.D. Hayes and J.B. Hattendorf, *The Writings of Stephen B. Luce* (Newport, RI, 1975), pp. 84, 91 and 177–8. Luce used this article in his own papers 'The Sovereignty of the Sea', *Potter's American Monthly* (November, 1876) pp. 345–63 and 'On the Study of Naval History (Grand Tactics)', *United States Naval Institute Proceedings (USNIP)*, **XIII** (1887), pp. 175–201, where JKL is quoted at length.

A. Gleaves, *The Life and Letters of Rear Admiral Stephen B. Luce USN* (New York, 1925).

[3]'Naval Signals' and 'Naval Tactics' from *Johnson's Cyclopedia* (New York, 1878).

which you will find I give your country credit for having the best system in the world for training man of war's men, and we have probably the worst.[1]

From the pamphlet I send, you will observe that we have been trying to get up something like the United Services Institution. But our officers are so few and so much scattered that it has been found difficult to get enough together for discussing professional questions.[2]

I would not mislead you in regard to my paper on tactics, it is simply a brief historical sketch exposing no opinions. It is now in the hands of the publishers; as I am struck off I shall take great pleasure in forwarding you a copy.

I observe in the pamphlet sent me a reference to your essay in naval tactics, published by the Junior Naval Association.[3] If in a convenient form for mailing I should be very glad to see a copy of it. I cannot altogether agree with some of the views put forward, in the *United Services Journal*, nor yet in the *Gun, Ram and Torpedo*.[4]

If your officers are adrift on the question of modern fleet tactics, what must be we – who never have any practical experience?

Thanking you again for your kind favor, I am:

3. *Laughton to S. Luce*

10 August 1875

I have to thank you very much for the vol. of the *Proceedings of the U.S. Naval Institute*, which I have just received. I shall be pleased to have the paper on Tactics of which you speak: as to my own essay on the subject to which reference was made in the paper I sent you, it is that which is published with *Gun, Ram & Torpedo*, which, I gather from your letter, you have already seen. I may in connection with this subject refer you to some papers of my own, in which I have endeavoured, however feebly, to carry out my idea of The Scientific Study of Naval History – De Suffren X in *Colburn's United Service Magazine* May & June 1867: Colbert X *St. Paul's Magazine* December 1868:

[1]S.B Luce, 'The Manning of the Navy', *USNIP*, **I** (January, 1874), pp.17–37.

[2]Luce was the prime mover in the foundation of the United States Naval Institute in 1873.

[3]The Junior Naval Professional Association, a short-lived but highly significant junior officer led naval intellectual group. JKL was an active member. See *Foundations* pp.40–44.

[4]However, Luce would make much use of Laughton's contribution to *Gun, Ram and Torpedo*. The three JNPA prize-winning essays are usually attributed to Gerard Noel, author of the first essay (see Hayes and Hattendorf, p.71).

DuQuense X *Fraser's Magazine* November 1874: & *Fraser's Mag.*[1] will also shortly have one on Lepanto, which is now in type.[2] I have also contributed one on Naval Archaeology which will shortly appear in *The Edinburgh Review*.[3] I see by the number of your *Proceedings*, that Com[modo]re Parker has been writing an essay on Lepanto.[4] I shall look forward with eagerness to its publication.

X [I] have seen, L[uce].

4.   *Laughton to Vice Admiral Edward Gennys Fanshawe CB,*
President of the Royal Naval College[5]

13 March 1876

The Director of Studies[6] having acquainted me with the purport of the letter from My Lords Commissioners of the Admiralty, dated February 24th 1876, proposing that I should deliver; each year, a course of lectures on Naval History; and have, as consideration therefore, an increase to my pay of £31.10.0 I would beg, very respectfully, to point out to you that this sum would be a very inadequate remuneration for the additional work which such a course of lectures, as I would wish to understand it, would necessarily entail upon me; and that, on pecuniary grounds, I should feel obliged, however reluctantly, to decline an appointment which it would otherwise be my ambition to hold; were it not that Dr. Hirst has explained to me that the course of lectures being limited to six, must and ought to be essentially the same, year after year, and that thus, the work of preparation will be comparatively light. With this understanding and limitation, my objection on the score of pressure of work and insufficient remuneration vanishes, and I would be perfectly willing to undertake the duty of the proposed lectures.

---

[1]These essays were all reprinted in J K Laughton, *Studies in Naval History* (London, 1887): 'Suffren', pp. 94–147; 'Colbert', pp. 30–58; 'Du Quense', pp. 59–93.

[2]'The Venetian Navy in the Sixteenth Century', *Fraser's Magazine*, **LXLII** (1875), pp.483–500 (not reprinted in *Studies*).

[3]'Lindsay's *Merchant Shipping*', *The Edinburgh Review*, **CXLIII** (1876), pp. 420–55.

[4]Commodore Foxhall Alexander Parker USN (1821–79); the leading American naval tactician of the Civil War and Post War era; he died while Commandant of the US Naval Academy. His essay was eventually published in his book *The Fleets of the World* (New York, 1876); Luce reviewed it in *USNIP*, **III** (1877), pp. 5–24.

[5]Admiral the Hon. Sir Edward Gennys Fanshawe, second President of the College (1876–78).

[6]Dr Thomas Archer Hirst (1830–92), Cambridge physicist, appointed first Director of Studies at Greenwich by First Lord George Goschen on the recommendation of Thomas Huxley. See A. Desmond, *Huxley: Evolution's High Priest* (London, 1997), p. 43.

I would, however, express a hope that this arrangement may prove to be only temporary; and that it will, before long, be found possible to extend the course beyond these limits; and in any case, I would wish to record my opinion that a rigidly fixed course of six lectures is altogether insufficient to answer the requirements of a subject so extensive, and of such direct professional interest and value, as Naval History; that in such a course many most important points must necessarily be left entirely unnoticed, and others be but barely mentioned; and that the repeating this omission, systematically, year after year, will be tantamount to removing them altogether from the cognizance of our younger officers:– for though, very evidently, the class of officers at the College is, each year, individually different, it is still so far the same that the individuals are thrown together in the closest intercourse; and the subject matter of this and other courses of the College instruction will, beyond doubt, be freely discussed; so that I conceive, lectures at the College are addressed not only to those actually present in the body, but, indirectly, to the whole service.

In this way, then, I think, that when circumstances will permit its fuller development, the yearly course of lectures on Naval History ought not to consist of less than ten; and that; with ten, it would be quite possible to attack the subject satisfactorily; varying the lectures each year in some essential particular. I would propose to base such a course of lectures on the six which will be delivered this year; being a general outline of naval history, as illustrating the science of naval war; and to expand some one or two of these, each year, so as to make the course include, in addition to the general outline, the detailed examination of some particular period.

The present course of six is arranged as follows:

I.   Ancient and Medieval war with galleys, in the Mediterranean; down to the battle of Lepanto.
II.   The origin and early organisation of western navies; and the history of medieval war in western seas; down to the death of Queen Elizabeth.
III. The development of navies in Europe during the 17th century; including the wars between England, Holland, France and Spain: down to the Treaty of Utrecht.
IV.   The wars of the 18th century, down to 1780.
V.   The War of American Independence, with more especial reference to the year 1782.

VI.   From the Peace of 1783 to the present time: including the War of the French Revolution.

To these I would wish to add, as occasional lectures:–

A.   Actions between frigates, single ships or small squadrons.
B.   Strategical value of cruising against the enemy's commerce.

Now, each of these lectures is capable of very considerable expansion, the course of ten, which I submitted, in the first instance, to Sir Cooper Key, last June, was constituted as follows:–

I	II	III	IV	V	A	B	VI
1	2	3,4	5	6	7	8	9,10

and other courses of ten could be arranged at pleasure, each year, and based on the original six, according to the following scheme:–

I	II	III	IV	V	A	B	VI
2	2	5	5	5	1½	1½	6

the numerals underneath the Roman characters denoting the number of lectures into which each of the original could, and should, be occasionally expanded. The complete course would thus consist of about 28 lectures, that number being still capable of increase, did experience show this to be desirable.

Such a course would, I think, properly and fairly represent the subject in the College curriculum: and it is such a course that I would wish to understand as the duty of the Lecturer on Naval History; but at the same time, it is a course which would bring on him a very considerable amount of work, and necessitate much laborious, and even expensive research; and would therefore, I conceive, render him entitled to a proportionate increase of pay.[1]

[*Endorsed*:] 14th March. For information and any observations E G Fanshawe
Director of Studies.
The full course of lectures [proposed here] must necessarily be of a tentative character. It may be desirable to transfer to this extended scheme here sketched on some future occasion.

T. Archer Hirst

---

[1]This letter followed one from the Admiralty to the President of the Naval College of 24 February 1876, reporting that the Treasury objected to making any extra payments for Laughton to provide the Naval History lectures. However, the Admiralty was prepared to add £31.10.0 to his salary for providing the course.

5.   *John Allan to Laughton*

Allan & Souter, Solicitors, Banff, 21 December 1876

I have your letter of the 18th. I shall be always delighted to assist you in the research you are engaged in and you need have no hesitation in asking my aid. I have referred to the Council Book for the year 1757 and particularly to October of that year, but regret to say I find no trace of Thurot.[1] Indeed there is no minute between Sept. 1757 & April 1758. I hope in the course of a few days to have time to look into some other books about this date & shall advise you of the results.

6.   *Commander Cyprian Bridge to Laughton*

HMS *Audacious*, Hong Kong, 1 February 1877

[fragment starts at p. 3]
I am going to make a hot attack upon views as to the College *curriculum*; so be prepared for the worst. The examination for Lieutenant, as at present established, is cruel, useless, and uncalled for, besides being highly injurious to the service. You know me well enough to know that I am not the man to disparage book learning, but rather to encourage its diffusion; I see in their mania for setting up theoretical tests (I mean tests in theoretical subjects) of merit in a profession, which is worse than useless if its members be not practical, the germs of incalculable damage to our naval pre-eminence. The system of examination is arranged in a lubberly way; you want to make all hands submit to the same enquiries; you ignore variety of taste, of disposition, of talent, of habit of mind. You say, the successful passer of X shall have the rewards of the service poured into his lap; the first rate seaman, the first rate gunner unless he be a first rate hand at work which very rarely, perhaps never, has been of use to a practical naval officer, or any other doing naval officers work, shall be of no account; a 1,1,3 is of no use, a 1,3,1 gains several months in promotion: the third term in the infernal expression being always the college work.[2] How are we poor devils who have, or have had the responsibility of taking Her Majesty's Ships about the world and disci-plining and training their crews got an ineradicable idea into our heads, from which all the professors on earth will not extract it by any process

---

[1]French privateer, Francis Thurot (see *Studies*, pp. 324–62).
[2]Bridge is referring to the enhanced promotion that was given to any sub lieutenant gaining first-class marks in the gunnery, navigation and seamanship examination. See R. Bacon, *Earl Jellicoe* (London, 1936), pp. 41–55 for this process.

of evolution known to man, that we want our officers to be seamen first,
then gunners, then perhaps engineers, then perhaps surveyors, and – no
one objects – Algebraists and arithmeticians about last of all? I should
say a good linguist is of infinitely more use in the Navy, and would find
his services more frequently required, than five senior wranglers. I want
to have the Senior Wranglers too: there is room even for these poor out-
casts in our Great Navy, but I do not want to have a service composed of
senior wranglers and failures to become such. Yet that is what the Professors (I use the term as being the most opprobrious I can think of) desire
to make of the young officers of the future. Of course you will say that to
call men who possess the <u>modicum</u> of mathematical learning possessed
by even a "three ones" Senior Wrangler is absurd, but I deny the absurd-
ity; I say that to get lads of 19 who left school at 13 and have been
perpetually at sea in the interval, learning many totally different things,
to pass an examination of the sort you set them so as to give themselves
any hope of future success in the service, is to expect quite as much –
nay! a deuced sight more – from them as from probable wranglers at
your old University.

The transcendent importance of getting first class at College now
puts every other idea out of a youngsters head. The knowing ones, the
unpleasant boys with unnaturally precocious prudences, with old heads
on young shoulders – I speak of the things I do know, and testify of that
which I have seen – just lay themselves out to learn as much as will pay
and leave the rest, such as their proper duty, to be learned by the well-
disposed lads who are only trying to make themselves sailors and good
officers. The impossibility of teaching a midshipman who is "going in
for a first at College", (the process has got its slang already, you see)
any part of an officer's or seaman's duty that cannot be learned by heart
out of a book like Nares' or Alston's[1] is fearfully disheartening to us
poor devils who are given up to the superstition that in the Navy we
want <u>practical</u> men in considerable numbers. The seaman-gunner who
knew all about "radius" did not prove very useful when the mainsail
had to be reefed in a gale of wind: and thank God the seaman-gunners
of to-day are put through a more practical course than he was. I have
had a pretty large experience of midshipmen, after 10 years service as a
second in command in both ranks, and as an instructor of youth, and I
am deeply grieved when I see who the future "lucky" men are.[2] Here
we have perhaps the best lot, certainly the most carefully selected lot of

---

[1] Admiral Sir George Strong Nares, Arctic explorer and author of the standard seamanship textbook. Alston was the other seamanship text of the day.

[2] This is very revealing; the generation Bridge is referring to included Jellicoe and
most of the senior commanders of 1914–18.

midshipmen in any ship. They were 20 in all; but some have passed. Now out of the lot about 5 are pretty sure of three ones. One is a first rate fellow, and is one of those rare people, very rare in my experience, who combines the practical turn with the faculty of succeeding in branches of theoretical learning. The other four (who will soon be Lieutenants, and God help their Captains!) are just worse than useless on a ship's deck. But, you say, how do they get their first class in seamanship? By learning it out of a book, say I; the confounded college examinations having impregnated all the others so that they are rapidly assimilating.

Now I will go farther than even the professors (to whom this time I will not give a capital initial) and say we do want Civil Engineers, Naval Architects, even naturalists, geologists and students of languages; there is room for all, and the greater diversity the better. Had sailors been able to make Keyham and Devonport yards they would certainly not have made them without a safe landing place for a boat during the prevailing winds. But we do not want our good practical men turned out of the service because they are not Isaac Newtons or Rowan Hamiltons.[1] The two best midshipmen I know are nearly sure to fail at the College 'till the service is quit of them, and much it will lose when they go. Some of the next best will only do poorly there. Now is this sensible – at least the united wisdom of our great universities declares it to be so:– have a simple test examination with a view to be passed not to be failed in; and then have honour examinations in your beloved mathematics, and also in other subjects, and let the <u>volunteers</u> (mark the word, I pray you) who choose to pass in them be rewarded – not by the ruin of their brother officers, which going over their heads really means – but by money prizes. If the College authorities ("authorities in education" they would like to be called I suppose, but they do not educate, they only torture) have persuaded the country to reward young X class let the country do it at its own expense and not at that of those who merely do their duty well and uphold the credit of the Navy.

No doubt your friend, the Superintendent of Police,[2] is quite right. He can, I will not dispute it, prognosticate the exact place in the pass lists of each sub-lieutenant by his own nocturnal pass-list of those who enter at the narrow gate which, like that leading to paradise, is only open in the evening. (The Peri – you will remember – stood disconsolate at the gate in the <u>morning</u>, it being shut). But what does he say of

[1]Sir William Rowan Hamilton (1805–65), Dublin-born mathematician, who was then considered to have made the most fundamental change in the study of mathematics since Newton, in a book of surpassing complexity.
[2]At the Naval College.

the chaps who will show men the way aloft in a gale, who will jump overboard at sea to save life, who will board an armed dhow with Arabs showing fight. I fancy they will not be found exclusively amongst those who burn the midnight gas *vice* Todhunter and Snowball.[1] If he is right, then it only shows that the College is harmless; that it weeds the service. But such a plan of weeding is infernally expensive. To pay £38,000 a year to weed out a few ill behaved sub-lieutenants is paying dear for a rake: why in China we will do the job for you at the trifling cost of a Judge Advocate's and Provost Marshal's fees. You say Captains lack the moral courage to do this dirty work. Believe me John, you are wrong. No Captain – remember I shall never be a Captain and am bitter – ever loses a chance of trying an Officer by Court Martial if there is a possibility of doing it. Even here where every one can do as he darn pleases, we do draw a line, and "screwing up" is not yet a lost art. The fault of the Service now is the tendency to trim young officers, not distinguishing between boyish freaks and the culture of wild oats and real viciousness.

The fact is, dear John, long residence ashore has corrupted you. We who serve at sea – I shall soon have no part or lot with them – suffer in every respect from the gentlemen who live at home at ease. Professors spoil our youngsters; Admiralty clerks bewilder us with circulars in gibberish which have no meaning; and young gunnery Lieutenants in the *Excellent* thrust upon us drill which is impractical in sea-going ships. I know you will say that at College Mathematics is not the only subject taught. Say it, and yet you will not refute us; for its importance overshadows all others. If you have had a heart hard enough to read as far as this, you will think me too great a bore. I hope I have not been abusive; but my treatment here has developed a fine capacity for swearing and I will not say that I have not occasionally used strong language; but I feel strongly, and even as I quit it, I hope to do some little good to a service in which I have wasted a life and ruined a career.[2]

We are to leave for Nagasaki about March 10th or 15th – it depends on the arrival of the Mail steamer – and go via the Inland Sea to Kobe and Yokohama. I will send you the Japanese things with pleasure. Japan

[1] Isaac Todhunter FRS (1820–84), wrote the standard textbooks on the key areas of mathematics used by the navy: *Algebra* (1865), *Integral Calculus* (1858), *Plane Trigonometry* (1859), *Spherical Trigonometry* (1859), *Mechanics* (1867), *Mensuration* (1869). J. E. Snowball, *Elements of Plane and Spherical Trigonometry*. (10th edition, London, 1863). These were the standard texts used for examination 'cramming'.

[2] Bridge was the Commander of the China Station Flagship, HMS *Audacious*, a second-class ironclad. The Admiral, Alfred Ryder, and his flag captain, Philip Colomb, were both important contributors to the intellectual revival of the service. Bridge's problems with them are unspecified.

is an enchanting country, but it is spoiled by Europeanisation; which the Japs call civilisation. You can tell Hildreth & Co[1] to transfer the amount to my credit when I send you the bill.

(Feb 6th.)

I heard yesterday by telegram of their Lordships approval of my application to be relieved. Parr,[2] I expect, will be my successor. Whoever is will have an easy time coming at this 11th hour. The thought of really leaving this odious ship has put me in better spirits than I have been in for months, though I am rather less well just at present than usual. It is not very long since I left a sick bed.

Give Mrs Laughton my very kind regards; and tell Master Leonard[3] to be prepared to stand an examination in recitation when we meet.

Yours very truly, as of old.[4]

7.   *Edmond Warre[5] to Laughton*

Eton, 3 August 1877

I hardly know how to apologise to you for having kept you so long without an answer, and without returning the paper of Capt. Luce which you sent me on May 11.[6] On three several occasions I have made the effort to answer (and the unfinished letters are by me) but I have been interrupted, and the grind of our mill is so incessant that it is hard to get time to do anything else but attend to it. My holidays begin today and I am now going into camp with my Volunteers at Medmenham, near Marlow.

If I can get an hour or two next Sunday to spare I [will] put together the memoranda I have made on the ancient signalling and send them to you.

I am the more interested in this question as I have lately invented a system of signalling myself, which I trust would do very well for the Navy. It is easier than the Morse, and very suitable to a semaphore. I

[1]G.J. Hildreth, 41 Charing Cross; Bridge's naval agent.

[2]Commander Alfred A.A. Parr RN, replaced Bridge with effect from 17 February 1877; a Commander of 1876.

[3]Leonard George Carr Laughton (1870–1956), the only son of Laughton's first marriage.

[4]Bridge's forebodings about the imminent end of his career were misplaced; he was promoted Captain in September 1877 and went on to serve in a variety of important posts afloat and ashore. See C.A.G. Bridge, *Some Recollections* (London, 1918).

[5]Edmond Warre (1837–1920), then a tutor at Eton, later Headmaster and Provost; an Oxford rowing blue and noted authority on galleys.

[6]This would be Luce's review of Parker's *Fleets of the World* in *USNIP*, **III** (1877), pp. 5–24.

have adapted flags, lanterns and electric instruments to it so that it can be used under most circumstances.

Should you be free and able to pay a visit at camp I would be very glad to receive you and would put you up, if you would not mind being *sub pellibus*.

With many apologies for my long delay.

8.   *E. Warre to Laughton*

18 August 1877

I seize the opportunity afforded by a wet day to fulfil my promise of writing to you respecting "Ancient Naval Signals". I hope that you received safely Capt. Luce's letter and the American Monthly Magazine. I am quite ashamed of having kept them so long.

I read Capt. Luce's paper with interest but notwithstanding the instances he produces am afraid that I must still adhere to my previously expressed opinion, that it is not possible for us now to discover the principle of the ancient codes. At the same time I cannot readily agree with the conclusion apparently arrived at in your letter "that it is doubtful whether the Greeks or Romans either had any notion of signalling for the guidance of large fleets beyond the most primitive". It seems to me that the evidence of Ancient authors is sufficient to establish the fact that signals were used for the purpose of manoeuvring. There are many passages, for instance in the *Strategemata* of Polybius, not to mention others scattered through the historians and poets which are I think conclusive upon this point. With regard to the famous passage in the *Tactica* of the Emperor Leo,[1] which Capt. Luce rightly notices as the 'locus classicus' on the subject, it should be remembered that Leo wrote as late as the ninth century AD, nearer to our times than those of Phormio, and if we are to believe Zosimus his *Dromons* were *biremes*, and the ancient triremes had been completely lost. Still he had no doubt access to ancient authorities on naval subjects and a living tradition upon such matters. Some of his directions addressed to the Admiral on the subject of signalling are worth quoting as shewing that the manoeuvring of a fleet by signal was familiar to him. He says Sec. 40 'You must have a signal placed in your dromon, whether pennant or burgee or something else, in a conspicuous place so that when you signal what is to be done the rest

---

[1]Byzantine Emperor Leo VI 'the Wise', lived between 865 and 911; author of the *Tactica*.

may at once understand the manoeuvre intended, whether to attack or to retreat, or to extend for the purpose of encircling the enemy, or to succour any portion of your fleet that may be in distress, or to slacken or to increase speed etc, etc, in all cases they must receive all signals from your flagship and take instructions as to how they are to act'. In Sec. 41 he gives reasons as to why signalling is necessary, the noise etc. preventing by means of sound being available. In Sec. 42 he enters into the detail of the methods of signalling by means of varied position, shape and colour of flags shewn and with regard to this last he makes the observation 'as formerly was the practice among the ancients'. In Sec.43 he directs that all the Captains of the Fleet are to be exercised in the Admiral's system so that they may be conversant with his code.

After comparing these passages with those of older writers I do not think that any other conclusion can be arrived at but that the ancients had systems of signalling by which fleets could be manoeuvred, probably by the use of different coloured flags, but that with the exception of the red battle flag, we do not know what the colours were or in what order or combination they were used.

There is surely no prima facie objection considering the civilisation to which they had attained, and the fact that they were far ahead of "primitive" methods in most things, to their having had as elaborate a code as we ourselves can boast of. Even barbarous tribes are known to have attained to a code of signalling. The Maoris, I am assured by a friend of mine, who was in the New Zealand War, had an elaborate system of flashing signals which they used at night. The code given by Polybius Book X [is] an elaborate system for signalling purposes by which words were spelt out, and it is hardly conceivable that such men as Phormio, Iphicrates & [Clabicas ?][1] in the command of large squadrons were unequal to the task of devising the means by which their orders could be communicated by signal to those under their command. It is indeed possible that each Admiral had his own method, and that there was no state code for each navy. The Emperor Leo's direction in Sec.43 rather points to this. The mention of preconcerted signals and their interpretation is frequent.

I am afraid that I must leave the matter here for the present. Perhaps wider and more careful reading may throw a clearer light upon it at some future time.

Can you by chance inform me if there is any authority for a statement which I find in a note in M. Joly de Mainzerot's edition of Leo's

---

[1]Noted ancient naval commanders.

Tactica[1] to the effect that to James II of England was owed the perfecting of the naval signals in use in the 18th century?

9.   *E. Warre to Laughton*

18 November 1877

I must seize on the "Dominical Letter" day at once in order to reply to your kind letter, for fear lest if it once fall into the 'by and bye' drawer, it remain as long unanswered as your last to me, which was even more than three months before, to use the American Capt's phrase, it could get the "oil from my journal".

I should indeed much like to have a talk with you over the many subjects in which I am sure we take a common interest, but until the 23rd of Dec'r I am a prisoner here and the whole holidays in prospect before that date are very few, and on those I fear that my Volunteer Corps will keep me employed.

I intend to be here however part of the Xmas holidays, and it would give me great pleasure if you could spare a couple of days and pay us a visit here. Will you let me know what time you will be free so that if possible we may arrange it ?

I should like to shew you a system of signalling that I have invented which I think would be useful at sea. It works with flags, lanterns and electric telegraph and is especially suited for semaphore. It is based on the ancient system indicated in Polybius, but simplified. I should like to ask you about Kempenfeldt,[2] if you know whether he has a twin brother who lived on the banks of the Thames in Berkshire. There is a legend about him which lends itself to a 'pretty conceit' as the Elizabethan writers would say, in verses.

I should enjoy much a visit to Greenwich and above all to be able to be present at your lectures. At present, however I do not see my way. I must manage it some time. I was in town yesterday and called at the United Service Institution & saw Sullivan, who told me that you are

---

[1]De Mainzerot's standard modern edition of the text, published in France in 1758, at a time when crediting James II with such developments would have been a popular, if not necessarily accurate claim. As Lord High Admiral, Commander-in-Chief and Fleet Commander James's contribution to the development of tactics was highly important. See B. Tunstall, *Naval Warfare in the Age of Sail*, ed. N. Tracy (London, 1990), pp. 20–50. For a discussion of Leo's text and the contemporary Byzantine navy, see A. Toynbee, *Constantine Porphrygenitus and his World* (Oxford, 1973), pp. 292–5 and 323–45.

[2]Rear Admiral Richard Kempenfelt (1718–82); a major influence on the development of British naval tactics and signalling; drowned when the *Royal George* sank (Tunstall, pp. 135–56).

often there on a Tuesday. Could you manage to come on & dine & sleep say Tuesday week? or the week after? I hope to go on with the ancient galleys after a while; but my signalling has exhausted my spare time this year. Hoping ere long to see you here.

10. *Laughton to S. Luce*

6 January 1878

I have to thank you very much for the papers on Tactics & Signals which you have been good enough to send me.[1] I have read them with a great deal of interest, & quite agree with most of what you say. I think (for instance) that you are right in your correction of Mr. Warre's account of Arginusa. Warre's paper on ancient galleys is undoubtedly clever, but he has pinned his faith too closely on Graser,[2] who is somewhat fanciful: I do not think anyone who knows what work in a hot climate is will believe that the ancient rowers could keep up for hours in a stifling box such as he describes.[3]

I have done myself the pleasure to send you a copy of the current number of *Fraser's Magazine* with an article by me on Thurot, an interesting episode in Naval History, though of course from an English point of view.[4]

11. *J. C. Tuxen[5] to Laughton*

Copenhagen, 4 May 1878

I have great pleasure in telling you the correct names of the ships you want, but no need however, as you have got them quite correct your-self.[6]

---

[1]Luce, 'The Fleets of the World', *USNIP*, **III** (1877), pp. 45–24; 'Signals and Signalling', *Potter's American Monthly*, **VIII** (1877), pp. 297–392; and 'Naval Signals' and 'Naval Tactics', *Johnson's Cyclopedia* (New York, 1878).

[2]B. Graser, *De veterum re navali* (Berlin, 1864).

[3]Modern research and experience with the reconstructed trireme suggests Warre was right.

[4]Laughton's paper, 'The Early Development of Naval War', was reprinted in two parts in *Colburn's United Service Magazine* in 1889.

[5]Tuxen, who had studied at Greenwich under the Naval Architect William White, went on to become Chief Constructor of the Royal Danish Navy. See F. Manning, *Life of Sir William White* (London, 1923), pp.351 and 379–80.

[6]Laughton was researching his biographical essay on Tegetthoff. This letter concerns the Battle of Helgoland between the Danish and Austrian fleets on 9 May 1864; see *Studies*.

Commanding the squadron was Com[modo]re E. Suenson

Niels Juel[1]	[Flagship]	Capt. Gottlieb
Jylland[2]		Capt. Holm
Heimdal[3]		Commander Lund

I shall be very happy to give you any other information you may desire and as I am at present appointed in the Dockyard, I shall stop at this address for a long time yet. In a few months a young brother officer of mine will go to London, to enter the College in October, and he is very well up in our Naval History.

P.S. The 9th this month we are going to launch in our dockyard, the largest ship we have ever built, her name is *Helgoland*,[4] in memory of the fight.

12.   *William White to Laughton*

Admiralty, 8 May 1878

On enquiry I find that the <u>tonnages</u> given in the Austrian official account of the battle of Lissa are the <u>displacement</u> in metrical tons. A metrical ton is 2204 lbs, as against 2240 lbs in an English ton: so the correction is scarcely worth making for your purpose. The *Affondatore*,[5] is an exceedingly narrow ship: hence her comparatively small displacement in proportion to her length.[6]

13.   *W. White to Laughton*

16 May 1878

Search has been made, but as the *Re d'Italia*[7] has disappeared from the Italian Navy List, I cannot send you her dimensions. I fancy you may find them in Admiral Paris's *L'Art Naval en 1867*.[8] You may take it as a mistake to say that she was a bigger ship than our *Prince*

---

[1] 1855 screw frigate, 2,300 tons, 42 guns.
[2] 1858 screw frigate, 2,300 tons, 42 guns, preserved in Denmark.
[3] 1856 screw corvette, 1,170 tons, 16 guns.
[4] Coast defence battleship of 5,300 tons.
[5] Italian warship, British-built turret ram, 4,300 tons, launched 1865.
[6] White taught at Greenwich between 1875 and 1885. He and Laughton were clearly on close terms. They would remain close until White's death (Manning pp. 59–76).
[7] Italian ironclad, American-built broadside ship, 5,800 tons, sunk at Lissa.
[8] François Edmond Paris (1806–93), French Vice Admiral and author; after 1871 he was Director of the Musée de la Marine.

Consort. The *Ferdinand Max*[1] was (or is) 270 feet long, 43 feet broad, about 23½ feet mean draught and 5,200 tons displacement. 5 inch armour.

I am sorry to be unable to help you more.

14.   *Captain Compton Domvile*[2] *to Laughton*

8 December [1878 ?]

Thank you very much for your slips; they are very interesting, I wish I could recall some personal trait of Tegethoff. I only remember him as a rather tall, fine looking man with light beard, rather English in his appearance and very fond of anything that was English and a great admirer of Sir Wm. Martin,[3] and I believe that his notice for drills etc. was always carried out in his squadron. If I can see old Admiral [M. or Mc ...] I dare say I may get out one or two stories about him, as he was a great deal with him during the time we were lying at Salamis.

15.   *Laughton to the Secretary, Royal Geographical Society*[4]

RNC, 3 March 1880

I enclose a nomination for Captain Fagan;[5] which I would ask you to put in train. Besides Capt. Church,[6] we do not seem to have a Fellow of the Society here just at present: but if you would fill up the vacant signature, I should be obliged.

---

[1]Austrian Flagship at Lissa, broadside ironclad, was 10 feet broader than White suggested.

[2]Admiral Sir Compton Domvile (1842–1924), then Captain of the RNC; ended his active career as C-in-C Mediterranean 1902–05.

[3]Admiral Sir William Fanshawe Martin (1801–95), C-in-C Mediterranean 1860–63 and pioneer of steam tactics. JKL served on the *Algiers* with Bridge under Martin's command.

[4]In 1880 this would have been Clements Markham or R.H. Major. The familiar references to the Naval College make Markham the more likely recipient.

[5]Captain Christopher Fagan Royal Marines, then a student at Greenwich.

[6]Captain Edmond J. Church (1878), then a student at Greenwich.

16.   *Laughton to Clements Markham*

28 April 1880

I have great pleasure in assenting to our President's wish, so flatter-ingly conveyed in your note of yesterday's date. If I can be of any use on the Council of the Society, I shall be happy to serve.[1]

I received the *Voyages of Davis* [2] yesterday; but was in doubt whether to thank you or your cousin for the very acceptable present. To me, as you are probably aware, all matters connected with naval history and archaeology have an especial interest; and this book cannot but be a valuable and suggestive addition to the literature of the subject.

17.   *Captain Cyprian Bridge to Laughton*

26 July 1880

I knew all along that you and I were really at one about the entering and training of naval officers. I was very much afraid that some expressions used by you would have led to your being ranked by the workers of mischief to the service amongst themselves. The mischief doing clique is an active and a vigilant one. The fact that more 'time' is given in the *Britannia* for mathematical learning than for seamanship, and that the lieutenant's commission prize really depends on the College Examina-tion must and do tend to lower seamanship – as a necessary qualification – in the eyes of youngsters. Only a few days ago an officer whose duty takes him aboard nearly every ship in the service told me that for some time past it had been evident to him that youngsters took but little interest in matters of seamanship and a great deal in those of 'scientific' matters, which it is only necessary that a limited number should be proficient in, and only possible that a few can be made so. The cause of course is the greater weight of the 'scientific' matters in the frequent examinations which our youngsters have to pass. My own experience as a first lieutenant and commander – second in duration I believe – to a very few, is that, with a few exceptions which undoubtedly are to be met with, the better a midshipman is at his book work the more useless

---

[1]In early 1880 the President was the Earl of Northbrook, First Lord of the Admiralty. His senior professional advisor was Cooper Key, Laughton's long-term patron. Clements Markham was then Secretary of the RGS; his cousin Albert Markham was a Captain in the RN and a famed Arctic explorer.

[2]The credit for *The Voyages and Works of John Davis the Navigator* belongs to Albert Markham. The volume was issued by the Hakluyt Society in 1878. It would appear from this letter that JKL was, rather surprisingly, not a member of that Society.

he is on deck. The reason no doubt is that the mental power of most boys being limited, only a few of them excel in several different branches of learning; and the more their thoughts are occupied with mathematics &c the less they can think of pure seamanship. You must remember that in the pre-Crimean period the delight of the youngsters was to run about aloft when permitted; I can assert that no-one goes aloft now unless he is sent or wants to verify an answer to an examination question as to rigging. How many youngsters were there when you first went to sea who were without a 'spike' or 'pricker'[1] as a constant companion, and in whose pocket was not to be found a bit of white-line or six thread stuff with a matthew walker[2] or a splice in more or less rudimentary state? How many are there now who would care to possess either? Of course knotting and splicing are not the whole of seamanship; but the state of things shows how the wind blows.

I quite agree with what you say, as to the deplorable ignorance of our naval youth, in spite of all that has been done for education within the last twenty years. There can be no question that foreigners e.g. Americans, are far better educated.[3] It is even more certain that nevertheless, our ships are in infinitely better order than those of any other navy; all foreigners will tell you the same, and in strong terms. This is, however, no reason why we should be ignorant. The vice of the present system of education is in the attempt – foredoomed to inevitable failure – to put every one through the same mill. Raise the age of entry, do away with all special schools like the *Britannia*; have a low compulsory 'book' test, and very high ones of the sort for those few who desire to submit to them, and who will be wanted for a limited number of special posts; keep your youngsters at sea as much as possible and when there let them do seaman's work; these things are wanted to improve the knowledge of our rising generation. I do trust that something will be done; the present state of things is really deplorable. I hope to leave town tomorrow or Wednesday.

18.   *C. Bridge to Laughton*

48 St. Aubyn Street, Devonport, 23 October 1881

I have been so 'driven' that it was literally impossible for me to avail myself of Mrs Laughton's kind invitation and run down for an evening's chat and farewell with you at Greenwich.

---

[1] A marlin spike.
[2] A stopper knot.
[3] Compare this with Luce's lament of 26 July 1875 [2].

You will now be aware that I was Morley's naval contributor.[1] I need hardly say that this is one of those dead secrets that I hope you will not even reveal in the confessional which you frequent. I have mentioned it to no-one.

The line I took was something like this: our navy is in splendid condition, there never was such a body of men as the present bluejackets, sifted thro' a dozen sieves and trained from boyhood; everybody is well drilled and in most respects fairly up to his work; no foreigner in matters of <u>personnel</u> comes near us; the weak points are the rotten educational system and the divorce between navy and the real reserve – the merchant service; the <u>materiel</u> is superior to that of all the world, but naval Architects are getting too much power and have been permitted to indulge in a kind of artistic rivalry with those of other countries in turning out 'triumphs of naval architecture', hence such awful mistakes as the *Inflexible*.[2] We are stronger and in a better state for war than any other power, and comparisons of the naval strength of France with ours – when made absolutely – are ridiculous, tho' France is gaining on us now. But no note has been taken of the enormous growth of our maritime interests and we are positively in a worse position than formerly considering what we have to defend.

The distribution of our forces is altogether obsolete, and so is the constitution of our distant squadrons. Our fleet is copied in every particular – as to <u>materiel</u> and <u>personnel</u> – by all nations; there is a remarkable exception to this – our armament. It is atrociously inefficient, and far below that of foreigners'. It will not be without interest to know that this is the one item provided by a department distinct from the Admiralty. My tongue was tied as to guns; you should speak out; the inefficiency (and not improbably the corruption) of the department of the War Office charged with the duty of supplying the navy with guns &c is appalling. No improvement is ever permitted unless they see that they cannot resist it; every recent amelioration of guns &c is due to the Admiralty's determination to insist on being heard. The Director of Artillery's department can beat Tom Pepper[3] into fits. The favourite lies are that the Navy prevented the introduction of breech-loaders and long guns; lies which I invariably contradicted when I heard them and based my contradiction on proofs.

[1]John Morley (1838–1923), then editor of the *Pall Mall Gazette* and later liberal statesman, Viscount Morley 1908, biographer of Cobden and Gladstone.

[2]British battleship, 11,800 tons, completed 1881; noted for her immense 16-inch muzzle-loading guns, and 22-inch thick iron armour; took part in the bombardment of Alexandria in 1882, commanded by John Fisher.

[3]C.F. Briggs, *The Trippings of Tom Pepper*: American satirical essay collection, published in serial form in 1848.

I have been converted to the view that Admiralty is the most efficient and (which can be proved by figures) most economical state department in existence.

You may be able to handle a point which I could only nibble at – the 'denavalisation' of Britain. The rise of the military as against the naval spirit is remarkable. You may have seen lately in the *United Services Gazetteer* an allusion to a little plot – under the late Ben Jingo – to put Portsmouth, &c under the Generals; this was very nearly done.

I have many of my contributions to the *Pall Mall* somewhere, if I can find them I will send them to you to read, but please let me have them again.

The following books may be of use

Die Marine
Das Schwimmende Flotten Material Marine Almanach
Carnet de l'officier des Marine
King's *Warships of the World*
Very's   "   "   "   "
Clode's *Military Forces of the Crown* (especially to see how the supply of Ordnance comes under the War Office).
Treatise on Construction of Ordnance (Official 1879)
Report of Naval Officers who witnessed Krupps' Experiments 1879
  "   *Military*   "   "   "

The two latter are blue books. I advise you to ask Orde-Browne[1] for a list of blue-books, but do not tell him you write on the subject. He is the gun man of *The Engineer* and – but for a strong bias in favour of Woolwich – writes well. Adm. Vesey-Hamilton[2] could – if he would – tell you a good many things, why not write to him without mentioning the *Pall Mall*? Our people are a good deal too much under the influence of Armstrong & Co.[3] who have done much good but are lagging behind now. The great man at Woolwich, Maitland[4] – is a mere pretender, but is thought a sage.

PS I am glad you are going to help Morley. You can often make a guinea whilst waiting for your wife to finish dressing.

[1]Captain Charles Orde-Browne, Royal Artillery.
[2]Admiral of the Fleet Sir Richard Vesey-Hamilton (1829–1912), later First Sea Lord, 1889–91.
[3]Armaments Company founded by William, later Lord Armstrong (1810–1900), after his development of rifled breech-loading cannon; see K. Warren, *Armstrongs of Elswick* (London, 1992).
[4]Major General Eardley R. Maitland (1833–1911); Director General of the Royal Gun Factory 1888–89; Superintendent 1880–88.

19. *Laughton to Leslie Stephen*[1]

10 November 1882

I have just seen in the *Times* the announcement of the Biographical Dictionary which you have undertaken. I think I may probably be of use to you in respect of Naval subjects, and would therefore offer you my services. I may say that for some years back I have been working up our Naval Records by special permission of the Admiralty with the view of bringing out a History of our Navy that may have some pretensions to accuracy and exactness.[2] In doing this I have accumulated a considerable mass of Biographical material, which probably no one except myself is acquainted with.

I should be glad to think that there was a chance of the memories of our naval worthies being cleared of some of the cobwebs of fiction; and the chance that it may be so leads me to trouble you with this note, and must be my apology for so doing.

20. *Laughton to L. Stephen*

9, Gloucester Place, Greenwich S. E.,[3] 24 December 1882

Your letter in yesterday's *Athenaeum*[4] leads me to repeat what I wrote to you some time ago; – that I have devoted a good deal of special study to <u>Naval</u> biography, and that I think I am in a position to render you effective service in this branch of your projected undertaking.

As you have already noted my offer do not trouble to answer this until your scheme assumes definite form; but if you want my assistance, I shall be glad to know your decision in good time.

---

[1]Leslie Stephen, editor and literary biographer; Founding Editor of the *Dictionary of National Biography*. See Lord Annan, *Leslie Stephen; the Godless Victorian* (London, 1984).

[2]A task that would be forever out of reach, as growing access to archival resources demanded ever greater effort.

[3]JKL's home while he worked at RNC Greenwich.

[4]A weekly Journal 'of English and Foreign Literature' founded in 1830; it changed to fortnightly in 1915; and ceased publication in 1921.

PROFESSOR OF MODERN HISTORY, 1885–90

After his enforced retirement in 1885, Laughton secured the post of Professor of Modern History at King's College, London, succeeding his friend Samuel Rawson Gardiner.[1] Although Gardiner was widely considered the leading professional historian in Britain, the post he had just resigned was not particularly prestigious. King's College occupied a peculiar position in the academic world, half-way between the public schools and the ancient Universities. It did not offer degrees, and was not part of the London University. Many of its students were being trained for religious or administrative careers, while others were passing between school and university.[2] The relatively modest demands the post made on Laughton's time were reflected in the very modest salary he drew, even when supplemented by additional payment for each student [34–5, 49]. Consequently his published output was large, but diffuse – a steady stream of paying articles and reviews, rather than the major texts that would more quickly have established his enduring fame [26]. However, the post placed him at the heart of the newly professional body of English historians. He would be a founder member of the *English Historical Review*, and a contributor to the work of the Royal Historical Society and the Camden Society. In all three enterprises he worked closely with Gardiner, who became a close friend as well as colleague [31]. He also discussed the subject with the Cambridge historian Oscar Browning [30, 47], Charles Yonge [36–7], Charles Hadfield Firth [54], then working for the *Dictionary of National Biography*, and John Robert Seeley [56–7].

The references Laughton secured to support his application were impressive [21a–i], but in the next five years his circle would widen to include the leading academic historians, senior naval officers and others who were drawn into his research. Many of the letters from this period relate to his ongoing labour for the *Dictionary of National*

---

[1]Samuel Rawson Gardiner (1829–1902); one of the leading academic historians of the period, best known for his pioneering studies of the early Stuart Monarchy and the Civil War.

[2]F.J.C. Hearnshaw, *The Centenary History of King's College, London* (London, 1929), p.381.

Biography [50–52, 54–5, 58].They show how he supplemented the available sources through family, professional and other personal contacts. He also continued to correspond with Luce. The two men were already discussing Mahan's work before it was published.[1]

However Laughton missed the Naval College, and his daily contact with the service. He would remain, at heart, a servant of the Royal Navy to the end of his life, using the academic community to enhance and expand his work. His links with the service leaders of the present and future remained vital; he discussed recent memoirs with Lord Alcester [32–3]; with Bridge he discussed history [38], the doctrine building role of education [40], his new book [44] and the recent manoeuvres [53]. He also kept in contact with his old friend Admiral Sir Geoffrey Phipps Hornby [58]. By contrast the Dean of St. Paul's, for all his literary attainments, had no idea why he wanted to look at some old flags [42–3], missing the quasi-religious significance of trophies.

One area where Laughton's naval/academic role proved vital was in opening the naval archives held at the Public Records Office. Access to these records had been severely restricted by the Admiralty and, even when permission was granted, it was restricted to individual papers, which had to be requested in advance. As a result, naval history was being written without access to the most basic resource. In 1879 Laughton exploited his friendship with Admiral Sir Astley Cooper Key, then First Naval Lord, to secure a more general access for himself. Recognising the immense importance and sheer scale of these collections, Laughton persuaded Key to grant general access to other scholars in 1885, for the period down to 1793.[2] In 1886 that access was so little known that Laughton still received invitations to use the records from senior officers who were consulting them [32]. Once established that access generated new opportunities, and new friends like Hubert Hall, Head of the Search Room, who frequently located new treasures for Laughton to inspect [45]. By contrast, his work with the Royal Meteorological Society came to an end.

Luce [46, 52, 60–63] was still in frequent contact, and was supplied with a steady diet of information and ideas, which he would use to further the cause of American naval modernisation. In August 1889 he

---

[1]Alfred Thayer Mahan (1840–1914), American Admiral and strategist. See R. Seager, *Alfred Thayer Mahan: The Man and his Letters* (Annapolis, 1977) and J.T. Sumida, *Inventing Grand Strategy and Teaching Command: the Classic works of Alfred Thayer Mahan reconsidered* (Washington, 1997); which provide distinctive approaches to this pivotal figure.
[2]Lambert, *Foundations*, p. 74.

warned Laughton that Mahan's first major book, *The Influence of Sea Power Upon History, 1660–1783* was about to appear. Laughton responded by noting that he expected much from the author of *The Gulf and Inland Waters*, which he had reviewed in 1883. When he read the new book it struck him as 'very able', but he queried the historical veracity of the evidence [60].

21a.   *Laughton to Council, King's College, London*

6 July 1885

I beg to offer myself as a candidate for the Professorship of Modern History advertised as vacant by the resignation of Mr S. R. Gardiner.
I am a member of the Church of England;[1] am now 55 years of age, and graduated at Cambridge as 34th Wrangler in 1852.

I have been serving, since then, as a Naval Instructor in the Royal Navy; and for the last 19 years have been employed on the staff of the Royal Naval College, first at Portsmouth, and afterwards at Greenwich. I have thus had a very large experience both in teaching and in lecturing, as well as also in examining.

For the last 10 years I have also held the office of Lecturer and Examiner in Naval History at the Royal Naval College, at Greenwich: and during the same time I have been a frequent contributor of historical articles to the *Edinburgh Review*, the editor of which[2] has been good enough to send me a memorandum, which I enclose.

I have recently retired from my office of Naval Instructor at the Royal Naval College, but retain the Lectureship in Naval History; and should wish still to retain it, if now selected by you for the Professorship at King's College. As its duties are limited to a lecture once a week during one term in each session; they would not in any way interfere with the duties of the Professorship.

I enclose a copy of the official letter relieving me from my duties as Mathematical and Naval Instructor at the Royal Naval College. I can produce the original, if called on to do so, but cannot definitely part with it.

In addition to this and Mr Reeve's memorandum already mentioned, I enclose other testimonials according to the annexed schedule;

List of Testimonials enclosed:

---

[1]This was a stipulation of the College.
[2]Henry Reeve (1813–95).

1. Copy of official letter from Vice Admiral Luard CB President of the Royal Naval College.
2. Memorandum from Mr Reeve, Editor of the *Edinburgh Review*: with list of contributions to the Review attached.
3. From Rev'd Brooke Lambert, Vicar of Greenwich.
4. From Rev'd Thomas J. Main, formerly Director of the Royal Naval College, Portsmouth.
5. Letter from Dr. T. Archer Hirst FRS, late Director of Studies at the Royal Naval College, Greenwich.
6. From Admiral Sir Edward G. Fanshawe KCB, late President of the Royal Naval College.
7. From Captain T.S. Jackson RN Naval Assistant to the Inspector General of Fortifications.

6th July   J.K. Laughton

21b.   *Luard to Laughton*

27 December 1884

In consequence of the reduced number of voluntary officers studying at the College, and the altered conditions of their course of Instruction, it has become necessary to make a corresponding alteration in the teaching staff of the Establishment.

I am therefore directed by their Lordships to acquaint you that your services as Mathematical and Naval Instructor will not be required after Easter, and I am, at the same time, to convey to you the expression of their Lordships' satisfaction with, and approval of your past services.

The Treasury have been requested to sanction your retention of the post of Lecturer in Naval History ... [Laughton left out the financial details]

I desire to add my own personal opinion of the work you have performed at the College; an opinion equally shared by the Director of Studies.

21c.   *Reeve to Council*

3 July 1885

I understand that Mr J. K. Laughton is a candidate for the Professorship of Modern History in King's College.

It gives me much pleasure to state that he has long been a contributor to the *Edinburgh Review* on historical subjects, not merely naval, but extending to the whole political history of Modern Europe.

If these articles had not appeared anonymously they would justly have obtained for him a considerable reputation as an historical writer. They relate chiefly to the events of the 17th and 18th centuries with which Mr. Laughton is perfectly acquainted. I have no objection to his submitting to the Council confidentially a list of his contributions to the *Review*.

The Indian Navy	Oct. 1878
The King's Secret	April 1879
Queen Anne	April 1880
Pepys Diary	July 1880
Charles James Fox	Oct. 1880
Gustavus III	July 1881
The Bonapartes	Jan. 1882
Baron Stael	Jan. 1883
Frederick II & Maria Theresa	Apr. 1883
John de Witt	Oct. 1884[1]

21d.   *Brooke Lambert*[2] *to Council*

1 July 1885

Professor J.K. Laughton of the Royal Naval College, Greenwich has asked me to testify that he is a member of the Church of England and that his character is such as becomes a Professor of King's College.

I can with confidence give my testimony to the fact that he is a member of the Church of England and that his character is in accordance with his profession.

I leave others to speak of his scientific qualities, of his earnestness and energy.

---

[1]This list leaves out 6 papers on Arctic exploration and contemporary naval issues. see Appendix 3 for a full bibliography of Laughton's output.
[2]Brooke Lambert, Vicar of Greenwich 1880–1901; had been a student at King's 1853–54.

21e.   *Thomas Main to Council*

3 July 1885

I have been requested by Mr. J K Laughton, a candidate for the Professorship of Modern History at King's College, to give my opinion of his
qualifications for that office. He took a Wrangler's degree at Cambridge in 1852 and entered the Naval service as 'Naval Instructor' and
he soon became well spoken of throughout the Naval Service as a
careful, conscientious, efficient teacher and although I had but little
personal knowledge of him at that time I considered it my duty, when a
vacancy occurred at the Royal Naval College Portsmouth (the Institution which was under my Direction) to make strenuous efforts to ensure
his being appointed to fill it. His duties required extensive knowledge
of scientific and mathematical subjects and I have always had reason to
be thankful for the assistance he gave me by his clear intellect and
accurate knowledge.

Our connection ceased by the removal of the college to Greenwich
and my own superannuation. It was, I believe, partly through my recommendation that he was removed to Greenwich and his sphere of
duty, which while at Portsmouth was chiefly confined to mathematical
subjects, became largely extended and among other things embraced
Naval History. I have always found him a sound and patient teacher in
every branch of education he has taken up. He is, I may say, extremely
accurate in his knowledge, much more so than the great majority of
teachers. As to character he is, as far as my intimate knowledge will
enable to speak, a man of unblemished reputation and he is also a
member of the Church of England.

21f.   *Thomas Archer Hirst to Laughton*

1 July 1885

I have great pleasure in bearing testimony to the fact that, during the
ten years of my tenure of the Directorship of Studies in the Royal Naval
College, Greenwich, you worked harmoniously and efficiently with me
as Instructor in Mathematics and Lecturer in Meteorology.

It was also your duty to give, annually, a course of lectures on naval
history; and I have reason to know that your lectures on this subject
were highly appreciated by the naval officers who attended them.

21g. *Admiral Fanshawe to Council.*

Mr J K Laughton late Lecturer in Naval History at the Royal Naval College Greenwich, being a candidate for the Professorship of Modern History at King's College, has appealed to me, as former President of the R. N. College, to express my opinion as to his qualifications for the office he desires to hold; and he informs me that the Council desire that testimonials should be specifically addressed to them, with reference to this application.

I can with full confidence state that Mr Laughton is a gentleman of high character who, after taking a Wrangler's degree at Cambridge, has been engaged with great credit in the educational branch of the naval profession:– latterly for several years at the Royal Naval College.

In his lectures on Naval History I was very favourably impressed by the learning and diligence with which he had collected materials and the skill and ability with which he deduced just conclusions from the data thus collected.

I also think that his aptitude in imparting knowledge rendered his lectures highly instructive and satisfactory to his hearers.

21h. *Captain Thomas Sturges Jackson[1] to Council*

30 June 1885

Mr J K Laughton RN is, I believe, a candidate for the Professorship of Modern History at King's College, London. As an old pupil of his, and also an old pupil of King's College School, I have great pleasure in testifying to his fitness for the appointment.

Before Mr Laughton devoted himself to the study of the subject, Naval History existed in two forms; fairly accurate but decidedly meagre accounts of actions at sea; and thrilling, but somewhat mendacious narratives apparently written with the view of propagating a belief in the inherent superiority as seamen of Englishmen over foreigners. Mr Laughton has succeeded in giving us history worthy of the name. Hitherto the results of his labours have only appeared in the form of lectures and occasional papers, but it is the hope of our service that before long these fragments may be welded together and may be published in a complete form. It is possible that the particular line taken by Mr Laughton may have prevented his talents as a historian from being

---

[1]Admiral Sir Thomas Sturges Jackson (1842–1934); taught by JKL as a midshipman 1856–58; then a Captain in the Ordnance Department; later C-in-C Devonport 1899–1902.

generally known. I have therefore thought it my duty to bring them to your notice at some length.

As to Mr Laughton's capabilities of imparting instruction, I will content myself with assuring you that I have the highest opinion of his powers as an instructor, and that I owe much of my success in the service to his teaching both at sea and at the Royal Naval College.

21i.   *Key[1] to Council*

6 July 1885[2]

Mr J K Laughton has informed me that he is a candidate for the Professorship of Modern History at King's College.

I am glad to have the opportunity of recording my opinion as to his qualifications. During the three years that I was President of the Royal Naval College at Greenwich Mr Laughton held the posts of Instructor in Mathematics – Lecturer in Meteorology and Naval History.

These duties he performed much to his own credit and the benefit of the naval service. His high character, thorough knowledge of the subjects on which it was his duty to lecture, and clear manner of imparting his knowledge to his pupils render him, in my opinion, well qualified to fill any similar position.

22.   *Laughton to J. W. Cunningham[3]*

6 July 1885

Sir Edward Fanshawe & the Rev'd Brooke Lambert have informed me that they have sent their testimonials in my favour direct to you. I have included them in my list, appended to my application, and should be obliged if you would put them with the others.

I had expected one or two more, but the time is short, & the people apparently away from home. So what I send must suffice.

---

[1]Key had retired as First Sea Lord on 1 July and was still occupying the official residence.
[2]Written from the First Sea Lord's official residence at that time, 65 Spring Gardens.
[3]Secretary to the Council of King's College.

23. *Laughton to Cunningham*

8 July 1885

I will call on you, as you request, on Friday at 3 O'Clock. I find that Sir Cooper Key has also sent a testimonial to you, which I hope you added to the others.

24. *Laughton to Cunningham*

11 July 1885

I have to acknowledge your note of last night's date, acquainting me that the Council of King's College had been pleased to elect me to the Professorship of Modern History.[1]

I should wish to talk over the detail of the duty with you as soon as may be; and would call on you with that view, on Tuesday or Thursday afternoon next, about 3 O'Clock if that time & either of these days would be convenient to you. If no, kindly fix some other time, but not for Monday or Wednesday.

25. *Laughton to Cunningham*

17 July 1885

I am glad to learn that Professor Gardiner has already proposed the subject & the period for the Essay & the Scholarship. His selection of both seems perfectly satisfactory, and I do not see that it could be improved on.

26. *Book Contract*

This Agreement made this 21st day of August 1885 between J.K. Laughton Esq. of 9 Gloucester Place, Greenwich on behalf of himself, his executors, administrators and assigns of the one part, and Messrs. Longmans, Green & C. of Paternoster Row, London on behalf of themselves, their heirs and assigns, of the other part, whereby it is mutually agreed as follows:–

---

[1]On 10 July 1885 the Council elected Laughton to the position on the verbal recommendation of the Committee formed to consider the application (KCL:KA/C/M/B p. 431). There is no indication in the College archive of any other applicants (KCL:KA/IC/L59).

1. The said Messrs Longmans, Green & C. shall publish at their own expense and risk an edition of one thousand Copies of a work entitled *Studies in Naval History*[1] by the said J. K. Laughton in one volume of four hundred (400) pages printed like the specimen page herewith annexed subject to the payment to the said J. K. Laughton of a Royalty of Three Shillings (3/–)[2] per copy on all copies of the English Edition sold beyond the first five hundred (500) copies, and one half of any profits that may be realised from the rights of Translation and Reproduction on Stereotype plates of the said work to the United States or elsewhere.

Provided that should it be thought advisable to dispose of copies of the said work in America or elsewhere, or of the remainder at a reduced price, which is left to the judgement and discretion of Messrs Longmans, Green & Co. the Royalty to be paid to the said J. K. Laughton is to be reduced accordingly.

2. The general management of the Production, Publication and sale of the work shall be left to the judgement of Messrs Longmans, Green & Co. including the power of making on such terms as they may think advisable, or of declining arrangements with reference to the Production, Publication, Translation and Sale of the work and Translation thereof in India, the Colonies, America and other Foreign Countries.

3. Corrections above twenty shillings per sheet of thirty-two pages on the average to be charged to the said J. K. Laughton and deducted from any Royalty that may become due to the said J.K. Laughton.

4. Accounts to be made up annually to midsummer, and rendered as soon as practicable after that time, and the balance due to be paid on the following 4th of December.

5. The said J.K. Laughton shall be entitled to Six Presentation Copies of the said work.

J.K. Laughton
Longmans, Green, & Co.

It is understood that the above mentioned work is to be published at half a guinea.[3]

---

[1]The book consisted of a series of essays written over the past two decades, and largely used as lectures at Greenwich. It was, in effect, a College textbook.
[2]£0.15 in modern currency, but more nearly £15.00 in modern value.
[3]Half a guinea would equal £0.525.

27. *Laughton to Cunningham*

24 September 1885

I am obliged by your note with the reference to the Warneford Scholar-ships.[1] Not knowing what to look for, it had escaped me. I see the exam in History is two hours. Setting the paper, as I said, rather in the dark, I have made it rather long; but if you will be good enough to send me a proof, I will consider if it is necessary to shorten it.

Will you kindly let me know what I am to do about my cap and gown. I mean as to where it is to be kept. Is there a room for the use of the Professors? If I order these things to be sent to me at King's College, where shall I find them? Pray excuse my troubling you about this, but I am quite a stranger to the place.

28. *Laughton to Cunningham*

10 October 1885

I should be much obliged if you could send me a few copies of the Prospectus of the "University Lectures at King's College". I am as yet in doubt as when my own course is to begin, though I understood it would be on the 30th.

29. *Laughton's Service Record*

Laughton, John K. M.A. 55 in 1885. Retired Naval Instructor, service 30 years and 145 days.

At Fatshan, June 1857, Canton December 1857, Taku Forts, May 1858. Long service at R.N. College, Greenwich, and writer of various professional books and papers, of which *Physical Geography in relation to the prevailing winds and currents* and *Introduction to the practical and theoretical study of Nautical Surveying* are accepted text books at R.N. College.

Nothing against him

5 Children, 10 to 16 years of age, dependent.

No private income but has £50 as Lecturer in Naval History at R.N. College & a doubtful £160 from literary work, including a Professorship at King's College.

---

[1]The Revd Dr S.W. Warneford had presented £5,000 to the College in 1850 to endow medical scholarships, to be secured by passing an examination in Divinity (Hearnshaw p.185).

Recommended by Admiral Sir A. C. Key GCB
Retired pay £400 per annum.

30.   *Laughton to Browning*

28 May 1886

Some of my critics have been saying that they don't see the use of such a book as mine.[1] The fact that it has induced you to examine Nelson's letters, which you probably shrunk from doing when they were only to be seen in seven large 8os [Octavos] is a complete and satisfactory justification, if I had felt that I needed one.

The question you raise is one which I had asked myself.[2] I think I should say No; not to blame; although we can now see that it would have been better if he had waited. But arguing after the event, we are perhaps too apt to suppose that the French Expedition was necessarily bound for Egypt and that no-one, in a position to judge, could think otherwise; too apt to forget that Nelson had no information, and that Corfu or Constantinople both seemed possible aims, and Sicily still more so: thus when he found that notwithstanding their long start, they had not been heard of near Egypt when he arrived there, he suspected that they had either gone 'Up the arches' to Constantinople, or more probably had doubled back to Sicily. But Oh how changed the history of that period would have been if he had the wished for opportunity, of trying Bonaparte on a wind (p.144).[3]

I have not seen the original of the intercepted correspondence – it was published I quite forget whether by authority; but probably – I don't know whether it is rare. There is a copy in the Library of the United Services Institution.

I see some critics are very angry with me for rejecting the *Arethusa* letter: they have been unable to see that it could not be written by the same man who wrote the letter of 23 July (p.145) and that this last is certainly Nelson.[4]

---

[1]*Letters and Despatches of Horatio, Viscount Nelson* (London, 1886).
[2]About the Nile campaign.
[3]Of Laughton's edition.
[4]A typical example of Laughton's robust source criticism.

31. *Samuel Rawson Gardiner*[1] *to Laughton*

10 October 1886

Can you help me to two points about Arthur Chichester, afterwards Lord Deputy of Ireland.[2]

1. He is said in Sir F. Fortescue's *Life* to have been Captain under Lord Sheffield in the fight with the Armada.[3] What is a Captain under another Captain (for Lord Sheffield appears to have been Captain of the *Bear*) and is there any record of inferior officers?

2. Chichester is also said to have been Captain of one of the Queen's ships, & of 500 men in Drake's last voyage. His name does not occur in the list of Captains in Monson's narrative, nor is he mentioned in Hakluyt's account.[4] I rather fancy he commanded landsmen & was not Captain of a ship. Is there any list of such commanders.

I am doing Chichester for the N. Biog., & want to be as correct as I can be.

32. *Lord Alcester*[5] *to Laughton*

4 November 1886

I have just read your review in *Longman's Magazine* of the *Sketches of My Life*, by Hobart Pasha and I entirely agree with you that he was in the habit of confusing his dates – more so perhaps even than you give him credit for.[6] Thanks to Sir Gerald FitzGerald, the Accountant Gen-

---

[1]Samuel Rawson Gardiner: Editor of the *English Historical Review* 1890–1902; Laughton's predecessor as Professor of Modern History at King's College; a close personal friend and intellectual supporter. Gardiner's new 'Scientific' German historical professionalism provided an authoritative stamp of approval for Laughton's self devised 'scientific' historical methodology.

[2]Gardiner was writing an entry for the *DNB*.

[3]Sir F. Fortescue, *Life of Arthur Chichester, Lord Chichester of Belfast*; cited in Gardiner's *DNB* entry on this subject (1563–1625), vol. X (1887), pp.132–4.

[4]Sir William Monson (1568–1643), Elizabethan and Stuart admiral. His *Naval Tracts* were a major published source on the period. The work was carefully re-edited and published in a new edition by the NRS between 1900 and 1914. Richard Hakluyt (1552/3–1616), English collector and publisher of travel narratives, notably *Principal Navigations, Voyages etc of the English Nation* of 1589.

[5]Admiral Sir Frederick Beauchamp Paget Seymour (1821–95); created Lord Alcester after the Bombardment of Alexandria in 1882; popularly known as 'The Ocean Swell'.

[6]Captain the Hon. Augustus Charles Hobart, later Hobart-Hampton (1822–86); Captain RN 1863, American Civil War blockade runner; from 1868 on in the Turkish service as Hobart Pasha; commanded the Turkish fleet during the Russo-Turkish war of 1877–78.

eral of the Navy, I have been furnished with (an official) abstract of Hobart's service in the Navy between 1835 & 1845. I knew him from the time he first entered it in February 1835 in HMS *Rover*, Commander Charles Eden, in which ship he came to the South American Station, as it was then called, where I saw a good deal of him. I cannot help thinking that the *Sketches of My Life* were written as the groundwork of a novel, for Hobart most decidedly never was in certain actions (notably those of the Vuelta del Obligado in 1845) in which he says, or implies, that he took a part.[1]

His ships as a Volunteer 1st class and as a midshipman were but two, the *Rover* in the Pacific and the *Rose* on the S.E. Coast of America, as a mate he served in the *Excellent* and in the *Dolphin* from which latter ship he was appointed to the Royal Yacht a year before the Obligado was fought. The duels, elopements & so forth are nearly all purely imaginary, as are some of his statements respecting the state of the Navy when he first joined it. It was bad enough in some ways, but that story about the Captain flogging his cook because his pea soup was not hot was a stale one when I joined the service a year before Hobart did, & every one who was in the navy in 1841 knew how the story of the breakfast, as Hobart calls it & its results originated; *Vernon* 1840. I am so glad that you have spoken of Sir William Martin as you have. The service, in my opinion, owes more to him than to any man alive, and I speak impartially as I never liked or approved of some of his ways, or his means of obtaining information, but he rescued the Navy, and especially the Mediterranean Station from the slough of despond, he had the courage of his opinion, and he was very nearly being a great man.

This however has nothing to do with Hobart Pasha.

On page 35 of your review an extract from Hobart's *Sketch* implies certainly that he was in the action of the Vuelta del Obligado, it was fought in Oct. or Nov. 1845 & he had left the *Dolphin* to which he refers in September 1844. I have not seen the *Sketches of My Life*, but I have written for it.

Please consider this communication as confidential & believe me.

PS. I have an Admiralty order to the Keeper of the Public Records authorising me to see any logs or papers therein. Would you like to come with me?

---

[1] The battle of Obligado took place on 20 November 1845. See Sir W.L. Clowes, *The Royal Navy: A History from the Earliest Times* (7 vols, London, 1897–1903), vol. VI, pp. 336–44.

33.   *Alcester to Laughton*

8 November 1886

I am now in a position to state & prove, if necessary:

(1)   that A. Hobart was a Lieutenant of the *Rattler*,[1] Commander Smith, in Portsmouth Harbour on the day that the action of the Obligado was fought.

(2)   that he never served ashore in Spain under Lord John Hay.[2]

(3)   that he never commanded a ship of any kind after he was promoted from First lieutenant of the *Duke of Wellington*[3] in September 1855, until he was appointed to the *Hibernia* Stationary Guardship at Malta in 1857, and that consequently his statement that he commanded one in the Black Sea during the latter part of 1855 'too late to do anything' is a _____.

(4)   A.C. is Arthur Cumming of course. The official report of his capture of a slaver in a boat of HMS *Frolic* makes no mention of the *Dolphin*'s boats being in company & I do not believe that Hobart was in the business at all, but I will ascertain. I do [not] credit for one instant Hobart's story about his having shot the captain of the slaver who tried to murder him, or of his, H., having captured a schooner full of slaves while in charge of a prize. It was done once on the coast of Africa in the *Felicidade* case & a pretty business came of it.

I think that you might hint to Mr. Longman that the *Sketches of My Life* are not to be accepted as gospel.

34.   *Laughton to Cunningham*

130 Sinclair Road, West Kensington,[4] 9 November 1886

I presume that one of the clerks ought to have let me know that the College was closed today, and neglected to do so, thus occasioning me a needless journey. May I request that in future I may be informed

---

[1] Wooden screw sloop, 800 tons; the first screw propeller warship. See D. Griffiths, A. Lambert and F. Walker, *Brunel's Ships* (London, 1999), pp. 336–44.

[2] Captain Lord John Hay commanded a squadron of British warships on the north coast of Spain, supporting Queen Isabella against her uncle Don Carlos, in the 'Carlist wars' in 1837 (Clowes, vol. VI, p. 276).

[3] Wooden steam battleship, 131 guns, 3,500 tons; flagship in the Baltic campaigns of 1854 and 1855.

[4] Laughton's new address, after moving from Greenwich.

of departures from the routine which affect the usual course of my work.

35. *Laughton to Cunningham*

27 November 1886

I enclose the copy of the paper for my share of the Christmas Exam. Mr Low[1] will send you his in the course of a day or two.

When I last saw you, you were good enough to ask my opinion as to the appointment of a successor to Mr. Low. My connection with the College has been so short that I feel some diffidence in offering any opinion, but in looking at the Calendar (p. 51) I notice that from 1876 to 1883, there was no *Lecturer*; and it has occurred to me, considering the small numbers in the Department, that there might be no difficulty, & some advantage in amalgamating the two classes into one. The office of Lecturer seems (at present) unnecessary, & the emoluments are so small as to make it scarcely worth the while of a capable man; nor would their addition to those of the Professor raise them to an excessive amount.

However, this is merely a suggestion which I offer, in case no other arrangement has been made or resolved on.

36. *Charles Yonge[2] to Laughton*

7 December 1886

I hope you will excuse me for troubling you, but I have been reading your article on Byng[3] in the Biographical Dictionary, and also on Admiral Boscawen,[4] and I wish to point out to you that you are mistaken as to Boscawen's opinion respecting the sentence passed on Byng, and its execution. When the Duke of Somerset's[5] Board applied

---

[1]Sir Sidney Low, student at King's 1870–75, then lecturer in History; returned at the end of the century to lecture on Imperial History; also a journalist and a barrister.

[2]Charles Duke Yonge (1812–93), Regius Professor of History at Queen's College, Belfast; biographer of Lord Liverpool; father of the popular novelist Charlotte Yonge. His claim that he had been asked to write the history of the Navy is open to doubt, as Somerset's Board refused him access to the archives after 1840.

[3]Admiral John Byng (1704–57); court martialled and executed for the strategic defeat off Minorca in 1756.

[4]Admiral the Hon. Edward Boscawen (1711–61); victor off Lagos in 1759.

[5]Edward Adolphus Seymour, 12th Duke of Somerset; First Lord of the Admiralty 1859–66.

to me to undertake the compilation of the History of the Navy, which after its completion they adopted as the standard work on the subject, (being in fact the only one which goes back to the Saxon times, and down to their own) they gave me access to all the dispatches in their possession, whether at the Admiralty or at Somerset House.[1] But besides those stores of information I sought for private records wherever they were obtainable; and a friend of mine also the heir and present representative of Admiral Boscawen obtained for me from his cousin, Lady Arthur Somerset, a great body of the Admiral's correspondence of which I was able to make considerable use. But you have evidently overlooked a note of mine Vol. I p.241 in which I maintain that Boscawen's letters on the subject are evidence that he <u>disapproved</u> of the sentence – of course his signing of the death warrant was a mere formal act as Commander in Chief at Portsmouth which he could not refuse to perform, and which therefore affords no indication of his opinions.

I have pointed out that H. Walpole[2] was manifestly mistaken in attributing the suggestion that Byng would be condemned because the adherents of the late ministry had a majority to Boscawen; but Lord Shelburne[3] in his autobiography implies that it had been made a party question; since he says Lord Hardwicke[4] sacrificed Byng to save his own son-in-law Lord Anson.[5] West[6] was a cousin of Lord Temple,[7] which explains Boscawen's statement that, after being cashiered, he was re-instated 'through interest'. Lord Stanhope's[8] account of the action is, like all his narratives of naval operations, ridiculously meagre and defective. His account of the battle of Malaga is actually taken from St. Simon, whose narrative is only valuable as a specimen of how much a courtier of Louis le Grand was expected to believe, and so Lord S. represents it as a drawn battle and the fleets as nearly equal in numbers; though he might have learnt from Charnock's work on marine architecture that the French force nearly doubled ours; and that 5

[1]C. D. Yonge, *A History of the British Navy* (2 vols, London, 1863).

[2]Horace Walpole, later 4th Earl of Orford (1717–97); politician and diarist.

[3]William Petty, later 2nd Earl of Shelburne (1737–1805); Prime Minister at the end of the American War.

[4]Philip Yorke, later 1st Earl of Hardwicke (1690–1764); Lord Chancellor.

[5]Admiral Sir George, later Lord Anson (1697–1762); outstanding naval commander and later First Lord; son-in-law of Lord Hardwicke.

[6]Vice-Admiral Temple West (d. 1757).

[7]Richard Grenville-Temple, Lord Temple, later 1st Marquis of Buckingham (1711–79).

[8]Philip Henry, 5th Earl Stanhope (1805–75); minor politician and historian. The reference is to his *The History of England from the Peace of Utrecht to the Peace of Versailles: 1713–1783* (7 vols, London, 1836–1854).

of the French ships were destroyed (see *Naval History* I p.140). One of Boscawen's letters, giving an account of his capture of the *Alcide* and *Lys* I have given, as you are probably aware, in the appendix to my first volume. My paging in this letter is from the 2nd or 3 volume edition).

Renewing my apologies for thus intruding on you.

37. *Yonge to Laughton*

12 December 1886

I am much obliged by your kind letter; Admiral Boscawen's letters, to which my note refers, were nearly all to his own wife the celebrated Mrs Boscawen; and therefore not 'letters of courtesy' but to his own wife they must surely have expressed his real opinion. It was to Lord Hardwicke the Lord Chancellor, not <u>Lord Temple</u> that Lord Shelburne attributes the sacrifice of Byng to save Lord Anson. If, in my letter to you I wrote 'Lord Temple' it was a strange slip of the pen. Lord Temple could have had little or no importance at that time. Lord Shelburne, who was very young at the time, probably got his view of the case from Pitt,[1] who, as is well known, made every effort with the King to save Byng & no man was more zealous for the honour of the nation than Pitt.

As to Malaga, which is a matter of greater importance now, our fleet was <u>53</u> ships of <u>all</u> classes, the French fleet consisted of 50 sail <u>of the line</u>, 17 frigates & fireships & 25 smaller vessels, in all 92. This is Charnock's[2] account, who gives the names of the ships of both fleets; and he also gives the names of the 5 French ships which, on his authority, I mention in my account of the battle as having been sunk (see my Vol.I p.140 2nd Ed.). As for the French having told a lie about the *Marlborough* in 1744 that does not prove that they told the truth about their own ships in 1704. Voltaire in his *Siecle de Louis XV* remarks that in these reports of battles the English 'do not diminish their own losses, & do not exaggerate those of their enemies', evidently meaning to imply a difference in this respect between them and his own countrymen. Charnock was a very careful writer and my impression certainly is that in such details he is thoroughly to be relied upon. And it is not a slight proof that the battle was more decisive than St. Simon states that Louis never sent out any naval expedition of importance

---

[1]William Pitt, 1st Earl of Chatham (1708–78); statesman and leader of the wartime coalition of 1757–61.

[2]John Charnock (1756–1807); naval biographer and naval architect. The reference is to his 6-volume *Biographica Navalis* of 1794–98.

afterwards. I am naturally anxious that in your article on Rooke[1] justice should be done to the navy in this instance, & to the Admiral himself; whom I regard as the most successful sailor we had had up to that time; unless indeed it may be thought that Lawson's[2] novel tactic of breaking the Dutch line, June 23rd, 1653 puts him on an equal level. It was exactly Rodney's[3] manoeuvre anticipated; though Rodney had never heard of Lawson's exploit. I imagine that in nautical skill both Lawson & Rooke were probably superior to Blake[4] (who had had no early naval training) though no one could surpass him in hardihood and enterprise.

I may add that before drawing up my account of the Battle of 1653 I showed the reports of Lawson's manoeuvre to Sir Michael Seymour,[5] & one or two others of our most brilliant officers of that day, & they all agreed that it was precisely the same as Rodney's.

38.   *Bridge to Laughton*

HMS *Colossus*,[6] 20 December 1886

When I was Leonard's age I strongly held the opinion that the Christmas Holidays were greatly improved by the receipt of a tip. As that opinion may not have become obsolete amongst young gentlemen of his years, will you kindly offer him the enclosed with my love? I should like to hear from himself how he is getting on with his studies.

I have just got the 2nd edition (published in 1793) of John Payne's *Naval History* in five volumes. Do you know anything about the book? The engravings, which are good, seem taken from Hervey's *Naval History*.[7] At p.270 vol. ii he says that – in Charles II's time 'Sir Tobias Bridge' with six ships from Barbadoes 'took Tobago', who was Sir Tobias? An ancestor of mine was Tobias Bridge, a Cromwellian General.

---

[1]Admiral Sir George Rooke (1650–1709); captured Gibraltar and won a strategic victory at the battle of Malaga.

[2]Admiral Sir John Lawson (1605–65); Parliamentary and later Royal Naval Commander.

[3]Admiral Sir George Brydges, later Lord Rodney (1719–92); best known for his victory at the battle of the Saintes (12 April 1782), when he exploited a shift in the wind to pass through the French line.

[4]Robert Blake (1599–1657), greatest of the Parliamentary 'Generals at Sea'.

[5]Admiral Sir Michael Seymour (1802–87). Laughton served on his Flagship during the Second China War, and considered him one of the finest sea officers of the century; he kept Seymour's portrait in the room where he worked.

[6]Turret battleship, 9,460 tons; completed 1886; broken up 1908. Jellicoe was then her Gunnery Lieutenant.

[7]George Augustus Hervey (pseud. John Payne, d.1787), *Naval, Commercial and General History of Great Britain* (5 vols, London, 1779).

I find that – in my family till comparatively recently the S was often put, also Y and even U for I, though the present spelling was most common.

Since I last saw you I have come into possession of several family portraits, one is of a certain Guy Phillips afterwards a captain in the Guards who married an ancestor of mine, Jemima Bridge, whose portrait and another of Guy are in possession of a cousin of mine. Guy was uncle or brother of the Phillips[1] who was shot for the loss of the *Nottingham* and who was doubly connected with me, my great-grandmother being a Phillips. Can you give me the date of the execution? I go to Cokethorpe, Witney from 22nd to 27th.

39.　*Thomas Nesham[2] to Laughton*

6 February 1887

I start away for Winchester tomorrow – on [a] house hunting expedition – with my wife, & all my gear was packed up two days ago, so I cannot refer to books. I had taken some notes on [the] French Navy of last century, when at Greenwich two years ago. I think however, I can answer your question from memory. The French had no three deckers during 7 Years War (vide Charnock & Schomberg[3]). The eighties were a new, powerful class of 2 decked ship; French 36 pounders on the lower deck, 24 pounders on main deck. E[ngland] caught two of them, viz:– *Formidable* & *Foudroyant* – and destroyed others at Lagos, *Ocean* (or *Orient*) *Soleil*, not *Soleil Royale*, (vide Troude[4])

	length on main deck	Breadth	Depth	Tons	
Capt. 1758 *Foudroyant*	180.5	50.3	23.0	1979	taken to pieces 1787
Capt. 1759 *Formidable*	188.0	49.3	21.5	2007	taken to pieces 1767

Like many French ships *Formidable* though of beautiful model & proportions was built of poor materials & badly put together, – she was, after being opened up for repairs, deemed unworthy of the expense.

---

[1]Lieutenant Baker Phillips; shot for cowardice after surrendering HMS *Anglesey* on 28 March 1745. It has been suggested that the severity of his sentence reflected the suspicion that he was a Jacobite.

[2]Captain Thomas Peere Williams Nesham, promoted for meritorious service on the West African coast in 1876.

[3]Isaac Schomberg, *Naval Chronology* (3 vols, London, 1812).

[4]O. Troude, *Battailes Navales de la France* (Paris, 1867).

In seventeen hundred [&] forty something a splendid 3 decker on the stocks at Brest *Royal Louis* was accidentally burnt. No other 3 decker was built until peace [in] 1763; when the merchants of Paris stood the cost of *Ville de Paris* 90 guns vaisseau a trois ponts <u>sans gaillards</u>. She was afterwards built up with Q[uarter] deck, Forecastle armament and Poop so as to carry 104 guns, as such we took her 12 April '82. See *James*[1] for this. Our second rates 1759 *Sandwich,* '61 *Blenheim & Ocean,* '66 *London,* '69 *Barfleur & Queen,* '72 *Prince George,* '73 *Princess Royal,* '76 *Duke,* '77 *Formidable* were 90 gun ships – only 2 6 pounders on the Forecastle, nothing on [the] Quarter deck or Poop: until '78 when *London* and later ships had 8 6 pounders put on Quarter Deck making them 98 gun ships. In '77 [the] French launched *Invincible, Terrible* & I think another 3 decker and a few years later a half dozen more (*Bretagne, Etats de Bourgogne, Dauphin Royal, Commerce de Marseilles*) Query *Majesteux,* large ones. Spaniards at the same time built several, chiefly at Havana.

Bien Aimee is the nickname for Louis XV. There was a 74 of that name. I think she was in East Indies – before Suffren's time. She was either left as a hulk at Isle de France, or else came home & was razee in '93 Query called *Agricole. James* has a list (not quite correct) of French liners & frigates 1793.

I don't think I can say any more on the subject. Junior United Service Club, St. James' will always find me.

P.S. The French even before the Revolution were rather fond of altering names of ships. <u>Possibly</u> one of the new 3 deckers was for a short time called *Bien Aimee.* A three decker was laid down at Chatham, in '82 & was called the *Umpire*! On the *Royal George* coming to grief her name was changed.[2]

40.   *Bridge to Laughton*

HMS *Colossus*, 8 February 1887

I have been greatly struck by Lieut. Snell's paper so kindly sent by you.[3] It is one of the ablest documents, in my opinion, ever prepared by a Naval Officer. At last there is a prospect of working out a practical sea

---

[1]William James, *A Naval History of Great Britain* (6 vols, London, various editions since 1822).

[2]See D. Lyon, *The Sailing Navy List* (London, 1993); p. 63 confirms this story.

[3]Commander William C. H. Snell, then commanding the station yacht HMS *Imogene* in the Mediterranean. There is no indication in the letter whether the paper was published, and it cannot be traced in contemporary publications. It may have been a hand-written essay.

war-game. Some of Snell's maxims, are admirable e.g. 'successful naval strategy is the concentration at the right time and place of a force superior to the enemy'.

He makes one assertion of great importance – strategy, as far as we are concerned, is of more importance than tactics. This he bases on the opinion that all modern improvements have been more advantageous to our enemies than to ourselves.

I have long been of opinion that strategical combinations are of more moment to us than ever. Is not our naval history something like this?

The middle of the 18th century was the era of the strategists, the end, and the beginning of the 19th that of the tacticians. Anson, Hawke,[1] Boscawen, or their superiors, took advantage of the greater numerical strength of our Navy and generally engaged the enemy when he had a smaller force. The tacticians worked under very incompetent strategists at headquarters, and therefore, notwithstanding the numerical superiority of our fleet, they nearly always fought at a disadvantage as regards mere numbers. Their immense tactical skill more than redressed the balance. As soon as we were engaged with an enemy nearly on an equality with us tactically, due to his equally good seamanship and sea-experience, (American) we found that something more was wanted than mere tactics and that the *bon dieu* had not lost any of his preference for big battalions. Is this view right? Can you give me a few dates to support it?[2]

I have just sent in a sketch of a plan of 'mobilisation' (damn the ugly foreign word!) and expect to be spiflicated for my cheek.[3] Why do not you write in *The Times* on naval subjects?

41.   *Rear Admiral Sir Francis Leopold McClintock[4] to Laughton*

9 February 1887

At his lecture, on Lord Nelson last evening Mr J.W. Dixon, who very highly praised your *Life of Nelson*[5] stated his disbelief in the aspersions

---

[1]Edward, 1st Baron Hawke (1705–81), outstanding fleet commander; victor at Quiberon Bay, 1759.

[2]The combination of ideas and questions in this letter reveals much of the underlying creative tension in the relationship between Bridge and Laughton.

[3]Bridge was already becoming known for his organisational skills, and these would secure him the post of Director of Naval Intelligence. Mobilisation planning had become a central feature of modern war since the Franco-Prussian war of 1870–71. See Robert E. Mullins, 'Sharpening the Trident: The Decisions of 1889 and the Creation of Modern Seapower' (unpublished Ph.D. thesis, University of London, 2000).

[4]Sir Francis Leopold McClintock (1819–1907); Admiral; best known as an Arctic explorer.

[5]*Letters and Despatches of Horatio, Viscount Nelson* (London, 1886).

which have for so many years clouded the memory of the Hero; and he read Lord Nelson's letter to Mr Davidson from your book, shewing that in 1801 he had separated from his wife.

In conversation with Mr Dixon, he expressed to me his great regret that no-one had written a vindication of Lord Nelson; and he thought, that if no-one else did it, he would perhaps try to do so himself. If England has for nearly a century so deeply wronged the memory of Nelson, it is only just, to make what reparation we can even now. And not only for his sake, but for the cause of Religion, which has suffered through this slander. I believe Lord Nelson was deeply imbued with veneration for sacred things, and entertained strong religious convictions, and I cannot believe in the gross [immorality?] attributed to him.

If you entertain similar views, I will only add that your great research into the history of his life and times justifies me in saying that no-one could undertake such a service to our country's history, and the cause of true religion, than yourself.[1]

42. *Revd R. W. Church[2] to Laughton*

15 June 1887

I shall not be in town 'till next week, when I will enquire about the flags.[3] But I may say at once that I never heard anything about them during the time that I have been at St. Paul's: and I am afraid that there is no record, as to what became of them.

But I will make enquiry as soon as I can.

Would not the French Admiralty give information as to the flags worn at that time, if they were approached from our Embassy in Paris?

43. *Revd R. W. Church to Laughton*

30 June 1887

I have had enquiry made about the flags, but with no success.

It appears that the captured flags used to hang in an upper room in the Cathedral, called the Trophy Room. Some 50 or 60 years ago the use of this room was required as a place of deposit for a number of wills, which were removed from the old 'Doctors Commons' which

---

[1]Laughton's *Nelson* in the 'English Men of Action' series (London, 1889) would address this task.
[2]The Very Revd Dr R.W. Church, Dean of St. Paul's since 1871.
[3]These were the French, Spanish and Dutch flags taken in the period 1794–97.

was pulled down. These papers were piled up in the Trophy Room, 'till a permanent place was found for them in Somerset House some 12 years ago. But none of our present officials or servants knows what was done with the flags. One remains, a large Spanish ensign; but all the rest have disappeared.[1]

It is just possible that they may turn up in some store chambers of the cathedral, but I fear that they are lost. It is possible also that they may have fallen to pieces: but I am very sorry that I can find no record of them.

[JKL endorsed the letter, in red ink]

The reply to my letter asking about the flags captured 1 June, St. Vincent & Camperdown, deposited in St. Paul's 19 Dec. 1797. (Schomberg's *Nav. Chron.* iii p.49) Unsatisfactory; very –

44.   *Bridge to Laughton*

HMS *Colossus*, Cattaro, 5 October 1887

Your kind and welcome letter and your most acceptable book reached me last evening.[2] I am very grateful to you for sending it and shall read it with pleasure and interest. I am very glad that you have republished the papers and hope that you may give us further instalments of previous publication. I rather regret not seeing in the volume just received the essay on the 'Sovereignty of the Sea'. It will, I hope, reappear some time later.

Accept my congratulations on the birth of your son,[3] who, I trust, will live to be an honour and a comfort to both his father and his mother.

I wish you could find a spare minute or two to protest in *The Times* against the abolition of the title of <u>Vice Admiral of the United Kingdom</u>, latterly held by your distinguished old chief Sir M. Seymour.[4] There is now no pay attached to it; but its abolition is simply another step, otiosely acquiesced in by an over-worked lot of Naval Lords of the Admiralty – taken by the jealous and aggressive military party. It and the 'Rear Admiral' ought to be conferred on men on the active list,

---

[1]See LGH 53 for a drawing of a Spanish flag sent in by Church on 30 June 1887.
[2]J K. Laughton, *Studies in Naval History* (London, 1887).
[3]Francis Laughton, the eldest son of his second marriage.
[4]Admiral Sir Michael Seymour (1802–87).

Geoff Hornby[1] for example – its abolition tends, with a multitude of other small things, to diminish the consideration in which the Navy is held, and thus to check its efficiency.

We are just off to Argostoli for some manoeuvres and I am more than usually busy. Our cruise has been interesting but hurried.

P.S. I will certainly look out for the N. Biog.[2] and your Collingwood.[3]

45.   *Hubert Hall[4] to Laughton*

Public Record Office, 10 December 1887

I have just found Capt. Cook's logs i.e. Officers Logs & Journals of *Endeavour, Resolution, Discovery* &c I don't know whether this is of any importance but the fact was interesting to me as bearing on my hobby of the necessity of original authorities for every kind of historical or biographical work.[5] From this point of view I made a short precis of each of the *Resolution* journals (6) and *Discovery* ditto (2) for account of Cook's death &c and the recovery of his remains (Feb. 14–22 1779) and was much amused to note the variations which occur in these 8 independent accounts and in the printed versions i.e. King[6] & Ellis.[7] I thought of sending this to *The Athenaeum* to draw attention to the importance of the subject – and it was at this juncture that I discovered you were Cook's biographer (Nat. Dict.)[8] & therefore possibly interested in these journals. From my point of view no Edition (popular or not) of the Classic *Voyages* could possibly be satisfactory unless the journals of Cook &c which form the basis of the present list were collated with all the other journals which survive. I wish you would take the matter up and give us a realistic edition <u>a la mode</u>. Sampson & Low might encourage it, as I think Routledge brought out the latest edition.

[1]Sir Geoffrey Thomas Phipps Hornby (1825–94), Admiral of the Fleet.
[2]*Dictionary of National Biography.*
[3]Cuthbert, 1st Baron Collingwood (1748–1810); Admiral, second in command at Trafalgar and close friend of Nelson. The reference is to Laughton's essay in the *DNB*.
[4]Hubert Hall, Head of the Search Room at the Public Record Office; Editorial Director of the Royal Historical Society 1891–1938. A close friend.
[5]James Cook (1728–79), Captain RN and outstanding navigator. See also LGH 47 for Hall to JKL 20 December 1887 and more notes on this subject.
[6]James King, *A Voyage to the Pacific Ocean* (3 vols, London, 1784).
[7]W. Ellis, *Narrative of a Tour Through Hawaii* (London, 1827).
[8]For modern interpretations of this evidence see J.C. Beaglehole, *The Life of Captain James Cook* (London, 1974), pp. 668–72; and G. Dening, *Mr Bligh's Bad Language* (Cambridge, 1992), pp. 168–71.

Anyhow I thought I would let you know at once that you might appropriate the discovery if such it be. I happen to know however that there have been lots of opportunities to see these logs though no use seems to have been made of them except for scientific purposes, and that is what made me think of vindicating their importance for textual purposes. Shall I (or will you) send a paragraph to *The Athenaeum* that you are engaged here upon as these things soon get abroad and the Australasian historians are always anxious to secure them? Also shall I (or will you) give a small enticement to the literary public, such as contradictions in re. Cook's death mentioned above? I said something about it to McColl and have got something in hand but will hand it all over to you if you prefer, only let me know soon (or see you better still) in case McC hunts me up about it.[1]

46.   *S. Luce to Laughton*

USS *Richmond*, New York, 22 December 1887

Please accept my sincere thanks for your kind consideration in sending me a copy of *Studies in Naval History*. I had already gathered together a number of these essays, as they came under my notice in the current literature of the day; and am now very glad indeed to possess them all under one cover.

We, on this side of the water, have undertaken, in a small way, to set up a Naval College.[2] As an evidence of the high esteem in which your work is held I have sent you a copy of one of my crude efforts in the way of a lecture, wherein may be found liberal quotations from your articles.[3]

Absence from the ship has precluded an earlier acknowledgement of your courtesy.

47.   *Laughton to Browning*

6 April 1888

A young fellow who has been attending my lectures is meditating trying for one of the King's College (Cambridge) history scholarships

[1]Unknown.

[2]The United States Naval War College, which Luce had played the major role in securing.

[3]S.B. Luce, 'On the Study of Naval History (Grand Tactics)', *USNIP*, **XIII** (1887), pp.175–201, reprinted in Hayes and Hattendorf, pp. 66–97.

and has consulted me about his chances. May I venture to ask you to trouble yourself so far as to get me a set of old Exam papers, and to send me any further information that you can. He tells me the next exam is in December, by which time he ought to do fairly well. He is an intelligent lad and seems inclined to work.

I am trying to busy myself about the Armada Tercentenary, but our work has scarcely begun yet. The Lord Mayor is to receive a deputation on the 17th, which I hope will give us a start. You may perhaps have seen that I am to discourse on the subject at the Royal Institution.[1] I think I have some interesting and comparatively novel matter to produce.

48.   *Commander Thomas Hull[2] to Laughton*

11 June 1888

Many thanks for your interesting paper on the *Invincible Armada*. I saw a very good notice of it, I think in *The Times*, cut the same out and stuck it in my 'cyclopedia, but now I have the real thing. You have given the old orthodox account a bit of a shaking, cut the trimmings off, made it something like Mostin's coat in the *Tale of a Tub*[3] after they had cut off the fringes. Yet I am bound to say yours reads as the true account of the matter. As our old friend Jack Falstaff says 'Lord, Lord, how this world is given to lying' How the Armada story has been lily painted and gold-gilt you might write at the head of your paper.

Mark now, how a plain tale shall put you down! Well for the poetry of the affair I shall stick to Kingsley's yarn in *Westward Ho!* But yours shall be the flame that has made the smoke.

Well 'twas a very good deed as it stood without varnish.
I've always thought we should have had a tougher fight of it if Santa Cruz had lived. At the same time [I] agree with your remark on p.8 'that had Drake been permitted, etc, etc would have effectively prevented the invasion which was now on foot'. That Old Queen Elizabeth must have somehow spawned the modern Admiralty, her tricks are their tricks. Another good meeting in the City that I tell everybody

---

[1]'The Invincible Armada', Royal Institution Lecture, delivered and published (London, 1888).

[2]Staff Commander Thomas Hull had helped Laughton with *Physical Geography*. He had been superseded at the Hydrographic Branch at the instance of Evans (for Evans see fn. 1, on p. 58) in December 1879. See G.S. Ritchie, *The Admiralty Chart* (London, 1967), pp. 343–4.

[3]Satirical story by Jonathan Swift written during the War of the Spanish Succession, 1702–13.

that asks me that it is no good voting money until the present Admiralty Department is *utterly destroyed*. So long as that abode of respectable rascality lasts, so long will there be the same God forgotten tricks and messes.

I generally fancy things can be reformed, but I look on the Admiralty as hopeless. Makes you understand the 'Why' of Sodom and Gomorrah. You could not find ten righteous men to save the place. It would demoralise the Archangel Gabriel. There is nothing but to make a Dead Sea or sink of respectability of the place, with the First Lord turned into Lot's wife for a remembrance of this peril to the nation.

Jars my soul when I look back at the tricks Evans[1] did and naturally [recognise ?] that other sections are like him. I fancy we may see Famine among us yet. Evans studied the place, knew the men he had to deal with, was wise in his generation, saw how to get on, what they liked etc. so was CB'd and KCB'd and his pension doubled. Promised to be the best 'Dust thrower' they ever had. A bogus Chart builder, a hinderer of good, a selector of incapables: this sick flower spreading from the muck heaps of the Admiralty Administration.

By this fruit I know them! Here are some lines from one of Edwin Arnold's translations from the Sanscrit. A king having got to heaven will not stop there because he finds the Gods to have admitted a man who he knows to have been a scoundrel. Hear him:

> If he attains, he attains – yet not the less,
> Evil he told and ill he died, a beast
> Impious and harmful, bringing woes to all
> To friends and foes – this was the curse which cost
> Our land its warriors, horses, elephants;
> His the black sin that set us in the fields,
> Bringing for rightful vengeance – Ye are Gods,
> And just, and ye have granted heaven to him,
> Show me the regions, therefore, where they dwell
> My Brothers, those the noble-souled, the strong,
> Who kept the sacred laws, who swerved no step
> From virtue's path, who spake the truth, and lived
> Foremost of warriors.

There's an epitaph for the Admiralty Darling!

Not my wrongs old chap that puts the spirit of the old Greek Erinnyes into me, but because I see plainly unless this horror, this blasted re-

---

[1]Sir Frederick John Owen Evans (1815–85); Captain RN and Hydrographer of the Navy 1874–84.

spectable iniquity is purged out of our midst some calamity must come upon us. So I cry with the prophet of old 'Shall I not visit for these things? Shall not my soul be avenged on such a nation as this?' There I'd better pipe down. Curses come home to roost.

49.   *Laughton to J.W. Cunningham*

24 June 1888

Of the four essays sent in for the Stephen Prize,[1] I would recommend the one, with the motto 'Amor patria' as the best. The one with the motto 'Quod potui perfies' comes next; but does not evince the same study and care.

The writers of the other two are apparently trying to qualify themselves for post on the staff of the *Daily Telegraph* or *London Journal*.

I return the Essays herewith.

50.   *Captain Walter Kerr[2] to Laughton*

28 March 1889

In reply to your note asking me to inform you as to the motive power used for the heavy guns of Sir William Peel's[3] Naval Brigade during the Indian Mutiny, I write to say, that on the line (of) march they were drawn by oxen, though occasionally when sufficient of them were not available, by Elephants, two to a gun.

To the large guns from 11 to 13 yoke of oxen were allowed. These were not the small country bullocks, but a magnificent breed of cattle specially raised by the Government for use with heavy artillery. They were far superior to the ordinary native cattle both for purposes of draught and as beef, in which latter sense an occasional casualty among them, a misfortune not wholly without compensatory advantages in the eyes of us midshipmen, gave an opportunity of attesting.

---

[1]Prize funded by Sir George Stephen from 1840. The annual interest on his donation of 50 guineas was given to the best English essay (Hearnshaw, p.158).

[2]Lord Walter Talbot Kerr (1839–1927); Admiral of the Fleet; First Sea Lord 1899–1904.

[3]Captain Sir William Peel RN, VC (1824–58). Son of Prime Minister Robert Peel, he demonstrated uncommon skill and valour in the naval brigade batteries before Sevastopol, and in the failed assault on the Redan. His Naval Brigade in the Indian Mutiny provided the heavy artillery, and was a critical element in the suppression of the insurrection. He died of small-pox.

Sir William Peel's letter well describes the idea that ran in his mind when he settled to take the *Shannon*'s[1] guns up the country with him and points out the purpose to which he hoped to apply them viz. of using these heavy guns as field artillery in the advanced line instead of in fixed positions or trenches usually employed for siege guns.

Once on the scene of action out came the bullocks and in went the guns crews (20 to a gun) who continued to work them until a long move was necessary. In the event of a hitch or a bit of heavy ground the nearest Regiment always gladly lent a Company or two to man the drag-ropes until the difficulty was surmounted.

It is no small tribute to Sir William Peel's genius that he should have originated this novel application for a frigate's main deck guns, and have foreseen when forming the Naval Brigade at Calcutta the useful purpose to which they could be, and subsequently were, applied.

There was probably no prouder man in the whole force than Sir William Peel when on Feb. 17th, 1858 on the way to the capture of Lucknow, all his difficulties having been at length overcome, and the whole of his heavy guns at last mounted on field carriages and fully equipped and manned, he brought the Commander in Chief, Sir William Mansfield and the Headquarters Staff and with them Dr. Russell, the correspondent of *The Times* to witness our evening parade and see the men go through their exercise.

The facility with which the guns were worked and manoeuvred must have been a surprise to them, as it was indeed to all of us.

Nothing was wanted to make us prouder of 'the Captain' than we were already, but had such been required his triumph, so markedly demonstrated on that day, over the almost insuperable difficulties that appeared to stand in his way and which would have daunted any man with less of the energy and pertinacity of purpose which were so prominently his characteristics, would have more than supplied what was wanting to establish his claim to the affectionate respect and pride of those whom he commanded.

The cry of sorrow that went forth throughout India at the time of his death, I have no hesitation in saying, is as fresh now as it was at the time in the hearts of any that remain of us, of the *Shannon*'s Naval Brigade.

[1]HMS *Shannon*, 50 gun, screw steam frigate, named for the ship that captured the USS *Chesapeake* in 1813.

51. *Evan MacGregor[1] to Laughton*

4 May 1889

I beg to thank you for so kindly letting me see the proof of the notice in regard to my grandfather Admiral Sir Thomas Hardy.[2] I sent it to my mother and I enclose her reply (which can be torn up). I am sorry we are not in a position to afford accurate information. I may remark that having looked at the dates of the Admiralty Patents I find that Sir Thomas was appointed First Sea Lord in November 1830, and remained at the Admiralty until 1834, when appointed Governor of Greenwich Hospital.

I return the proof.

52. *Laughton to Luce*

11 August 1889

I can answer your query about Sir George Seymour[3] definitely, so far: he was not in the *Penguin* in 1814, being at that time a captain of 8 years seniority. In 1814 he commanded the *Leonidas,* a 38 gun frigate in the West Indies. You will see a memoir of him (George Francis Seymour) in O'Byrne's *Naval Biographical Dictionary,*[4] which you probably have access to. The present Lord Alcester[5] is his nephew; & if you like to send me the name of the officer you speak of as Sir George's personal friend, I will ask him if he can throw any light on the subject. He was in the *Collingwood,* as his uncle's flag lieutenant, & will be pretty certain to know something about it. If you prefer writing to Lord Alcester yourself, the address:

United Service Club
Pall Mall
London S.W.

will find him.

I have delayed for a few days replying to your letter in order to see the number of the *London Shipping World & Herald of Commerce*

---

[1]Sir Evan MacGregor (1842–1926); Permanent Secretary to the Admiralty 1884–1907; Hardy's grandson, his mother being one of Hardy's daughters.

[2]Sir Thomas Masterman Hardy (1769–1839); Admiral; Nelson's Flag Captain at Trafalgar.

[3]Sir George Francis Seymour (1787–1870); Admiral C-in-C Portsmouth 1856–59. JKL wrote his *DNB* entry.

[4]London, 1849.

[5]See above [32, 33].

which you asked me to look at. Unfortunately on applying for it at the British Museum I found it was at the <u>Binder's</u>, so as it may be some little time before I can see it, I wait no longer – but I have no doubt the illustration will give a fair idea of the building, or rather buildings for there are *four* distinct blocks. The work of the College was admirably described a few years ago in a Report by Professor Solly (*sic*);[1] & though it is slightly modified from year to year, the changes are of no great consequence. I am sure the Director of Studies (W.D. Niven Esq.) will be happy to answer any questions you may address to him. For myself – though continuing to take special interest in the study of Naval History – I have been retired from the College at Greenwich; & am now Professor of History at King's College, London, the work of which is by no means so interesting.

I am glad to hear of the probability of Captain Mahan's lectures being published. His little work (The Gulf & Inland Waters) as a contribution to "The Navy in the Civil War" has already impressed me with a high opinion of his ability & clearness. Latterly I have been a good deal occupied with contributions to our "Dictionary of National Biography" for which I have done most of the naval officers; but I have recently edited, for The Camden Society, a fragmentary memoir of Lord Torrington (Admiral Sir George Byng)[2] which is curious. You have probably seen a couple of articles I contributed to *Colburn's United Service Magazine* in the Spring, on the very vexed question of the share which Lady Hamilton had in contributing to our naval successes.[3] For those who read my articles, I think I have set the matter at rest: but unfortunately, on this, as on most other subjects, people prefer to talk out of the fullness of their ignorance.[4]

[1] James Russell Soley (1850–1911); Professor at the United States Naval Academy; author of the *Report on Foreign Systems of Education* (Washington, 1880). This report had been influenced by Laughton's lectures and articles.

[2] *Memoirs Relating to the Lord Torrington*, Publications of the Camden Society XLVI (1889).

[3] 'Nelson's Last Codicil', *Colburn's United Service Magazine*, **II** (1888), pp. 647–99, and **III** (1889), pp. 10–23.

[4] This letter is particularly revealing. Laughton had already read Mahan's first book, as he notes, and had recognised his ability. The review is in the *Edinburgh Review*, **LVXI** (1883).

53.   Bridge to Laughton

23 August 1889[1]

You may like to see this well-written and accurate description of Fleet Evolutions.[2] Was there a ship on the Navy List in the early part of the last century called the *Mary* and qualified as a yacht? If so what was she, a Royal Yacht or a small fighting craft?[3]

I am here from 8 a.m. till 11 p.m. and have a bed here, though I have only slept here once. I shall not be sorry when the manoeuvres are over. The latest from the 'British' Fleet. Tracey's defeat and the chase of Darcy Irvine. – The Battle of Bull's Run.[4]

54.   Charles Firth[5] to Laughton

26 October 1889 [?]

I wrote to Mrs Ashington mentioning the two points, on which you would require information amongst others, and she answers that she will be pleased to give you any assistance as soon as she gets back to her papers. Anytime after Christmas that is. So that when ever you have the article in the rough I shall be pleased to assist by forwarding any questions you choose to ask.

The company with which Osborn[6] was connected was, I believe, the Telegraph Construction & Maintenance Co.

When I was at Waterloo Place last week I saw the proof of your article on Jenkins. I have a curious book connected with the subject – entitled *England's Triumph: or a complete History of the many signals victories gained by the Royal Navy & Merchant Ships of Great Britain, for the term of 40 years past over the insulting & haughty Spaniards* by Captain Charles Jenkins, who has too severely felt the effects of Spanish tyranny. London 1739.

[1]Bridge had just been appointed Director of Naval Intelligence, a post he retained for nearly six years. This was, in professional terms, the apogee of his career; subsequent periods of sea service were of peripheral interest.

[2]For these manoeuvres, see Arthur J. Marder, *The Anatomy of British Sea Power* (London, 1940), p.109, fn.9.

[3]The *Mary* was a yacht of 155 tons, and 8 small guns, built at Chatham in 1677; rebuilt in 1727 and 1761; broken up in 1816.

[4]A reference to the 1889 naval manoeuvres and the commanding Officer, Admiral Sir Richard Edward Tracey (1837–1907); founder of the Japanese and Chinese navies, 2nd in Command, Channel Fleet 1889–92; President of RNC, Greenwich 1897–1900.

[5]Sir Charles Harding Firth (1857–1936); later Regius Professor of History at Oxford.

[6]Captain Sherard Osborn RN (1822–75); Arctic explorer; Crimean and Chinese Service; turret ship pioneer.

Facing p.64 is a folding plate representing 'A Spanish Guarda Costa boarding Capt. Jenkins' ship & cutting off his Ear'. It is evident that this Capt. Jenkins claimed to be the hero of the story, but your article in the *Eng. Hist. Rev.* as far as I remember proved the man's name was Robert.[1]

The book is perhaps worth referring to. I enclose a few more naval notes & a broadside you may care to have if you have not got it.

55.   *E. Warre to Laughton*

3 April 1890

I must apologise to you for not answering your letter before this.
I sent it to the Provost who has all the old books etc. under his charge. He only returned it yesterday with the accompanying note. I am afraid therefore that we shall not be much help about Lord Howe.[2] It is curious how absolutely indifferent as to the preservation of records, the School seems to have been in those days.

[*Enclosed*]

The Lodge, Eton, 2 April 1890

My dear Warre,

I return Mr. Laughton's letter. We have nothing, I am sorry to say, about Lord Howe. Only the Colleger Registers exist for that time; and he was not a Colleger. We have no portrait of him, only a print in the gallery.

If he came to Eton early, at 8 or 9, as boys often did then, he may just have been at Eton with Gray and Horace Walpole.

Lord Howe was born in 1723, Gray left Eton in 1734.

Yours very sincerely,
J.J.H.[3]

---

[1] 'Jenkins' Ear', *English Historical Review*, **IV** (1889), pp. 741–9.
[2] Richard, Earl Howe (1726–99); Admiral of the Fleet; the pre-eminent master of fleet tactics in the late eighteenth century; victor on the Glorious First of June, 1794.
[3] James John Hornby (1826–1909); brother of Admiral Sir Geoffrey Thomas Phipps Hornby; provost of Eton.

56.   *Laughton to John Seeley*[1]

8 June 1890

Our friend Hales[2] has forwarded me your query as to the Elizabethan Naval War, which it gives me pleasure to answer, to the best of my power.

The history of the war, properly so called, has never been written, of what passes for naval history, the best is – I think – Lediard's, which is fuller than Burchett's, Southey's *Lives of the British Admirals* has some value, principally for the references: so also Campbell's *Lives of the Admirals*. The other comprehensive histories e.g. Entick, Hervey, Schomberg, are worthless.

We have then to go back to the originals. the principal facts, as they appeared to Englishmen at the time, are chronicled in Hakluyt and Purchas, Ralegh in *History of the World*, goes more into the meaning of things than anyone else of his day; but only incidentally. Monson's *Naval Tracts* (in vol. iii of Churchill's *Voyages*) are also suggestive; but his historical instances seem to be often based on a confused memory or very imperfect knowledge. So also Sir Richard Hawkyns *Observations &c* republished by the Hakluyt Society in *The Hawkins' Voyages*: his historical references are often spoken of as most valuable; but I fear they are almost worthless. One stock example is his account of his father's conduct at Plymouth in 1567, which is fiction. The truth in details is only to be got at from the *State Papers*. I have myself done a good deal, but it only amounts to scratching on the surface. Some of my work is published in the articles on Drake, Sir John Burgh, Clifford Earl of Cumberland and perhaps some others, in the *Dict. of Nat. Biog.* Greynvile will be (I suppose) in the next vol. Hawkyns and Howard will not be published for some time. My Armada Lecture, you have possibly seen; but in case you have not, I take the liberty of enclosing a copy. Devereux's *Lives of the Devereux, Earls of Essex*, you probably know. Barrow's *Life of Drake* might easily be better. Duro's book is, I think, quite the most valuable contribution of recent times: his essay is very fair, and the State Papers he

---

[1]John Richard Seeley (1834–95); Regius Professor of History and Cambridge 1869–94. Letter in the Manuscript Collection, Palaeography Room, University of London.

[2]On 6 June Seeley had written to his friend John Hales, Professor of English Literature at King's: 'I believe you often see Professor Laughton, I write to ask you, next time you see him to say from me how much obliged I should be if he send me a list of the books most necessary to be read on the naval war of Elizabeth, Armada included. He will be able to judge how far I want to go into the subject, as a political historian who wants to get the opinion of naval experts without professing to be anything of the sort himself' (LGH 18/21–2).

gives are very valuable. If I remember right, it is catalogued in the British Museum under Fernandez, but it is a book to study.

I am afraid you will think all this not very satisfactory: really it amounts to this, that the truth in the details, which often are the key to the grander events, is still buried in the *State Papers, Dom. & For.* of the period. Some of Admiral Colomb's papers on 'Naval Warfare', now running in the *Naval and Military Magazine* (Allen) may be worth your looking at; but if I remember, his account of the Armada – independent of his strategic deductions – is mainly made up of excerpts from my lecture.[1] His strategic reasoning however, is always interesting. He has a good article in this month's *Murray*.[2]

P.S. I am putting also another lecture of mine which may perhaps interest you, though it has nothing to do with this Elizabethan business.[3]

57.   *Seeley to Laughton*

10 June 1890

I feel really obliged by your response, so prompt and so thoroughly satisfactory, to my appeal. It will encourage me to apply to you again, if I need your help. I think the work you are doing is most important, and that we have long wanted a writer who should blend, as you do, the qualifications of a historian with those of a thorough naval expert. I bow to your criticism on my somewhat sketchy remarks, but I venture to dispute what you say at the opening about religious prejudices.

Many thanks also for the other interesting lecture, and for the references to the *Dictionary of National Biography*. I trust soon to master most of what you have produced.

58.   *Admiral Sir Geoffrey Hornby to Laughton*

12 June 1890

Yours of the 10th and inclosure have just reached me. Many thanks for them. If the whole Biography is as accurately and concisely written as the article on my father it will be a very valuable and interesting record of

---

[1]This was indeed the case. The essays later appeared as *Naval Warfare* (London, 1891).

[2]A literary journal.

[3]Laughton's own essay 'The Elizabethan Naval War with Spain', in the *Cambridge Modern History*, vol. III (Cambridge, 1907), remains an excellent survey and discusses the extant sources in detail.

our old Sea Kings. I see no omission except his service as 2nd Sea Lord in the Duke of Northumberland's Board of Admiralty in 1852. I do not carry the dates of its existence in my memory. But if I may suggest an addition, that I can ask for only on personal grounds, it would be that his other son should be named also viz. the Provost of Eton.[1]

59. *Laughton to J. W. Cunningham*

29 June 1890

I enclose my list. Gooch[2] is very well entitled to the Brewer Prize.[3] He has been the head of the class throughout the year. Gray is a good second, & has been so all along. I have recommended him for a Certificate of Distinction.

The Junior Division is terribly weak: but appears here ever weaker than it is, from the fact that two of the best of them, Taylor & Lynch having attended *both* classes, & chosen to go up for the senior paper. I should like to recommend Taylor for a Certificate of Approval, but scarcely know whether the rules allow it. It is, that he belongs to the second division, has attended the second division lectures by right, & the higher class voluntarily, & has, as you see, done very creditably. I shall be obliged if you will take the Principal's opinion on this point.

P.S. Will you please give Fisk directions about the Certificates at once, so that he may have them ready for me to sign in the afternoon.

60. *Laughton to Luce*

3 August 1890

I am much obliged by your letter of the 21st July, calling my attention to Captain Mahan's book, which, however, I have already read with much interest. With the author's main argument I am quite in accord, and the way he has worked it out strikes me as very able. In the details, I notice some trifling mistakes, which he will easily be able to correct,

---

[1]Laughton had sent Hornby the draft *DNB* notice on his father Admiral Sir Phipps Hornby. He amended the entry as Hornby suggested, noting both Admiralty service, and the name of his brother in the entry as printed. The draft is in the Laughton MS.

[2]The historian George Peabody Gooch, who studied under Laughton at King's between 1888 and 1891. Laughton then introduced him to Seeley.

[3]Prize of books awarded from the interest on a fund collected to commemorate the memory and the long service at King's College of Professor John Sherren Brewer who died in 1879.

e.g. in Byng's unfortunate action, the wind (as sworn at the court martial) was SSW and the ships' heads about WbyN which would turn his plan round through 8 or 10 points: otherwise, it is right enough.

But minute criticism apart, I think it quite the most important contribution to naval literature which has appeared for very many years; and if Captain Mahan cares to know my opinion, you are quite at liberty to repeat it to him.

I saw the notice in the *Saturday Review* which seemed to me inadequate. I did not see those in the *Morning Post* or *Admiralty & Horse Guards Gazette*; but neither of these papers carry any weight. I may say (in strict confidence) that I have been asked to write an article on it for the *Edinburgh Review*, which will appear in either October or (I believe, more probably) in January next. But this ought not to be spoken of in advance. I shall take the liberty of reproducing some of the sentences in your letter, as to the origins and purpose of the work. I agree with you and (so far) with the *Saturday Review*, that the title is not the best possible.

Many thanks for your pamphlets which have also reached me. The one on 'The Future of the Navy' is to me especially interesting.[1]

61.   *Laughton to Luce*

12 August 1890

I have to thank you for the cutting from *The Critic* which you have been good enough to send me.[2] I hope I shall be able to do Capt. Mahan justice on this side of the water. His chapters on strategy and policy are excellent: the details of his history he has, I think, taken too exclusively from French sources, and many of them are certainly inaccurate.

I see *The Critic* refers with disapproval to Clark Russell's *Life of Nelson*.[3] It is no doubt a scandalous performance, and I took the oppor-

---

[1]'Naval Administration', *USNIP*, **XIV** (1888), pp. 561–88, and 'Our Future Navy', *USNIP*, **XV** (1889), pp.541–52. Both in the Laughton pamphlet collection at the Admiralty Library; the second is a signed copy.

[2]The cutting from *The Critic* was Luce's unsigned review of Mahan's first seapower volume, which appeared on 26 July 1890 at pp. 41–2 (reprinted in Hayes and Hattendorf, *Luce*, pp. 101–3). I am indebted to Prof. John Hattendorf of the Naval War College for sending me copies of these letters.

[3]The reference to Clark Russell's book concerns a passage where Russell wondered if Nelson's genius can any longer be of use behind steel plates. This, as Luce argued, 'would sap the very foundations of the science of war'. It was to Mahan's credit, Luce argued, that he had shown that the reverse was the case. As Luce had exercised a large influence over Mahan's work, his comments, in an unsigned review, were aimed more at the audience than the author.

tunity of saying as much in *The Athenaeum* of 31st May, which you may perhaps have seen.

I am sending you by this post a copy of the *Memoir of Lord Torrington,* which I hope you will do me the favour to accept.[1]

62.   *Luce to Laughton*

NMM: LGH 16/ 5–7

Newport Rhode Island, 10 November 1890

I have bit just returned from an 'outing' in the White Mountains, and hasten to avail myself of the first opportunity to thank you for the copy of the story of *Trafalgar* which is always entertaining reading.[2] Your treatment of the subject, giving details not to be found in general naval history, invests the story, which cannot be too often told, with fresh interest.

I take heart to ask if you can kindly inform me if there are, in accessible form, returns of British commerce from 1803 to 1815? similar to that given in Macpherson's Annals which come down to 1802 only.

In addition to this I would be glad to have the names of any works containing information in regard to the losses of British vessels, by capture (the number and tonnage); the number of privateers in given years, the number of them taken; and the like information in regard to the Chief maritime enemies of Great Britain during these eventful years 1803–1815.[3]

If any such works exist we may be able to procure them through our agent in London, Mr. B. F. Stevens,[4] 4 Trafalgar Square.

In a recent discussion reported in the *United Service Magazine* in which Admiral Tryon led off, Mr Hubert Haines, a lawyer, stated that G. Britain lost, between the years 1793 and 1815 10,381 vessels by capture. Such exactness implies data. Where is it to be found? None of this information is given in Macpherson's Annals.

---

[1]Publications of the Camden Society, vol. XLVI (London, 1889); see [52].

[2]*The Story of Trafalgar* (Portsmouth, 1891). An early example of a commissioning book, written for a new ironclad battleship.

[3]This research query was indirectly from Mahan.

[4]Stevens, an antiquarian, had been appointed US Dispatch Agent in London in 1866. He also acted for American libraries and private collectors and provided a vital link between the American Navy and British Naval intellectual activity. In addition to acting as a forwarding house for specific queries, it would appear that he collected relevant material from the press and publications. More work is needed on this important figure. He would later be a councillor of the NRS between 1895 and 1899.

I look forward to the appearance of your review of Captain Mahan's book with much interest.

[*Annotation by JKL*] G.R Porter (George Richardson) *The Progress of the Nation* 3rd edit. 1851 especially see Chap. 1 p.30
Parliamentary Papers: *Report from the Select Committee appointed to consider the means of maintaining and improving the foreign trade of the Country 1820* (300) (Consideration of the Navigation Laws)

63.   *Laughton to Luce*

7 December 1890

As far as the returns of British Commerce are concerned, I think you will find all you want in Porter's (George Richardson) *Progress of the Nation*, (published by Murray, 3rd Edit. 1851), more specifically in S iii Chap. ix – but much information on the subject is scattered through the whole book.

The 'Report from the Select Committee appointed to consider of the means of maintaining & improving the foreign trade of the Country', July 1820 (300) A Parliamentary Paper (or Blue Book) scarcely bears on the subject of your enquiry, but may be worth your looking at, if (as is probable) you have access to a collection of our Blue Books.

Your second question as to the returns of our losses etc. during the Great War is more difficult to answer satisfactorily. I do not know of any book that gives such information except Norman's *Corsairs of France* (Low, Marston & Co. 1887) Appx. pp. 429–53; & the body of the book is so feeble that I hesitated to recommend any part of it to you. But yesterday, making enquiries at the British Museum, I was referred to one of the assistants who was employed by Norman to draw up these tables from scattered information, & he assured me that, to the best of his knowledge, they are as correct as is possible. The form is meagre & unsatisfactory: but I know of nothing else – should I find out anything more complete I will let you know.

I reviewed the book, unfavourably, for the *Athenaeum* of 5 Nov. '87: but, as I have explained, the tables stand on safer ground.

My article on Captain Mahan's book is in the Oct. number of the *Edinburgh Review*. You will know that the book has excited much interest here.

3

THE NAVY RECORDS SOCIETY, 1891–95

By 1891 Laughton had settled into his new post, and his new profession [66], building links with historians at other Universities. His work for the *Dictionary of National Biography* continued apace, with the steady progress of letters, reaching the mid-point around M in 1893. In this work he employed his naval contacts, many of whom would also be drawn into his most important creation, the Navy Records Society of 1893. This body grew out of Laughton's opportunities to inspect the Admiralty Archives, and the increasing body of historical papers in private hands that had been revealed by research for the *DNB*. Even so, he did not always have the time or the inclination to follow up the opportunities for new research that the project threw up. Although he was offered access to the papers of Admiral Sir Charles Napier, he spurned the chance to consult them, and wrote his entry on the basis of old gossip and ill-informed prejudice dating back to his own first sea service. When taken to task by Napier's formidable daughter he came close to admitting his error, but left an entry that has done lasting damage to the reputation of a brilliant officer [70–71, 112–13]. The Royal Naval Exhibition of 1891, and Alfred Thayer Mahan's second *Sea Power* book of 1892, dramatically increased popular interest in the Royal Navy and its history. Recognising a priceless opportunity to improve the quality of naval history, Laughton marshalled his forces and launched the Navy Records Society, a body based on the model of the Royal Historical, the Camden, and the Hakluyt Societies [79–85].

The objects of the new body were evident in the prominent role of Laughton's oldest friend, Admiral Cyprian Bridge. Bridge was then serving as Director of Naval Intelligence, and effectively Chief of Staff at the Admiralty. As co-founder Bridge ensured that the Society became an unofficial historical branch for the Admiralty. The large number of distinguished names, spanning the naval, military, academic, newspaper and political worlds, that Laughton and Bridge were able to secure for the inaugural meeting of the Society ensured its success. The accession of each group helped to persuade others that the exercise was valid, credible and durable [79]. However, Laughton made the key contribution to the foundation and development of the Society. He took on the thankless task of Secretary, acted as editor, edited the first two volumes, recruited members, solicited support from outside, and drew on all the various strands of his life to make up the critical membership. With the current First Lord of the Admiralty as President, and the support of the Duke of Edinburgh, the senior Royal Admiral, the Society achieved instant prestige. Not everyone was convinced; James Anthony Froude proved a difficult man to please [80, 83, 85]. Nevertheless, by the end of 1893 the Records Society had been established, and was ready to carry out the quiet, yet vital, work of informing naval policy, and enlarging knowledge of the critical role of the Navy in national policy to the leaders of the nation. Over the next 20 years, with Laughton at the helm, the Society published more than 40 volumes. From the beginning the majority were deliberately focused on the historical dimension of contemporary issues; the very first volumes studied the Armada, a timely case study when the Army was, once again, claiming that there was a need for more fortification. Other studies ranged from tactics to administration, but the influence of the contemporary Navy was ever present. In addition to developing the understanding of the Navy, the Society targeted the leading statesmen and spokesmen of the day, bringing together as members Joseph Chamberlain, Rudyard Kipling and the naval correspondents of all the major newspapers. In consequence, while the Society remained a small body, rarely more than 500 strong, it had a far wider constituency, and acted as an intellectual opinion-former. Here it stood in complete contrast to the Navy League of 1894, which quickly degenerated into a noisy, populist pressure group of a type that Laughton despised.[1]

With Laughton as Secretary, the Record Society recruited new scholars of note, such as Julian Corbett [86, 88, 104–6, 111–12], and persuaded the great men of the day, like Samuel Rawson Gardiner [108, 109, 113, 123], to edit naval material, to an agenda set by Laughton. This marked a major shift of emphasis in his work. From the 1870s he had been anxious to provide a complete and reliable naval history; exposure to the documentary sources had widened the scope of his project, but not the ultimate aim. Because it was based on primary evidence, Laughton considered history could be placed on the same foundations as the natural sciences. This new 'scientific' history would be the basis from which to develop a coherent written doctrine for the

---

[1]W.M. Hamilton, 'The Nation and the Navy: Methods and Organisation of British Navalist Propaganda, 1889–1914' (unpublished Ph.D. thesis, University of London, 1986).

Royal Navy. With this ambition, it is little wonder he could rely on the support of naval intellectuals like Philip Colomb [73], Bridge, Battenberg and Vesey-Hamilton. In addition, he had the ear of the leading men, most significantly Admiral of the Fleet Sir Geoffrey Thomas Phipps Hornby [93–5, 103]. With leading politicians and statesmen holding dignified office in the Society, and the naval writers for the major newspapers as Councillors, his list was complete. Only Laughton could have brought these disparate elements together.

Beyond the British Isles he recruited Mahan [75, 78, 87]. From the beginning of their remarkable correspondence it was clear that Mahan deferred to Laughton as 'the' historian, while Laughton recognised the American as a strategist and commentator of the first rank. In his typically unselfish way Laughton laboured mightily to improve Mahan's appreciation of, and access to, the archives, and helped him with secondary sources. He took his reward in the greatly increased recognition that Mahan secured for naval history. The two men would work together on many issues, but none to more purpose than the life, career and character of Admiral Lord Nelson [92, 97–8, 116–18]. Both men produced important studies of the great man in the mid-1890s, and found themselves acting in his defence against a resurgence of ill-informed and partial complaints [123].

Laughton's work also involved him in legal proceedings. His damning review of an anonymous attack on the naval service saw him called to account in the High Court, where he was able to call Hornby as a character witness, and demolish the claims of his prosecutor, H. J. B. Montgomery, a disgraced former Royal Navy paymaster who had served time for theft [91, 93–7]. However, the cost of the case threatened irreparable damage to his invariably straitened finances. This led a group of his friends among the officers of the Royal Navy to launch a Guarantee Fund, inviting every officer to show his appreciation of Laughton's stand [102].

Laughton tried to make more money through his writing, contracting for books on Strategy, Flags and Signals, but never delivered the manuscripts [105, 108], simply because he was too busy with the *Dictionary of National Biography* [90, 102], the Records Society and the *Edinburgh Review* to finish such tasks. He was forever finding the lure of new subjects took him away from profitable, but unoriginal work. Even his two lives of Nelson, his most popular books, were filled with insight and original material, as Mahan recognised [116–18].

Thus, throughout the early 1890s Laughton advanced his cause on all fronts, and with remarkable energy for a man past 60. He had occasional bouts of eye trouble [100–101], and was often weighed down with family and financial pressures. But through it all he remained positive, dynamic and outgoing [112], driving forward his scheme for 'scientific' naval history – of benefit to both the Royal Navy and the historical profession.

64.   *Henry B. Wheatley to Laughton*

29 May 1891

I am editing a new edition of Pepys' diary for Messrs George Bell & Sons which will contain much matter not hitherto printed and which I hope will be the standard edition. I am adding a good many new notes and as I know that you are well acquainted with the ins and outs of the Diary I venture to ask if you happen to have any corrections or notes on passages, which you would be willing to let me have the benefit of. I write this however to ask one particular question. On Dec. 9 1666 the Comptroller (Sir R. Slingsby) showed Pepys, among other things, 'a design of his, by the King's making an order of Knights of the Sea to give encouragement for persons of honour to undertake the service of the seas, and he had done it with great pains and very ingeniously'. I cannot find any other reference to these proposed Knights of the sea, and I hope therefore you will excuse me for troubling (you) with an enquiry respecting them. Perhaps nothing further was done – but I suppose Slingsby's papers are preserved somewhere.

65.   *E. Delmar Morgan[1] to Laughton*

Hakluyt Society, 22 June 1891

Will you excuse my troubling you with the following query. We are about to edit the voyages of Keymis[2] to Guiana 1596, and wish for some biographical particulars of this navigator. To what family did he belong, his place of birth &c, &c. Edwards & St. John speak of him as a Wiltshire or Somersetshire man, but Collinson in his history of

---

[1]Morgan had supplied JKL with information for his *DNB* entry on Kemys; Secretary of the Hakluyt Society 1887–93, but quarrelled with Clements Markham and resigned. No such volume was produced.
[2]Lawrence Keymis, or Kemys as JKL characteristically entered him in the *DNB* on the evidence of his signature (d. 1618). A follower of Raleigh, he committed suicide after Raleigh blamed him for the failure of the Guiana expedition.

Somersetshire does not mention him, nor does Colonel W. Kemmis in his monograph of the family of Kemys of Wales.

Several families of this name are given in G.T. Clarks' *Genealogies of Morgan and Glamorgan* but Lawrence Keymis does not appear among them. He went with Raleigh in his first voyage to Guiana and on the 'Island Voyage', was his messenger to Cobham in the Arabella Stuart affair – was threatened with the rack at Raleigh's trial and was in the Tower for a short time. He was Steward at Sherborne and a commissioner in arranging Raleigh's compensation for Sherborne. These are the few facts that we know about him, also that he committed suicide when reproved by Raleigh for the disaster at San Thome.

It occurs to me that as you have been writing the biographies of our Naval worthies for the *Dictionary of National Biography* you may have found out more about his personal history. I would be very grateful for any assistance you can give. With many apologies for troubling you.

66. *Laughton to Cunningham, Secretary of King's College*

7 October 1891

I have to request you to bring the following under the consideration of the Council.

Very early in last session Mr G. P. Gooch[1] consulted me as to whether he was eligible for the Brewer[2] Prize a second time, having received it in July 1890; and after carefully reading the instructions, as laid down in the Calendar, I told him that he was eligible. At the same time, I advised him to try rather for the Inglis History Scholarship, as being better worth his while. Mr Gooch replied that he had no wish for the Scholarship, but that he would try for the prize if there was no objection to his doing so. I again assured him that the instructions were perfectly clear, and that there was no bar to his winning the prize a second time.

Mr Gooch's work during the whole session was in the highest degree satisfactory & even brilliant. In the mid term papers, in the term examinations & in the final examination in July, he was always first, with full or nearly full marks. I am firmly convinced that he

---

[1] F. Eyck, *George Peabody Gooch: A Study in History and Politics* (London, 1982). Gooch went on to study with Acton at Cambridge, and became a major figure in the historical profession.

[2] Revd John Sherren Brewer (d. 1879); Classics, History and English Lecturer at King's from 1840; editor of *State Papers during the Reign of Henry VIII* (Record Commission on Historical Manuscripts, London, 1830–52).

could have won the Inglis Scholarship in either 1890 or 1891, had he chosen to compete, & I believe he did not compete, as not wishing to stand in the way of men to whom the money payment might be of importance. All the more on that account do I think him deserving of the Brewer Prize, which – until yesterday – I was under the impression had been awarded to him; and I would respectfully urge that he is entitled to it under the provisions laid down in the Calendar, in which no exception is made to a student who has previously won the prize on p.135. I would also quote the case of Mr. Newnham, who was twice awarded the Jelf[1] Medal, in 1887 & 1888, as – to some extent – a precedent.

67. *Augustus Phillimore[2] to Laughton*

28 October 1891

I have not got Sir William Parker's papers by me, so I must trust a little to my memory.

I believe in Sir W. P's journal or log it is mentioned that the *Amazon*[3] delivered Lord Nelson's plan of attack to each ship while at sea.[4] The manner of doing this was described to me by Sir Wm. Parker himself.

I have always taken it for granted that it was the same as that given in the *Nelson Dispatches* Vol. 6 p.443. I have never had the pleasure of reading your abridgement: but it is quite possible that you may be right. I think Sir W. Parker told me that two of Lord Nelson's ships were three decked ships (90 guns) and this was much considered by Lord Nelson. There is however no allusion to this: and perhaps no allusion was likely? I do not think that the word Admirals in the plural is decisive. ·On arrival in the West Indies Lord Nelson expected to be joined by more ships: and Admiral Cochrane did put himself under Lord Nelson's orders on his arrival. At page 467 Rear Admiral Louis was in company on July 1st.

So I think it but natural that Lord Nelson's orders were framed so as to include any flag officers who might join his flag before an action.

---

[1]Richard William Jelf, Principal of King's College 1844–68.
[2]Vice Admiral Sir Augustus Phillimore (1822–97); Parker's Flag Lieutenant and later biographer: *The Life of Admiral of the Fleet Sir William Parker, 1781–1866* (3 vols, London, 1878–80). Parker was a protegé of Nelson's, as well as St Vincent's nephew.
[3]The frigate that Parker commanded.
[4]While on passage to the West Indies in 1805.

Your suggestion raises a point of considerable interest. Though there are many letters and papers from Lord Nelson I do not think that I could have overlooked so important a document, had it been there; so I feel sure no other plan of attack is given, among Sir William Parker's papers. The difficulty of communicating at sea without delaying the Fleet would be so great that the plan of attack might not be given to the Captains of frigates, but only to Ships of the Line. I only mention this as a suggestion in case your surmise is right as to there being another plan of attack not yet published.

68.   *Bridge to Laughton*

21 December 1891

I have just found out that the signal made by Nelson, as you have given it, is wrong. You have given the flags as they were numbered in the 1808 Signal Book. Nelson used them as they were numbered in the 1799 book, but with the signification of Sir Home Popham's book of 1803. I have seen both the 1799 and 1808 signal books and there can be no doubt about the numbering.[1] A happy Christmas to all your circle

P.S. I have made inquiry about the status of paid off officers and may get some information. I am told that mates paid off and not re-appointed were legally discharged down even to 1869!

1799

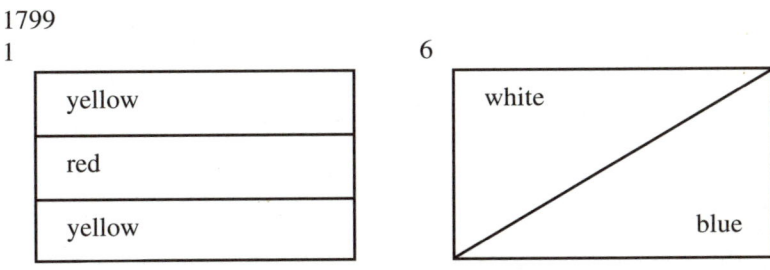

1   6

<hr />

[1]This must have been in his *Trafalgar* of 1890. See the frontispiece of J.K. Laughton, *The Nelson Memorial: Nelson and His Companions in Arms* (London, 1896) for a repetition of this mistake.

69.   *C. H. Firth to Laughton*

9 January 1892

I am much obliged to you for your letter of Dec. 27th and your suggestions about Monck, and shall be thankful for any help you can give me
in regard to his naval career.[1] I am inclined to think that he probably
served in the Cadiz expedition as a gentleman Volunteer under Sir
Richard Grenville, and in the expedition to Re he was first a Gentleman
Volunteer and afterwards I believe an ensign. But, not having my books
here I cannot be absolutely certain about my facts.

The Clarke papers give me ample material for the history of Monck's
government of Scotland, and I have all the information necessary about
his share in the Restoration. As to his merits as an Admiral, I am not able
to form a judgement and if you have written anything on the subject
should be glad of a reference to it. I have a number of notes on Edward
Montagu, Earl of Sandwich which I will collect and send to you when I
return to Oxford. Are you writing Sir John Mennes?[2] The present Earl of
Sandwich has a couple of volumes of Montagu's papers including journals of his naval expeditions in 1659 and after the Restoration.[3]

70.   *S. P. Oliver[4] to Laughton*

30 March 1892

As you are probably preparing the notice of Admiral Sir Charles Napier
for the *Dictionary of National Biography* I beg to inform you that Mrs
H. Jodrell,[5] the only daughter of that gallant commander, has in her
possession all the correspondence of her father, in which many most
important letters are included which were suppressed at the time of the
publication of his *Life and Correspondence* by his step-son, and in
Earp's *Baltic Campaign.*[6]

[1]Firth was composing a life of George Monck, Earl of Albemarle for the *DNB*.
[2]JKL did write this entry.
[3]Sandwich's Journal was subsequently published by the Record Society. The Life of
Montagu composed for the then Earl of Sandwich did not impress JKL, who reviewed it
in the *Edinburgh Review* of October 1912, his last contribution.
[4]Captain, Royal Artillery, NRS Councillor 1893–1896. He had written on 8 July 1890
about Admiral Robert Drury (LGH 31/ 44–5).
[5]Frances Napier, later Mrs Henry Jodrell (1818–1915).
[6]G. Elers-Napier, *The Life and Correspondence of Admiral Sir Charles Napier KCB*
(2 vols, London, 1862); G.B. Earp, *A History of the Baltic Campaign of 1854: From
documents and other materials furnished by Vice Admiral Sir C. Napier KCB* (London,
1857). Mrs Jodrell had directed the production of the *Life*, and personally suppressed or
destroyed many of the papers from her father's archive.

Mrs Jodrell lately entrusted me with a large portion of this correspondence in hopes of getting it published, but after negotiations with
Blackwood, Bentley, Seeley & other houses, I have reluctantly been
forced to return this correspondence to the owner. I have recommended
Mrs Jodrell to mention to you that she possesses this correspondence,
and impressed on her the importance of giving the writer of the biography for the *Dictionary of National Biography* an opportunity of
reinstating the great name of her father, who suffered so much injury
from political opponents at the end of his famous career. I told her that
I would let you know of my suggestion, and I sincerely hope you may
see your way to make use of this material for the small biography, and,
indeed, if you could for a fuller vindication of the Admiral's rights.

P.S.
Mrs Jodrell's address is: Gisleham Rectory, Kessingland, Lowestoft.

71.   *Frances Jodrell to Laughton*

4 April 1892

Understanding from Capt. Oliver that in all probability you will write
the memoir of Admiral Sir Charles Napier for the *Dictionary of National Biography* I beg to inform you that all the correspondence of that
officer was left to me, his only daughter, and that I shall have great
pleasure in placing whatever portion of it you may require for reference
in your hands.

As a considerable portion of this correspondence has not been published and as I am most desirous that the good fame of my dear Father
should be fully vindicated, I beg that you will not wholly rely on the
published accounts of my father's career for the facts of his biography.[1]
The biographer of Admiral Sir Charles Napier, after perusing the private and official letters in my possession will be able to give to the
world the true relations which existed between the Admiral and the
Board of Admiralty during the Baltic Campaign of 1854.

Should you, on further consideration, consider that there is sufficient
material to publish in a less abridged form I shall be most thankful if
you can bring it to the notice of your publishers and recommend them
to bring out a true memoir of my father.

---

[1]In the event JKL chose not to exploit this opportunity. He relied on the ill-informed
gossip he had heard on board HMS *Royal George*, notably from Captain Henry
Codrington. It was a decision he would regret, leading to an ill-considered article that
has done lasting damage to Napier's reputation.

72.   *Hubert Hall to Laughton*

Public Record Office, 3 May 1892

I put Sconius[1] on the track of your man and he has got out the whole story. The papers are waiting here for you and I think are worth your seeing, but the long and short of it is that Marryat when commanding the *Ariadne* in Nov. 1829 was fascinated by the beautiful lines of a fast Yankee Schooner [named] the *Samuel Smith*, which had put in with a hole in her bottom.[2] He bought this craft for the Navy Board and put a crew on board under P. Salmon 'Master's Assistant' (we have all the names). The Ship was never heard of again and Captain Rennie who succeeded Marryat asked to have their names struck off his books. This led to an inquiry and the whole story came out rather to friend Marryat's disadvantage. (Is it not like our way that this should have been transformed into a noble deed – a slaver gallantly taken, &c &c all probably because the said schooner's lines were suspiciously fine.)

I hope to see you some day. We have got a paper at the Historical[3] on 19 May by Professor M. B.[4] on the Gascon Rolls. You ought to hear it so I will send you a card. He may have something to say about the Channel pirates.

73.   *Philip Colomb[5] to Laughton*

26 July 1892

I believe the extract is all wrong. What Marryat did was this:– He drew up a code of signals for the mercantile marine (date?) on the plan already existing in the Navy. Part of this had gradually grown up from time immemorial, but the important part was the invention of Capt. Sir Home Popham & was completed by him for the Navy in 1816.[6] Marryat

---

[1]Sconius: presumably a researcher at the Record Office.

[2]This letter would have been a reply to an enquiry by JKL about Captain Frederick Marryat RN, the popular novelist. See O. Warner, *Captain Marryat: A Rediscovery* (London, 1953), pp. 82–4 for this incident.

[3]Royal Historical Society, of which JKL was a member.

[4]Montagu Burrows, Chichele Professor at Oxford, ex Captain RN. See *Autobiography of Montagu Burrows* (London, 1908).

[5]Vice Admiral Philip Howard Colomb (1831–98); signals specialist; later an authority on tactics and strategy. His *Naval Warfare* (London, 1891) was a major navalist text, and a worthy companion to Mahan's more famous work.

[6]H.A. Popham, *A Damned Cunning Fellow, Rear Admiral Sir Home Riggs Popham, 1762–1820* (Cornwall, 1991).

introduced nothing new, he only adapted what he found, copying directly to a great extent from the naval signal code.

His code & the flags for use with it slowly found its way into merchant ships, but other codes such as Reynold's also found their way in.

Marryat's code was gradually superseded by the 'Commercial Code' published (date?) This code was ultimately made official in England (?date) under the name of the 'International Code'. It is now, & has been for years the sole code in use in the mercantile marine. It has new features in it, but, the real inventor was Home Popham. Marryat's Code had a good run while it lasted, it may have been translated into foreign languages, but my impression is that the French used Reynold's code until it was superseded by the 'International Code'.

I dare say French merchant ships have been in time past & may be now, compelled to carry a code.

The man who can give you dates & details is Larkyns. He was in the Board of Trade & lives somewhere in the West End of London. You will find him in the Red Book.

Page 2 [*may not be same letter*]
I have written to [the] *Army and Navy Gazette* in answer to his absurd article on Wilmot's paper.[1] Wilmot was only advocating what you & I have before advocated:– i.e. that we should carefully consider how far we should go in distributing force in several ships, or concentrating it in single ships. They have taken him to say that if you are going to design a single ship you must begin by setting her displacement.

74.   *Henry Sulivan to Laughton*

21 November 1892

I did not recognise you as one [of] whom my brother had spoken to me. Thanks you for your letter. I will try and get to London someday and have a look in at the United Services Institute. I will also try a French publisher. There must be some French history of the Baltic Operations, I should think.

The objection to the Legion of Honour was, I think, from there being no exchange. Yes, see enclosed page 12. I have marked my Father's

---

[1]Captain, later Admiral, Sidney Eardley-Wilmot RN; Deputy Director of Naval Intelligence 1887–90, and NRS Councillor and a frequent contributor to the policy debates of the era. His *An Admiral's Memoirs* (London, n.d.), pp. 80–88, contains a brief discussion of his intelligence and literary career. In addition Chapter 14 is almost entirely based on Laughton's historical writings.

own cases 12 & 13. I cannot find the special copy or I would have copied down the real names of persons referred to.

As to Admiral James's life I agree with you – there is not a yarn published that can equal it. It would take enormously. I have pressed my brother to publish it and I think I have now induced him to set to work with the preparation.[1]

Kingston has rather spoilt it, but I think we could begin from the beginning over again, with a mere reference to K. There is no literary work needed about it, a plain copy, cutting perhaps a little out here and there and explaining a little of the history of the campaigns and their origins. So I hope now we shall see them soon in print. The Feasting and Drinking habits of our Ancestors rather influenced my brother against printing the logs, but I hope now he has overcome the prejudice!

I have for 27 years urged the publication, for I want the proceeds to pay for my Father's life.[2] It rests with my brother and I think he is even now having the logs type-written out and then they will be more easily edited.

75.   *Laughton to Captain Alfred Thayer Mahan*

King's College, London, 11 March 1893

I venture to hope that you will not be annoyed at receiving a letter from me thanking you for the pleasure I have derived from your works, & more especially from your last on the *French Revolution & Empire*.[3] It is a great work, & ought to open the eyes of many on this side who are obstinately blind to many of the truths you have so clearly put forward.

You will probably have seen Admiral Colomb's collected essays, lately published.[4] It is interesting to note the general agreement between your views & his, though there are some points of difference, which are possibly more apparent than real. The most important & real is that which Colomb has expressed at p.37, and which does, I think, directly controvert the view you have put forward at i. 327–8.

---

[1]J.K. Laughton and J.Y.F. Sulivan (eds), *Journal of Rear Admiral Bartholomew James (1752–1828)* (London, NRS, 1896).

[2]H.N. Sulivan, *Life and Letters of Admiral Sir Bartholomew James Sulivan 1810–1890* (London, 1896). Sulivan was the outstanding fleet surveying officer in the Baltic campaigns of 1854 and 1855; H.N. and J.Y.F. Sulivan were his sons.

[3]*The Influence of Sea Power upon the French Revolution and Empire* (2 vols, Boston and London, 1892). This was JKL's favourite among Mahan's books.

[4]P.H. Colomb, *Essays on Naval Defence* (London, 1893).

I think myself there is much to be said in support of your opinion. Our loss of the North American Colonies seems a case in point – but I fancy most thinking men here would endorse Colomb's.

I have been asked to read a paper at our United Services Institution on 'Recent Naval Literature', which will necessarily be mainly on your two books. It will not of course be critical, but rather, as bringing up some of your arguments & conclusions for discussion. If we are fortunate this may be interesting. As your name will of course be mentioned I should be very glad to learn, on your authority, the proper way to pronounce it. Opinion here varied as to whether the accent is on the first or the last syllable. M'ah~an or M~aha\n. Of course authority alone can settle it. How do you pronounce it?

You probably learned from Admiral Luce that I wrote the article on your former book in the *Edinburgh Review*. I have been guilty of similar presumption as to this latest. I believe the article will appear in the April number of the Review.

If you see Admiral Luce will you kindly make my compliments acceptable to him; and believe me.

76.   *Bridge to Laughton*

Admiralty, 14 March 1893

My belief is that Sir Wm. Martin's[1] representations led to the introduction of a C[ontagious] D[iseases] Law at Malta.[2] I do not know for certain that he did. I suppose you know that the operation of these laws – at home and in Crown Colonies was suspended by the Conservatives, of course with the natural and expected result of an enormously increased sick list.

Sir W. Martin was the introducer of an evolutionary system suitable to steam fleets. He was the introducer of the present system of giving men leave according to classification for behaviour. Before this, men, as you know, were prisoners on board with opportunities merely for an occasional debauch.

He was the introducer of the Uniform Watch Bill, Station Bill etc.
He was the introducer of a uniform scale of punishments for offences.

[1]Admiral Sir William Fanshawe Martin (1801–1895). Bridge's letter gives a very good impression of this outstanding officer's contribution to the 19th-century Royal Navy.
[2]Legislation for the compulsory inspection of prostitutes in garrison and dockyard towns, introduced to combat the high levels of venereal disease. Later repealed on civil liberties grounds. See E.L. Rasor, *Reform in the Royal Navy: A Social History of the Lower Deck, 1850 to 1880* (Hamden, CT, 1976).

He made cleanliness in the matter of bedding and exactness in seamen's uniforms general.

The well-known 'white-working rig' we owe – at any rate its general use – to him.

He made silent performance of work the rule.

He found many, if not most, of the ships in the Mediterranean in a state of mutiny. They were manned, as you know, by hastily raised 'bounty-men' and you will remember into what admirable order he brought his fleet.[1]

It is a remarkable proof of his genius that he carried all his reforms, and diminished leave breaking, and stamped out mutiny less by severity than by discretion, and that under him – and especially in his own ship – punishment was smaller than perhaps it had ever been. Sir T. Brandreth would know more about him than I do.[2]

Have you noticed Mahan's curious defence of large size in the *Revolutionnaire* case, p.128 of vol. I?[3] The big ship lost 7 times as many men as her opponents, was thoroughly beaten, only did not surrender because Lord Howe called off her antagonists, and had to run back to port. A desire to persuade his countrymen to have huge armour-clads clouds even Mahan's clear historical vision.

77.　*Bridge to Laughton*

15 March 1893

I like this immensely, better even than your review of the earlier work.[4] Chevalier, Lois, and other writers, not with standing, I am convinced that the French Navy at the beginning of the war was as well manned as, or even better manned than ours. Of course we had an enormous superiority as regards quality of officers; and discipline had died out during the early years of the Revolution.[5]

---

[1] JKL and Bridge served together on board HMS *Algiers* under Martin's command.

[2] Admiral Sir Thomas Brandreth had been Captain of the Fleet under Martin.

[3] A.T. Mahan, *The Influence of Sea Power Upon the French Revolution and Empire* (2 vols, Boston and London, 1892). The example comes from the 'Glorious First of June', where the French three decker beat off numerous smaller opponents. The contemporary significance of the point is particularly important.

[4] Bridge is referring to JKL's 'Mahan on Maritime Power', *Edinburgh Review*, **CLXXXIV** (1893).

[5] W.S. Cormack, *Revolution and Political Conflict in the French Navy 1789–1794* (Cambridge, 1995), demonstrates that the French were short of seamen before the war (pp. 24–5), and that they had to adopt draconian disciplinary measures in 1793 to keep those they had in service (pp. 252–3).

But we may call Chevalier and Lois themselves to witness that there were a considerable body of men in France who had had a man-of-war's training. What became of them? We know that they did not go to sea in merchant ships, because there were no merchant ships for them to go to sea in. We may feel quite certain that they were suffered to stay at home. If they were sent to the armies you may feel pretty confident that it was they who were sent back as 'soldiers' to the fleet.

I have heard too many competent officers abuse the inefficiency of our own absurdly over-trained men not to know that statements such as Adm. Martin's[1] about his crews at Toulon require to be heavily discounted. As for our service, remember the sort of crew Pellew[2] had in the *Nymphe*. For 7 or 8 years before the war began we had on average some 15,000 seamen and 4,000 marines. In 1794 we had 73,000 seamen and 12,000 marines. Is it conceivable – even without the evidence of Pellew's case – that even half of the above increased numbers could have been either men-of-war's men or seamen?

I have made several easily erasible pencil notes in the margin.

P.S. Mahan quite contradicts his view as liking ships advantages on the same page as that on which he attributes them to the *Revolutionnaire* and again in his allusion to the *Orient* at the Nile.

78. *Mahan to Laughton*

Naval War College, Newport, R.I., 21 March 1893

My dear Sir,

I beg to express the extreme gratification caused me by your letter of the 11th, received yesterday. Your distinguished reputation as a master of naval history, and writer on matters of naval warfare has of course long been known to me, and adds greatly to the value your kind expressions have for me. I knew from Ad. Luce that you were author of the article in the *Edinburgh* and which I may now perhaps thank you for thinking what you were there kind enough to say. I may mention that I greatly appreciated your good opinion. I shall wait with impatience for next April's number.

With regard to the particular question you ask – as to the pronunciation of our name – we put the accent on the last syllable. I fancy this arose from a mistake – my father having been a child of Irish parents, though born in this country – but the usage with us is well settled.

---

[1]French Admiral commanding in the Mediterranean, 1794–95.
[2]Admiral Sir Edward Pellew, later Viscount Exmouth (1757–1833).

I have not yet seen Ad. Colomb's essays, having for some months been on detached duties, but shall send for them at once. He and I differ in more than one point, as is naturally to be expected. The most important perhaps is summed up (his view) on p.172 of *Naval Warfare*. What he then considers the strength of the Allied strategic position is to me its weakness, and I think Napoleon agreed with my view. I cannot, alas, go as far as he does in estimating the deterrent force of the smaller and weaker fleet, when the stronger lies between it and the operation which the stronger wishes to cover. One can admit to excellence of Torrington's management in 1690, without being convinced, as I am not, that it was possible for Herbert to prevent the crossing of the force at Cherbourg if Tourville held his ground in mid Channel. All this, however, simply amounts to saying that there are two sides to most questions; and, indeed, I feel, without the least shame, that a careful reader will find me contradicting myself from time to time, simply because I look now on one side, now on the other. The dangerous man in war is he who gets hold of one side of the truth and thinks himself then equipped with a pass key to unlock all problems. To my mind the solution of the difficulties of war, (and for that matter of most problems in <u>practical</u> life), is not to attempt to strike a mean between the two opposite sides of a truth, but to hold them both, and under the influence of both to decide a particular case.

I am pleased to hear that you will bring forward my books in your intended paper for the Royal U.S.I. I presume you may by this have seen a *Life of Adm. Farragut* by me, published last fall. I advised the publishers, who wished to bring the series of which it is one before the English public, to send a copy to you, as one of the few recognised experts. While I did my best to bring Farragut's personality forward, my habit of thought has made it rather a military study of a military character – as such it may perhaps interest you.

Adm. Luce is at present in Europe, having gone as Commissioner to the Madrid Exposition, sometime last summer. What his present whereabouts, or his intentions as to returning, I know not. We do not correspond regularly, although I had a letter from him in December last. I think very probable that you will see him in London before we do here.

Before closing, may I express the hope, uttered by Prof. Burrows in his *Life of Hawke*, that we are some day to have from you a history of the British Navy.[1] I had occasion to realise the need of it during many painful hunts for details – and you must, with your particular and intimate knowledge, have seen that I have practically given up in many

---

[1]M. Burrows, *Life of Admiral Lord Hawke* (London, 1883), p. iv.

cases, accepting ignorance of details as not material to the broad lines I wished to draw. Still, without Nelson's *Dispatches* and Napoleon's *Correspondence* I should have been in a bad way. It was upon them, not upon any published naval history that I built my work. Immense as is the task I hope you have undertaken it.

79. *Laughton to Earl Spencer*

Catesby House,[1] Manor Road, Barnet, 13 June 1893

My Lord,

I have the honour to inform you that at a meeting held this afternoon at the Royal United Services Institution, it was proposed by Admiral Sir Edward Fanshawe, and seconded by Prince Louis of Battenberg,[2] 'that a Society be, & is hereby formed for the publication of rare or unedited works relating to the Navy; & that the Right Hon. Earl Spencer KG[3] be requested to accept the office of President of the same'. This was carried unanimously & by acclamation, and I am accordingly to convey to you the request of the Society to accept the office of President.

Other resolutions appointed a provisional Committee to frame rules, draw out a list of Council, determine on the name of the Society and to report to a general meeting on Tuesday 4th July, at 3 pm. Sir Edward Fanshawe is the Chairman of this Committee, in the absence of the President, it was agreed that I should prepare a draft of rules & Council list, and send a copy to the several members of the Committee, prior to our meeting them.

May I express a hope that you will be able to comply with the request of the Society as embodied in the resolutions I have transcribed? In which case, though we can scarcely hope that you will be able to take any active part in the work of the Committee, it will be my duty to inform you of its progress.

encl.

Proposed by Sir R. Vesey-Hamilton,[4] seconded by Mr Hubert Hall. That the proposed Committee* consist of the President and;

---

[1] On leaving Greenwich Laughton had moved, presumably to a larger house.

[2] His Serene Highness Admiral Prince Louis of Battenberg (1854–1921), later Admiral of the Fleet the Marquess of Milford Haven.

[3] John Poyntz Spencer, 5th Earl Spencer (1835–1910), at that time First Lord of the Admiralty. See P. Gordon (ed.), *The Red Earl: The Papers of the Fifth Earl Spencer* (2 vols, Northampton, 1981 and 1986).

[4] Admiral Sir Richard Vesey-Hamilton (1829–1912); First Sea Lord 1889–91.

Battenberg, Prince Louis.
Bridge, Rear Admiral.
Clarke, Major George S. KCMG.[1]
Colomb, Vice Admiral.
Fanshawe, Admiral Sir Edward G. KCB (Chairman).
Hannay, David.[2]
Laughton, J. K. (Secretary)
Loraine, Sir Lambton, Bart.
Robinson, Commander C.N.
Wharton, Captain W. J. L. FRS.[3]
Wilmot, Captain S. Eardley
of whom five shall form a *quorum*.

[*Endorsed*] I approve, reply.[4]

80.   *James Anthony Froude[5] to Laughton*

12 June 1893

I have not as a rule found that much valuable historical work is produced by Societies. Fine historical work is like fine poetry, and can
only come from individuals who have gifts for it. But I dare say that
such a body as you are forming may discover and publish old letters of
interest and I will become a member of it with pleasure.

81.   *Laughton to Spencer*

21 June 1893

I enclose a draft of the laws & Council list which I have prepared for
the consideration of the provisional committee. It is to meet on Tuesday
next at 3 pm at the RUSI & should you not be present Sir Edward
Fanshawe will preside.

---

[1]George Sydenham Clarke (1848–1933), Royal Engineers; later Lord Sydenham of
Coombe; First Secretary of the Committee of Imperial Defence; noted writer on defence
issues.
[2]David Hannay, leading popular naval writer and journalist.
[3]Wharton was the Hydrographer of the Navy.
[4]In Spencer's hand, a direction to his secretary. Lambert, *Foundations*, Chapter 6
examines the foundation and early years of the Record Society.
[5]James Anthony Froude (1818–94), Regius Professor of History at Oxford, one of the
last great historians from the 'literary' age. See W.H. Dunn, *James Anthony Froude: A
Biography* (2 vols, Oxford, 1963).

I should be glad to have your instructions about the General Meeting on 4th July at 5 pm. the hour being fixed by the requirements of the Institution.

The object of the meeting is to consider the Report of the Provisional Committee & elect Council.

If you can take the chair on this very important occasion I am certain your doing so would be highly esteemed, but if that is not possible, I should be obliged if you would tell me who you think should be asked. Sir Edward Fanshawe is the Chairman of the Committee: it would therefore be perhaps better that he should not be in the chair at the meeting. The Marquis of Lothian[1] would probably consent, of course, if you could ask the Duke of Edinburgh,[2] it would give us a hoist into public notice that might be worth a great deal to us.

[*Attached draft reply of 23 June. Spencer would be unable to attend, and suggested that the provisional committee should select a Chairman.*]

82. *Laughton to Spencer*

15 July 1893

I have the honour to enclose a copy of the rules of the Navy Records Society.

The Marquis of Lothian took the chair at the meeting of the 4th July, which passed off quite satisfactorily.

We had a Council meeting last Tuesday, when 107 names were approved as members of the Society. I was instructed to draw up a prospectus setting forth more fully the aims & objects of the Society, and also a list of members. These are now at the printers, from whom I hope to have them in the course of a few days. I have arranged to dispose of a large number (about 10,000) of the Prospectuses, as leaflets slipped into the several copies of the *Geographical Society's Journal*, & of the *Journal of the United Service Institution*. In other ways I hope to place another 5,000 from all of which I think we may fairly expect a considerable increase to our numbers.

We have a committee meeting on Wednesday to consider about getting some publications under way, so as to get a volume out as soon as

---

[1]Schomberg Henry Kerr, 9th Marquis of Lothian (1835–1900); geographer, diplomat and educationalist.

[2]Alfred, Duke of Edinburgh and Saxe Coburg (1844–1900); Admiral of the Fleet, second son of Queen Victoria.

possible after the New Year. Till we actually make a beginning, we cannot expect to hear anything from libraries & clubs etc. which I have little doubt will join us, if we do well.

83. *Froude to Laughton*

23 July 1893

In giving you my name in support of your Society I express merely my approval of its purposes. I must see however, the character of the work which you produce before I bind myself to an annual subscription.

84. *Michael Oppenheim[1] to Laughton*

24 July 1893

It quite makes one gasp to hear that Camden[2] susceptibilities will be hurt by our touching the Cadiz voyage! However I have no particular desire to treat it. I will only remark that the majority of their naval works have been edited by men who have much the same sort of knowledge of the sea that a bookseller has of literature and that it is a great pity they have not left them alone.

[Oppenheim proposes to reprint three Elizabethan pamphlets for the NRS]

I am disappointed at seeing from the list sent me that there are only about 100 members and that less than half of them are naval men. Although it is perhaps really better that they should be readier to make history than read it.

---

[1]Michael Oppenheim (1853–1927), historian of the Tudor Navy, edited *Naval Tracts of Sir William Monson* for the Record Society. In an incomplete letter contemporary with this Oppenheim declared: 'I suppose that, from a naval point of view, Mahan's may be considered one of the great books of the world. I am sorry it was not written by an Englishman.' and in another fragment: 'I may be taking an exaggerated view but I fancy that even Mr. [Samuel Rawson] Gardiner has hardly done justice to the weight of the fleet in the Civil War. Indirectly it stopped Rupert at Brentford and, to go back yet earlier, one hardly sees how London could have dared to revolt at all if the navy had not been on its side.'

[2]The Camden Society (1869–97), historical publishing society, amalgamated with the Royal Historical Society in 1897. Gardiner was the Director at this time.

85. *Froude to Laughton*

29 July 1893

In explanation of my last letter I think it better to say that I read in some newspaper an account of the purpose and intention of the Society which diminished the interest which I had at first been inclined to feel. In my opinion the thing needed is the exact text of important papers with a minimum of commentary. The editors in such cases usually economising the selection and giving us a great deal of themselves with a limited quantity of original matter.

It appeared to me from what I read that you are proposing to imitate those societies which I had regarded as the worst offenders – and therefore I wished before definitely committing myself with you to see what you really meant to do.[1]

86. *Laughton to Julian Corbett*[2]

8 August 1893

So many new members were coming in that Lord Spencer thought it would be best to approve them at once; which has been done.

I have just been reading your 'Doughty' article with much interest.[3] You seem to make out a strong case in support of your theory, which is probably as good a one as can be framed. Do you know how <u>John</u> Doughty got back to England. His name is not among those of the *Golden Hind*, who testified in favour of Drake – which is not to be wondered at. I called attention to this in the *DNB*.

P.S. Have you yet seen Froude's papers on the Elizabethan seamen in *Longman's Mag.*?[4] They are worth reading, of course, though they contain much with which I cannot agree. In the last, just published, he suggests that Doughty was in <u>Spanish</u> pay: which is possible enough:

[1]Froude died on 20 October 1894, not long after the first NRS volumes were published.

[2]Sir Julian Stafford Corbett (1854–1922); historian and strategist. Corbett built on Laughton's legacy, and learnt much of his working method from him. See D.M. Schurman, *Julian S. Corbett* (London, 1981).

[3]J. S. Corbett, 'The Tragedy of Thomas Doughty; his relations with Sir Francis Drake', *Macmillan's Magazine*, **LXVIII** (1893), pp. 258–68. Doughty was executed by Drake.

[4]Lectures delivered at Oxford, Easter terms 1893 and 1894; reprinted as *English Seamen of the Sixteenth Century* (London, 1895). The reference is to chapter 4 'Drake's voyage round the world'.

but I think, on the whole, I prefer your suggestion, which seems to me very happy. By the way if you have any short copies of that article, I should be very glad if you could spare me one.

87.   *Mahan to Laughton*

Southampton,[1] 16 August 1893

I thank you most heartily for your letter of the 14th and for the interesting, and from my point of view most valuable, excerpts you send me.[2] It is under such side-lights that the real figures of men and women gradually emerge. In this way I have found the Hamilton letters conduce much to the development of her character and appreciation of the influences that affected her. Vague still, I see 'men like trees, walking', but I have encouragement to believe that I shall gradually reach some close approximation to the nature of the woman who so powerfully and for so long swayed the career of the hero. I cannot yet divest myself of the hope that something more worthy – or less degrading – than mere animal passion underlay such a sustained devotion – may somewhat extenuate the lamentable blot on his name.[3]

88.   *Laughton to Corbett*

28 September 1893

I am obliged by your note. The Banker's order came to hand all right – before my card could have reached you, I think.

I like your idea of the papers of the Spanish War subsequent to the defeat of the Armada. I believe there is a good deal. Salisbury[4] was speaking to me – only a few days ago – of much material relating to the Expedition to Cadiz in the Cecil Papers at Hatfield, which he is calendaring for the Hist. MSS. Comm. and the S[tate] P[apers] Dom[estic] & Holland, must have a good deal almost if not quite unknown.

I doubt if there is anything like enough matter relating to the Dutch in the Medway in '67: but I hope before long, we shall attack the Dutch Wars systematically. There is a mass of material, both MS. and printed

---

[1]Where Mahan had arrived as Captain of the USS *Chicago*.

[2]This reference is obscure, the intervening letter from JKL is not preserved in Mahan's archive.

[3]The key problem for Mahan and JKL in using Nelson as the basis of naval education remained his personal life.

[4]Mr Salisbury, transcriber, worked at the Public Record Office.

relating to the First Dutch War of the greatest interest. If no-one else wants particularly to do it, I shall take it up, when I have to do another volume.[1] I have rough notes for a good deal of it. It would perhaps be a matter to consider whether it would not be better to attack this rather large subject in chronological order (I mean the Dutch wars): but as our volumes are and must be distinct from each other, it is not of much consequence.

Are you often at the R[ecord] O[ffice] [?] Now I am a good deal there, looking about the Armada papers, and we may perhaps meet – especially if you will send me your card when you think of going there.[2]

I hope you had a good time in Norway.[3] Here our weather has been perfect.

P.S. I suppose your present address is an accidental one. You must let me know if I am to change it in the list.

89.   *Bridge to Laughton*

30 October 1893

I looked in the *Dictionary of National Biography* today for Admiral Guise and could not find him.[4] He was Lord Cochrane's colleague and – I think – successor in the War of South American Independence.

The part that Englishmen took in that contest – especially in Venezuela, Colombia and Peru, is not often remembered. General Miller,[5] whom I met at Honolulu, was a very distinguished soldier. See Pillings' translation of General Mitre's book.[6]

---

[1]He persuaded Gardiner to take on the task.

[2]This approach to correspondence would explain the relative paucity of Laughton's archive for those who he met regularly in London.

[3]Corbett was a passionate fisherman.

[4]Martin Guise, Peruvian Admiral in the Peruvian War of Liberation; killed in action at Guayaquil in 1829. Not qualified for inclusion in the *DNB*.

[5]General William Miller (1795–1861); served in various South American Wars of Liberation against Spain and Portugal; later British Consul in the Pacific, 1843–59.

[6]B. Mitre, *The Emancipation of South America* (London, 1893), a translation of a life of General San Martin.

90.   *Laughton to Sidney Lee*[1]

23 November 1893

I should have liked Pepys,[2] of course; but I quite recognise Mr. Stephen's prior claim, so there can be no soreness about his getting it. Otherwise it's a very poor batch.

I fancy Pullen[3] was a surveying officer, he may have done more work than I know of. At any rate, if you like to put him down to me, I'll look into his services.

I think the proposed dinner to Mr. Smith[4] a capital idea: I would suggest some more convenient place than Richmond as desirable. Limmer's I can recommend from personal experience: & his charges are quite reasonable.

P. S. We passed the recommendations of the Committee (at which you were present) at the Council of the NRS (when you were not). It was perhaps as well that the Council was composed entirely (with the exception of Colomb & myself) of those who were not at the Committee Meeting. It made the work longer, but perhaps gives more weight to the decision. We settled that Spottiswoode[5] should print, no publisher – no sales by the Society – Quaritch & G. P. Johnston[6] admitted as members, but no member to have more than one copy, unless he *subscribes* for more.

If you have the *Life of Palavicino, Sir Horatio*, in I should be glad to have a very short abstract of it, to put in a note to some of his letters – shall I call and make it myself?[7]

The Mayor of Weymouth in 1588 was Richard Pitt: of Exeter, John Peryam.

---

[1]Sidney Lee (1859–1926); long-serving second editor of the *DNB*.

[2]To write this entry for the *DNB*, being a longer notice it paid better.

[3]William John Samuel Pullen (1813–87); Vice Admiral and Arctic explorer: JKL wrote the entry, which appeared in 1896.

[4]George Smith, publisher of the *DNB*. See J. Glynn, *The Prince of Publishers: George Smith* (London, 1986).

[5] This arrangement persisted until 1977.

[6]Booksellers.

[7]The request concerning Palavicino was for the Armada volume.

91.   *Louis J.V. Amos[1] to Laughton*

28 November 1893

Montgomery[2]

I now beg to enclose your copy of Counsel's opinion as to the defendants being represented by the same solicitor & counsel. He has likewise expressed his opinion on your article; that opinion is full of censure, but it must be remembered that he has not yet read the book.

Can you send me a copy of 'Another view of the British Navy in the present year of Grace' by 'A Lieutenant RN'?

92.   *Mahan to Laughton*

U.S.S. *Chicago*, Genoa, 1 December 1893

I had ordered through Stevens a copy of your lecture sent me, and received it two days before the one from yourself came.[3] I beg to thank you for the latter. It will not, I hope, be necessary for me to enlarge upon the gratification I feel at being spoken of in so flattering a manner by a person of your attainments in our particular field.

I am glad to see some qualification made and accepted in Colomb's first presentment of a general deduction from Torrington's strategy. That the latter's <u>conduct</u> was perfectly correct, and also his general contention with the Admiralty, must be conceded. The inferior fleet should certainly fall back on its reinforcements, and avoid action; its 'in being' has doubtless its utmost effect while unimpaired by battle. I think Torrington in pleading his case naturally overstated his position; and of Colomb's endorsement the ill-effect appears to me in the recent *Quarterly* article, where 'the fleet in being' theory is accepted practically without qualification.[4] My treatment of Torrington excited more adverse comment than any point in my first book, which certainly did not do him justice – but I have never conceded the position that his fleet after – or before Beachy Head (though certainly more before than after)

---

[1]Laughton's Solicitor, of 39 Great Marlborough Street, London.

[2]Henry James Boyle Montgomery, disgraced ex-Paymaster RN and author of the scurrilous book *The Navy in the Present Year of Grace*, referred to under the pen-name of 'An Undistinguished Naval Officer' of 1885. He was suing JKL for libel following a severe review in the *Army and Navy Gazette*.

[3]J.K. Laughton, 'Recent Naval Literature', *JRUSI*, **XXXVII** (1893), pp.1161–82.

[4]'The Battle of La Hogue and Maritime War', *Quarterly Review*, **CLXXVI** (1893), was also by JKL.

prevented Tourville's action, in the crossing of the French Army. Of course, if men want to make war without running any risk, a very small force will deter them – Tourville may have been, I think was, a man of that stamp. In my opinion, it was possible, with Tourville's fleet occupying the channel abreast the Isle of Wight, to have passed across a force quite sufficient to endanger the new settlement – and that the probabilities were much against Herbert's being able to prevent it. Running risks, in Napoleon's sense, I conceive to mean taking chances, not merely of being killed but of a great disaster – or as he elsewhere phrased it, 'The Art of War consists in getting the balance of chances on your side'.

I think Dundonald falls into a similar exaggeration – though my knowledge of his career off Spain is not precise enough for a final opinion. I think he compounds operating on a line of communications with diversion. In Spain he did the former; off the Biscay coast he could only have accomplished the latter. A dozen ships of the line off the Biscay coast would not have endangered a single route through France, or landed a force that could have gone inland ten miles without being destroyed. The predatory or destructive work they might have done would not have employed fifty, I doubt if more than twenty thousand men. But when the French in 1809 were crawling along shore in the first year of the Peninsula war, their advance depended upon a very narrow line, through a hostile country easily struck from the sea – like the Corniche in 1796. Cochrane made their communications most perilous – he might have burned some villages, but he could not have stopped a wagon train in France. Such diversions as he could have made Napoleon would not have regarded an iota, and they would, I believe, have ended in failure or disaster.

With regard to the *Revolutionnaire* incident I am not contentious. As a rule the same force in one hand is superior to the same in two or more – chiefly because of the difficulty of unison between the several. This the *Revolutionnaire* illustrated – six ships detailed to attack her, several of which did not get in. Apropos of the general question, do you recall Hardy's remark to Parker (*Last of Nelson's Captains* p.146).[1] Personally I myself favour ships of moderate size, for the very reason you give. We cannot sub-divide a ship once built; we can bring together two separate ships for joint action. I may mention that in lecturing at our College I took the historical ground. Our predecessors had 120 and 64 gun ships – they found by experience the 74 to be the best working type. The big

---

[1]A. Phillimore, *The Last of Nelson's Captains* (London, 1886); an abridged version of Phillimore's monumental 3-volume life of Admiral Sir William Parker.

ships had a function, however; they strengthened the important points of an order as no combination of weaker ships could have done.[1]

Your incident of Holmes and the Great Civil War are both admirable and to me wholly new.[2]

Nelson gets on with appalling slowness owing to the mass of petty administrative work I have. I own, too, that it seems no light task to present a new life, that can justify itself, in face of the constant repetition in the previous ones of the same anecdotes.[3] Whether my painful pondering over his letters will produce any result worth the trouble remains to be seen.

93. *Hornby*[4] *to Laughton*

29 December 1893

I was brought up under the Old Articles of War,[5] which I greatly prefer to the present Naval Discipline Act. In the former was a clause calling on every man, under heavy penalties, 'to assist a known friend in view to the utmost of his power'.

I shall be glad to look through the book you mention: and to give evidence on your behalf. I will write my opinion of the passages quoted with as much precision as I am capable of.

94. *Laughton to Hornby*

31 December 1893

Very many thanks for your most kind letter.

Pending your reply, I sent the book and papers to Sir Vesey Hamilton, and will forward them to you as soon as I get them back – probably tomorrow.

I have written also to Sir Thomas Brandreth, to Cox Edwards and Harboard (the present and last Chaplains of the fleet) and to Lloyd,

---

[1] JKL had clearly passed on Bridge's point on the *Revolutionnaire* incident; see [76].

[2] See JKL's entry on Robert Holmes in the *DNB*; and R. Ollard, *Man of War: Sir Robert Holmes and the Restoration Navy* (London, 1969).

[3] A.T. Mahan, *The Life of Nelson: the Embodiment of the Sea Power of Great Britain* (2 vols, London and Boston, 1897).

[4] Admiral of the Fleet Sir Geoffrey Thomas Phipps Hornby (1825–94); the pre-eminent sea officer of the age, he and JKL had been friends since the early 1880s, when Hornby served as President at Greenwich.

[5] See N.A.M. Rodger (ed.), *The Articles of War* (Havant, 1982), for these basic instructions, one of the building blocks of doctrine.

Director of Hospitals, asking their opinion as to the statements about chaplains and doctors. But I shall be surprised if you don't pronounce the whole book extremely scurrilous.

95. *Hornby to Laughton*

4 January 1894

I have posted to you today, from Chichester, Mr Montgomery's silly scurrility, & the manuscript you sent with it. On the margin of this latter I have attached a few lines of condemnation, & hope they will reach you safely. I hope this packet will reach you safely. I have been passing the day in [a] bitter cold Law Court, & feel groggy.

96. *R. V. Hamilton to Laughton*

Royal Naval College,[1] 14 January 1894

It is a wonder to me how any Naval officer could have read more than two or three pages of such a tissue of lies, scurrility, and maliciousness; as is contained in Mr Montgomery's book, – or how he could have got a publisher. I am glad to hear however the latter got the profits. I have made my remarks on the paper and sent them this evening to Mr. Amos. I could not do it before as we had a dance on Friday and they required consideration. I have told him I can see him on Tuesday, Thursday or Friday about 2 pm. if he would like to see me.

The first vol. which I have read, and the extracts constitute what morally, whether legally or not, I can't say – one big lie – as he attacks classes never individuals.

I must got to the Admiralty and find out his history. I fancy I was at the Admiralty when he was tried.[2]

97. *Mahan to Laughton*

Villefranche, 31 January 1894

At this season I presume you are more or less in London, and occasionally at the [British] Museum. If so, it may not greatly inconvenience

---

[1]Hamilton was then President of the College.

[2]Montgomery's Service Record shows two court martials for theft, imprisonment and dismissal from the service with disgrace.

you to do me a favour. You may remember that Mrs Salmon let me have some proof pages of the Nelson–Hamilton letters, and undertook to let me have the other pages as they came out.[1] Since then – August last – I have had nothing. If you could, without too much trouble ask if there be any hitch in the matter, I should be greatly obliged. I sent to him once through Stevens, at least three months ago.

I certainly shall make no *chronique scandaleuse* – but Nelson with Lady Hamilton left out may be a military study, yet can scarcely be a portrait. I have also a theory in the matter which I can scarcely test without seeing his letters to her &c.

I make but slow progress – the infinite and infinitely small details of a modern ship consume time while yielding small results. I have only got him through the siege of Bastia. To be sure the following ground is, from the military standpoint, much more familiar to me. If this cruise ends, as we expect, next summer I can then make rapid progress.

My address is always B.F. Stevens, 4 Trafalgar Square.

98.   *Mahan to Laughton*

Naples, 18 February 1894

Your kind letter of the 4th, being directed to Villefranche, must have reached there after our departure, and I only received it day before yesterday. My surest address is B.F. Stevens 4 Trafalgar Square, who is kept informed of the ship's movements by telegraph.

I am very glad to know that I shall receive the remainder of the Nelson–Hamilton correspondence. I am in no hurry, but I feel that she being, as you say, such a liar (how could she be else?) I can never get at the truth of his feelings towards her except by this means. The character of the relations existing between them is to me comparatively immaterial, though I regard them as beyond doubt since your being convinced.[2]

I wish you all success with your life of Nelson. With your intimate acquaintance with the whole subject – both his career and the general naval history of the period – no one is so well equipped as you for the work. I should of course have regretted to find so formidable a competition, if we were running on the same lines, but I don't think we are at all.[3] The subject grows upon me much, and the steady effort to look

---

[1]A. Morrison (ed.), *The Collection of Autograph Letters and Historical Documents formed by Alfred Morrison* (2 vols, 2nd series, privately published, 1893).

[2]This expresses both Mahan's deference to a higher authority, and his standard of proof.

[3]Laughton, *The Nelson Companion* (London, 1896).

into his character and emotions tends to produce somewhat the same charm that he exercised in life.

These modern ships, however, and yet more the complicated administrative methods growing up in our navy – I fancy in all others as well, not only use up my time but also tire my brain. My progress is consequently very slow – I am ashamed to admit that I have only got him through the siege of Bastia. If I succeed in bringing the book up to the mark at which I aim, it will stand as the work of my life – I so intend it.

If you think of it when at the Museum, would you kindly express to Mrs Salmon my sense of her kindness.

99. *Laughton to Hornby*

3 April 1894

I have just received the enclosed from the Solicitor who is conducting my defence against Montgomery.[1] Will you please let him know when and where he can see you? Of course if you are likely to be in town within a few days it will be more convenient.

We had hoped the fellow was going to let the matter drop; but he has lately shown signs of life and has moved for a trial.

100. *Mahan to Laughton*

Gravesend,[2] 22 May 1894

Pray forgive me for my neglect to reply more promptly to your kind note of welcome. The truth is your fellow countrymen have been so hospitable that I have been on the clean jump throughout my stay, and as your letter required no reply in the nature of an understanding to be reached, it gave place to the R.S.V.P's. I am sorry to hear of your gout and trust it may not prevent your attendance on Thursday, when I shall hope to see you. I myself have the fell disease in the orthodox place – enough to annoy but not cripple me. I can imagine nothing could be more painful, nor, to a writer, vexatious than to have it in the eye. I hope your *Nelson* is progressing well. Mine has ceased to grow, but will not, I hope, die in youth.

P.S. Do you know of any portrait of Lady Nelson?

---

[1] Louis J.V. Amos of 39 Great Marlborough Street, London.
[2] This letter was placed out of sequence when the Mahan letters were bound.

101. *Mahan to Laughton*

13 June 1894

I reproach myself for not having got down to Barnet to see you, but I took too much for granted that your trouble would be sooner over, and that we should meet in town. Latterly I have been driven beyond the bounds in the attempt to run the ship and follow up the social racket, as well as official, into which I was incautiously drawn to a degree that has taxed my head as much as it has my body.[1]

I am truly distressed at the continuance of your trouble, which is so sorely disabling to a literary man – and can but trust that the disease will, at the least soon shift its base to a more manageable spot.[2] I knew nothing of the meeting of the NRS till I saw it in this morning's paper – but the fact was immaterial. I could not possibly have gone.

We leave tomorrow for Antwerp, thus closing a visit which has been most pleasant. I need scarcely say how deeply I have valued the many kind expressions of appreciation I have received from your people. It is an epoch in my life.

I run over next week to take my degree at Oxford – but when the ship will return – if at all – I don't know.

102. *Lee to Laughton*

DNB: 13 June 1894

We are all indebted to you for your admirable action in resisting the impudence of the person who had the audacity to bring the action against you which you <u>had</u> so triumphantly terminated as far as you are concerned yesterday afternoon. Both by your original article and by your conduct of the case you did very good service to many interests and I cannot resist my desire to offer you my warmest and heartiest congratulations.[3]

I trust that your eyes are better and are ceasing to give you trouble.

Many thanks for Nelson, which is very good looking, as it needs must be when major subjects are considered. A proof will reach you very shortly. You do not seem to have forwarded Sir John Norris (1674–1749).[4]

---

[1] A reference to the Banquet at St James Hall to the officers of USS *Chicago* 24 May 1894 (NMM Corbett Mss. Box 2; added by Brian Tunstall).
[2] This must refer to the early signs of Laughton's eye problem, which seems to have been iritis.
[3] The Montgomery Case had been settled in JKL's favour on 12 June.
[4] *DNB* entries.

103. *Hornby to Laughton*

16 June 1894

As I think I told you before; I hold entirely by the old Articles of War, and am bound to assist a known friend in view to the utmost of my power. I was very glad to go to town to uphold what was right and true, and if any reward was due, I got it fully in the very emphatic condemnation the judge gave of the nature of the attack on you.

It is indeed a scandal that a worthless scoundrel, like Montgomery, should be able to levy Blackmail on any responsible person, he being practically irresponsible, but I think the law, and our institutions generally want a great deal of altering.[1] At present an honest man finds it hard to live in England; while rogues and vagabonds flourish. Bright's[2] works, a cheap free press, and a lying edition of the great truths that Adam Smith taught – have gone far to ruin the country, and until a body of statesmen can be got together, to tell the truth and nothing but the truth, I fear we shall not be better.

The sort of truths I want to see taught in Schools are, that authority, on the one hand, and subordination on the other areas such as natural laws as that trade winds blow from SE in the Southern Hemispheres, and that so far from 'all men being equal' (just?), the dogma is not fully quoted, the important words 'in the [eyes] of the law', being omitted; but that probably no harder task could be put on any one, than to have to find two men who were equal. I have known two men so like that one took himself for his brother; but they were not equal.[3]

I hope the Navy Records Society may succeed. I fancy our forefathers were more careful than we are about telling the truth, and therefore the more we can retain of what they recorded, the better.

---

[1]In December 1894 the Laughton Guarantee Fund printed a Notice calling for subscriptions to pay JKL's legal costs: (NMM: Hornby MS PHI/120d). Henry James Boyle Montgomery was imprisoned for five years in 1899 for stealing close to £1,000 from a Company that had employed him as Secretary. (*Morning Post* cutting, 11 January 1899). Laughton's marginalia reveal a vindictive streak.

[2]John Bright (1811–89), liberal politician and advocate of an expanded franchise.

[3]The tone of the letter reflects the fact that Hornby could never afford to live in his father's house, as well as his strong conservative political views.

104. *Laughton to Corbett*

3 January 1895

I am much obliged by your kind note. Without undue modesty I think myself the volumes give us a good start and the get-up is highly respectable.[1] You will have the 2nd volume before now. It has been delayed for nearly a month by the pressure of Xmas work among the binders, and the inevitable drunk after it.[2]

As to the latter part of your letter. I should have liked to print the State Papers for the 'Spanish War' instead of merely the Armada Year, but the opinion of the Council was decidedly and probably correct, that it would be better to begin with the Armada, as likely to be a more popular subject, the rest might follow. Whilst working at these volumes I have been more than ever impressed with the desirability of printing these other papers, both before and after, and had intended to consult you on the subject. I had thought you might perhaps be willing to undertake a volume say 1585–87 or 1589 – really it ought to include 1596, and perhaps selected papers afterwards to 1605 which would probably require quite two volumes. If any part of this scheme commends itself to you, I should be glad to know. It would not, in any way, militate with, but rather assist, your scheme, and though the Society would scarce be able to print the volumes for some years it might help you in the way of transcripts.

With Drake's earlier period – Nombre de Dios, and the World Encompassed – I do not think the Society need meddle for some time to come, though there are some interesting papers about the San Juan de Lua business, and I am anxious to get at the Spanish account of it. That Hawkyn's account contains much falsehood is clear enough.[3]

However, if you will consider about a volume of 1585–7 papers I shall be most happy to bring it before Council.[4]

---

[1]J.K. Laughton (ed.), *State Papers Relating to the Defeat of the Spanish Armada* (2 vols, London, NRS, 1894).

[2]JKL's severe Calvinist morality led him to abhor drink.

[3]Sir John Hawkins (d. 1596). Corbett took this on in his *Drake and the Tudor Navy* (London, 1898).

[4]Corbett edited *The War with Spain, 1585–1587* (London, NRS, 1898).

105. *Laughton to Corbett*

5 January 1895

I am very glad that you are willing to undertake a volume of the Elizabethan Papers. It seemed to me when I suggested it, that it would really be a great help to you in the important work you contemplate.[1]

The Society pays the cost of transcriptions made under the Editor's superintendence. The plan I worked on was precisely that which you describe. With these Elizabethan papers great care was necessary in collating the transcripts, and I fancy I went over them word by word, in which task I had the very valuable assistance, in cases of difficulty, of Mr Salisbury. Several of the '88 papers are so much faded and such bad condition that the making them out was a very difficult job – so much so, in some cases, (eg. ii 146) that the transcriber struck, and I had to do it myself. As far as I have seen, this difficulty does not apply to the earlier or later papers, certainly not to the same extent.

I think it would be better to have the 85–7 period first, though it does not really matter. Should you decide on this I will bring it before the Council at an early date, and have no doubt they will authorise it. The transcripts could then be made when you chose; but I do not see that we could print the volume 'till '98 unless it was thought well to hold Oppenheim's *Henry VII* over.[2] If that is issued in '97 the other volume of '97 ought to be of a lighter, or rather more modern sort; for which I hope we may get a volume of Jervis's letters – but nothing has been decided.

I do not myself see the smallest reason to doubt the essential truth of the Nombre de Dios adventure, though the Spanish version, if we had it, might put a somewhat different colouring on it. I fancy I have seen a reference to the Spanish account of San Juan de Lua – possibly in Duro[3] – but I cannot lay my hands on it at this moment. There are several Spanish papers in Paris, in getting at which Spont would, I have no doubt, assist.[4]

If you are likely to be in town I could generally meet you at the Record Office, and we might talk over the matter more fully.[5]

---

[1]An excellent example of JKL's enlightened patronage, using NRS funds to support research and publication.

[2]M. Oppenheim (ed.), *Naval Accounts and Inventories of Henry VII* (NRS, London, 1896).

[3]C. Fernandez Duro, *La Armada Invencible* (2 vols, Madrid, 1884).

[4]Alfred Spont, French historian and editor for the Society.

[5]Such meetings, rather than correspondence, would appear to have been JKL's basic method of working with NRS editors.

106.　*Laughton to Corbett*

1 February 1895

We had a meeting of Council on Tuesday, when your proposal to edit the State Papers 1585–7 was considered with some others, and the whole referred to a small committee to examine in more detail. Practically your proposed volume was approved, but it was felt that great care would be necessary not to give the members too much of any one period; and it so happens that we had before us besides the volume which Oppenheim is to edit (1495–7), a proposal of M[onsieur] Spont to do the War of 1512–3 and the question not yet dead, of Anthony's pictures (1546).[1] All these are important and most interesting; but we must distribute them so as to give our members a taste of all, or rather to give something to different tastes. This will be for the committee to consider carefully; so that though you may consider that the Council is much obliged by your offer and gratefully accepts it, it may possibly be three or four years before it can publish it. When the Committee has gone into the matter I will let you know. At any rate, when it has decided and the Council has approved you will be able to have the transcripts made. My experience is that doing work of this kind is a race against time, is much more onerous and engrossing than we have a right to expect anyone to undertake. To complete my volumes in the time obliged me to put all other work on one side, with the result that I now have the Editor of the *DNB* ramping for my copy – and not without just cause.

107.　*George Bell & Sons to Laughton*

23 February 1895

We have the pleasure of enclosing, in duplicate, the memorandum of agreement relating to the book which you have kindly undertaken to write for Capt. Robinson's series of Naval handbooks.[2] We have inserted nine months as the time by which the MS. will be delivered, as that is about the period which the other contributors think sufficient, but we are quite willing to suit your convenience in this matter if you require a somewhat longer time.[3]

---

[1]While Spont's volume appeared soon afterwards, the Anthony Roll was only published by the Society in 2000.

[2]Charles Napier Robinson (1849–1936), Captain RN Retd; a long-time friend and coadjutor of JKL.

[3]The title was *Naval Strategy and the Protection of Commerce.* It was never published, but the essay 'On Convoy' in *Brasseys' Naval Annual* (London, 1894) was almost certainly a fragment.

We have also inserted 'about 4/6d' as the price of the books, but we intended, if possible to make them 3/6d, though we have thought it better to allow some latitude in this respect in case there should be unexpected expenses in the illustration of some of them.

Kindly keep the copy that we have signed and return the other with your signature.

108.   *Gardiner to Laughton*

11 April 1895

I am now working up the Dutch War,[1] and want to ask your opinion as to whether the fighting practice (at least up to the end of 1652) which is as far as I have yet reached, had not absolutely deteriorated since the fight with the Armada. In 1588 keeping out of the enemies fire must have necessitated, I suppose, a fight in line varied with occasional advances in pursuit, or at all events as each ship fired its broadside at its own sweet will, it did so at the enemy from outside.

In the newspapers dealing with the fights in 1652, I find the only thing commended is that certain English ships break into the enemy's fleet. Each ship not only acts for itself, but throws itself into the middle of the enemy, thus losing all advantage of superior guns and firing which is usually set down as being on the English side.

I do not know whether there was any change in 1653, but if there was the credit would not go to Blake.

Capt. Mahan speaks of the promiscuous fighting as a mistake, but does not compare it with the Armada fighting.

On the political side I think that the importance of the English claim to search Dutch vessels for French goods has been too much ignored. It did more than the Navigation Act to bring on the war.

109.   *Gardiner to Laughton*

14 April 1895

Thank you for your letter, especially for your references to the instructions for fighting in Penn's MS. They are not those referred to in

---

[1]JKL had persuaded Gardiner to combine research for his long-running history with the editing of naval papers on the First Dutch War (1652–54). The use of Society funds to secure Dutch transcripts and translation was the key to the successful recruitment of such an eminent scholar.

Granville Penn's book[1] as originating with Penn, but earlier ones ema-
nating from Blake, Monk and Deane, therefore I suppose before the
Portland fight. They are instructions for forming a line, each ship in the
track [*JKL* wake][2] or grave [*JKL* grain] of the one before it, upon a
given signal. There is a good deal about the movement in the army
which brought about the appointment of the three generals in Panluzzi's
despatches (R.O.) There seems to have been an uprising of the soldiers
against the management of the war, and they not only carried the
change of generals, but also a change in the Council of State.

Where do you find your account of the two divisions tacking to join
Blake? [*JKL* Penn vol. I p.478 distinctly & II 614] The Contemporary
letters in the pamphlets do not say anything about it. [*JKL* Generals
Desp. Penn I p.474 implied the whole picture, but no details] Perhaps it
may be the Dutch accounts.

Have you seen the unmutilated despatch of the Generals printed
anywhere? The earlier paragraphs are left out in all the printed copies I
have seen. The original, which is amongst the Tanner MS states that the
whole fleet was spread out between Portland and the Casquests in order
to make sure of intercepting Tromp on his return.

Can you tell me where the 'Singles' are by which occurred the fight
in which Blake was beaten by Tromp? They must be somewhere near
Dungeness. They can't be the Shingles between Hampshire and the Isle
of Wight.

I think the explanation of the difference between the fighting of 1588
and 1652 is to be found in the account by Pallavicini in your 2nd
volume.[3] He says that the English kept outside the enemy because of
the smallness of their own ships. This looks as if it were considered the
proper thing to go in promiscuously, and the ships being bigger in 1652
there would no longer be any reason for not doing so.

110.   *MacMillan & Co. to Laughton*

15 April 1895

We are obliged to you for sending us your paper on 'The Heraldry of the
Sea' and write to say that if you will extend it somewhat and will supply
us with material for the illustrations we shall be glad to undertake the
cost of publishing it in book form and to give you half of whatever profit

---

[1]G. Penn, *Memorials of Sir William Penn* (London, 1833).
[2]Sections enclosed and marked (*JKL*) are JKL's notation on the original letter, linked
to the relevant section of Gardiner's text.
[3]J.K. Laughton (ed.), *State Papers Relating to the defeat of the Spanish Armada*.

may be derived from the sale.[1] If this arrangement is satisfactory to you we will send you a formal Memorandum of Agreement for signature.

111.   *Laughton to Corbett*

8 May 1895

The Council desires me to convey to you their grateful acceptance of your proposal to edit the State Papers of 1585–7. They are unable, at the present, to decide on the time for the issue of the volume; but in any case, you can get on with it at your convenience. The Society will, of course, defray the cost of transcripts etc.

I enclose you the resolution of Council as a guide to Editors; but I would suggest further, in the case of letters, references etc. might be advantageously arranged as in the Armada volumes, to which your volume will have such a close affinity.

If you are in doubt about a transcriber, Hone who did mine at 3½d a folio, will (I think) be glad to undertake it for you. Having done mine he will be more *au courant* than another. He has my volumes too for reference.

My critic in *The English Historical Review* p.367 (April '95) refers to and quotes from Add. MS 28,420 and Cotton Galba C.V. Spanish letters of great interest; which though not within your date might very well come in an Appendix, if I had known of them, I should have been tempted to give them myself.

11 May 1895

I had this written to you waiting 'till I could get the resolution of Council for the Guidance of Editors printed, but send it now – the other will follow. The Add. MS referred to seem to embody some of the information you want. I know of nothing in print – I am sending your letter on to Oppenheim and asking him to answer it to you. He has gone much more closely into this matter than I have. My impression is that many vessels were spoken of as galleys by reason of their being flush decked. It appears so in Anthony's Declaration.

---

[1]J.K. Laughton, 'The Heraldry of the Sea: Ensigns, Colours and Flags', *JRUSI*, **XXIV** (1880), pp. 116–48. The book never appeared, although there is a significant collection of material among JKL's papers.

112.   *Laughton to Corbett*

20 May 1895

I am truly sorry to hear of your illness. I hope by this time you are on the mending hand, though this bitter weather intruding on our summer is anything but favourable for a convalescent.

In the roll of the Navy of Henry VIII which Elgar[1] is going to reproduce for us, are pictures of some of Henry's galleys, from which you will see that it was but a name for flush decked and comparatively small ships. The pictures in Magdalene College Cambridge we cannot get leave for: but those of Henry's ships which are not in the museum are there, and seem quite trustworthy as far as the hulls are concerned: the rigging, I fancy, is only an indication.

Of galleys rightly so called, we had very few. The *Bonavolio* was the only one going in 1588, and she was useless. The type of vessel was a mistake in northern seas: but as they did some damage in 1545 it was thought well to try them.

I was hoping to get a clearer exposition of the matter from Oppenheim, but he is out of town. I fear, like yourself, something of an invalid.

When you are about again I can easily meet you at the R.O. but there is no hurry.

113.   *Gardiner to Laughton*

28 June 1895

You must have for your Dutch War an account of the Battle of June 2–3 1653 in Nicholas's hand, and almost certainly written by him.[2] He got his information from the person charged with Tromp's despatch. It is in the Clarendon MS. . . .

He describes the fight as a reversion to the Armada tactics. The English having larger vessels and guns keep outside the Dutch fleet and pound it, the Dutch not being able to close.

It is curious that the first attempt at skill should be made in Blake's absence. The two soldiers in command cannot have thought of it. Was it Penn's idea?

---

[1]Sir Francis Elgar (1845–1909); Royal Corps of Naval Constructors; Director of the Royal Dockyards. He was to have edited the Anthony Roll.

[2]Evidently Gardiner had yet to take on the task of editing the material. Sir Edward Nicholas was the Royalist Secretary of State.

Anyhow, it is an interesting matter, and when I get back to London it will be curious to see whether anything in Penn's life, or in the Dutch histories, newspapers &c throws any further light on the matter.

I go back to Bedford tomorrow.

114. *Gardiner to Laughton*

1 July 1895

Since I wrote to you I found several other papers relating to the war in the Clarendon MS and a good many entries in the very valuable news letters there.[1]

Whenever you come to this point I shall be happy to give you any information about them. It is the more necessary as Macrae has taken a dislike to any information about the War, and deliberately leaves out all reference to it whenever he possibly can.[2] The result is that in this regard the Calendar is quite worthless. I told him what he had done last Saturday. When he does say anything he sometimes goes astray, confusing, for instance, de With with De Witt, but he is a good fellow, and as a rule very careful and accurate.

The English accounts of the Portland battle seem to me to err in omitting all notice of Tromp's deplorable want of powder and shot on the third day under Cape Gris Nez.

I am going back to Oxford tomorrow for a few days to work on at the Clarendon MS.

P.S. I am glad to hear your Kensington class is doing so well.
It's all right about Cromwell I am from Bridget and Ireton, Col. Chester worked out the genealogy for me with references, deeds, &c.[3]

115. *Oppenheim to Laughton*

26 July 1895

Not the least of the surprises of the year is your change of address. I associated you with the stern and hardy North, and I find you in the degenerate South![4]

---

[1]Edward Hyde, 1st Earl Clarendon (1609–74); Royalist statesman.
[2]W.D. Macray, historian and editor of the *Calendar of Clarendon State Papers* (Oxford, 1872).
[3]Gardiner was delighted to discover that he was a descendant of Oliver Cromwell.
[4]JKL had moved from Barnet to Pepys Road, Wimbledon.

I am entirely in your hands about any volume. Writing the introduction would not, I think, take me long; difficulties of editing would be greater. Therefore if the Council decide on it I should like the transcripts as soon as possible. And I suppose it would be the third and last issue of the year.

I have been away off and on (I hope you received my letter with enclosure from Wateringbury) but I am now in that loathsome Reading Room[1] wading through verbose and useless Spanish books in the hope of obtaining some relative light on the formation of our early navy. I am trying to piece out and date the ship lists of Henry VIII from insufficient material. I have a strong idea that several of his ships were like members of a poverty stricken theatrical troupe and did duty under more than one name.

That Review in the *Quarterly* is well written but I should take exception to several of his views. Seeing that even in 1559 and 1560 Elizabeth spent £106,000 on the navy she can scarcely be said to have been ignorant of its value, even if there were no other arguments against the statement. But anything that bangs into the Electoral head what the Navy is to England is yeoman's service.

Government by see-saw appears to be the outcome of democracy everywhere. As a republican (not a radical, please) I don't know whether France, America or this presents the most hateful example.

P.S. I see that I have stated that the *Nomendator Navalis* and Manwaring's Dictionary are the same. Doubtless at the time I compared the M.S. with the printed volume.

116.　*Mahan to Laughton*

Quogue, Long Island, 14 August 1895

The memorandum of your change of address, accompanying the Navy Records Report, came to me very apropos, as I had for some time, purposed writing to you for some information. To my great regret, as a consequence of an unnecessary curiosity about the date of Nelson's entering the Navy, I attempted to calculate back from the times he served on board various ships, as given by Nicolas.[2] This led to my observing, what I had always over-looked and wish I had not found,

---

[1] The British Library. Oppenheim preferred to work at home.
[2] Sir N.H. Nicolas, *The Dispatches and Letters of Lord Nelson* (7 vols, London, 1844–46).

that his age in passing for lieutenant was stated by the passing Captains to be 'by certificate' more than twenty years; whereas he actually lacked eighteen months of that age. He could hardly have been himself ignorant of this incorrect statement, which I presume would scarcely have been made had there not been some requirement it was intended to meet. It was scarcely gratuitous, I know from memoirs of officers of his time that custom justified the attributing <u>constructive</u> service, in childhood, as <u>real</u> service, for the purposes of passing. Tolerated abuses remove the moral stigma in such cases; but what is there to justify a false statement about a man's age?[1]

I wanted also to ask you what possibilities, and what facilities, there may be of getting copies of ships' logs now preserved. They are often – nay, generally – dry as dust; but at the same time there lies scattered among them hints which often solve difficulties. The question of speed in and before battle is often essential to understanding the conditions. I should greatly like to have the logs of vessels at St. Vincent, Copenhagen, Nile and Trafalgar for three days before, during and after each battle; if I could arrange to have them copied for me.

Although I have not myself seen the announcement of your *Life of Nelson*, my English publishers have mentioned the fact – so I suppose it will soon be out.[2] I shall look forward with pleasure to seeing it, and feel the advantage of having before me the views of one so thoroughly master of all the facts. How do you get through all the work you accomplish?

The last volume of the 'Records' (Hood) was to me most interesting.[3] I was particularly struck by what seemed to me a strong similarity of <u>professional</u> temperament between him and Nelson – <u>presumably</u> the latter must have been more likeable. Despite lack of achievement, Hood has gradually assumed in my opinion the second place to Nelson among British admirals. I once asked Sir Geoffrey Hornby, whom he placed second. He replied 'St. Vincent, if second'. I gathered that he thought Nelson erratic. I formerly placed St. Vincent second; now, though with reservations, I should say Hood, but there is little choice.

If the copying of the logs is feasible I should like to have Stevens make the arrangements for me, asking suggestions from you.

---

[1]Mahan's fastidiousness reflected his concern to present Nelson as an unblemished teaching aid for the modern officer. Any hint of improper behaviour would ruin his plan.
[2]*Nelson* in the 'English Men of Action' series, (London, 1895).
[3]D. Hannay (ed.), *Letters of Lord Hood 1781–1782* (NRS, London, 1895).

117.   *Mahan to Laughton*

28 August 1895

Your very kind letter of the 8th was received a few days ago, and was closely followed by the book. I thank you extremely for the latter, appreciating the advantage to myself of such a forerunner of my proposed Life by one so thoroughly master of all the facts. It arrived just in [time] to forestall my intention of ordering a copy from McMillan in N.Y.

I shall refer to your work at each stage of my own, as a beacon to warn me of possible mistakes as to facts. In reading it, I noticed more than one instance in which my impressions are different from your statements, and I may need to write to you on the matter. There is one point on which I would be glad to know more – at your leisure, viz: (p.162) that the British ships at Copenhagen retained their positions till nightfall, which would I suppose be about 6.30 on April 2. This was wholly new to me, and does not yet seem reconcilable with Stewart's narrative (Nicolas IV 311, 312).[1] You will of course have seen the account in *McMillan['s Magazine]* for last June – and although by a midshipman, and evidently written in error as to clock time, the general tenor seems to me to support Stewart: that the movement of the ships began by full daylight, and the implication in both, of an *arriere pensee* [*sic*] on the part of Nelson, is sufficiently strong to render a justification of his whole action in the flag of truce desirable, from one as free as I am in the matter of space – and a foreigner to boot. I am by no means myself willing to believe he took an unfair advantage, and the Dane Lindblom, writing so soon after the event, expressly disavows the opinion; but still the contrary view is largely held.

In matter of opinion, I own to thinking Nelson's course towards Hughes[2] justified upon the whole – that Hughes orders were illegal, and that Nelson owed it to his own position in one case, and to his country's interest in the other to do as he did. The question of disobeying orders is doubtless delicate – but the average naval officer, like the average man, will not sin on the side of involving himself in trouble. At St. Vincent also I think that a flag officer, at any rate, was justified in the independent action Nelson took. Towards Keith his conduct was not to

---

[1]Lieutenant Colonel William Stewart of the Rifle Battalion, commanded a detachment of troops and produced an eye-witness account of Copenhagen.

[2]Admiral Sir Richard Hughes, Nelson's Commander on the Leeward Islands Station 1784–87. See Mahan's *The Life of Nelson: The Embodiment of the Sea Power of Great Britain* (2 vols., Boston and London, 1897), Vol. 1, pp. 43–72.

be justified – it was not independent action, but express disobedience, the onus of justifying which rests on the offender.

I am glad to see that you detect in his letters to Mrs Nisbet[1] the lack of ardour I myself have noted. It explains much to my mind – she was utterly beneath the plane of the ideal in which Nelson habitually moved.

As regards Hood, I believe I mentioned, in the letter which has crossed yours, that I had come to look upon him as the second to Nelson. His comments on the Chesapeake affairs prove to me (forgive the egotism of an author) that had he been in chief command Cornwallis might have been saved (*Seapower* p.476) He doubtless would have been.

I have been pretty entangled with other matters since I came home – but I have so arranged that after Sep. 20 I may give myself exclusively to the *Life of Nelson*.

118.   *Mahan to Laughton*

2 September 1895

Thank you for very much for your prompt reply to my questions, received yesterday. The prevalence of such a custom of falsification is astounding, to use your very just word; but while the custom was abominable, its general acceptance greatly lessens the individual delinquency – and Nelson, about whom alone I am concerned, was not then of an age to be better than those around him.

What you say of the difficulty of valuing, comparatively, officers of different ages is most true – and nothing exemplifies the difficulty more than Hood's case. What he did we know, and also what he proposed to do at certain critical moments; but the achievement was small as compared with men of calibre, to my mind, inferior. To place them in a relative order which would be generally accepted would require an analytical argument few would be likely to read; and any other acceptance must depend upon the mere authority of the person upon whose opinion it is based. I think with you that Howe was over-valued in his day, but perhaps under-valued now. Considering his age I think his conduct on May 28 and 29 wonderful.[2]

I have not yet come to any decision about the logs – being somewhat discouraged by perusal of those for Trafalgar, quoted by Nicolas. Yet

---

[1]Lady Nelson, she was a widow when they married.

[2]In the opening phases of the battle that culminated on the Glorious First of June, 1794.

curiously enough I received a query from your side about a statement of Alison's that Nelson had made a general signal at Trafalgar to cut away the sails on coming into action.[1] Did Alison make such a statement? I shall know before you get this – having no copy here to refer to – but as regards the studding sails, one ship mentions cutting them away and another taking them in.

119. *Bridge to Laughton*

HMS *Orlando*,[2] Australian Station, 23 September 1895

Your *Nelson* was very welcome, you may feel sure. I am most grateful to you for it; but as it reached me only 3 or 4 days ago I have not as yet been able to read it, having hardly found time to cut the pages and glance at it.

I am delighted that you should have brought out a life of Nelson in so convenient a form and in a style which brings its purchase within the means of almost every officer.[3]

It must be satisfactory to you as it assuredly will be to every member, that the Navy Records Society is in such a flourishing condition.

With regard to Nelson's Arms it may be said that of course the Heralds made out, whenever they could, that arms not registered in their Colleges had no real existence. This they were, and perhaps are, obliged to do by the law of their being; but the truth is – and the additions to every new issue of an 'Armorial' almost proves it – that many families had arms which they would not report at 'visitations' for fear of taxation and demands to register which in the Herald's College they would have considered mere impudence. Arms existed long before the College and the older coats were not registered till they had been borne for generations and probably were only registered in time by younger, distant, or doubtful branches of the greater arms-bearing houses. I know the modern craze for documentary history, we have seen what that can come to in Froude's case; and Freeman[4] supplies a needed corrective; but we are not obliged to either over value or under value 'documents' or 'diplomatics'. All that registration in the College of

---

[1]A. Alison, *A History of Europe* (London, 1833–42). There is no foundation for this assertion.

[2]An 8,000-ton armoured cruiser launched in 1888 and sold in 1905.

[3]Bridge means that the book was compact and cheap.

[4]Edward Adolphus Freeman, Regius Professor of History at Oxford and self-appointed public critic of J.A. Froude, who, ironically, would succeed him in that position after his death in 1893.

Arms proves is the fact that Arms were borne at the time of registration, it proves nothing or but very little, as to previous rights to them. As bearing on historical precision this is more important than is generally thought. I have recently, for family reasons, been watching the discussion of the Washington[1] pedigree, and could not help seeing how wildly astray undiscriminating reliance on 'visitations' and Herald's registers leads a man.

I have just returned from a long and interesting and grievously hot and unpleasant cruise amongst the South Sea Islands. I see that some wiseacre has just realised, and tells the world, that old maps and charts contain records of geographical discoveries long before they appear in literature or even in the S[ailing] Reports. Of course they do; why, to this hour, out here people are making discoveries in the South Sea Island groups which will not be noted in print for years, except in 'sailing directions' and not even in them till months after they have been noted on charts. The pre-Columbian discoverers of this *Terra Australis* no doubt made notations more or less right on such charts as they used; but they did not write in the daily papers or offer Histories of their voyages to the leading publishers.

In 1883 I got, in the Marshall Isles, one of the native charts made of strips of wood and pebbles which were then, and perhaps still are in use amongst a race of navigators who could not write a word to save their lives.

There is too much 'society' and entertainment on this Station to make the command a satisfactory one to any officer who has work to do. The plan of having the Headquarters of a squadron in a luxurious city[2] of 500,000 inhabitants anxious to display newly-acquired riches, has never been tried before and the result seems to me to be a long way from satisfactory.

I had a conversation at the Observatory a few days ago with Mr Russell, the Government Astronomer. He spoke in flattering terms of your Meteorological and geographical work. That man in the *Quarterly* seems to make too much of the Dutch fleets co-operation in preventing Parma's crossing.

P.S. Are you the God-father of Pepys Road?[3]

---

[1]George Washington, first President of the United States.
[2]Sydney, New South Wales.
[3]A reference to JKL's new address.

120.   *Corbett to Laughton*

Imber Court,[1] 4 October 1895

I find myself obliged to quarrel with you for saying in the *DNB* that there is no evidence that Drake discovered Cape Horn and that he could not have been so far south.[2]

Have you not been misled by what Burney calls the 'uncouth and unconnected' narrative of Prety in Hakluyt, who says they discovered the southernmost island when they were driven to 57°, at this time Clife, who was aboard the *Elizabeth*, says they were about 90° west of England and therefore not nearly westerly enough. But Drake did not claim to have made the discovery the <u>first</u> time he was driven south. It was not till he had regained the Straits and the *Elizabeth* had parted company. He was then the <u>second</u> time driven south on a lee shore and therefore probably by a WNW gale, which would naturally, continuing as long as it did, have carried him to the Horn from the mouth of the Straits.

Can we say in the face of the authorised narrative, Fletcher's original notes; Richard Hawkins report of his talk with Drake; Honduis's note and Molyneux's in the maps, that there is no evidence that he did make the discovery. We may reject the evidence, but it is certainly there.

Burney had no doubt of it after very careful examination of the case (*South Sea* I 327 et seq.)[3]

I did not know it was ever denied that he did discover some islands in the latitude of Cape Horn. The way the old geographers tried to reconcile Pretey's and Silva's narratives with the others was by placing an imaginary Elizabethides group west of Tierra del Fuego (see note in Burney ib).

You know Drake gives the latitude of Cape Horn exactly right ie 56°, it being really 55° 48′ also that in sailing back they discovered on the second day a group of detached islands that corresponds exactly with the Ildefonso group.

Do you claim that the <u>second</u> forced voyage south of the Straits is all an invention; and if not what is your reason for doubting the evidence which was satisfactory to Hondius and Hakluyt? Hondius certainly did not feel quite sure, but only because the Spaniards and Cavendish continued to assert that Tierra del Fuego was a continent.

---

[1]Corbett's family home, before his marriage; now the Metropolitan Police Training Academy.

[2]On his circumnavigation.

[3]Rear Admiral James Burney (1750–1821), companion of Cook. J.A. Burney, *Chronological History of the Voyages and Discoveries in the South Sea or Pacific Ocean* (2 vols, London, 1803); see Vol. I.

I am very sorry to bother you, but your name has so much weight with me, and every one else, that I cannot pass the point without a note on our difference of opinion – unless that is we can manage to agree on your view or mine.

121. *Laughton to the Librarian of Gonville and Caius College*[1]

21 October 1895, Trafalgar Day

I hope that the College will do me the honour of accepting the accompanying little book as a contribution to the library, and as a small mark of my affection for the place to which I owe so much.

122. *Laughton to Browning*

16 November 1895

When we have our next Council, early in December, I want to get the publications for '97 provisionally settled. Will it suit you to have Rooke's Journal[2] among them? It would suit very well if it could be first; put into the printers hands about this time next year so as to be issued before Easter: but it must depend on your convenience. Of course the arrangements will be only provisional, but it will be better to have some understanding about the year's work.

At the last Council meeting we agreed to bring out **three** volumes next year. Oppenheim's *Henry VII* being the third; and as it is very archaic, it would be well to follow it by one of more modern interest. We shall, I have no doubt, be in a position to continue three volumes a year, with perfect prudence. £150 is a full estimate for the cost of a volume all told, binding, issuing etc. included, and we have now close on 500 members, with a nest egg at the end of this year of about £300.

123. *Gardiner to Laughton*

17 December 1895

I should like to hear what you have to say on the references. There are also a letter of Nelson's to the Council at Turin in [BL] Add. MS.

---

[1]This note is still pasted inside a copy of his *Nelson*. JKL was in Cambridge seeking election to the Regius Chair in succession to Seeley.

[2]This volume would cause JKL more trouble than any other NRS volume published during his 20-year tenure as Secretary.

34,963 which combined with the opinion in Nicholas iii 384 favours Badham's view.[1] As for the trial see Foote's letter of June 26 in Add. MS. 34,912[2] and Acton's letter of June 20 in the same vol. Acton's letter of Aug. 1 says that H. M.'s[3] impressions of Ruffo were ['rou(?)] by Nelson's and Acton's[4] observations i.e. were subsequent to the events at Palermo.[5]

[1]Francis Badham had just launched his attack on the interpretation of Nelson's actions at Naples presented by Mahan and JKL. He had written a paper, and submitted it to the *English Historical Review*. Gardiner became involved in the debate as Editor of the *EHR*.

[2]British Library, Additional Manuscripts call mark.

[3]Ferdinand I, King of the Two Sicilies.

[4]Sir John Acton (1736–1811); English-born Neapolitan Prime Minister.

[5]A typically dense and occasionally cryptic postcard from Gardiner.

FIGHTING FOR NELSON, 1896–1900

With the Navy Records Society established and rapidly maturing into a successful venture, Laughton found he had taken on a heavy workload of editing, administration and related tasks, one that filled every waking hour, and would have filled more, had they been available. While much of the work was enjoyable, and relatively straightforward, two of his editors wasted undue amounts of his time and energy. Oscar Browning was the most troublesome. Browning's badly edited *Rooke Journal* was based on a poor transcript. He did not bother to harmonise spelling, despite Laughton's numerous pleas, and did not check the original documents. The volume caused much upset, once its deficiencies had been revealed [124, 138–40, 142, 145–7, 154–5, 163–5] though it had the positive outcome of a considerable tightening of editorial guidance. It also demonstrated to other editors the penalties of poor work. As Michael Oppenheim observed [160], it 'could be used as a gamekeeper do vermin', by which he meant it should be hung up on a fence as a warning to others!

Admiral Sir Richard Vesey-Hamilton failed to deliver his projected two-volume study of the *Blockade of Brest*, so Laughton hired John Leyland to carry out the work for a fee [125]. The importance of blockade as a contemporary question[1] led the Council, dominated by the Naval Intelligence Department, to approve this use of Society funds. Vesey-Hamilton would also fail to meet his commitment on the Greenwich textbook, *From Howard to Nelson*, which Laughton and Philip Colomb developed, leaving Laughton to bring his chapters on Hood and Rodney up to the mark [131–3]. Laughton also supported Colomb's research into the career of Lord Torrington, a project which Colomb did not live to complete [183, 187, 195]. Laughton even considered completing the project.

On the evidence of the surviving letters Mahan became Laughton's principal correspondent in this period. Mahan came to rely on 'the naval historian' as a living resource from which to draw information,

[1]A.J. Marder, *The Anatomy of British Sea Power* (London, 1940), pp. 107–15 discusses this issue.

archival advice, support and companionship [126]. He was occasionally less than gracious in acknowledging the support he received, once describing Laughton as a 'rummager of records' [162]. Nevertheless, over time their relationship deepened as the two men recognised their mutual interests, and their distinctive, mutually reinforcing approaches to their work [143]. A key project in this process was Mahan's chapter for William Laird Clowes's massive *The Royal Navy*. In order to write this the American strategist would have to make himself a historian [148–9, 174, 186]. Laughton, who sent his own notebooks across the Atlantic to help, would be so pleased with the results that he spent a decade persuading Mahan to have the piece republished as a stand-alone volume.

However, the dominant concern of both men in this period was Nelson. With the centenary of his greatest achievements many aspects of the great Admiral's life and career were thrown under the spotlight. A debate about who was 'responsible' for the nature of the attack at the Nile [136–7, 141] was only a foretaste of what was to come. Unfortunately in his *Life of Nelson*, published in 1897, Mahan had criticised an account of the Naples affair, written as self-justification by Captain Edward Foote.[1] His comments provoked Foote's grandson, Francis Pritchett Badham to mount a formidable, if ill-conducted, assault on Nelson's veracity, and, as a side-line, on the integrity and scholarship of Mahan and Laughton [150–53, 156–7, 179, 185, 190, 196–7, 201]. Both men were determined to protect Nelson's good name from the slurs of Badham, and those contained in the older biography by Robert Southey,[2] which was drawn into the controversy, because they placed Nelson at the pinnacle of naval command, and used him as an example to teach the officers of the next generation.[3] They could not use Nelson as an example if his conduct was open to the criticism of immorality, either for his treatment of the Neapolitan Jacobins, or for his affair with Lady Hamilton. The former matter has remained a problem for Nelson scholars to this day. In essence, the Neapolitan Revolution was adopted by Italian liberals as the beginning of national regeneration and independence, 'when modern Italy, the new Italy, our Italy was born'.[4] The first account of the events by a republican participant appeared as early as 1801, deliberately attempting to shape

---

[1]E.J. Foote, *Vindication of his Conduct when Captain of HMS Seahorse etc. 1799* (London, 1807).

[2]R. Southey, *Life of Nelson* (London, 1814).

[3]J.T. Sumida, *Inventing Grand Strategy and Teaching Command: the Classic Works of Alfred Thayer Mahan Reconsidered* (Washington, 1997), pp. 36–9.

[4]J.A. Davis, 'The Neapolitan Revolution, 1799–1999: Between History and Myth', *Journal of Modern Italian Studies*, IV (1999), pp. 350–58; the quote is by Croce (p. 350).

the judgement of posterity.[1] This attempt, and those that followed would appear to have worked, for by the late nineteenth century liberal historians who addressed the issue, led by the Neapolitan Benedetto Croce,[2] made it a moral and ethical question. Because he restored the corrupt Bourbon regime, suppressing the movement for Neapolitan autonomy, the mythical basis for Italian unity, Nelson's actions have always been portrayed by liberal Italian nationalist historians in the darkest terms.[3] The Italian sympathies of British liberal historians and intellectuals have reinforced this message, creating a dark shadow on an otherwise distinguished career. Unaware of these deeper themes in the literature Laughton and Mahan addressed the evidence, and began to uncover the confused history of the issue.

For three years the two men joined forces, overwhelming first Badham, and then the legion of ill-informed, hostile critics who seemed to dog the hero's heels. Badham had sent his Nelson paper to Samuel Rawson Gardiner, editor of the *English Historical Review*,[4] who, after agonising over the evidence, as it appeared, concluded that Laughton and Mahan were wrong. Having published Badham, he was mortified to find that his old friend and the famous American had been right all along, and advised using the Records Society, of which he was a Vice-President, to settle the matter. While Laughton worked at the sources, Mahan prepared a series of retorts and papers that culminated in the comprehensive revision of his two chapters on Naples in the second edition (1899) of his *Life of Nelson*. These were longer, and adopted a scholarly approach to the use of evidence. This was the only time Mahan ever rewrote one of his books. Eventually the two men amassed enough evidence to secure a victory, and Laughton set H.G. Gutteridge, a young Cambridge graduate, to work on the Italian archives [199–200]. The Records Society volume produced by Gutteridge in 1903, *Nelson and the Neapolitan Jacobins*, would be the culmination of their efforts. The book followed a suggestion from Gardiner, and was encouraged by Mahan, who was anxious for support; but, as usual, it was Laughton who carried the main burden.

Gardiner was also editing documents relating to the First Dutch War for the Society [157, 161, 166, 168–71], but the majority of the corre-

---

[1]J. Roberston,. 'Enlightenment and Revolution: Naples 1799', *Transactions of the Royal Historical Society* (VIth Series, Vol. 10, Cambridge, 2000).

[2]Croce (1866–1952); historian and philosopher of history; briefly Italian Minister of Education 1920–21. His *La rivoluzione napoletana del 1799* (1st edn, Naples, 1887) is not mentioned in the Laughton correspondence, but was clearly a powerful influence behind the Nelson debate.

[3]Davis, ibid., pp. 350–58.

[4]Samuel Rawson Gardiner: editor of the *English Historical Review* 1890–1902. A close personal friend and intellectual supporter of Laughton.

spondence relative to this volume has been omitted for, unlike that concerning Nelson, it was uncontentious, being largely concerned with questions of fact and revealing little of Laughton's aim or methods. Other Society editors relying on Laughton included Michael Oppenheim, then beginning a long-term relationship with the *Naval Tracts of Sir William Monson*. For the same reasons this correspondence has been largely omitted, the exceptions relating to Laughton's arrangement for the republican Oppenheim to gain access to the original manuscripts in aristocratic collections, and an opportunity to experience the speed trial of a destroyer [160, 176, 180]. Despite being on the other side of the world, Laughton's oldest friend, Cyprian Bridge, kept up a regular correspondence, their exchanges including the Records Society and their mutual friend Henry Reeve. Reeve had died in 1894, and Laughton was compiling his biography, a task in which he involved Bridge who had known the *Edinburgh* editor longer [128, 178, 182].[1]

In this period Laughton became much closer to his new friend Julian Corbett, who would take some of the load from his shoulders in future years. Corbett still sought the older man's advice for his projects [202]. By the end of the period, Laughton had also drawn closer to Mahan, who was able to repay some of the favours Laughton had bestowed on him, carrying out useful fieldwork for him in Holland [189, 191, 193]. At this stage Laughton's son Leonard also became involved in his research and correspondence [167].

By the end of this hectic half-decade Laughton had reached 70. In many ways the turn of the century would be the turning point in his life. His great work was now nearly complete. The central directing body of the Royal Navy, the Naval Intelligence Department, had available to it a growing body of historical material invaluable to the shaping of its thinking. In the process Laughton had created a discipline, and a professional body, bringing together the new profession of historian and the old one of sea-service, assembling the great and good, the able and the industrious. The Records Society was not a popular pressure group, it worked through influence at a high level, and was far too discreet to be noticed by those outside. Nevertheless, naval education, doctrine development and the formulation of national strategy had all been given a historical base, and by 1914 could be taught through case studies of previous wars to officers already familiar with the tactical precepts of their predecessors.

---

[1]Henry Reeve (1813–94); long-serving editor of the *Edinburgh Review*, one of the first journals to encourage naval writing, and the forum for most of Laughton's paid reviews. Reeve's testimonial to Laughton's standing as a historian played an important part in securing him the post of Professor in 1885. Laughton was then writing a two-volume biography of Reeve which appeared in 1898.

124.   *Laughton to Browning*

24 January 1896

I have seen Spottiswoode's man about the maps, & he will get them done as soon as he knows exactly what is wanted. If you will let me have the limits of each I will get him to work. The man that will draw them works for the Hydrographic Office, & will take them from the charts. I should say that all modern improvements should be left out – and the modern fortifications. Are any old batteries etc. to be put in? If so it will be necessary for you to send him an indication. I will see about the Index for you. In the revise you have near enough for it – as to the pages, I mean. If so, I will tell Spottiswoode to send me a set of the sheets, & put the girl to work. I am glad to hear you will be able to finish it off now: & we can bring it out as soon as you like. It would do very well to come out before Easter.

As to the spelling, the recommendation of the Council, for the sake of uniformity, is to adopt the modern spelling; but when place names are obsolete, to give the obsolete names in the text & the modern name in a note. I can't see myself that the vagaries of Rooke's Secretary are of any interest – and the writing is (I fancy) all his. By the way, have you found out his name? or anything about him?

125.   *Laughton to Lee*

26 February 1896

Just a hasty line to thank you for the pretty copy of your lecture. I read the notices of it in the daily papers & was looking forward to read it in its entirety in the *Cornhill*, which this copy pleasingly anticipates.

I was sorry you were unable to be at the Council of the NRS last week. However, we settled the business, satisfactorily, by agreeing to offer Leyland – he is the sub-editor of the *Army and Navy Gazette* & a very capable man – remuneration at the rate of 20/– a sheet to do the *Brest Blockade* of 1803–05.[1] I have not heard from him accepting the offer, but he had told me beforehand that he would do it.

---

[1]Admiral Sir Richard Vesey-Hamilton had agreed to compile this volume, which was of the greatest contemporary significance for naval planning, but found himself unable to complete the task. JKL persuaded Council to fund Leyland to continue the work. The influence of the Director of Naval Intelligence, who was represented on the Council, can be seen in this development.

Gardiner takes the *Dutch War* off my hands, and by & by, I will do instead a vol. (selected) of 18th C. Courts Martial.[1] This (supposing Leyland accepts our offer) provides us with vols at the rate of 3 a year 'till the end of 99, which is far enough ahead.

P.S. I can make nothing of James Ralfe. I fear I must give him up, unless you think it well just to mention him as the author of the two books & one or two pamphlets.[2] There has been no sign of him in *Notes and Queries*. There never is. JKL

126.   *Mahan to Laughton*

160 West Eighty Sixth Street, 20 March 1896

Your two letters came in rapid succession, and some little time after I received the logs from Stevens. I am very much indebted to you for your kind attention in the matter. As you forewarned me some time ago they do not throw very much light on tactical details, but I think are upon the whole complementary of the Danish accounts in the particulars about which I was curious. As I think I said to you before, if the Danes statements are correct, they are even more creditable to your people than the English are. Nelson's own plan was admirable, but as you know missed fulfilment.

What you tell me of the Bridport Papers[3] aroused mixed feelings. I am reasonably sure that no letters of Nelson's own will throw new light on his character, though they might possibly throw light on incidents, and I own that – from the point of view of a life of him, in which I am trying to circumscribe the narrative to that which is necessary to illustrate the man, I shrink from going through letters <u>to</u> him. Yet, on the other hand, how is one to reconcile himself to leaving unexamined such a mass of possibilities. The truth is, I shrink from further delay, partly because I have already been so long, partly because I want to finish, and partly also because it seems to me we are approaching an age in which events of great political interest will occur – before your and my generation goes under the sod. I feel the impulse more and more strong

[1]This, like many of JKL's NRS projects, came to nothing. He was always prepared to move on when new materials appeared, or more important issues needed to be addressed.

[2]In the event, JKL produced for the *DNB* a very short note on Ralfe (fl. 1820–29), whom he described as 'a writer on naval history'. Ralfe's main work was a *Naval Chronology of Great Britain*.

[3]Nelson material recently acquired by the British Library from the Hood family, to whom it had passed through marriage.

to turn my attention to the future, from the point of view of Sea Power and to address the public through magazines. Our system is in Egyptian darkness, from my point of view, as regards its place and mission in the world. I hope by the way your people are determined to take their own way in Egypt with all diplomatic courtesy, but resolvedly. When I look at the powerlessness of movement which seems to attend the European concert, I wonder how any one expects aught from a Permanent Tribunal of Arbitration. Let each nation keep its hands clear for action, and its conscience under its own guidance.

With my laborious painstaking, and from many interruptions, I have actually only got Nelson through Tenerife. I estimate that, however, as nearly half way, for though the rest of his correspondence is voluminous it contains an immense amount of repetition.

As the situation develops of the Bridport papers I would be glad if you would drop a line to me personally, or to Stevens. Though I have no fixed plans, it is not impossible that I may come to England a twelvemonth hence, but I should regret the postponement of publication till then. Perhaps some middle course may suggest itself.

The really interesting data that may yet exist would I think be in letters from persons about Nelson's person to their correspondents. What do you think of Parson's Nelsonia?[1] I think the man is telling the truth, as far as his memory serves him – but you would be a better judge.

P. S. Having had many narrow escapes myself I felt for you in finding any mistake like that of the withdrawal of the ships.[2] 'What perils do remain, the man who meddle with cold' facts! [*sic*] I have tumbled in more than once, but not badly hurt.

127.   *Laughton to William Laird Clowes*[3]

31 March 1896

I'm not at all sure that a joint stock history, such as I understand you are contemplating, quite commends itself to me: but I am saved the

---

[1]G.S. Parsons, *Nelsonian Reminiscences; Leaves from Memory's Log* (London, 1905; reprinted 1998). This material originally appeared as a series of magazine articles, to which Mahan is referring here.

[2]At Copenhagen: see [117], Mahan's letter of 28 August 1895.

[3]Sir William Laird Clowes (1856–1905); naval historian and journalist; educated at King's College, London; editor and largely author of *The Royal Navy: A History from the earliest times to 1900* (7 vols, London, 1897–1903). Laughton's copy is in King's College Library.

trouble of examining the scheme by the impossibility of my taking part in it, as you are good enough to ask me to do.[1] I have already on hand fully as much as I can do, and dare not to attempt to increase the amount. This compels me to decline your flattering proposal.

128.   *Bridge to Laughton*

Admiralty House, Sydney,[2] 21 April 1896

Type-writing out here is 2/– per 1000 words and the MS belonging to Dr Cox would cost rather more than double what you mentioned if it were type-written. In view of this fact – and of your doubt as to its importance, it does not seem advisable to commit the Council to the necessary expenditure without further instructions. You said £5, the real cost would be £10 16s 0d, say £11.10.0. for copying writing and sending. If the Council would still like to have the MS. copied and will send the money, I will see to it.[3]

I have been looking to see what number of dear old Reeve's letters to me I can put my hand on and can find only four.[4] These I will send to Mrs Reeve, but I fear that they have not much general interest. I confess that I should like to find some mention in his life of my 23 years friendship with him. I first dined with him in 1872 after the contribution of an article on the Marquis of Pombal which I wrote at Lisbon in 1869 and kept for a long time before offering it to the *Edinburgh.*

I am much obliged to you for the slip about the unfortunate Baker Phillips.[5] One part of your article is contrary to what I have always been told. Phillips, we believe, left 2 little girls – one an infant. One became a Mrs Clarke, I have her miniature painted, if I remember right, in 1767. The other daughter married my great grand father, one of whose grandsons, still living at Ventnor, Isle of Wight, is also a Baker Phillips Bridge.

I had always understood that the Lieutenants widow married again, her second husband being a Mr Gibson, some relative of my family. My

[1]Clowes had invited JKL and Michael Oppenheim to write for his *The Royal Navy, A History,* but JKL did not like Clowes, who had fallen out with his old friend Charles Napier Robinson. The Laughton name did appear on the volumes, as Leonard Carr Laughton wrote some sections in Vol. II. The pay was one guinea per 1,000 words.

[2]Bridge was C-in-C of the Australian Station between November 1894 and November 1897.

[3]No action was taken.

[4]JKL was just beginning work on his *Memoirs of the Life and Correspondence of Henry Reeve* (2 vols, London, 1898). Bridge had introduced the two men.

[5]JKL 'The Study of Naval History', *JRUSI,* **XXXX,** (1896), pp. 795–820 at p. 800. Phillips was related to a distant ancestor of Bridge.

grandfather, 2 of his brothers, and 1 sister inherited £90,000 from a Gibson. I have miniatures of 2 Gibsons, one a Captain in the 62nd killed in S. Carolina in 1781.

129.   *Mahan to Laughton*

1 May 1896

I am so extremely busy now myself that I feel reluctance to intrude on one always as occupied as yourself, but can you give me any clue to the reasons of the Government for refusing medals for Copenhagen? Addington's[1] letter (Nicolas[2] IV 526 note) seems to imply that Nelson's own reputation might be involved, although it may also mean merely that his letter to the Lord Mayor was liable to injure him. I own my sympathies are very strongly with him as far as indications now open to me go.

I have received with much interest the last Navy Records volume, *Adml. James journals.*[3] I wish the spirit had moved him to give a little more fully the daily inside life at Yorktown; as it is the occasional gleams make one want for more. The family is to be congratulated on having you for its Secretary. I hope you will not wholly dismiss my suggestion about the papers called for by the House of Lords about 1782, relative to naval affairs about the Yorktown year. The list of titles published in Stevens' 'Clinton–Cornwallis Controversy' made my mouth water when I was writing my first Sea Power, but I could not get hold of them and don't know where they may exist.

[*Endorsed by JKL*: '*Campaign in Virginia 1781.*Vol. ii 263–99 inclusive.']

130.   *B. H. Chevalier[4] to Laughton*

17 May 1896

As all the money due to Mr Amos has been paid, the Committee wish me to send you the receipts for the different sums and also to enclose the Bill of costs. This, I hope, the last you will hear of the matter.

---

[1]Henry Addington, 1st Viscount Sidmouth (1757–1844); Prime Minister 1801–04.

[2]Sir Nicholas Harris Nicolas (d. 1847); Lieutenant RN, lawyer and naval historian; his *The Dispatches and Letters of Lord Nelson* (7 vols, London, 1844–46) remains the bedrock of all Nelson studies.

[3]Which JKL had edited with Commander J.Y.F. Sulivan.

[4]Naval officer and secretary of the Laughton Guarantee Fund; see *Foundations*, pp. 116–21, for the details of this issue and the handbill of the Fund.

131.   *Philip Colomb to Laughton*

7 September 1896

The passage you allude to re Colpoys[1] gale of wind must be *United Services Magazine* for January 1896 pp.386 et seq. I go by the logs of all the ships concerned. Colpoys proceedings are to me inexplicable.

Should Fitzgerald do anything?[2] He has finished Tryon, but they are fighting over the difficulties of the last chapter as I told Fitzgerald was certain.[3]

There is in fact only one explanation by which justice can be done to Tryon's memory. He had always followed Hornby in disbelieving in the certainty of steamships movements. Both Admirals were certain that the movements of the ships depended on the skill of the Captains, and that it did not matter what you called on the ships to do. Tryon had no idea that the movement he ordered was an impossible one – no more had any of his Captains – except perhaps Custance.[4] They all knew it was risky, but they thought Tryon would be able to do impossibilities with his ships, and Tryon thought so to. Note that he had never actually tried what he could do. Nor would Hornby ever try unless he was driven to it. In both men's idea it was all very well to have a rough idea of the 'diameters' of the ships' circles', but this was only a sort of rough guide for a Captain or an Admiral. It did not mean that all the skill and judgement in the world would not alter things. Naturally, no doubt, the ships would do so and so, but in the hands of a skilful Captain the natural movement was quite under control.[5]

P. S. If I think of any possible Admiral I will let you know. I think I you said you had some St. Vincent notes which might be useful to me. I

[1]Admiral Sir John Colpoys (1742–1821), a central figure in the Spithead Mutiny. The reference would appear to be to the escape of the French fleet bound for Ireland in 1798, while Colpoys was blockading Brest.

[2]Colomb and Laughton were collaborating to produce the book *From Howard to Nelson: Twelve Sailors* (London, 1899), which was written by Laughton, Colomb and other flag officers, and edited by Laughton. It was designed as a textbook for The Royal Naval College.

[3]Vice-Admiral Sir George Tryon (1832–93), who perished when his flagship, HMS *Victoria*, was sunk in a tragic collision with HMS *Camperdown*. Fitzgerald's biography was published in 1898.

[4]Reginald Neville Custance (1847–1935); later Director of Naval Intelligence and Admiral and author of several texts on Naval Policy.

[5]For the latest thoughts on the disaster, see A. Gordon, *The Rules of the Game: Jutland and British Naval Command* (London, 1996), pp. 243–314, which includes a discussion of Colomb's thinking.

have done him and a great part of Nelson in the rough, but I am open to any new points.[1]

132. *Montagu Burrows[2] to Laughton*

26 September 1896

I ought to have included an historical question in my letter of this morning. If you look at your 'Blake' in N Biog. You will see that you ignore Blake's cruise to the North Sea in April & May 1653, which is spoken of in all the common, but very inaccurate accounts of the times. You mention first his illness, then his appearing to do Admiralty business, & then his being too late for Monk's battle of June 2. Have you discovered that he was not on that cruise to the N. Sea? Either way I think it is clear that he did not separate himself from Cromwell as the books suppose.

133. *C. P. Fitzgerald[3] to Laughton*

28 September 1896

Can you recommend me some good <u>concise</u> general history of Rooke's time? I expect I shall be bothering you a good deal for the next month or two, but is your own fault for asking the country mouse to write.

It is doubtful now whether Sir George Tryon's life will be published at all. Lord Ancaster (Lady Tryon's brother) has strongly recommended her not to allow it to be published. He has read the last chapter only, and gives his advice on the strength of that, which seems scarcely fair. I undertook to write the book mainly because I believe that Sir George's name was known to the great majority of the British public <u>only</u> as the man who was responsible for the <u>loss</u> of the *Victoria*, and they know nothing (or very little) of the many eminent services which he rendered to his country; and it was with the view of rescuing his memory from this unjust estimate that I took the job in hand.

Blackwood[4] thinks I have succeeded; but Lady Tryon seems inclined to listen to her brother, and of course I can have no thought of publish-

---

[1]These were the two subjects on which Colomb wrote. His essays are examples of his best work.

[2]Burrows, the Chichele Professor of History, at Oxford compiled a life of Blake for *From Howard to Nelson*.

[3]Admiral Charles Cooper Penrose Fitzgerald (1841–1921), nicknamed 'Rough', a fine sea-officer and a prominent contributor to the policy debates of the era.

[4]The publisher.

ing the book without her consent. The worst of it is that as I have been going far and wide in England and Australia to collect information, a good many people know that the book is being written, and if it is now suppressed they will ask why. The truth is sure to leak out, viz. that the family put their veto on it. Then the public will think there must be something worse than they already know. So the last state of the case shall be worse than the first!

134.   *Mahan to Laughton*

To be returned[1]

6 November 1896

I recognised your hand on the envelope enclosing the notice of the *Nelson Memorial*,[2] which told me that you had been again tempting fate in tackling the life of your great admiral. I trust that the memento, both of recognition and pecuniarily, may adequately repay your venture. I feel the rashness of such attempts – dealing with a character of so much mingled strength and weakness – the more vividly, now that my own manuscript has left my hands. I sent it to the publisher a week ago today, and as it is not to appear till March [there is] before me a winter of proof-reading, besides lots of other work. I have undertaken immediately a course of lectures – fairly popular – on Naval Warfare; hoping, if successful I may get a comfortable yearly order.

Nelson will be long – about the same as my *French Revolution;* but I soon made up my mind that unless I was to be dry I must cast aside compression. A brief life, like that you have[3] so well done, is one thing – vividness of outline compensates for meagre detail, but beyond a certain length, detail only can lighten the burden of the way. Have you seen Sloane's *Napoleon* – it is an instance in point.[4] It is, I suppose, a very valuable and accurate presentment of facts, but many tell me, unutterably dull. Reason, I think, not room enough for all the facts of so full a career. Besides, I fancy, Sloane is too frigidly impartial. I don't believe in attempting the biography of a man for whom you do not feel enthusiastic admiration from some point of view. The *Century Magazine* ran this through 24 months, and I was told, before eight of them

---

[1]Annotation in JKL's hand.
[2]Annotation by JKL: 'a mistake. I didn't send it.'
[3]Annotation by JKL: 'in "Men of Action" series.'
[4]William Milligan Sloane (1850–1928), American philosopher and historian. His *Life of Napoleon* (4 vols, New York, 1896) was first published in serial form in *The Century Magazine*.

were over people at the Railways Stat[ion]'s were demanding maga-zines 'that had nothing about Napoleon'. *The Century* offered to undertake a book for me serially. I had only *Nelson*, & that I declined, for many reasons; amongst others because I dared not believe that interest could be sustained for every number.[1] Pecuniarily, I shall prob-ably lose by this; but I don't regret the decision & I fancy the magazine is blessing its stars for it now.

135.   *Alfred Lyall[2] to Laughton*

18 November 1896

I am much obliged to you for sending to me a copy of your Address on 'The Study of Naval History'. I have always followed with interest your successful endeavours to extend our knowledge of the subject, and I think the Naval Records Society a most valuable national institution.

I see that you refer to some French writers on naval affairs. You are of course well acquainted with, though you do not mention, Jurien de la Graviere's book *Guerres Maritimes*,[3] to which it seems to me that Mahan was much indebted in writing his recent work upon the French Revolution and the Empire. In fact I venture to think that the French Admiral led the way which Mahan afterwards followed, in his criti-cisms on the battles of the great French War.

136.   *R. V. Hamilton[4] to Laughton*

15 December 1896

Many thanks for your offer. I have not troubled you as much as I should have done, had you been a man of leisure.[5]

I am aware repetition is one of my faults – also how very difficult it is to correct proofs – one very prominent one in my *19th Century* Article on Invasion Scares escaped the Reader – Sydenham Clarke & myself – and I detected it at the last correction, if I mistake not. I

---

[1]This was an unusual act on Mahan's part, for most of his major works were initially published in this form.

[2]Sir Alfred Comyn Lyall (1835–1911); Anglo-Indian administrator and later histo-rian of British India; Councillor and Vice President of the Navy Records Society 1893–1907.

[3]Admiral Jurien de la Gravière, *Guerres Maritimes de la Révolution et de l'Empire* (2 vols, Paris, 1881–86).

[4]Hamilton had been First Sea Lord in 1889–91, succeeding Hood.

[5]He was writing Rodney and Hood for *Twelve Sailors* and once again let JKL down.

haven't mentioned Rodney's 2nd marriage, nor have I given the reference. Print is so much easier to correct than writing.

I see your war has commenced with Mr Herbert.[1] When were the Hon'ble G[eorge] E[lliot]'s memories written, evidently not at the date – but I see he is first of all signal mid. and then Captain's ADC, two not very compatible posts.[2]

In your narrative of Nelson p.146 in the note you refer to ante p.7 Q[uer]ly should it not be App'x IX. Today is the first time I ever heard of the *Zealous* and *Goliath* being 50 minutes ahead of the Ad[mira]l – fancy if a calm came on – with 2 ships against 13 – unable to receive assistance from the rest of the fleet – unless [the] French repeated De Grasse's blunder against Hood's Van Squadron[3] – we should not have won the Nile. Miller's statement is very clear, his proper station was next the leader on one tack evidently and he was [tacking?] into station. Speaking the *Mutine* is very different to picking up a boat full of pilots 'In about 5 minutes after bringing to the Adm'l made sail again.' This letter from an unimpeachable authority is worth the Hon'ble's Memoir. 'More spoken of by the French than by the English' says G.E. of *Goliath* and Hood being so far ahead – where is the authority? for the statement. Have you ever seen it? 'As we got pretty nearly abreast the shoal at the entrance, being within hail of Ad'l he asked me if I thought we were far enough to the Eastw'd to bear up & clear the shoal' (don't look as if Ad'l was far off) 'I told him I was in 11 fathoms – had no chart of the bay but if would allow me I would bear up & sound with the lead to which I would be very attentive & carry him as close as I could with safety – he said he would be obliged to me. I immediately bore away & rounded the shoal, the *Goliath* keeping on my lee bow[4] until I found we were advancing too far from the Admiral – then shortened sail & found Ad'l was speaking to a boat, soon after he made the signal to proceed *Goliath* leading & as we approached the enemy shortened sail gradually, the Ad'l allowing *Orion* to pass ahead of *Vanguard*. The van ship of enemy being in 5 f[atho]ms expected G[oliath] & Z[ealous] to stick fast in the shoal every moment & did not imagine we should attempt to pass within her. As the van engaged with the mortar fired regularly at us Foley intended to anchor abreast of the van ship – but his sheet anchor cable being out of the stern-

---

[1] J.B. Herbert, *Life and Services of Admiral Sir T. Foley* (1884, privately printed). The argument would have been about the credit for the opening move of the Battle of the Nile.

[2] Admiral Sir George Elliot's *Memoirs* (London, 1863; reprinted 1891).

[3] In the action of 9 April 1782, three days before the Saintes, De Grasse failed to press his advantage against the detached British van.

[4] Annotation by JKL: 'see chart *Naval Chronicle*, vol. I, 521 no scale'.

port, not dropping the moment he wished he brought up abreast of the second ship having given the van one his fire. I cut away *Zealous's* sheet anchor and came too exactly in the situation Foley meant to have taken' a sure proof everything had been previously arranged – 'I directed a heavy discharge into her bow' Van ship within musket shot a little after six – her foremast went by the board in a few minutes just as the sun was closing the H.U. on whole squadron gave three cheers'. I think you will have a good rejoinder to our friend – moreover if the pamphlet is not Berry – there is no doubt as to Miller's & Hood's account, I presume however logs will settle this matter – as they have many other erroneous statements.

I have also a strong idea Saumarez did not approve to attacking inside and outside, but would have one on the quarter and one on the bow of each French ship. I have just been reading Hood's letter to Lord Hood,[1] have written to Hood to ask to be allowed to send it to you. The whole letter is very long – but if Hood of Avalon[2] consents I will send it to you.

P. S. I shall be very glad to put anything [in the Fortnightly?] *Mag.*

137. *Hamilton to Laughton*

18 December 1896

I heard from Lord Hood this morning; and he has no objection to the publication of Capt. Hood's letter – which I think will set the matter at rest. It is certain if it had not been so arranged previously none of Nelson's Captains are likely to have acted so independently, nor would he have left them so long unsupported – it might have been magnificent on Foley's part – but not war.

By Miller['s] letter Foley rounded *Guerriere* at 6.40 and at 6.44 Miller also did the same – and as *Zealous, Orion* and *Audacious* came between, pretty close order must have been kept. *Vanguard* came to a few minutes [after?] *Theseus* – so could not have been 50 minutes behind *Zealous* as G[eorge]E[lliot] writes. Berry[3] & Miller[4] agree fairly and Hood's certainly corroborates them – and contradicts G.E.

---

[1]Three different Hoods are mentioned in this sentence: Captain, later Vice Admiral, Sir Samuel Hood (1762–1814) of HMS *Zealous* at the Nile; his cousin Samuel, Lord Hood (1724–1816), Nelson's mentor; and Lord Hood of Avalon, one of JKL's near contemporaries.

[2]Admiral Arthur William Acland Hood, 1st Baron Hood of Avalon (1824–1901); First Sea Lord 1885–89.

[3]Captain Edward Berry, HMS *Vanguard*.

[4]Captain Ralph Miller, HMS *Theseus*.

It is worth while getting real time of sunset – as all mention but Berry is 6.01, Hood & Miller 6.44 more likely to be right at that time of year. If I can be of any assistance to you shall be very glad.

138.   *Laughton to Browning*

31 January 1897

I will do what I can with the later sheets, in the course of a day or two. I don't quite understand what I am to do with sheets B–E which you have sent. Are they for Index? In that case don't trouble: I'll tell Spottiswoode to send me a set. I don't gather that you have passed them for press. I hope not, at any rate; for at a casual glance several of the names on pp.24–5 are certainly mis-spelt, & most of the Dutch seems to me exceedingly suspicious. Hopsonn most certainly wrote his name with two n's Vlisseuzen is clearly the Secretary's or transcriber's or printer's error for Vlissingen. I fancy you will find all these ships in *De Jonge*.[1]

There is no pressing necessity to get the book out by Easter; but it is very desirable that it should be out before the Annual Meeting in June. So if you can manage to have it issued in May pray do.

P. S. I suppose we can hardly expect to see you at the Council on Tuesday. We begin the year with 541 members net. The list corrected, that is, for deaths, resignations, & names removed for non-payment. I fancy our balance is pretty much as it was last year: the issue of three big volumes must take the best part of our income: & there have been many payments for forthcoming volumes two or three years ahead. But altogether our financial state is very satisfactory.

139.   *Laughton to Browning*

2 February 1897

This is very good news. I hope now we shall be able to get the book out in very good time, if not before Easter. I am sure that your Introduction will be interesting & valuable, and congratulate myself on having – as Secretary – the prospect of seeing an advance copy.

---

[1]J.C. De Jonge, *Geschiedenis van het der Nederlandsche Zeewesen* (2nd edn, 5 vols, Haarlem, 1858–62); then the standard history of the Dutch Navy, and the only one to use the archives before they were accidentally burnt.

I fear I have been appearing negligent about your proof sheets.[1] The fact is that for the last week or two I have been so oppressed with odd jobs of one sort or another – including the Nansen[2] functions at the Albert Hall, which stole a whole valuable evening – that I have scarcely known which end of me is uppermost. I am now just starting for Uppingham, where I have been asked to give a lecture to the boys on the centenary of the Battle of St. Vincent. I'll take your sheets with me & look them through in the train.

I have had a letter from Dr. Murray[3] – to whom I was instructed to send a copy of vol. VIII[4] – saying how valuable it is for his work & regretting that he had not had it long ago.

140.   *Laughton to Browning*

18 February 1897

I am sending you sheets B–E and I–N, F–H I haven't got. O–End I have; but I have not yet been able to look over.[5]

I am afraid you will think I have been going outside my commission: but some of the words & spellings seemed so peculiar that I took the sheets to the Record Office & compared them. Several of the misspellings were the natural errors of the transcriber, not knowing the names. e.g. the MS. has Cascais which the transcriber has read Cancais and to any one not knowing the name it was as like n and sc. So Stukeley was misread Shekeley. The man's signature is Stucley.

I have not been able to go to the Museum to see *De Jonge*. I suppose they have it in the University Library. Some time since I noted his spelling:
Callenburgh
van Almonde
Evertsen
I have not corrected these, though I think it ought to be done.

The most important thing is the sentences which have been printed in the margin. They are not aperstilles, but merely sentences omitted, or written in afterwards; but should have been printed as part of the text. Where you will have them, it is for you to decide, but I am afraid they

[1]JKL would regret this bitterly: see *Foundations*, pp. 158–61.
[2]Fridthof Nansen (1861–1930), Norwegian explorer and scientist. He had just returned from his attempt to reach the North Pole.
[3]Editor of the *Oxford English Dictionary*.
[4]M. Oppenheim (ed.), *Naval Accounts and Inventories in the Reign of Henry VII* (London, NRS, 1897).
[5]At this date books were sent for proofreading in the form of uncut sheets.

must come out of the margin. Are you going to print the Robinson transcripts as an Appendix, or are they embodied in the Introduction?

I will send two or three sheets in a day or two. I have not by any means exhaustively corrected the things that caught my eye.

141. *Mahan to Laughton*

23 February 1897

The *Nelson Memorial* got into my hands a little too late to quote Collingwood's (probable) remark, without upsetting the paging through-out a couple of chapters or more; you know how sometimes there is no room for an insertion without more rearrangement than the case seems to demand. I am the more sorry because among some extracts of letters written by Lady Saumarez from Bath in 1797, and sent to me by the present Lord de Saumarez,[1] I stumbled across a remark which, coupled with the one given by you from the *Excellent*, would have indicated how public opinion tended. It does not exactly affect Nelson, except as showing how the estimation of St. Vincent and the Admiralty triumphed over petty misjudgment.

Mr J. B. Herbert sent me recently a copy of his *Memoir of Foley*,[2] together with all his controversy with you. You have easily held your own and more, and he betrays that imperfect knowledge which is more dangerous than none, laying himself open to retort. I have just written to him that the impression left upon my mind (without diminishing the credit I have before given Foley) is Nelson had more share in the detailed plan than I had previously thought; and I have recalled to him that Pousielgue, the French Commissioner says that Aboukir was the only Bay on the whole coast of Egypt; and that it is scarcely likely, as such, that Nelson would have overlooked it as a possible anchorage, alternative to Alexandria, the difficulties of which he doubtless knew. I must congratulate you on the force and directness of your argument – no words wasted or miss-fired.

I incline to think that Berry was not much of a seaman, and that Nelson was sorry to lose Hardy for him when the *Foudroyant* came out in 1799.[3]

---

[1]James St. Vincent, 4th Baron de Saumarez (1848–1934), Captain in the Grenadier Guards.

[2]Herbert, *Foley.* See [136].

[3]Edward Berry and Thomas Masterman Hardy, Nelson's Flag Captains in the period of the Nile campaign and his sojourn at Naples. Just before Trafalgar, Nelson remarked to Hardy that Berry was a 'blockhead', although a very brave man.

My book is now through the press all but a little of the Index, but the publishers tell me that owing to copyright exigencies it will not appear till April. When it does I promise myself to send you a copy, which I hope you will accept, not only as a token of friendship but also as an acknowledgement of my indebtedness to your previous labours, and mastery of the subject, in guiding my footsteps. Your 'Life' has been a great security to me.

142. *Laughton to Browning*

28 February 1897

I return the Introduction, which I think will do very nicely I have made one or two short notes, of no great consequence. Personally, I should prefer uniformity of spelling throughout, but if you won't have it, the sin be on your shoulders. Only Köge is a manifest mistake for Kiöge.

As soon as I get the corrected sheets I will set the girl to work at the index. So that perhaps, after all, we might get out before Easter, or very shortly after. May will do very well.

143. *Laughton to Mahan*

21 April 1897

I have today received from Sampson, Low & Co. the handsome set of volumes you have been so good as to send me, & which I value more for the little autograph on the flyleaf.[1] The book itself I have read in the rude set of advance sheets which previously reached me. I congratulate you most heartily on the result of your labours, first & chiefly, because it is really good work, & those will value it most who know most about the subject, even if they do not always agree with your conclusions: & secondly, because I understand from Marston that it is having & likely to continue to have a remarkable commercial success. When a publisher goes out of his way to tell that to a comparative stranger, I suppose it is not credulity to believe that he is speaking the truth.

I see Clowes's 1st vol. is announced, but I don't think it is yet out.[2] Marston wrote to me that you had longer time for your contribution

---

[1] This letter refers to Mahan's two-volume *The Life of Nelson* published in 1897, which Laughton reviewed for the *Edinburgh Review*. Sampson, Low & Co. were Mahan's English publishers.

[2] W.L. Clowes, *The Royal Navy: A History from the Earliest Times* (7 vols, London, 1897–1903).

than you supposed, & that therefore left it to you to decide about those letters of Sir Charles Douglas.[1] In one he gives an interesting & curious account of forcing his ship up to Quebec through the ice. Beatson mentions the fact, but without detail.[2]

Did I tell you that I have got hold of Sir John Narborough's journal as flag captain to the Duke of York in the Battle of Solebay & during the campaign of 1672? I have had it copied, & it will be published by the N.R.S. at the earliest opportunity.[3]

Gardiner's work is likely to be extremely interesting. So also is Spont's.[4] I saw some of the French letters which are very curious.

With kind regards & very many thanks, always sincerely yours

144. *Mahan to Laughton*

29 April 1897

I received today your enclosure of cutting from the *Athenaeum* reviewing the *Life of Nelson*. A copy had already been sent me by another person, but I am glad of a duplicate. You will permit me to say that not only have you given me a very generous meed of praise, but, what I value much more highly even, a discriminating appreciation of what I have tried to do which is very grateful. I am glad to think that you are to have the ample space allowed by the *Edinburgh* for further notice. We differ in points of course. I presume that if you and I had known Nelson long and intimately in the flesh, say as first and second captains, that our estimates would have varied in some points materially. How much more when we rely on letters and deal with disputed episodes.

Your controversial friend Herbert has done a very singular thing by me, in publishing a letter I wrote him in reply to his sending me the correspondence in the Foley discussion. Because I did not write by return mail to a request for permission, he, to use his own words, inferred that silence gave consent, and gave to *The Times* a letter written off-hand without thought of publication. A day or two after came my peremptory refusal and a statement that I had no wish to go into a discussion that could lead nowhere, on a point essentially secondary. As I kept no copy, I don't know just what my words were and whether

---

[1] Rear Admiral Sir Charles Douglas (1725–89); Captain of the Fleet at the battle of the Saintes, 12 April 1782.

[2] R. Beatson, *Naval and Military memoirs of Great Britain from 1727 to 1783* (6 vols, London, 1804).

[3] It did not appear.

[4] A. Spont (ed.), *Letters and Papers Relating to the War with France 1512–13* (NRS, London, 1897).

they give room to misunderstanding. I trust not for I don't want to go into the business any further, but now I shall have to hunt up the papers, to see what I have been forced into giving the public.

I wish by all means that you would have me sent the copies of Douglas's letters, and I will write Stevens to discharge the bill on hearing from you.

May 1

I meant to have mailed this last night, but forgot. Today I have yours of the 21st and am glad to know the book has reached you safely. I will repeat that I shall be glad to have Douglas's narrative as soon as convenient to you, and also shall be grateful for any hints you may give as to other sources of information probably not known to me, concerning war of 1778.

145. *Laughton to Browning*

5 May 1897

I fear I have been very lax, but really I have not had a minute to myself till dead beat at night so as yet I have not been able to look at your proofs. I hope to do so this evening, & will get them off to Spottiswoode as soon as I possibly can. I had hoped to get the volume out before the annual meeting, but that I fear is now impossible.

146. *Laughton to Browning*

6 May 1897

I forgot to say that I know nothing about Corry. His name is new to me and except that he apparently died before 1732, when the *Gentleman's Magazine* obituary begins, I cannot guess who he was. At that time an Admiral's Secretary was most commonly a civilian, so that the problem is very vague.

147. *Laughton to Browning*

8 May 1897

On pp. XV, XX, XXII, XXIV the name Rheenskield is spelt in 4 different ways. This is quite contrary to the letter & spirit of the Council's memorandum; & I should be glad if you could see your way to uniformity, even if you don't know how the fellow spelt it himself. I fancy these pages have been sent to you.

Also on p.XV you have Seeland & Sealand. Neither is strictly right, & neither is the usual English form; but if you prefer one or the other it does not much matter: only it would be as well to keep to one.

148. *Mahan to Laughton*

21 May 1897

I enclose a list of books at my disposal which I expect to consult with reference to my contribution to the Naval History being edited by Laird Clowes.[1] Can you suggest any others which I <u>ought</u> to see; and could see without crossing the Atlantic. My subject is substantially the major operations of the war of 1778; for though it reads in the prospectus 1763–1793, the strategy and tactics are pretty much all confined to the period after war with France broke out in /78. I remember that in your review of my first *Seapower* in the *Edinburgh* you pointed out several errors of detail in particular battles. I want of course to eliminate all these as far as I can. In working the business up in our library here I find myself entangled by my prepossessions for the '*Influence*', and prone to forget that I am now the military – or naval – historian, pure and simple; and that, however critical my narratives may be, I must dismiss the political bearings in great measure.

I find in out of the way corners of our Astor Library odd things – a Defence of Admiral Graves, 1781; two journals of French officers with de Grasse, '81 and '82; with de Ternay at Newport &c; while in the Parliamentary Ry. of 1781 and 2, quite an extraordinary number of official papers, in which as usual much chaff and little wheat. <u>Any</u> suggestion will be most acceptable; but especially is it indispensable to me to know of any greater authority I may have overlooked? My impression is that there is no valuable general history of that War. If you would be good enough to write to Mr R.B. Marston[2] any books of especial value that you would yourself think indispensable, I will write him by this mail to procure them for me, if possible.

---

[1]'Major Operations of the Royal Navy, 1762–1783' in Vol. III (1898), pp. 353–564; published as a separate volume in 1913.

[2]Roy Marston, publisher at Sampson, Low & Co., Mahan's London publisher, and publisher of the Clowes *History*.

P.S. I have made out fairly well with the Lake Campaign of 1776 – have nearly all Arnold's[1] letters, with some English; quite sufficient to understand the whole.

[In] English
Ekins
Beatson
Matthew's Nav. Battles
White's Nav. Researches
Clerk's Naval Tactics
Hood's Letters / N.R.S.
James's Journal /
Drinkwaters Siege of Gibraltar
Biog. Rodney, Saumarez, Pellew, Keppel, Howe, Nelson

I have access also to Nav. Chronicle, Colburn's U.S. Mag., Annual Reg. &c &c. perhaps you may indicate to me some articles, like those of Sir H. Douglas 1829–30.

[In] French
Troude
Chevalier
Lapeyrouse-Bonfils, Hist. Man.
Kerguelen, Guerre Mar. 1778
La Serre Essais Hist. Nav.
Isuerin
Bouclon, Mar. de Louis XVI
Cunat's Suffren

149.   *Mahan to Laughton*

Quogue L.I., 24 June 1897

By your kindness I have received through Stevens the copies of Sir Charles Douglas's letters from Quebec. They have been of considerable assistance in preparing the account of the Lake Operations in 1776. When Clowes asked me to include this I was rather bored, but I have become quite interested and even enthusiastic over it. It is now finished and makes a very decent prologue. If our scoundrel Arnold had been decently honest, and had a chance under Nelson, he would have filched a G.C.B. at last.

[1]Benedict Arnold (1741–1801); American commander on Lake Champlain during the War of Independence; later joined the British.

150. *Mahan to Laughton*

28 June 1897

The mail had just taken off my letters to you of Friday last when yours of the 11th arrived, followed the next day by the three note books. These I have carefully put aside, and will look after well, as well as use them. I am extremely indebted to you for them.[1]

I feel some hesitation about asking the loan of the Radstock pamphlets in the U.S.I.[2] Perhaps, after thinking, it over, I may feel less reluctant; but it is a good deal to ask of them to trust these, which perhaps could scarcely be replaced, across the Atlantic. All the same I am much obliged for the hint.

I suppose you saw the letter of 'F.P. Badham' in the *Saturday [Review]* of May 15, in which he condemns you, as well as me, very magisterially. I got Stevens to have me copies of any letters of Hamilton[3] to Grenville,[4] between June 5 and July 14 in the Record Office. Today I have the return, and also of a search of the Br. Museum. There is in them nothing, either to Grenville or Acton;[5] and in the dispatches to Grenville absolutely nothing bearing on the question, additional to the despatch of July 14, 1799 which I quoted in the *Life*. As Badham misquotes Foote[6] (garbles) and is clearly not familiar with Nicolas, I am tempted to ask you if you know who Badham is, and if you have any suspicion of what may be in those 'extant letters from Hamilton to Acton & Grenville', whereof he speaks, which are not in the Records Office, nor the Museum, nor Morrison.[7]

I wrote to Lord Acton,[8] while preparing Nelson. I had had the pleasure of meeting him. He did not reply, and I thought wiser not to renew my request for papers &c.

---

[1]JKL had sent his notebooks for Mahan to use.

[2]Admiral Granville George Waldegrave, Lord Radstock (1786–1857), left his important collection of naval pamphlets to the RUSI.

[3]Sir William Hamilton (1730–1803), British Minister at Naples.

[4]William, later Lord Grenville (1759–1834); Foreign Secretary 1791–1801.

[5]Sir John Edward Acton (1736–1811); Chief Minister of Naples in the Revolutionary War era; grandfather of the historian Lord Acton.

[6]E.J. Foote, *Vindication of his Conduct when Captain of HMS Seahorse* (London, 1809), critical of Nelson. Badham was Foote's grandson.

[7]A. Morrison (ed.), *The Hamilton and Nelson Papers* (2 vols., London, 1893–94).

[8]John Emerich Edward Dalberg Acton, Lord Acton (1834–1902); historian; Regius Professor of History at Cambridge 1895–1902.

151. *Mahan to Laughton*

Quogue, 3 August 1897

I am much interested to know that you think of answering Badham and Herbert. The former's letter is chargeable, I think, with grave careless-ness or bad faith – garbling. I enclose a sheet from a reply I drew up in which I point this out – you will of course test my statement, which I have marked in lead pencil for you. Furthermore, I got Stevens to go through the Record Office and get me all Hamilton's dispatches, and any letters from him to Grenville or Acton, from June 1 to July 14. He sent me all to be found having, he said, received every help from the officials of the Office. There were no letters from H[amilton]. to the two men, and nothing of consequence in the dispatches. H's dispatch of July 14 I had when I wrote *Nelson*, and I quoted from it considerably. This Badham seems to have overlooked – that I used it – for his charges seem partly based on it. I would advise you to read it in full, as I think it shows clearly that Nelson had received full <u>verbal</u> powers during his two hours stay in Palermo, the written to follow later. Time pressed e.g. Hamilton says in his dispatch : the King[1] 'entreated Lord Nelson that he would immediately go to Naples, with H.M's. whole squadron <u>and prevent, if possible</u>, the Cardinal[2] from taking any steps or coming to any terms with the Rebels[3] that might be dishonourable to their Sicilian Majesties and hurtful to their future government.' Was there anything that was not possible to Nelson's force, and if so, were not these full powers? I don't of course know what out of the way documents Badham may have come across, but I think his misquotation, and suppression, are clear.

As regards Herbert, he has sent me a copy of the *U.S. Mag.* The letter, p.426, is I believe what he published in *The Times*, and I believe the 'eminent critic' p.425 refers to one of the several replies I had to write him. He does not quote, however, and scarcely could after my expressed annoyance at the publication in *The Times* [of] one of my latest letters. I then said that I had paid little attention to the point, which I considered minor, until he involved me in correspondence; but that upon the whole, my opinion inclined to become firmer that Nelson had discussed <u>all probable</u> situations and I added, what I commend to your consideration, that M. Pousielgue, the French Commissioner (you

---

[1]Ferdinand I, King of the Two Sicilies (1751–1825).
[2]Cardinal Fabrizio Ruffo (b. 1739), Calabrian-born Prince of the Church; led the Neapolitan Counter-Revolution in 1799; reconquered Naples.
[3]Neapolitan Jacobins.

doubtless recall the name) had said Aboukir Bay was the only available anchorage on the coast of Egypt – except Alexandria. If this be true, and I think it is, Nelson must have known it, in a general way; and, although there was no good chart, probably had some idea of the general character of the anchorage. I think it a very probable inference, taken with Berry's story, that Aboukir Bay and its possibilities were discussed. I have an impression that I have somewhere seen that the chart they did have, La Graviere's 'Esquisse' was taken from a vessel that they boarded the day after leaving Alexandria, on the first abortive search. You may know about this. If any of this seems useful to you use it as you please, without quoting me. I don't care to enter the discussion, but Herbert's pertinacity has bothered me so that I sometimes feel inclined to say of Foley what Nelson did of Brenton.[1]

Can you send me the text of the 21st article of the additional fighting instructions – the signal Rodney made on April 17, 1780, which caused so much trouble?

I did not write for the books in the U.S.I. list of which you kindly sent me, because I found great part of them in our Dept. Library: Keppel's[2] and Palliser's[3] Trials, Considerations on Naval Discipline, Brenton's trial, Letter to Admiral Keppel and Rodney's letters. Your note books I have found useful and not difficult to decypher.[4]

I will ask you to return me the enclosed at your leisure. I am, half inclined in an undertaking to deal with the question of Nelson in Naples some day; but I will not till I can find time to look over the Italian authorities, which will be a very long time. By the way, I forgot to mention that in Isaac Butt's *History of Italy* you will find the subject treated at some length.[5] This may be worth your while to look up.

[*Separate page*]

[1] Either Edward Brenton (1774–1839) or Jahleel Brenton (1770–1844), brothers and both RN officers. Edward Brenton, *Naval History of Great Britain* (5 vols, London, 1823), vol. I, p. 405 discussed this point, and relied on information from his brother, Jahleel, who was later Saumarez's Flag Captain. However, Nicolas demonstrated that he was in error in *The Dispatches and Letters of Lord Nelson*, vol. III, pp. 64–5.

[2] Admiral Augustus 1st Viscount Keppel (1725–86); commanded at the battle of Ushant, 27 July 1778.

[3] Admiral Sir Hugh Palliser (1723–96), Keppel's second in command at Ushant, but failed to support him properly.

[4] An example of JKL's generosity, and his desire to improve the quality of Mahan's work.

[5] Isaac Butt, *The History of Italy, from the Abdication of Napoleon I* (2 vols., London, 1860).

Final <u>Secondly,</u> replacing those sent on May 28 and June 1.

Secondly M. Badham controverts my statement, that the treaty which Nelson annulled had not been carried into execution. 'Here again' he says, 'the reverse of Captain Mahan's premise is true. When Nelson arrived at Naples the treaty was already thirty six hours old, and the greater part of the garrisons of the castles, Nuovo and dell'Uovo, had already retired home in accordance with the stipulations. Ruffo's letter and Foote's (see the latter's *Vindication*) state that of the 1,500 men who were in the castles when the treaty was signed, only 700 remained on June 24.' <u>I have diligently searched the first and</u> second editions of Foote's *Vindication*, and failed to find this statement. But granting it true, the terms read, 'The garrisons shall keep possession of their forts until the vessels destined to convey such as are desirous of going to Toulon are ready to sail. The evacuation shall not take place until the moment of embarkation.' If any withdrew before, it was not in accordance with, but in contravention of, the stipulations of the treaty; and a proceeding so irregular, and unauthorised by the terms, did not constitute an execution binding on the other party. Again, Mr Badham cites the evidence of two of the garrison 'that – also in accordance with the stipulations of the treaty – the approaches to the castles had been given up, and the hostages surrendered;' but he neglects the fact that these important witnesses [Nicolas gives them] (for they wrote within a month of the event) say that these things were done, – 'the capitulation <u>was begun</u> to be put into execution –, after the arrival of the British fleet in this road commanded by your Excellency'. '<u>After the arrival</u>'; whereas the signal annulling the truce was made some time before the arrival, in obedience to which Foote's ships had to haul down their flags of truce. Lord Nelson, says Foote, (*Vindication* p.71) 'made the annulling signal before it was possible for me to have any personal conversation with him'. Foote, having got his ships under weigh to meet the fleet went on board the flagship then about ten miles from Naples, at 4 p.m. The fleet arrived at 9. It was after this, their own statements, that the transactions mentioned by the prisoners occurred.

Mr Badham seems to have overlooked the fact that, although Nelson never receded from his decision to annul the treaty until the King's pleasure should be known, he did subsequently appear to allow the armistice to continue; but when Troubridge, who carried a message to this effect to the Cardinal, was asked to sign a paper pledging Nelson not to oppose the embarkation of the garrisons, he declined on the ground that he was not authorised to do so. It was during this armistice, this stand still time, while the garrisons were deciding what they would do under the changed conditions, that Hamilton (whose levity I have no wish to excuse) wrote the words (I depend for these on Badham) quoted by Mr Badham; 'if they refuse to embark', (evidently they still had the option), 'they break the treaty themselves, and we are at liberty to attack. Once they have embarked, if they do that, we can do with them as we please', &c Mr Badham continues, 'After reading this correspondence of Hamilton's, one cannot doubt that Foote was absolutely correct in stating that the garrisons were enticed out of the castles under <u>pretence</u> of putting the treaty into operation'. This charge against Nelson is so serious that the sentence should have been quoted entire as Foote wrote it: 'I <u>believe</u> (my italics) [*Vindication* 2nd Ed. p.39] it is but too true that the garrisons were taken out of those castles under <u>pretence</u> of putting the treaty I had signed into execution, (which, after having annulled the treaty, must appear truly singular).' Singular indeed! So singular that it is remarkable neither Foote nor Mr Badham should have seen that there could be no pretence in the matter, as Hamilton's words also imply.[1]

152.   *H. Hall to Laughton*

4 August 1897

All I know about F. P. Badham is (I know not how I knew it) that he is an Oxford man (Exeter) and of historical proclivities. Young, but at the same time old enough to know better than write such rot as I saw in the *S[aturday] R[eview]* likewise Stamp. He has not been here with a permit nor can I find he has been in the public room without one. If he saw the papers it was more likely through O.B. [Oscar Browning] who had lots of these copied in 1886 and wrote a paper I think an essay on this business. There is also Ch. Auriol (cf Montpensier) a learned man with many copies, but not earlier than 1804. To know more of F.P.B. write to Poole[2] and O.B. is my tip.

But I may tell you that Mahan is already prepared to smite him over his having employed B.F. Stevens to check these references, but neither he nor we could make head or tail of them.

---

[1]See: J. Roberston, 'Enlightenment and Revolution: Naples 1799', in *Transactions of the Royal Historical Society*, 6th series, Vol. X (2000), citing Carlo Knight, 'Sir William Hamilton e il mancato rispetto, da parte di Lord Nelson della "Captitolazione" del 1799', in *Atti della Accademia Pontaniana*, new series, **XLVII** (1999), pp. 373–97. Robertson cites Knight as implying that Hamilton was to blame for any 'trick'. However, Robertson makes the common error of claiming that in his conduct of Caracciolo's execution Nelson set a 'wretched example'.

[2]Reginald Lane Poole, historian.

These flare ups remind me of the sentimental lady who wrote pit-eously asking us to look up a certain ship's log at a certain date when she put into Gibraltar, to see if a letter was not sent to vindicate Lady Hamilton's good fame which depended hereon! Of course no such ship ever went near the Rock but she was not satisfied all the same!

153. *Laughton to Browning*

6 August 1897

A Mr Badham wrote some little time since in the *Saturday Review*, arraigning Mahan & myself – myself, perhaps, more especially – for not having presented all the evidences as to the conduct of Nelson at Naples in 1799 & virtually accused me of having wittingly ignored some letter in the Record Office, which put a very different colour on the business. His reference is, however, quite vague – in the Record Office, I think he says – such a reference it is impossible to deal with. I asked Hall about it, & he knows nothing of the letter alluded to, nor of Mr Badham who – he tells me – has not had any permit, or worked at these papers. Hall suggests that you may possibly know something about Badham. I should like to know what his meaning is.

 If you can tell me anything about the letters & his sources of information you would greatly oblige.

154. *George Sydenham Clarke[1] to Laughton*

8 August 1897

I have just been reading *Rooke's Journal* and can't make out what is the matter.

 I have an anonymous book of 1808 entitled *Naval Biography* and including a sketch of Rooke's Life. The author, fully quotes Rooke's journal of which he says 'the original is still in existence'. He begins to quote it from May 19 1692 and carries it on through La Hogue, picking it up again later on and down to the battle of Malaga. Of course the writer may have had access to the M.S. and it may not have been published. But taking October 12 1702 (the Vigo business) and compar-ing it with the same day in the Navy Records publication, I find that the entries are quite different, and that the one printed in my book is very

---

[1]Colonel George Sydenham Clarke, Royal Engineers, later Lord Sydenham of Combe (1848–1933); first Secretary of the Committee of Imperial Defence; founder member of the Navy Record Society, Councillor and Vice President.

much fuller, more interesting, and more like Rooke's own writing than the new version. My version concludes with the words 'therefore I do set it down for a maxim and rule without exception in our sea service that a huddle is a thing to be most apprehended and avoided'.

There is a naturalness about this and other passages which bespeaks the man, and I fear that we have got hold of only a semi-official journal kept by a secretary. The point is interesting, so I thought I would let you know.

I can't say I am impressed with Mr. Browning's editing which leaves much to be desired.

155. *Clarke to Laughton*

9 August 1897

Many thanks for your letter. In his Journal Rooke uses the word 'huddle' p.231, but the account of Vigo[1] is far inferior to that from which I quoted.

I have not the least doubt that this is genuine – the use of the word huddle seems to prove it – but I think that another was his journal in time [*sic*] and if it is still in existence we ought to get hold of it. The Malaga[2] part is interesting also.

Yes, I think B. has certainly made a mess of it, and the general reader will hardly know what it is all about. For all that, I find the volume very interesting.

156. *Mahan to Laughton*

Quogue, 16 August 1897

I suppose you have noticed that in the second paragraph of Herbert's article he associates the *Theseus* with the *Guerriere* and *Zealous*. How does he reconcile that with Elliot's statement that the latter two were alone for near an hour? How also Elliot <u>art</u> 15, saying the fleet was hove-to fifty minutes with Miller, art 35, saying 5 minutes.

Did I mention to you Butt's *History of Italy*, having in the appendix a discussion of Nelson at Naples? Also did I draw your attention to Hamilton's dispatch of July 14, in the Record Office as containing

[1]Spanish Atlantic port, the treasure fleet sheltering there was taken or destroyed by an Anglo-Dutch fleet led by Rooke in 1702.
[2]Battle of Malaga 1704, an Anglo-Dutch fleet led by Rooke defeated the French attempt to recapture Gibraltar.

words that clearly indicate that the King gave Nelson <u>verbally</u> a commission to act for him, by charging him to do everything in his power 'to prevent if possible the Cardinal from taking any steps <u>or coming to any terms</u> with the rebels that might be dishonourable to their Sicilian Majesties'. Is not this <u>full power</u>?

Mr Badham thirdly asserts that Nelson's reply to Fox's[1] accusation was made nearly a year after the event. True, but <u>he</u> had said, (and <u>I</u> in my life repeated), the same thing to Earl Spencer[2] in a letter written July 13 or June 27, and also to Keith[3] on one of those dates. I have not Nicolas here so cannot verify my dates.

I have now had two contradictions of the statement that no medals were issued for Copenhagen. One by the Rev. F. M. Millard, Otham Parsonage, Maidstone who says that his father had one. This was in the correspondence of the *Guardian* of June 16. The other is a Mr A.A. Borrodale, of 44 Victoria Road, Kensington, who writes to me that he has one dated 1847 issued to Lt. T. Furber who was in charge of the *Ardent*'s signals.[4] I have written to the latter that I will look the matter up, to know how they came to be issued, and would be disposed to add a note of correction to the chapter: but that I thought medals issued so long after the death of those who ought to have given them, and of most of those who should have received them, were practically not given. Have you any information you can give me in the matter?

157.   *Gardiner to Laughton*

10 September 1897

[paragraph dealing with the *Dutch War* volume omitted]

After I finished this letter, I received from Poole your article on Mahan which is very grateful to me. Would you however object to tone down some of the language, as the argument seems strong enough even with modifications. Would it not for instance be enough to say that Mr Herbert has 'asserted' material of interest, rather than argued, and 'I answered Mr Herbert' instead of 'I answered Mr Herbert's mistaken views – I will not call them arguments'. Your argument would I think

---

[1]Charles James Fox (1749–1806); politician and statesman; Prime Minister 1806.

[2]George John, 2nd Earl Spencer (1758–1834); statesman; First Lord of the Admiralty 1794–1801; papers published by the NRS in four volumes.

[3]Admiral George Keith Elphinstone, 1st Viscount Keith (1746–1823); Commander-in-Chief in the Mediterranean 1799.

[4]The Naval General Service Medal of 1847 had bars for all the major, and many of the minor, actions fought between 1793 and 1840.

commend itself the more by these changes, and there are several others which I should recommend with a full remembrance of the battle of ink that Round[1] presented me with by treating Archer like a black beetle.

How do you know that the letter was printed contrary to Mahan's wish? I suppose that you had a private letter from him. If so would it not be well to add 'as I have been informed by Capt. M. himself'? or if this cannot be said would it not be better to omit the assertion.

I have not read Mahan's book, and therefore perhaps I am a good representative of the unlearned mass, so I may freely represent that I should like a few more words to say exactly what Foley did. He did not, I suppose, suggest the whole plan of putting French ships like beef in a sandwich between two English ones.

It seems to me that I venture to think that there is no perhaps about it, is ambiguous. It seems to imply that Foley certainly invented what he did whereas I think from what follows that you mean that he certainly did not.

About Badham when you say he hasn't seen certain despatches in the Record Office I suppose this is on a statement from Hall. Can Hall's evidence be adduced without getting him into a scrape. If so, must not the argument, however tempting, be left out, as Badham will probably want to reply and will at once ask for the evidence.

Then again when you say that neither Badham nor you, nor Hall have seen certain other despatches in the R.O. the question arises in my mind whether it is more likely that Badham told a deliberate lie, which is practically what you accuse him of, or is simply a muddle-headed personage who saw the despatches somewhere else. Are they non-existent, or are they perhaps at the Museum?

I hope you will not think that I am unreasonably picking holes in your article, but I want to lessen the chances of controversy as far as can be done.

158. *Herbert Wrigley Wilson[2] to Laughton*

17 October 1897

I have written as strongly as I could, and have asked Beresford[3] also to intervene.[4] Moreover I have rained copies of *the Navy League Journal*

---

[1]John Horace Round (1854–1928); historian; a severe critic of Edward Augustus Freeman's scholarship.

[2]Herbert Wrigley Wilson (1866–1940), navalist writer.

[3]Admiral Lord Charles Beresford (1846–1919), co-author with Wilson of *Nelson and his Times* (London, 1897), which had appeared that month.

[4]To persuade a family to deposit a naval archive in the British Museum.

(!) and offers of *Nelson and his Times*, so that I hope we may bring it about that the MSS will be sent to the British Museum. It would be annoying if after all this, we found they were of small interest. Would you not suggest to Leyland as a peace offering to send his and Robinson's *Nelson*. Then the W.M.'s will be fairly stocked with that commodity.

Mr. W.M. is A.K. Cornwallis Wykeham-Martin, I think. All my correspondence has been with Mrs.[1] Still I feel some doubts whether they will let the letters go.

I came across a fascinating romance in the Record Office, yesterday. In Secret Letters of the Trafalgar period, there is a long and curious account of the escape and adventures of a French naval prisoner – who got out of Dartmoor – with a nice drawing of Dartmoor. Also some secret agents accounts of the Boulogne flotilla. This bundle has never been opened before, as it had to be stamped for me. You will easily find it – it is the only one.

I suppose you know that in the Bridport papers are one or two unpublished letters of Nelson at an early date. One, if you had not seen it – which I expect you had – exactly comprises p.17–18 of your little *Nelson* and shows Nelson owed promotion to his uncle's warm recommendation to Parker.

I have been reading Popes' *Napoleon* and the new letters. My opinion as to the Caracciolo[2] episode changes somewhat – tho' Popes does not know what you know of the facts.

159.   *Wilson to Laughton*

27 October 1897

I have written to Leyland and asked for an appointment.

I take the opportunity of sending you *Nelson* Part 1. Do you consider as the *Army and Navy Gazette* says, that the miseries of life in the Navy are overdone? I rely on:

(1)   Court Martials

---

[1]The papers of Admiral Sir William Cornwallis (1755–1819), now in the National Maritime Museum. They formed the basis of the NRS volumes on the *Blockade of Brest 1803–05* of 1898 and 1901.

[2]Commodore Francesco Caracciolo (1732–99), Neapolitan naval officer. He joined the republicans in arms against his King, was captured by Neapolitan forces, tried by his fellow Neapolitan officers and executed on board a Neapolitan warship. While Nelson has been widely accused of harsh, or hasty proceedings, due to the influence of Lady Hamilton and Queen Maria Carolina, Caracciolo had taken up arms against his legitimate sovereign, was tried by his fellow Neapolitan officers, and objected only to the method of his execution, asking to be shot instead of hung.

(2)   E. Thompson's horrible account
(3)   Oslear's *Exmouth* on food
(4)   References in Mundy's *Rodney*
(5)   Secret papers in Record Office on causes which led to mutiny of
      1797

But so highly do I value your opinion that if you think our account overdrawn we will try to modify it for future editions[1] – if any! Beresford is absolutely with me on this. He says even when he joined the service life in it was horrible.

160.   *Oppenheim to Laughton*

5 November 1897

I can imagine that you have been raging over that Vol. IX,[2] still your experiences as Secretary have not been altogether unfortunate; and you can use it as the gamekeeper do vermin. I have seen at the Museum several papers that ought to have [been] printed as an appendix – especially some copies of letters between Burchett[3] & the other Secretary, then at Bath, while the Vigo result was unknown, which shew that even the smug Burchett could make jokes & that the Admiralty did not lose an hour in sending off ships to try to meet Rooke returning from Cadiz and give him the information.

By the way I still want some explanation of the blunder which made every index reference to the Introduction of *Naval Accounts* wrong by a page. If it was my fault I want to know the 'how' so that it may be avoided for the future. If it was Spottiswoode's fault they owe the Society **and me** an apology.

With regard to the time of the Monson[4] I can only say that I don't want to be hurried. The *Naval Accounts* came out a year earlier than had been proposed, and in the result both it and the *Administration* suffered in quality, especially as I was more or less ill the whole of last year.[5] The manner of editing must be a subject for discussion; but what I have in my mind at present is to collate fully from all available sources, those expeditions where he was present on service, and merely

[1]Of *Nelson and his Times*.
[2]Browning's *Rooke Journal*.
[3]Josiah Burchett, Secretary of the Admiralty 1694–1705.
[4]Sir William Monson (1568–1643); English Admiral; wrote six volumes of *Naval Tracts*, which Oppenheim would edit for the Society, completing the task in 1913.
[5]M.A. Oppenheim, *A History of the Administration of the Royal Navy; 1509–1660* (London, 1896). Oppenheim was a hypochondriac.

to correct obvious errors where he speaks from hearsay. His account of 1588 had better be left alone altogether in view of the recent literature of the subject. Whether the collation should be in the Introduction or the shape of foot notes is another matter for consideration. Also I suggest the advisability of some outline maps in illustration.

I may be a faddist but I attach importance to 'atmosphere'. I don't like to see a 17th Cent. Book printed in the same prim, mechanical style of 1898. It doesn't suit the terms of expression, it is like putting a shell-back into evening dress. Of course Churchill's[1] is 18th cent. & as far as spelling goes is practically modern, but I think the liberal use of capitals characteristic of that period more consonant with the subject and style than cut & dried present day scholasticism. But that again can be considered.

Of course I have a Churchill but cannot sacrifice it for the Society. I fancy it is getting a rather rare book, but I will circulate it among some booksellers. Churchill, proper, is always in 4 vols; the so-called continuation or Harleian travels is really a quite separate book. Would it not be as well to get up Lord Leconfield's (I think you said) MS to the Museum; it may be an entirely different & much earlier version.

I think that this time I shall not add any notes till I have it in Spottiswoode's proof. It may cost the Society a little more – although not much in view of the numerous alterations required in proof – but it will save my eyes & temper in dealing with the vile Churchill type.

Spont was here the other night (vile locution) and expressed regret that he was not going to edit the papers of 1545–6. I don't know who is to do them, but I should think he could manage them better than any Englishman.

161.   Gardiner to Laughton

19 November 1897

From the Editor of the English Historical Review
Badham has sent me a request to insert in the Review a short article on Nelson at Naples. I have enclosed his *Saturday Review* answer to you. As far as I can make out there is a direct contradiction between you in that you say (*Review* p.809) that there are no such letters in the Naples Correspondence in the [Public] Record Office or Hamilton's despatches

---

[1]John Churchill, *A Collection of Voyages and Travels* (6 vols, London, 1732); the existing edition of Monson's work, which JKL and Oppenheim recognised was unreliable.

to Grenville & his letters to Grenville, whereas he says that there are such letters, and in the *Saturday Review* quotes 8 lines from one of them.

Perhaps however you meant that there were no such letters in which certain statements were to be found.

Again, he says that according to Hamilton's despatches Nelson had 'no legal powers'. This however is precisely what Mahan says, because though he begins his paragraph (p.429) by saying that Nelson had been given 'full powers' he goes on to explain that there was no time to give him a regular commission. That means, I suppose, that he sailed either with a verbal authority or, at least with such a note as would not give 'legal' powers.

Mahan adds that it is certain that letters were afterward sent, but as he gives no dates, I suppose they are not acceptable. Badham however says it was received on June 30. If so, & Caracciolo was hanged on the 29th & the forts surrendered on the 27th it does not affect the question, & the extract which Badham gives seems to confirm his argument for the absence of legal powers. As I am not up on the points I hope you will excuse this if it is wrong.

162. *Mahan to Laughton*

29 November 1897

On Saturday I started back to you, by registered mail, the three note books you were kind enough to lend me. I was somewhat disturbed to be told by Mrs Mahan that the package which I had put up with very great care, was opened at the District P[ost]O[ffice] when she mailed it, to verify contents. As it must go forward as soon as this, I hope you will notify me if it does not reach you in due time, or if in bad order, that I may make complaint.

The notes were of critical assistance to me in two or three instances – notably Rodney's April 17, 1780 – as well as in other minor matters such as a rummager of records, like yourself, can understand.[1] The signal records of April 17, the testimony of the flag captain and signal lieutenant, and the lacunae filled up in Rodney's letter in Mundy's *Life of Rodney* were the most distinctly valuable of all to me, and they were absolutely essential. As you will probably review the book you may have occasion to note the effect of them upon my account. As I have

---

[1]Mahan still tended to deprecate the value of research, although he was soon to learn a lesson on this subject.

overrun the words allotted to me I have marked for omission – if Clowes think necessary – much critical comment, and among it part of my remarks on this really interesting and illustrative action. If these be omitted, the account will suffer, but you will have in your notes the crucial data upon which I base my account. It is extremely difficult, in the plan of an action, to represent movements, in which the course drawn must be a compromise, between that actually steered and the change of relative positions in the contending parties; but you have so much experience of the perplexities of naval battles, that I can count upon your indulgence for the ease with which error enters into them.

I see that Badham has replied – like a trickster. His letter in the last *Saturday* that I have seen impresses me, as that of man of <u>meagre intellectual morality</u>, who expects to escape detection like a cuttle-fish, under a cloud of ink. He does not <u>meet</u> a single assertion. He has wronged you and me by an assertion of neglect of documents, not one of which he adduces; and an ignorant reader might suppose that the 800 & 700 of which he speaks had some existence in Foote. If they exist anywhere but in his own imagination, he owes it to all to give proof.

An interesting fact has lately been brought to my notice. In the *Life of Richard H. Dana* (II. 61)[1] appears the statement that his relative Captn. Dana fell in with the French fleet, and two days later with Nelson, was in the latter's cabin, and explained to him on the chart where he saw the French. A few weeks later he heard of the battle of the Nile. There may very well be confusion, the confusion that creeps into the reminiscences of old men – and second hand accounts; but, if such a meeting took place, it was between Syracuse and Alexandria; for at the former place Nelson expresses his <u>total</u> ignorance. A vessel was, however, spoken just after Troubridge went into Koron, and <u>may</u> have been Dana's. If so, Dana could only have reported them <u>in Aboukir Bay</u>, possibly in general terms as somewhere east of Alexandria; for it was only 48 hours before he met Nelson and the French were in Aboukir three weeks before the battle. At any rate I thought worth while to follow up the clue, so have written Adams, whom I know, and today he writes me that the Dana family are on the track of the vessel's name, voyage &c. It occurs to me you might choose some time in town to see if the *Vanguard*'s log gives name of nationality of vessels spoken between Syracuse and Alexandria. If such tally substantially with Dana's story we should not only have an interesting incident, but very strong proof that Nelson had some idea of the location and disposition of the

[1] C.F. Adams, *Life of Richard H. Dana* (2 vols, Boston, n.d.).

enemy. I must add I read your notice in the *Historical Review* with great interest and sense of obligation.[1]

163. *Laughton to Browning*

1 December 1897

The enclosed will no doubt annoy you at least as much as it does me. It is a sad pity. The question now is whether we can or ought to do anything. The Council [of the NRS] seemed to think that it might be necessary or right to issue the list of Errata to the members; but deferred its decision 'till it had the list before it. I rather incline to the opinion that it will be better to leave it alone. The review which, I understand, will appear in the *English Historical Review*, will necessarily attract some notice, but will soon be forgotten unless we emphasise it; but the Council may think differently.[2]

In any case, it is a sad misfortune.

164. *Navy Records Society Minute*

In accordance with the Resolution of Council passed on November 4 I have prepared, had printed and herewith forward a List of the Errata complained of in Vol. IX, independent of the proper names – ships, men and places – in the spelling of which great licence has been permitted to remain. J.K. Laughton; Secretary

165. *Laughton to Browning*

5 December 1897

There will be some differences of opinion as to whether it is advisable or necessary to issue the errata. Yorke[3] is strongly of opinion that it will be best – in the interests of the Society – to do nothing: that few concerned about the Society will see the review in the *EHR*, & that

---

[1]Laughton reviewed Mahan's *Nelson* in the *English Historical Review* in October 1897, p. 804.

[2]It appears that Gardiner, as Editor of the *EHR*, sent JKL an advance warning of J.F. Chance's severe review, which appeared in January 1898 at pp. 171–4.

[3]Sir Henry Francis Rehead Yorke KCB (1842–1914), Director of Victualling at the Admiralty, and Treasurer of the Navy Records Society. As a midshipman he served in the Baltic in 1855, like JKL.

what is said about it will soon pass over. I myself have no decided opinion: but I think that it would be mistake – if the errata are issued – to send out with them a detailed explanation such as you suggest. I think that something like what I have written overleaf would be very much better, would quite satisfy the members, & raise no controversy. And in any case, I could not accept, for myself, any responsibility for a work over which I had no control. I did, quite officiously, offer some advice on two or three points: I did verify, or correct by verifying, a few words that seemed to me to have escaped you: but – frankly it had not entered my head that you would accept any transcript as perfect.

I was not aware of the omissions and transpositions that you speak of; the omissions pointed out by Mr. Chance seem such as a transcriber might naturally make; & the transpositions I have not seen. Those, in the errata are transpositions – indicated in the MS but not made.

However, this shows that there might be a serious conflict of opinion between even us, with every desire not to have it, and therefore I repeat that in my opinion, something like that opposite would best, and sufficiently, meet the case. I hope you will be at the meeting: 'till then always sincerely yours,

Suggested:

The Council regret that owing to an unfortunate misconception, the text of the *Journal of Sir George Rooke* (Vol. IX) was printed from an uncorrected transcript. Since the volume was published several errata have been discovered, a list of which is now issued to the members.

166. *Gardiner to Laughton*

11 December 1897

I return Mahan's letter and also send a copy of a letter I have written to Badham which I should like to have back again. I have, as you will gather from it, come to the conclusion that he is a duffer, but he has sent me certain references which I ought to look up before finally rejecting him. He now says that he quoted Foote's *Vindication* from memory, and ought to have quoted somebody else. I think however I am justified in saying that Mahan ought to have made his means plainer, that the full powers he ascribes to Nelson cannot have been formally given. It is plainly to be inferred that he means this, but he does not say so in so many words.

Badham assures me that he did see the letters some years ago, and was then told that he could not see them again without a permit. Hall says that though he had no permit, he cannot answer for what may have been done in the Reading Room. I do not think we need doubt Badham's word on this.

[*Three paragraphs on Sir Walter Raleigh*]

167. *Laughton to Leonard Carr Laughton*

12 December 1897

In writing a review of Gardiner's vol. I have questioned his statement and diagram that Lawson[1] was astern of Blake in the Portland fight.[2] You said you had come to that conclusion also: on what evidence? Gardiner does not refer to any, and I take it has no other than the Saunders narrative quoted by Granville Penn which certainly says 'astern of the generals' but contradicts himself by saying that Lawson tacked and with the wind on his <u>larboard</u> side fell on the Dutch. The two statements are incongruous. But Gibson,[3] whose narrative is almost word for word the same, says astern of the genera<u>l</u> meaning (I think) Penn. If you have any other evidence than Saunders, let me have a reference.

In *Liverpool Privateers*[4] just published, there is an account of the capture of the *Fanny*, a Liverpool letter of marque belonging to Brotherston & Begg, and commanded by Captain John Laughton, in 1814. John Laughton's brother was 2nd mate, and was killed in the fight. Now the curious part of this is that my father, James Laughton, then and for many years afterward, commanded a ship owned by these same Brotherston & Begg, after the 1st of whom my brother was christened.[5] It was his amiable intention to have me christened after the 2nd, if I had been born ten years earlier than I was. As far as I can recollect, my brother was born in Sept. 1814 (it's in the big bible at the bottom of the cubic box) and I take it it's true that the Captain of the *Fanny* was my father. He would never have told me, but my mother must have known of it, and she would have told. I never heard that he

---

[1]Sir John Lawson (1605–65), Commonwealth and Restoration Admiral.

[2]Battle of Portland, 18–20 February 1653, First Anglo-Dutch War; a tactical victory for the English, but Tromp pushed his convoy through the Channel.

[3]Richard Gibson, seaman and purser in the Commonwealth navy. JKL had been loaned his manuscript journal by Admiral Sir Leopold McClintock. He made it available to Gardiner for the *First Dutch War*, and published it in *The Naval Miscellany* II (NRS, London, 1912), pp. 141–2, 149–68.

[4]G. Williams, *The Liverpool Privateers* (London, 1898), pp. 445–6.

[5]James Brotherston Laughton was some ten years older than JKL.

had a brother to be killed, so that I dare say the John is right; very possibly he may have been a cousin, but it's curious the two being in the same employ. I should think it possible this may be the John Laughton, the grandfather of the woman in Australia. I have written to ask the author of the book if he knows anything more.

Hannay's book[1] is about the most scandalously inaccurate piece of work I have seen – except perhaps his *Rodney*.[2] I have said something to that effect in about 4 columns of the *Athenaeum* which I think might be out this week, but I see it isn't. I take it Hannay won't love me any more for it, for he'll feel pretty sure that no-one else could have written it. It is a pity for the man writes well – if only he would stick to facts and curb his imagination.

If you have a clean bill of health, I shall be glad if you will ask as many as are in town – come down here for Xmas dinner – we can't very well put you up for the night – but we don't want any importation of measles.[3] Let us know in good time about it, and who are coming.

168.   *Gardiner to Laughton*

13 December 1897

I have been looking at Badham's documents, which seem to me of great importance. That Nelson should have condescended to a trick to get the men in the two forts into his hands is marvellous; but so it is. The King and Queen's letters to Ruffo of June 20 & 21 are very helpful. I don't say they support Badham. I saw him today at the Museum. I take him to be an honest man, who has not been trained to know what evidence proves. I can't write more as I have not finished my enquiry. It is a thousand pities that Mahan did not know of these letters.

169.   *Gardiner to Laughton*

14 December 1897

Having looked further into the documents published in Italian,[4] it seems hopeless to contend any further that Nelson had any powers to supersede Ruffo, or to break off a negotiation conducted by him.

---

[1]*A Short History of the Royal Navy: 1217–1688* (London, 1898).
[2]Published 1891, in the same 'English Men of Action' series as JKL's *Nelson*.
[3]The five children of his second marriage were in the house.
[4]Gardiner ascribed too much weight to these 'documents', which turned out to be, at the very least, appalling transcripts.

To make all sure, I have written to the Foreign Office for permission to see the papers in the Record Office, but unless they upset the Italian documents, I do not see how I can refuse to allow the evidence to be set for Badham. It is no doubt a difficulty that Badham should have the arguing of the case, because as I said, he sees too readily what he wants to see. But I think I can induce him to let me keep him straight in the matter of interpreting his documents.

Nelson, as I said, tricked Ruffo into sending the garrison on board the polacres by sending Troubridge and Ball to tell Ruffo that he would not oppose the embarkation of the Rebels and the people comprising the garrison of the two castles. When he got them on board he seized them. On June 28 Hamilton wrote to Acton[1] that Nelson having found that His Italian Majesty disapproved of what Ruffo had done in consequence of his instructions and that the rebels having gone on board *i Lord Nelson & e co dato cafficeatemnte autorizzato ad im patronissi della potoache ed a farle ancorace in mezzo all squadra Britannica clore rim arrave a disposizione de S.M.* [*Hamilton actually wrote, in English*: 'Lord Nelson, thought himself sufficiently authorised to seize all these polaccas and anchor them amidst the squadron, and there they will remain at His Majesty's disposition.'][2]

This seems to me entirely destructive of the notion that Nelson had any powers to overrule Ruffo.

170.   *Gardiner to Laughton*

15 December 1897

I am very glad that you are going to look up these things. The chief papers are jumbled in Vol. 4 of Dumas' *I Borboni in Napoli*.[3] This book has not yet been catalogued but if you will ask Wilson for it he will give it you at once. Obviously anything from the pen of Alexandre Dumas comes from a suspected source, but Badham tells me that the Archivist at Naples has certified to the correctness of the copies. Moreover, many of the papers are taken direct from the archives or other sources in the three books for which I enclose the tickets. In the *Archives Storico* you will find the relevant passages beginning at p.659.

---

[1] Sir John Acton (1736–1811), Prime Minister of Naples.
[2] H.C. Gutteridge (ed.), *Nelson and the Neapolitan Jacobins: Documents relating to the suppression of the Jacobin Revolution at Naples June 1799* (NRS, London, 1903), p. 270, quoting Hamilton to Acton 28 June 1799 in the original English version.
[3] Alexandre Dumas, *I Borboni di Napoli* (10 vols, Naples, 1862–63).

With regard to the trick, I shall be very glad if you can explain it away, but it seems to me to be traced in the words in the first two lines of Nicolas iii 395. A letter from Hamilton to Ruffo. Sacchinelli[1] 255 says the same thing.

The engagement by Troubridge and Ball[2] that Nelson would not oppose the embarkation is given in facsimile by Sacchinelli at the end of this volume. S[acchinelli] says that Troubridge wrote it. It seems unlikely that T[roubridge] was so good an Italian scholar and the hand looks to me more Italian than English. He adds that T[roubridge]. refused to sign it as he and B[all] were only authorised to deal with military affairs. This may or may not be.

Your argument about the right to arrest R[uffo] is strong, and it was discussed on the evening of June 2nd.

I have asked the F.O. to let me see the volume at the R.O. so as to discover whether there is evidence of any kind there.

171. Gardiner to Laughton

19 December 1897

I have just received permission to see the Foreign Office Papers at the R. Office up to 1830, and mean to go there tomorrow to see whether I can find up anything.

I left a note on your book on Friday of a letter which looks very suspicious, and I shall be glad to hear what you think of the whole matter.[3]

On one point you will be able to explain: that is, what was the relation between Nelson and the Neapolitan Commanders by sea and land irrespective of any special powers given at his visit to Palermo? It looks as if the sea-commanders were subordinated to him, but not those on shore.

It has taken up a great deal of time which I wanted for my own Fifth Monarchy men,[4] but if Badham is to write, I meant to have knowledge enough to control him. As far as I am present concerned, I can not but think that in his main contention he is right, but he evidently needs to be kept in hand.

When I was in Edinburgh Professor Kirkpatrick offered to look at any passages in our Dutch papers concerning which there was a difficulty. I was told that his Dutch was very good.

---

[1]Abate Domenico Sacchinelli, *Memoire Storiche sulla Viat del Cardinale Fabrizio Ruffo* (Naples, 1836). Sacchinelli was Ruffo's Secretary.
[2]Captains Sir Thomas Troubridge and Sir Alexander Ball, from Nelson's squadron.
[3]'T'dge' written here in JKL's hand.
[4]His work on the Commonwealth period, which he did not live to complete.

172.   *Gardiner to Laughton*

21 December 1897

I have left your letter at home, so I cannot reply seriatim, but I do not see how your idea that the two letters about letting the armistice be [executed] will stand with Hamilton's letter to Acton of June 28 (Dumas IV 94–6). He says at least in an Italian translation 'Lord Nelson, dunque, aveva mantenuto la parola data al Cardinale. Non erasi opposto all'imbarco della gaurnigione, ma la guarnigione una volta imbarcata, si vede che cosa re aveva fatto'. ['Lord Nelson . . . finding that his Sicilian Majesty totally disapproved of what the Cardinal has done contrary to his instructions with respect to the rebels in the castles, and those rebels being still on board of 12 or 14 polaccas.' *Dumas omitted the next section*: 'and it being in time to remedy that evil'.][1]

If that does not mean that Hamilton thought that a trick had been played, I don't see what language can mean.

Of course there is, as you say, the immense difficulty of accounting for Nelson's condescending to anything of the kind. My suggestion is that he was in a state of wild excitement, and did not consider what his action really meant.

Let me go back and show you how the whole chain of events presents itself to me. As W. Hamilton said of the Palermo visit 'We had full powers' one asks 'full powers of what?' Certainly not for annulling the capitulation because nobody at Palermo knew that it had taken place. Moreover Hamilton's letter of July 14 lets us know what was done. The King, he says, earnestly entreated Lord Nelson that he would go immediately with His Majesty's whole squadron to Naples and prevent, if possible, the Cardinal from taking any steps or coming to any terms with his Rebels, that might be dishonourable to their Sicilian Majesties, and hurtful to their safe government, and to assist in the reduction of the French garrison in the Castle of St. Elmo.

Then sailing to Naples Nelson receives news that an agreement has been come to. He comes to the conclusion that the mere presence of his fleet broke it (see the paper in Nicolas) and so tried to get Ruffo to act on this view up to the evening of the 25th. On the 26th he goes on a new tack. His order is that the Treaty cannot be executed because it has not been approved by the King of Naples. Also he may have taken it that if this was the case he might cajole Ruffo, whom he considered a disobedient scoundrel, in a cooler moment he would not have done this,

---

[1]Gutteridge p. 270. Dumas had garbled the text and omitted passages in his Italian translation; whether he did so deliberately or carelessly is not clear.

but he was not cool. Hamilton's letter 'Milord Nelson une prie d'assûrer Votre Eminence qu'il est résolu de ne rein faire qui puisse rompre l'armistice que Votre Eminence, a accordé aux Châteaux de Naples' [Lord Nelson begs me to assure your Eminence that he is resolved to do nothing which might break the armistice which your Eminence has granted to the Castles of Naples][1] is clearly meant to take Ruffo in. It might be interpreted to mean that Nelson would carry out the capitulation, literally it meant that he would not attack the forts by force.

Then comes in the Italian Note. I interpret it to have been drawn up by Ruffo or his secretary and when he asked Troubridge to sign it he wanted to get an engagement to do more than Nelson had said, i.e. to allow the embarkation of the garrisons. If Troubridge and Ball or either of them refused to sign it, it shows that they were only responsible for carrying out their orders.

Even if this view of the Italian writing be incorrect, still, Hamilton's letter which I quoted at the beginning of mine leaves me no doubt that there was a trick in whatever way Nelson may have reconciled it to his conscience. As to the 800 I do not see that it matters much, but there is evidence – good or bad – that there were 1500 men in the forts when taken and about 700 came into Nelson's power. It may be argued that if a capitulation was broken Nelson was bound to put the garrison back in the same position as it was when it was made and he could not do this as 800 had disappeared. But this is a small question.

I should imagine that Parker would do your collating at the Bodleian.

Mr G. Parker
Bodleian Library
Oxford

but he will want to be paid.

P.S. Can the trick as I call it have been suggested by Hamilton,[2] and rubbed in by Emma, if she was on board?

173. *Laughton to Browning*

18 January 1898

I am obliged by your note, and will enter Ryan's name.

---

[1]Hamilton to Ruffo, 26 June 1799 from Sacchinelli *Memoire Storiche*, translation by Gutteridge at pp. 231–2.
[2]See [151].

Those errata are an infernal bother. It was a most unlucky chance that led to it. Meantime I am anxious to know what he says in the *EHR*.

I had a note from Bridge a day or to ago. He hopes to be in England early in March.

174. *Mahan to Laughton*

11 February 1898

I have undertaken to write a magazine sketch of the career of Paul Jones.[1] In connection therewith I have seen that you say in the *Dictionary of National Biography* that, notwithstanding nominally equal force, the *Drake*[2] was really no match for the *Ranger*.[3] Does this depend simply upon the want of preparation and of officers, a perfectly valid argument, or was there disparity of armament, in the calibre of the battery? Can you tell me what the *Drake's* battery was? I would be greatly obliged if among your memoranda you have easily accessible any data – precise – as to the size of *Serapis's*[4] crew, number of killed and wounded, etc. I would not have you make any research, for the matter is not of sufficient importance, not to speak of your time; and moreover I myself cannot wait. I am expecting now to sail with my family on March 26, for Italy via Gibraltar, and I want to get this article into shape before we leave, so a prompt answer would help me. From Italy we expect to work slowly north, so as to reach England about the 1st of July, and to give the remainder of our time to your island, until our return at the end of September. My hands now are pretty full, closing up matters, and I have to read the proof of my contribution to Clowes's Naval. History. My *1812*[5] will have to wait till I come back though I have started it; so also my intended compendium of Sea Power.[6]

---

[1]John Paul Jones (1747–92), considered the father of the US Navy. JKL had been highly critical of him in *Studies*.

[2]HMS *Drake* a sloop of 275 tons, ex mercantile vessel, 14 or 16 four pounders; taken 24 April 1778 by Jones in the USS *Ranger.*

[3]USS *Ranger*, ship sloop of 308 tons, 8 six pounders.

[4]HMS *Serapis*, frigate of 879 tons built 1778–79; taken by Jones in the *Bon Homme Richard* off Flamborough Head on 23 September 1779.

[5]*Sea Power in its Relations to the War of 1812* finally appeared in 1905.

[6]This is a reference to a projected work which was not written, rather than the revised lecture series *Naval Strategy* of 1911, to which Mahan refers slightingly in documents [251] and [254].

175. *Gardiner to Laughton*

28 June 1898

I have just got from Poole the make-up of the reviews. I should very much like to have your opinion on Corbett's idea about the tactics of fighting in line ascribed to Drake by Corbett.[1] It seems to me the most important thing in the book is true. I could keep back the review 'till October, if you think you could give an opinion about this and have not time to do it at once. This is of course on the presumption that you have not dealt with the matter elsewhere.

I have sent off Part II of the Navy Records Society book to Spottiswoode and am getting along with Part III.[2]

176. *Oppenheim to Laughton*

15 July 1898

So far so good about the Leconfield animal.[3]

I am going away I expect next week for 2 or 3 weeks. I believe you have a copy of Duro's *Armada Invincible*; if you can spare it, & would lend it to me, I can take it with me & thus save the Museum working time.[4]

Does, by chance, any member of the firm of Thorneycroft[5] belong to the Navy Records Society? I should much like to be on a destroyer's trial trip – it must be a quite unique experience. If one does belong to the Society I would write to him to ask to be allowed to be on board for one.

Sunday

You are indeed kind. I received a telegram from Thorneycroft's yesterday, inviting me to join the *Ariel* from Chatham Tuesday. Need I say I'd jump? Apparently I shall stand a chance of an invitation from Yarrow[6]

---

[1]In his *Drake and the Tudor Navy* (London, 1898) JKL disagreed, and said so in his review for the *Edinburgh* in 1901.

[2]Gardiner always sent his books to the printers as he finished each section, rather than waiting to submit the whole book.

[3]Lord Leconfield's Monson manuscript.

[4]C. Fernández Duro, *La Armada Invincible* (2 vols, Madrid, 1884–85); an essential collection of Spanish documents.

[5]Destroyer builders, then based at Chiswick in West London.

[6]Destroyer builders, then based on the Isle of Dogs in East London.

also. The more the merrier. I suppose I ought to write a line of thanks to
Sir W. White.

[*Details for Monson Volume*]

31 July 1898

[*Details for Monson Volume*]

I attended a destroyer's speed trial on Tuesday, & on Friday went over
Thorneycroft's yard. The former was a striking experience in its sug-
gestiveness, but when one hears that only 7% of the energy in the coal
is applied to the water one does not know whether to praise the skill of
man, in obtaining it, or to smile at his folly in thinking it a success. But
nature wastes power more than man does I suppose. Yarrow wrote me a
nice letter, but I have deferred a visit there until I come back to town. I
wrote to Sir W. White thanking him.

177.   *Marquess of Bath to Laughton*

Longleat, 22 September 1898

I shall be very glad to comply with your request with regard to the
Naval Tracts and the Journal with the fleet – and send them to the
British Museum that you may collate them.

I shall be glad if you will first kindly send me the written consent of
either Mr Scott or Mr Warner to take charge of them in the Museum.

178.   *Bridge to Laughton*

13 October 1898

Many thanks for letting me see the proofs of the Clarendon letters and
the MS note, which I return with the others.[1] I had already noted the
passage (ii, p.393) to which you refer; and had not forgotten the circumstances. Still my firm impression is that, except in a few cases –
articles as corrected in proof went unaltered into the [*Edinburgh*] *Review*. Of course I only speak of those about which I know something,
and can quite understand that it may have been very different with
articles on what may be called 'argumentative' subjects.

---

[1]George William Frederick Villiers, 4th Earl Clarendon (1800–70); Foreign Secretary
1853–58, 1865–66 and 1868–70.

My confidence in my recollection of Reeve's remark about the Paris negotiations is quite unshaken. It was part of a long conversation, in which he was really taking the part of defender of the so-called 'Paris Declaration'[1] or 'Privateering is and remains abolished' etc. He was much pleased at finding, what he seemed not to have expected, that I agreed with him as to the policy of the Declaration. I may add, parenthetically, that I am sure that no belligerent ever has been, or ever will be bound by any Declaration or any other document, if he thinks he can get a real advantage by ignoring it. Reeve did not actually say so, but I began to think that he was perhaps not the author of the Declaration, but at least the cause of its adoption by the British representatives. I have lent a friend my copy of your book, so I cannot at this moment refer to it: but, unless my memory deceives me, his journal shows that Reeve was in Paris for several days in the early part of 1856. The negotiations, which lasted some time, began – I think – in the winter, so that there appears to have been no physical impossibility as to his really sharing in the negotiations, though he may not have been in the room in which the representatives of the several powers put the Treaty into shape.

Considering all that he had done Reeve, in conversation, was modest almost to a fault; and I think it highly probable that the part which he really took in the Paris negotiations was even more important than most of his intimates supposed. I have mentioned this to Mrs Reeve.

I dare say that neither he nor Mrs Reeve knew it, but old Count Hübner, the Austrian diplomatist, had a great dislike for him; this was, not unlikely, because Reeve got the better of him in the negotiations. Old Hübner probably knew a great deal more about the true relations between Clarendon and Reeve than the English public. By the way it might have been some consolation to Reeve, if he had become acquainted with Hübner's dislike of him to know that the old diplomatist hated Reeve's antagonist – Hayward[2] – still more.

I have got a full nut to crack in a late slip of Professor Gardiner's proofs. I enclose a copy. 'Synode' may possibly be wrongly written for something connected with the Seine (Seyne). A glance at the chart of the Channel will show that the meridian of Havre would make a very good intermediate line between others drawn from Dungeness to Calais and from Portland to the Caskets.

---

[1]Signed 16 April 1856; settled an agreed international legal regime for war at sea, but not signed by the United States.
[2]Abraham Hayward (1801–84), literary figure.

I see that 'Impress stations' existed at least as late as 1816. Yet, I suppose, there are still people who will insist – in spite of that and of Professor Laughton – that 'Impress' has nothing to do with 'Imprest' and has everything to do with 'Press-gang'.

179. *Mahan to Laughton*

4 November 1898

After so long an intermission, I should begin with a Latin 'Greeting'. I hope you have been well and prospering during this trying summer, which I see has been hot in England as well as here.

I write now on business, in which you may help me, at, I hope, no great trouble to yourself. My English publishers want to bring out *Nelson* in a cheaper form. The question still pends, chiefly upon business considerations; but I also say that in bringing out what will be practically a new edition, I wish first to study the criticism of the old, and the material on which they are based. Of these the principal one appeared in *Literature* in a series of some half dozen papers last spring. You probably saw them and know that they rest on the Bridport papers, now, I believe, in the British Museum. I have written therefore to Mr. R.B. Marston,[1] asking him to put himself in communication with you, to learn whether these papers are in such order as to permit copies made for me, with any suggestion you may add. My wish is to make this a purely business matter, except the favour of your advice, and I beg therefore that if it can be carried forward equally well by Marston, and through any third party in the Museum, you will say so to him and then discharge it from your mind. I have indicated him as my agent, to spare you the time and trouble of a transatlantic correspondence.

Besides *Literature* I have Badham's article in the *Eng. Hist. Review*, and a letter from Sir H. Nicolas, claiming that I have done injustice to his father (Vol. 1 p.105). Of course I undertook to investigate and make amends upon due opportunity. His letter is in my files, but my recollection is it is based upon the same papers as *Literature*. As to Badham, I do not, antecedently, anticipate much trouble. I believe that the legal, technical, justification of Nelson's action turns upon the terms of the capitulation, solely; and that all other allegations, of understandings and misunderstandings however operative in mercy, cannot affect the technical decision. In this, of course, I may

---

[1]Roy Marston, of Sampson, Low & Marston, Mahan's English publisher. Their offices were in Chancery Lane, hardly a stone's throw from the Public Record Office.

find myself mistaken. As you have been drawn into this, it may interest you to know that an Italian writer, in the *Rivista Maritima*[1] for June (p.526), while criticising sharply my justification of Nelson, says explicitly that he accepts my narrative, which has stated correctly the historical events in the transaction. As he seems to have written a *Storia Generale della Marina Militare* (p.535), I presume he has some historical knowledge to set off against Badham's imposing array of Italian authorities.

I have seen that your biography of Reeve is out, and congratulate you upon the termination of a long labor, successful, too, from the notice in the *Weekly Times*. The subject is most interesting – a man so in contact with life and with men; but I don't know when I shall get time to read it. The recent hostilities with Spain have involved me in magazine writing, which seriously handicaps my more regular work, as it is; and as I have now a certain influence on our public opinion, in particular directions, I feel almost compelled to take some part in the solution of our new problems, concerning which opinion is tossing rudderless. In such a condition, <u>drift</u> tells, as on a ship disabled; and the degree of drift we have done in six – in three – months, is not only measurable but startling. It resembles the silent growth of a plant, not a rational process; and to my mind such a change is both sounder and more durable than the results of a rational process, our intellects being what they are. Of course, the drift is in a direction which I approve, which will bring us ultimately with this China business, as a respectable naval power irresistibly drawn to back – or rather to side, with you – in the period of turmoil that must precede equilibrium.[2]

180.   *Gunton to Laughton*

Hatfield House, 16 November 1898

I am desired by the Marquis of Salisbury[3] to acknowledge your letter of the 23rd inst. & to say in reply that he will be happy to give you leave to have copies taken of the letters of Sir William Monson. He regrets however that he is unable to comply with your request to have the volumes removed from Hatfield.

---

[1] Italian naval journal, begun in 1868.

[2] See Mahan's *The Problem of Asia* (Boston, 1900), for a more detailed discussion of his ideas on this subject.

[3] Robert Arthur Talbot Gascoyne Cecil, 3rd Marquis of Salisbury (1830–1903); three times Prime Minister. See A. Roberts, *Salisbury: Victorian Titan* (London, 1999).

I shall be glad to make arrangements with your transcriber to give him access to the MS here at a convenient time. Or I can supply you with type copies of the letters at a cost of 4d a folio.

181. T. Sturges Jackson[1] to Laughton

25 November 1898

I have really today made a find at the R.O., which settles the question of the Battle of Camperdown. Duncan[2] evidently intended to attack in the time honoured manner, first by forming line parallel to the Dutch line, then bearing up together and each ship engaging her opponent in the enemy's line. The intention of the old man seems to have been frustrated by the slowness of his fleet to form on the line of bearing ordered, and by the proximity of the land. He then made a signal to bear up and for the van, i.e. Onslow's[3] Division, to attack the enemy's rear. By a happy blunder the signal lieutenant hoisted the signal to attack the enemy's centre, after a signal to attack the rear. It was interpreted as a signal for the Starb'd Division (which then by the bye came to port) to attack the Dutch centre. This last signal was hauled down directly the signal lieutenant saw it, but it was apparently acted upon by several ships, and was sufficient to bring an overwhelming force on the craft in the rear of the *Vryheid*, and to bring on a decisive action. Duncan and a few ships which were in his immediate neighbourhood were of course hard pressed; and the Admiral naturally expected every craft to be alongside her own particular opponent and not to spoil the game by interfering with the sport of others.

It seems pretty clear that Duncan simply went on the old fashioned lines. Log of the *Venerable*[4] gives the following signals:–

11.08 Form Starboard line of bearing
11.11 Come to Windward together on the starboard tack
11.17 prepare to take stations in the line as pendants are thrown out
11.29 Ships to windward to close
11.30 each ship to engage her opponent
11.35 Bear up & sail large

---

[1]Captain, later Admiral, Sir Thomas Sturges Jackson (1842–1934), a midshipman on board the *Calcutta*, and later taught by JKL at Greenwich. He was editing *Logs of the Great Sea Fights* (NRS, London, 1899, 1900).

[2]Admiral Adam, First Viscount Duncan (1731–1804), victor at the Battle of the Camperdown, 11 October 1797.

[3]Admiral Sir Richard Onslow (d. 1818), second in command at Camperdown.

[4]Duncan's flagship.

11.40 Van to attack enemy's rear
11.53 Pass through the line and engage enemy to windward

For the last 4 signals *Monmouth's* Log gives:–

11.25 each ship to engage her . . .
11.29 Bear Up
11.36 Lee Division engage the enemy rear
X 11.37 Weather Division engage centre of enemy
11.47 Pass through the line etc.

It struck me as odd that such an important signal as that marked X should be omitted from the signal log of the flagship. The minutes of evidence of the Court Martial on Williamson[1] explains everything. Renton, the signal lieutenant of the *Venerable* says 'there was no signal made for attacking the centre, the signal was made for the English van to attack the enemy's rear.'

Q: 'Was there not a total change by the signals of the English fleet, the van for the rear and rear for the van?'
A: 'It might be understood as the signal was made for the English Fleet (q[uer]y van of E[nglish] Fleet?) to attack the rear of the enemy that it was also meant for our rear to attack their van, though the signal was never made.'
Q: 'Was not the signal No. 39 made, and for what purpose?'
A: 'It was made, but hauled down instantly, being a mistake.'
Q: 'Was there not an annulling signal and, was not that made after No.39?'
A: 'There is such a signal, but it was not made.'

Duncan never got his line of bearing formed. Captain O'Brien, O'Bryen, or O'Bryan (which is it, by the way?) of *Monarch* says:– 'That signal (i.e. to form the starboard line of bearing) appeared to me to have been generally misunderstood. The *Monarch* took her station as by signal directed, and left a space by Quadrant for four ships between the *Monarch* and the Commander in Chief, which space was not filled but by the *Triumph*, who was the Commander in Chief's second.' Etc.

The Admiral began to arrange the fleet in a new order, but only hoisted two ships' pendants & then apparently gave it up and hoisted the signal for each ship to engage her opponent. Therefore Duncan was not a Nelson but an ordinary chap Q.E.D.

---

[1]Captain of HMS *Agincourt*, who failed to engage.

182. *Bridge to Laughton*

30 November 1898

This is very – indeed delightfully – interesting. Not, however, because of any 'discovery', for – in view of James's[1] somewhat remarkable date of publication, not to speak of Duncan's own letter and the extracts from the report of the Williamson Court Martial published by Lord Camperdown[2] – it is not quite easy to see where the 'discovery' comes in. Surely it has long been known that Duncan intended at first to form the orthodox line, but – in finding that that was not formed in time – in the end decided to fight out the thing differently. This discovery is exactly parallel to the great Foley – Nile 'discovery', about which you know a little. The Foley discovery amounted to this:– Nelson intended to fight the Nile in a certain way, it was fought out in the end in a different way. Therefore Nelson was 'but an ordinary youngish chap'. Of course, you know, similar discoveries have been made about Marengo, Waterloo, Sedan and, a few weeks ago, Omdurman.[3]

183. *Colomb[4] to Laughton*

19 December 1898

I am very busy looking up Torrington[5] and the history of that time, and I seem to be coming across very curious matter. I first looked up nearly all Macaulay's[6] references, but have found nothing to justify his fierce denunciations of Herbert as a man. As an Administrator and an Admiral, Macaulay knew nothing of him, and did not try to know anything of him, and so he is all over the shop – making Torrington responsible at the Admiralty when he was cruising off Brest and worse.

[1]William James, *A Naval History of Great Britain* (5 vols, London, 1822–24).
[2]Lord Camperdown, *Admiral Duncan* (London, 1898).
[3]Battle in the Sudan in 1898, won by the Anglo-Egyptian army of General Kitchener.
[4]This lengthy letter indicates why Colomb was known as 'Column and a half' to many of his naval contemporaries.
[5]Arthur Herbert, 1st Earl of Torrington (1647–1716); English admiral disgraced after his defeat off Beachy Head in 1690. Colomb had a high opinion of his tactical and strategic thought; especially the 'fleet in being' concept; see *Naval Warfare* (London, 1891). He was working on a biography of Torrington at the time of his death.
[6]Thomas Babington Macaulay (1800–59), leading literary historian of his day; JKL was critical of his treatment of naval affairs in general.

But I am getting startled by a suspicion that is gathering weight, that Nottingham,[1] Pembroke,[2] and Russell[3] were in a conspiracy to cause the total defeat of Torrington so as to make way for the return of James. Has this ever been noted? I have always understood you to say that Russell was a Jacobite.[4]

Where shall I get true first hand evidence? and what about Nottingham and Pembroke, and others of the Queen's[5] Council?

What is arousing my suspicions are several things which do not appear to have been published – some of which I have got direct from the Hague. Nottingham you recollect, when he sent off the Queen's order to Torrington, told him there were only 60 ships in front of him, when he knew Torrington had counted at least 80, while the Government had heard from Paris in April, that de Tourville[6] would have 80 ships, and in May their informant told them from Paris that the list was out and that there would be 82 'great ships' (the number Torrington and his flag Captain counted, as they were bearing down on the enemy on 3rd June) But on the 2nd of June, an express arrived from Plymouth with the news that Shovell,[7] with his own and Saunders' ships – 18 sail, was off the Lizard, and would join Torrington 'in three tides'. Charnock[8] cites a letter from Shovell to Torrington, backing him up after Beachy Head, and the fact seems to have a connexion with this express news: now one asks why, when Torrington was hoping to join or be joined by the Western Squadron, and when Nottingham knew that Shovell with 18 sail was actually on his way to the eastwards and that Killigrew[9] would turn up at any moment – the Queen's order for Torrington to fight if he got the weather gage, should have been sent off in such a hurry that Nottingham had not time to take a copy of his letter enclosing it? It all seems so very much as if, knowing Torrington's numerical inferiority, Nottingham was anxious to get a battle fought <u>before</u> he could be reinforced.

Even here are curious things. The Dutch admitted before the Court Martial, that if Torrington was to be blamed for not entangling himself

---

[1] Daniel Finch, 2nd Earl of Nottingham, 6th Earl of Winchelsea (1647–1730).

[2] Thomas Herbert, 8th Earl of Pembroke (1656–1733).

[3] Admiral Sir Edward Russell, later Earl of Orford (1653–1727); Herbert's rival, and successor; political admiral; victor at Barfleur/La Hogue in 1692.

[4] A follower of the Stuart dynasty, named for James II and his son James III (the Old Pretender).

[5] Mary II, ruling England in the absence of her husband and joint ruler, William III, then in Ireland.

[6] Anne Hilarion de Contentin, Comte de Tourville (1642–1701); French admiral; victor at Beachy Head, defeated at Barfleur/La Hogue.

[7] Cloudisley Shovell (1659–1708), English admiral.

[8] John Charnock (1756–1807), British naval biographer.

[9] Richard Killigrew (d. 1712), English admiral.

by too close action, so also ought Evertsen,[1] as he kept his flagship to windward, and did not suffer at all. Evertsen in reporting to the States General – so Lord Dursely says – (I have Evertsen's report, but it is not yet translated) – did not throw any blame on Torrington or the English. It seems that Nottingham's furious letter was the whole cause of exasperating the Dutch against Torrington, and prompting the violent behaviour of Shey and other Dutch witnesses before the Court Martial. That is confirmatory of the former suspicions.

Altogether I seem to be finding out things, can you give me any leads?

I suppose I shall get some in the *Dictionary of National Biography*. There, I have as yet only looked up your Torrington.

I have written a very full and close account of the battle for which the materials are better, and fuller than for any sea-fight I know of. I am bound to range Torrington as on the highest level as a tactician and think he would have beaten the French had it been possible; and had the Dutch not misunderstood. I used to think he only intended in any case, to fight a partial action, I am satisfied that he meant to beat them if he could, and had a fair idea that he was beating them until, having seen his rear into close action, he made sail to see how the van was getting on, and found that what he most dreaded had happened and that 9 to 12 ships had weathered on the Dutch and put them between two fires. I am also getting grounds to believe that Torrington was the real [hero] in founding Greenwich Hospital.[2]

184.   *Clements Markham*[3] *to Laughton*

4 January 1899

After I wrote to you we found a lot more letters from Lord St. Vincent. My cousin Lt. Col. Francis Markham (the owner) is coming to Eccleston Square about Jan. 28; and I will ask him to bring the St. Vincent letters with him. Then I will get you to come to luncheon and look them over, and if you think them sufficiently interesting, I would edit them.[4]

---

[1]Cornelis Evertsen (1642–1706), fourth Dutch admiral of that name; commanded the Dutch squadron at Beachy Head.

[2]The buildings had been begun as a Royal Palace, but were converted into a Hospital at Mary's order. They later became the Royal Naval College.

[3]Sir Clements Robert Markham (1830–1916), long-serving Secretary of the Royal Geographical Society.

[4]The correspondence was published as: Sir Clements Markham (ed.), *Selections from the Correspondence of Admiral Sir John Markham during the years 1801–4 and 1806–7* (NRS, London, 1904).

We also found a great number from Sir J. Duckworth[1] – a beautiful handwriting, but he seems to have been rather an old humbug; and about 200 from Lord Keith[2] when he was watching the proceedings of Buonaparte at Boulogne. There are also two of his returns of the ships under his command and their stations, Downs, Dungeness &c for two years 1803 and 1804. Did not Vesey-Hamilton once have a controversy with some one about the number of ships at that time?

185.   *Mahan to Laughton*

9 January 1899

I received some time ago your pamphlet – or address – urging general education on naval subjects to give the public understanding of their importance to the general welfare &c. I felt I should soon have a letter from you, & therefore postponed thanking you for the tracts and for your kind mention in it of myself. Now the letter has come & two weeks are gone, & still my reply tarries. Luckily you are so busy, you will be lenient to others. I am now fully busy, and for the first time find myself driven to some extent to alternate my subjects in treatment.

   The worst of my trouble comes from that wretch Badham. I would not so much mind if the bother he has given me were legitimate; but while I am much more master of the subject than before, I find not only my conclusions <u>not</u> impeached but that he has supported his argument by false deductions, mis-statements, and garbled quotations, not to speak of a phenomenal capacity for overlooking the bearing of different things. We are all liable to errors and oversights, certainly; but it is one thing to incur them when gliding quietly along a narrative apparently certain, and quite another when the paper is controversial and has for its object to assail the reputation of a man like Nelson. I am preparing two papers: one a substitute for the pages in the *Life*, intended to meet the points Badham makes, but not polemically, a simple narrative;[3] the other a magazine article intended to refute, and dealing with his paper. I sometime ago promised Knowles[4] that if I wrote such a thing he should have it, but I doubt it will be too long, for Badham's

---

[1] Admiral Sir John Duckworth (1748–1817).

[2] Admiral Sir George Keith Elphinstone (1746–1823), from 1797 1st Viscount Keith.

[3] The second edition of the *Life* is the only time that Mahan rewrote any of his texts; this reflects the serious nature of the threat posed by Badham's attack, and the importance he placed on the subject.

[4] Sir James Thomas Knowles (1831–1908), friend of Tennyson, founder editor of *The Nineteenth Century* magazine, and a pioneer of signed articles by prominent people.

blunders and misstatements are so numerous. Moreover, with such a writer, I must be prepared against a reply equally uncandid with his first paper; although, if I am as successful as I think I can be, in proving carelessness amounting to bad faith in his article, I should think the *Eng. Hist'l Review* would refuse him page room. I think *Literature* treated me rather badly, also. I don't know if you read the papers, but it seemed to me that, to accuse me of not reading Nicolas, because I failed to notice that Nelson's father <u>was</u> at Merton, was pretty large deduction, and showed that the critic had not read my book, which was built up – quarried – from Nicolas. I had a letter, properly civil, from the present Sir Harris, calling my attention to an injustice to his father (Vol.1 p.105) in saying he dropped a sentence from a letter to the Duke of Clarence,[1] when it was not in the copy Nicolas had before him. I have replied that Nicolas in his prefatory note said he had compared his copy with that in the Clarke & M'Arthur,[2] & that all variations were noted. Nevertheless the sentence <u>was</u> in Clarke & M'Arthur, & was <u>not</u> noted by Nicolas. This also *Literature* has thrown in my teeth, before I replied – and in this it is wrong again. As for Nelson's love for his wife, there is not a shadow of indication of any more than you and I said. If anyone will compare the new letters with those to Lady H, he must admit that the latter show not only animal passion at red heat, but an adoration of which not a sign ever appears towards Lady N. I said three years ago, and I say now after reading the new finds, there is not the least probability that any new discovery will throw additional light upon N's <u>character</u>; we have already too much matter to make new light likely. Incidents may be set right, e.g. the cause of her not going to Yarmouth; but nothing that *Literature* brought forward changes a light or a shadow in his portrait.

I have nearly completed my articles – now appearing in *The Times*.[3] As regard these, I see that Colomb says I have gone over. To me it appears that I stand just where I always did & that my books prove it. The best proof probably is the way Maurice[4] used me in his *National Defence*; and, *per contra*, the position with which I have been accred-

---

[1] Prince William Henry (1765–1837), third son of George III, later Duke of Clarence; ruled as William IV 1830–37. A friend of Nelson from the 1780s.

[2] J. S. Clarke and J. M'Arthur, *Life of Nelson* (2 vols, London, 1809). The first 'official' life.

[3] A series on the origins and conduct of the Spanish American War, which first appeared in the *New York Times*, reprinted later that year as *Lessons of the War with Spain, and Other Articles*. See J.B. Hattendorf and L.C. Hattendorf, *A Bibliography of Alfred Thayer Mahan* (Newport, RI, 1986), entries A7 and E26–40.

[4] Major General Sir John Frederick Maurice (1841–1912). His *National Defences* appeared in 1897.

ited as an advocate of Sea Power. The truth is I have always put forward fortifications and fleets as complementary giving both sides; but what can I do if people insist on looking upon only one, or overlook the other, and thence infer that I also disregard it.

11 January

This is a horrid letter, all about my work. Nevertheless it will have to go; I can't do more and you don't have to read. I am relieved to see that Clowes has not forgot in his Vol. III to acknowledge my debt to you, but I must repeat my thanks. In many places your note books helped me, but especially in Rodney's April 17,[1] I could not have deciphered the case without them. I enclose some cuttings that may interest you, written for a 'syndicate' of newspapers, supposed to reach the man in the street.[2]

186. *Laughton to Mahan*

23 January 1899

I had intended writing to you yesterday to say *how* much I had enjoyed your chapter in Clowes' big book, and at the same time thank you for your reference to me. What I did was so little that it was scarcely necessary; though in the matter of the 17th April, I know my notes – especially of the *Montagu* Court martial – must have been useful. However my intention was postponed; & this morning comes your letter of 29/11 so that I can clearly answer at once, but while I think of it, here is a small error which I discovered quite accidentally a day or two ago. On p.399 (Clowes iii) 'Howe during all those days (7th – 11th) was indefatigable, not only in planning, but also in personal supervision of details'. I think this has always been so described. As I read it, I took it 'connue', but last week, having to do Sir James Wallace for the *DNB.*, I turned up the *Experiment*'s log to see what it said about running through Hell Gate, & found that the statement (above) is not exactly correct. As to planning, that of course; but by *Expt*'s log

July 6th (after vict'ling at N. York) p.m. joined Admiral in the *Eagle* at Sandy Hook.

---

[1] His action with de Guichen in 1780, which was noted for the failure of Captain Carkett to comprehend the meaning of Rodney's signals.

[2] Probably his 'The War on the Sea and its Lessons', *McClure's Magazine*, reprinted in *The Times*. For alternatives, see Hattendorf and Hattendorf.

a.m. Adm'l went to New York.

July 11th a.m. French Squadron anchored at the back of the Hook. Adm'l in *Eagle* working down through the narrows.

the defensive position was not by any means taken at first: eg.

13th p.m. anchored in 2 lines along the W. side of Sandy Hook shore, abt. ¾ of one cable's length asunder, frig[ate]s, bombs, f[ire]ships & tenders to the S[outh]w[ar]d & the *Vigilant* at the Hook
a.m. shifted berth a little more in.

17th Our l[ine of] b[attle] ships moored in a line head & stern, one cable & half asunder, from the point of the Hook along the Channel to the W[estwa]rd.

22nd. a.m. The *Leviathan* came into the line & anchored close to the p[oin]t of the Hook. The Adm[ira]l & the line of b[attle] ships formed the line a bit more across the channel, nearly 10°N from the p[oin]t of the Hook. Ab[ou]t 8 O'C[lock] the Fr[ench] sq[uadron] got under way & began to work off shore – cleared for action. Noon the Fr[ench] standing to the st[arboar]d.

It does not appear that she was chased on Aug.20 by the Fr. fleet. She anchored in the sound: hogged[1] ship 21 p.m. & the next forenoon ran through Hell Gate to N. York.

There are some details here that I dare say will be interesting to you.

I have been so busy for the last twelve months, with Reeve[2] & the *DNB* mostly, that I have not had time to spare for Badham, though Gardiner asked me to write an answer to him. If you like to send him an article on the subject I am quite <u>sure</u> he will gladly insert it; but the *EHR* though a most creditable Review & in the highest degree respectable, does not pay for contributions.[3] Knowles, on the other hand, does: so I only suggest the *EHR* in case you have any thing which Knowles may think too heavy for the *XIXth Century*. By the way Nicolas's[4] son is not <u>Sir</u> Harris.

---

[1]Drawing a cable along the ship's bottom, to clean off the worst marine fouling.

[2]His biography of Henry Reeve.

[3]The *English Historical Review* became the basis of historical professionalism in Britain, and necessarily had to stop paying contributors, but this limited JKL's ability to write for it, and reduced Mahan's interest. His two EHR articles of 1899 and 1900 were essentially the chapters he rewrote for the second edition of Nelson (Hattendorf and Hattendorf, D48 & D60).

[4]Sir Nicholas Harris Nicolas (1799–1848), naval officer and historian, compiled the seven volume edition of Nelson's Correspondence, and completed two volumes of a major History of the Royal Navy before his death. The first archival scholar to work on naval history in Britain.

I don't know whether I have to thank you for the *McClure Mags.* which have reached me. I am glad to have these arts of yours – I have undertaken to write a book on Strategy for Bells' Series. I hope to get it done during this coming summer.[1]

187.   *Colomb to Laughton*

11 March 1899

Three weeks ago I was knocked over for the first time by influenza, and though I have been about and to town when I could not help it, I can't get the steam up, or I would have answered yours of the 6th before. What a blessing to have so careful an editor at one's back![2] I wish you had edited everything I ever wrote.

Prototype is first rate, no one but myself could have written it or passed it. But I don't see that the editor would have been to blame in any case. How you keep in your mind a detail, nay how you got hold of a detail – like that of Parker, I don't know, but I am much obliged for the correction.

Thanks also for the reference to the Hist. MS Com.[3] I will look it up. I found that Bray (*History of Surrey* 1814) credits Torrington with being the founder of Greenwich Hospital on the same grounds that I was inclined to. And I think it is significant that William gave Torrington in 1696 the fee simple of Oatlands and Weybridge of which the lease had been held from James II, by the brother [of the?] Chief Justice. Torrington left all his landed property to the Earl of Lincoln in trust for any wife he might marry, and then to any son of such marriage, failing that to Greenwich Hospital. He left all his books to the Bishop of Salisbury. This would have been Burnet's successor. How can I find out who the successor was?

I am afraid Macaulay would have hardly allowed a library to his *bête noire*.

Very remarkable that there should be such proof of William's favour to him. Was he playing a political part all through, or did he come to understand the truth later?

---

[1]Laughton's proposed book on strategy was never published. The series for which it was commissioned was abruptly terminated due to poor sales: see fn. 1, p. 108.

[2]For his two chapters in *From Howard to Nelson*.

[3]Royal Commission on Historical Manuscripts; long-running publishing project producing a wide range of reports and calendars of papers.

188.   *J.A.H. Murray[1] to Laughton*

11 May 1899

The question of <u>pressed, impressed</u> is very difficult. I am leaving it over to <u>Prest, Press</u> etc, as anything said now might have to be unsaid then. Our present position is that the connection with <u>prest</u> & <u>imprest</u> 'Com advance' is a later confusion. We see reason to conclude that the origin is the old adjective 'prest' – ready. Holders of feudal land were ordered to have their men 'prest', they had so many 'prest'; the men themselves were 'prest for service'. So also in Old French. As the <u>readiness</u> often probably generally was rather unwilling readiness on the part of the tenant, he not unnaturally felt that he was 'press'd' into service. At the same time there is evidence of pretty early 16th C. association of 'being prest' with 'prest-money' and it is because I cannot wait to work this out that I do not go into it under <u>Impress</u> when it can easily be referred on to the place where, in any case, it will have to be done *in cafsite*. I am profoundly ignorant as to the facts that underlie the thing: viz. How late did the feudal duty of having so many men 'prest' continue? When did the forcible seizure or impressing of men begin? When were prests or advances introduced? What is the first record of <u>prest-money</u> in any such sense. These are matters of <u>fact</u> that the historians must supply before I can deal with the word. But at present there is abundant early evidence for 'prest for military service' in the sense of 'levied, armed, & ready to march.'

P.S. I send proofs to show the various words under I<u>m</u> please return with any notes that occur to you.

189.   *Mahan to Laughton*

The Hague, 18 May 1899

In asking Stevens to send you Dumas Vol. IV, my object was to ask you to verify by examination the extraordinary putting of Dumas's words into the mouth of Hamilton by Badham. As I said before, I can scarcely believe my own eyes. I may add that application was made near a month ago to the Italian Record Office for a copy of the original, but so far without success. It seems to me therefore probable that Badham quoted from Dumas, & Lemoni[2] from Badham.

[1]Editor of the *Oxford English Dictionary.*
[2]Unknown.

P.S. Badham's reference is to Dumas & to the same vol. & <u>page</u> as in the volume used by me & sent to you. The enclosed from Stevens gives the authority for the translation of the 'ai castelli' letter as changed in my article.

190.   *Mahan to Laughton*

Hotel du Vieux, Dorlen, 23 May 1899

I have your letter with Gardiner's, & thank you much for them and for your action in the whole matter. I have written G. accepting all his suggestions, & the non-remuneration. I am not above dollars; but in this matter my chief wish is to put the whole story on a rock-bed foundation, not hereafter to be shaken. The question of the 500 (marines) on June 26 is explained as follows: when Nelson wrote, (first by Hamilton afterwards by himself) on that day, that he would observe the armistice as regards Uovo and Nuovo, he sent, with his own letter, Troubridge & Ball to arrange for the operations against St. Elmo, which was not included in the armistice. <u>When Ruffo was ready for that</u> he would land 1200 men. He ignored R's terrified request for reinforcements, for he doubtless realised, with his keen military sense, that they were not needed, and that the Rebel's plight was desperate. Later in the day, the Rebels decided to surrender, accepting Nelson's terms which were to submit to the King's decision. These had been made known to them in the letter 'ai castelli'. It became necessary, of course, to garrison the empty castles, & for this the 500 were landed on the 26. When all was ready for attacking St. Elmo the remainder was landed, & Nelson also asked that Neapolitans relieve the 500 in the castles, that those also might proceed against St. Elmo. I have written this to Gardiner.

You wrote me some time ago that Badham, you had heard reported, was Foote's Grandson; but you did not tell me positively. As regards the translation of the 'ai castelli' letter, being doubtful of my own Italian I asked Stevens to have it looked at by a competent hand, with the result you saw. I of course can't vouch. I wish Gardiner or you would verify also my quotes from Lemoni. I give the references, I think.

191. *Mahan to Laughton*

International Conference at the Hague,
Commission of the United States of America,
17 June 1899

I have been in a rage to find that your letter, inquiring about flag devices in pictures, has disappeared. I have only now had an opportunity to go to Amsterdam, since my visit there prior to your letter. Wont you send me word at once again, that I may have a chance to attend to it? I have just been released from Committee work, but know not how soon I may be entangled in the full conference.

I went at once to the gallery here, but the picture specified gave no information. It is a sea shore painting; that is, on the dunes in the foreground are peasants, & other onlookers, gazing at four streams of men pouring down in the middle distance to a beach. The ships are not much more than indicated in the distance, and no details at all.

I have read & returned the proof of the article for the *Eng Hist'l.*[1] A letter from my home publisher yesterday told me he was about sending you the Revised *Nelson*, so I hope you will very soon receive it. I have sent for and received *From Howard to Nelson* but have not yet had time more than to glance at it. In matters of correspondence I seem no better off than at home – quite as busy.

192. *Mahan to Laughton*

21 June 1899

I stole two or three hours to go to Amsterdam today, and have obtained some results which will be interesting, and I hope satisfactory. The picture to which you referred me was indeed full of flags, but nothing that bore upon the special matter. I had bethought me of the Hall of the Admirals, which I had once visited hurriedly, and there I found several details which I noted down as follows:

1. (472 Hague) Four Day's Fight, 1666, by Jan Abrahmez Beerstraten.[2] A large English ship in foreground, has rising from the bowsprit cap a

---

[1] Mahan, 'The Neapolitan Republicans and Nelson's Accusers', *EHR*, **XIV** (1899), pp. 471–501.
[2] As Beerstraten died in 1666 this identification is problematic. He did paint pictures of the First Anglo-Dutch War, 1652–54.

short mast (?spirit topmast) above which again a pole, or flag-staff, from which this flag, ½ white, ½ blue, thus:

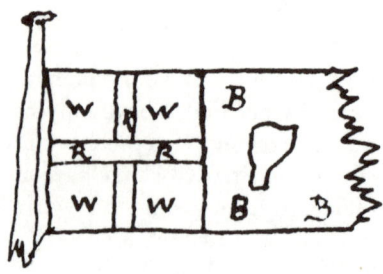

In the white a red cross, much like your present Admiral's flag, as I recall. The fly of the blue is frayed, but I could see no indication of a third color. In the blue is a harp. I may add that in the east Court of the Museum there are represented a number of flags, said to be English, more than one of which resembles the left hand half of the above, but I did not detect the blue half. I had seen them, however, before seeing the picture.

Another English ship in the same painting carries the same flag in the same position; also at the fore, on a pole above the F.T.G. [fore top gallant] truck, a flag apparently all red, possibly a small union (as we now say). At the U.T.G. [upper top gallant] she has an extraordinary flag – red field, in which a blue circle, and inside the circle a harp, also a small union in the usual place.

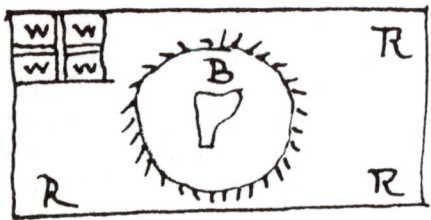

The circle seems to be surrounded by yellow rays, but I could not be sure whether this was not the work of wear on the paint.

Underneath this flag there flies also, from the M.T.G. [main top gallant] cap (or truck), a pendant; very long, but broad enough at the left to be bent to a staff. Colors, &c thus:

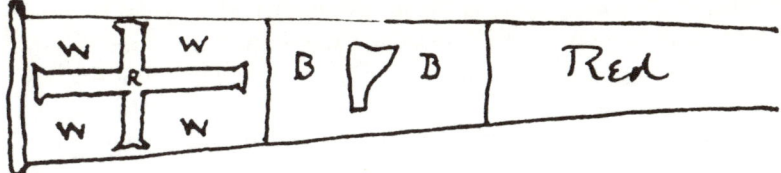

Harp again in the blue.

I omitted to say in the proper place that the first of these two ships carried also, from pole at F.T.G. [fore top gallant] head, a white flag with red cross; and at the M.T.G. [main top gallant] a blue flag, with a very small white union:

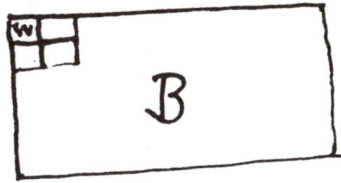

Generally, what we now call the union is much smaller than our present practice.

2. (359 Hague) A picture of the battle off Leghorn 1653, by R. Nooms. In this the flag half white, half blue, occurs very frequently, the harp always in the blue. The colors in this painting are much fresher than in the former, but in both are clear.

3. (367 Hague) The same battle, 1653, by Lingelbach. Affords comparatively little indication. There is one ship, apparently English, (I cannot make out the taffrail flag) which carries at the main T.G. a flag clearly white and blue, with red cross in the former, but I cannot make out the harp in the blue. The ship is rather in back ground. But in the corner of the picture Lingelbach has put a pedestal, on which is an allegorical claim of victory. A seaman, standing, carries high aloft a Dutch flag; at his feet two others are seated, hands tied behind their backs. Projecting forward from these, but drooping, are two flag staffs with spear heads, carrying flags partly furled, one red with white union and red cross, the other blue, with a harp in the place where the Union is usually. I don't know whether there was authority for this position, or whether, the flag being furled, he had to put it there to show it at all. The cross & the harp in this case seem to sum up the British forces.

4. Singularly enough, here is a picture of the Four Day's Battle (1496)[1] by W. v. d Velde the Elder,[2] in which some ships have at the bowsprit end something nearly like the present union – certainly a St Andrew's Cross. What can this mean? What was van de Velde's time?

I trust this may be of some help to you, and always at your service I am

193. *Mahan to Laughton*

4 July 1899

Thank you for sending me Badham's letter.[3] It is disfigured by faults much the same as those noted in the article in *E.H.R.* Though usually slow and cautious I have written off a reply for the *Athenaeum*, in which I take up a few points, and refer frequently to his previous blunders & their showing up in my article.[4] It seemed to me best in this case to strike at once. I hope Gardiner or Gutteridge may take the thing up; but personally I stop here. One can't be always refuting such mixtures of half truth, whole falsehood and monumental capacity for blundering.

I have found on the tomb of Tromp, at Delft Oude Kerk, flags in relief exactly like those described in the paintings, cross on one half, near the flag, and harp in the other. The lines were so fine I had to take an opera glass, the railing keeping me five feet distant. With the glass I made out several flags, but the lines so fine I should not have detected them but for my experience at Amsterdam. I paid a second visit, carrying glasses on purpose.

I can't get you a copy of Schwarzhoff's speech yet.[5] I heard it and it was admirable.

---

[1]This must be a mistake for 1665.

[2]1611–93.

[3]In the *Athenaeum* of 1 July. Mahan's reply of 8 July is noted in Hattendorf and Hattendorf, D46.

[4]Enclosed with this letter was a copy of Mahan's letter of 4 July 1899 to *The Athenaeum*.

[5]General Julius Gross von Schwarzhoff (1850–1901), German military delegate to the Hague Peace Conference. His opening speech condemned the Russian concept of non-augmentation of armaments. This conveniently saddled Germany with any blame of the failure of the conference, which suited the purposes of Mahan, and Admiral Sir John Fisher, the British delegate. See R.F. Mackay, *Fisher of Kilverstone* (Oxford, 1973), pp. 219–22.

194. *Laughton to Henry Newbolt*[1]

Lowestoft, 19 July 1899

I am here 'till the end of the month, with no books or notes to refer to; but I was myself up the Baltic in the fleet under Napier; & can say positively that he wore his *proper* flag (I dare say he was vice admiral of the blue, but I quite forget – that can easily be settled) with him in the *Duke of Wellington* was the Captain of the Fleet, Sir Michael Seymour, who was a Commodore of the First Class, & wore his red broad pennant at the main *when* (but only when) the Admiral was officially absent & his flag thus temporarily struck.[2]

I am quite sure that there was nothing irregular about the flag; nor – in any case – could the Admiral fly a pennant. When I get back to town I can easily tell you exactly what flag he did fly.[3]

195. *Colomb to Laughton*

21 August 1899

When Herbert, who had only become 1st Lord of the Admiralty on the 8th of March 1689, having been before acting for the whole Board, was appointed to command the ships in the Narrow Seas on the 14th of March, got down to Portsmouth about the 10th, he found his own flagship & the eastern ships had not yet arrived. H[erbert] at once wrote to Nottingham as Secretary of State to urge him to hasten up the contingent. Nottingham, by directions of the King, to [who] alone he showed Herbert's letter, sent it on to the Admiralty, who replied to Nottingham that they had given all necessary directions, & Nottingham informed Herbert accordingly.

There is a puzzle about it. When I found Torrington writing to Nottingham in 1690, I understood it was because of his special commission from the King. But I can't see why the 1st Lord of the Admiralty in 1689 should not have sent directions to his Board. Did Herbert definitely surrender his administrative functions when he took a sea command? How was it with Anson? What do you think?

---

[1]Henry Newbolt (1862–1938), poet and editor of the liberal *The Monthly Review* from 1900; a close friend of Corbett, volumes IV and V of whose *Official History of Naval Operations in 1914–18* he completed.

[2]Bridges had written to Newbolt on 17 July 1899 to ask if he knew whether Napier's fleet had flown a blue ensign. Newbolt evidently passed Laughton's letter directly to Bridges.

[3]This letter shows that even JKL occasionally took a holiday.

196.   *Mahan to Laughton*

160 West Eighty Sixth Street, 23 November 1899

Thanks for the *Speaker*[1] Oct. 14 sent me. I have received also a cutting from the same issue of Nov. 4, in which Badham, with his happy knack of assumption says I describe JKL as my agent. The opportunity was too good to be neglected, so I have squibbed off at him a letter which will be in time for the issue of Dec. 2. I never described you, needless to say, as my agent, despite the favours you have at times done me. It happens I remember the precise incident viz: that when Badham, in the *Athenaeum*, said if I had looked farther, I would have found an important letter of Ruffo's, I had not time to ascertain if there had been an oversight, & so wrote that if there were any, it belonged to the 'agent' I had employed, who was a copyist, employed by Stevens, in response to a cable I had sent for all Ruffo's letters between June 26 and July 1 – of which a memorandum had reached me. The fruit of this was the ai castelli letter; and that Gardiner, to whom I wrote by the same mail as to the *Athenaeum*, was good enough to verify the copyist's work, and so assure me there was no oversight. I then dared Badham to print his 'important' letter, a challenge he never accepted. I have asked Gardiner to keep me informed on his forthcoming work. He may prove to have something up his sleeve, but from his phenomenal capacity for misunderstanding & misstatement, I rather anticipate a series of assumptions and distortions, with not improbably something worse. You, of course, will be too interested to need a request for any help in your power to give. I am delighted with Gardiner's suggestion, if Badham's next spring fails, to print all the letters by the N.R.S.[2] I can conceive no worthier use of the Society's means than to gather in one accessible volume the demonstration of Nelson's integrity, & trust it may be feasible to do so.[3]

You may imagine with what keen interest and hearty sympathy I am following the British arms in S. Africa.[4]

---

[1]A short-lived liberal periodical.

[2]This resulted, largely through JKL's hard work, in H.G. Gutteridge (ed.), *Nelson and the Neapolitan Jacobins* (NRS, London, 1903).

[3]The object was, as it always had been, the education of modern naval officers.

[4]See the final chapter of *The Problem of Asia* and his *The Story of the War in South Africa, 1899–1900* (London, 1900) for his collected, and very pro-British, journalism.

197.   *Mahan to Laughton*

19 December 1899

In my letter in *The Speaker*, Dec. 2nd, I see I quote Maresca as saying Nelson's letter, of June 24, instead of 26. On referring to my rough draft, I find the error there. My impression is that the slip is Maresca's,[1] but having sent his letter to Gardiner, I cannot verify. If Badham catch at this, would you mind ascertaining from G. whether it is Maresca's, and if so writing a line to say so? I am perhaps over careful in this, and you will of course use your judgement as to the advisability of doing it at all; but I feel that in dealing with one so unscrupulous in inaccuracy, I can't be too chary of my own reputation for care. Of course, if B. says nothing, best let the matter lie.

I am greatly grieved over the news from S. Africa, and cannot but think it was a woeful mistake for Buller not to go in person with 40,000 men where he sent Methuen with 10,000 – or whatever it was. He would at least have done something somewhere, and my own belief is the Boers could not have been held at Ladysmith if your fellows to that number entered the Free State.[2] Of course, it is easy for a man at a desk to criticise, but I continually think of the Archduke in 1796. 'It don't matter if Moreau gets to Vienna, if I smash Jourdan'.[3] In view of your check all round this seems reasonable – and such an elementary teaching of war. Better have lost White & accomplished something than to stand still all round.

198.   *Laughton to Sir Charles Dilke*[4]

28 March 1900

I should have little doubt that Sir Peter Warren[5] is your man. He was never officially governor of any place – as far as I know: but he

---

[1]Benedetto Maresca, *La pace del 1796 tra le Due Sicillie e a Francia* (Naples, 1887).

[2]The operations leading up to 'Black Week' are open to much criticism.

[3]One of Mahan's favourite strategic examples, drawn from Jomini; see *Naval Strategy* (London, 1911), pp. 22–5.

[4]Sir Charles Dilke (1843–1911), Liberal cabinet minister, disgraced by a divorce scandal; became an important commentator on imperial defence. See *The British Empire* (London, 1899), chapters I and IX for an example of his work.

[5]Admiral Sir Peter Warren (1703–52), has been studied in depth in J. Gwynn, *The Enterprising Admiral: The personal fortune of Admiral Sir Peter Warren* (Montreal, 1975). Warren did harbour ambitions in New York, and for office in Britain, but did not succeed in either. Gwynn demonstrates that Laughton's assertion about his 'fortune' was well founded.

certainly was <u>de facto</u> governor of Louisbourg after its first capture. He had, by marriage, a good New York connection, & towards the end of his life was enormously wealthy. There is a letter to Anson (Add. MS 15,957) of about 1747 – as well as I can remember – saying that the appointment as Governor of New York would gratify him beyond anything else, & would he believed, be acceptable to the people. But he died, I think, before he could get it.

I don't remember any other Warren at all likely, the art[icle] in <u>Harper's Mag[azine]</u> – referred to in *DNB* – may be worth your looking at, written from an American point of view, it may give some detail which I omitted.

199.   *H. G. Gutteridge[1] to Laughton*

28 April 1900

I acknowledge with thanks the receipt of Gagniere and the 'Archive'. I have read your letter in the *Athenaeum* and will look out for Mahan's article in the *English Historical Review*. Palumbo[2] is so inaccurate that I do not think it will be at all necessary to use him, and I have Helfert[3] handy.

During the last few weeks I have been going through the Nelson papers but there does not seem to be much left of any importance. I have got hold of rather an interesting letter from the King to Nelson, specifying the powers and duties of Troubridge when employed at Procida. Also a letter, June 11, to Nelson from Caroline, and Northwick's account of the trial of Caracciolo, none of which I have yet seen in print.

So much was destroyed in 1860 by Bomba,[4] and at a later date sent to Vienna by Victor Emmanuel,[5] from the Naples Archives, that it is possible the missing documents will be hard to trace – I will make a thorough search when I have the opportunity. I once asked Lord Acton

---

[1]H.G. Gutteridge, then a student at King's College Cambridge, with a particular interest in this subject, a good working knowledge of Italian, and independent means, whom Laughton had enlisted in this vital cause. His *NRS* volume can be seen as the capstone on this debate.

[2]Raffaele Palumbo, *Maria Carolina Regina delle Due Sicillie, suo carteggio con Lady Hamilton* (Naples, 1877).

[3]Baron von Helfert, *Fabrizio Ruffo, Rivoluzione e Controrivoluzione di Napoli* (Florence, 1885).

[4]Ferdinand II (1830–59), the penultimate King of Naples; nicknamed 'Bomba' after bombarding his own people in Palermo in 1848–49; his son was deposed in 1860 by Garibaldi.

[5]Victor Emmanuele II, King of Sardinia Piedmont, and first King of Italy.

if he had any papers of 1799. He said he would see but I never heard if he had found anything.

If I employ a copyist will it be at my own expense or at that of the Society?

I am as yet unable to send in a report, though I have prepared a rough outline of what will be essential. I am hoping to be able to lay hold of some letters of Micheroux's[1] at Naples, as at present it seems to me that he is the real villain of the piece.

200. *Gutteridge to Laughton*

30 May 1900

Please excuse my not having answered your letter before this date as I have only just emerged from an examination.

I think it is just possible that the following MSS might be at Vienna.

a.   The original (probably in English) of Hamilton–Acton June 27, 1799 (Dumas iv. 87).

b.   A letter from Hamilton to Ruffo of June 27 printed in Rossi[2] [vol.] 1 237 speaks of a letter of June 26 from Nelson–Ruffo relating to action as to certain rebels.

Is there any chance do you think of the copy of the *Compendie* of Micheroux sent to Acton being there? I am not certain whether the copy printed by Maresca is anything more than a transcript for his own use.

Speaking generally, if anything has got to Vienna, most of the originals of letters printed in Dumas should be there. If you would like me to make a list of them I will do so, but have not Dumas to hand just now.

201. *Mahan to Laughton*

Quogue, 28 August 1900

I enclose our naval official directions for flag-making which will I hope give all the information you wished. There was a book once, written by Rear Adm. G.H. Preble of our navy, upon the history etc. of the U.S. Flag. Perhaps you may have a copy accessible; if not I <u>might</u> find one, though I don't know how rare it may now have become.

---

[1]Cavaliere Antonio Micheroux, Ferdinand IV's envoy to the Russian and Turkish commanders; negotiated the controversial armistice.

[2]Michele Rossi, *Nuova Luce risultante dai veri fatti avvenu I in Napoli pochi anni prima del 1799* (Florence, 1890).

I am today returning to Gardiner my review of the treatment of Hamilton's June 27. From first to last my object – subsidiary only to defence of Nelson – has been to destroy Badham's credit, by showing how he uses documents which he <u>accepts</u>. The validity of the document is less in question than his use of it; for, as I think I once heard you say, the only sufficient way of dealing with a man wholly unreliable – whether through inaccuracy or unscrupulousness – is to show him up. Badham being entirely unfettered by truth, I see no reason why he should not go on writing & asserting indefinitely; the only remedy is to convince others that he is not to be believed, and therefore not worth listening to. I think also that the one satisfactory solution is the NRS publishing as intended, making of it a really exhaustive & critical historical monograph.

I am very sorry to hear of your trouble with your eyes. So far mine keep very strong, but I use them so much, being no talker, that I don't know what I should do if even partially deprived. If you got to Holland,[1] you will have viewed with instructed eye, which I had not, the flags advising the sea fights in the Amsterdam Museum. I wonder did you visit Tromp's tomb at Delft. If you did I hope you took a binocular with you, I could not make out the tracing without one.

I told Gardiner that I would refrain from suggesting any solution for the contradiction in Hamilton between *ceri mattina* (like morning) and *questa sera* (the evening) but would be very pleased if he thought best to do so. I had already suggested one which could scarcely have reached [him] before the date of your last. Yours is certainly very plausible as regards <u>tense</u>, I am not sure there is a slip in <u>questa</u>.

[*Enclosure: two-page. Memo. on USN Flags*[2]]

202. *Laughton to Corbett*

11 November 1900

I fear I have been extremely remiss in answering your letter, which I put on one side when I had read it and could not find again. Today, in despair, I had a grand turn out and so brought it to light.

I am very glad to find that you are meditating the Navy of the Commonwealth. Why not take Blake as the central figure, as you have done Drake? No-one, to the best of my knowledge – is working at it,

[1] He had.
[2] LGH 14/ 88–9.

except of course, Gardiner, whose *First Dutch War* you will find helpful. His Dutch transcripts, as done with, are given to the B[ritish]
M[useum].[1] I was at Bridgewater a few weeks ago, at the unveiling of a
tercentenary statue to Blake, and found that they had got hold of a
hitherto unknown portrait, which <u>seems</u> to have a pedigree.

I can't quite make up my mind about that Ubaldino's MS.[2] I got it for
Lord Acton, but have not yet finished – I have been, in truth, waiting
for your volume which will be very helpful. Whether this MS is worth
printing in full or not, I feel doubtful: I cannot believe that Drake is in
any way responsible for it, though he may have given some information. At any rate, we do not want anything just now, having enough on
hand for the next three years at least. Towards the end of that time we
shall be glad of your help: in the meantime let me commend Blake to
you. No-one is so well prepared for the task as you are.

P.S. I have lately had some correspondence with Dr. Murray[3] about jib
for which I was able to give him some 17th C. quotations and to show,
as you have said, that the sail was used in small craft many years before
it reached square rigged vessels. Its origin, however, remains obscure. I
wonder if you could give him (through me if you like) anything bearing
on the point you speak of small craft having jibs in the 16th C. English
or foreign? Have you met the word 'jib' in the 16th C.?

203.   *Mahan to Laughton*

160 West Eighty-Sixth Street, 25 December 1900

There is always a relief to me when writing you a long delayed letter
that you are yourself so busy that you can allow for others' shortcom-
ings. I have been not only engrossed in my work, but sensible of a kind
of pressure from feeling that there is so much to be done, so much
ground to be gone over before I can really get to work, writing. I have
at last settled down – at least I hope so – to a re-presentation and
condensation of my two books on Sea Power; but while the argument –
main – remains the same, I rather propose considerable difference of
treatment, and in order to the completeness of my idea must strike its
roots a little further back, and carry the argument a little further forward; all which requires much reading and <u>you</u> know how that sort of

---

[1]Means British Library, then housed at the British Museum.
[2]Relating to Drake; published in S. Purchas, *Purchas, His Pilgrims* (1625, republished in 20 vols, Glasgow, 1905–7).
[3]See [188].

thing widens on you. Luckily, I am immensely interested, even absorbed, so though protracted the task is not tedious.

I read the account of the Hague Exhibition which you were good enough to send me.[1] It seems singular that it should not have attracted more visitors; but the truth, I fancy is that people know so little that they have no curiosity to know more. L'appitet vient en mangeant. To your instructed appreciation the interest must have been very great.

I hope I shall hear no more of Badham, but there is no limit to a man's writing when truth and accuracy have no grip upon him to limit his assertions. I am however comforted by Gardiner's opinion that I need pay no attention to anything further 'from that quarter'. I have hoped that Gutteridge might find time to search the Neapolitan archives, unless he does, this question will probably sleep for some time.

You will be very good if you take up Colomb's *Torrington*;[2] I can imagine few things less to my taste than to round out another man's work. If you do I can only hope that the service you will so do for the rest of us may be a sufficient reward, & that there may be also something substantial beyond it.

Thank you very much for your congratulations upon my receiving the Chesney Medal.[3] You will believe I greatly valued it.

---

[1]Which JKL had attended.

[2]Colomb had died in 1899, leaving his book unfinished.

[3]The prestigious gold medal of the RUSI, presented occasionally to historians of war. JKL received it in 1910.

5

WORKING TO THE END, 1901–15

At the turn of the century Laughton's remarkable working life continued unabated. He had a busy schedule of paying tasks, lecturing, writing, reviewing, and running the Navy Records Society, for which he was now paid, thanks to the Council's decision in 1900 to award him a salary of £100.[1] He certainly earned his money, picking up the pieces when editors failed, and continually pushing the cause that the Society served. In spite of this sustained effort, a number of important projects were not completed, and others changed direction [222]. This was hardly surprising. Laughton had always taken on more than he could complete. Up to 1900 he had usually managed to get through most of what he undertook, but after 1900 his reserves and resources were no longer sufficient. The most obvious problem was the gradual loss of sight in one eye [211, 212, 216], a problem dating back to the Montgomery affair. The effect of what appears to have been iritis was profound. Nevertheless, he still edited the *Du Cane Manuscripts* for the Royal Commission on Historical Manuscripts, two volumes of *Naval Miscellany*, three volumes of the *Letters of Lord Barham* and helped Admiral Vesey-Hamilton with the *Recollections of Commander James Anthony Gardner* for the Record Society. He also kept up his regular reviewing schedule. Julian Corbett offered to help [227], and provided more substantial fare [246].

Throughout the last fifteen years of his life Laughton's major correspondent would be Mahan; half the letters in this chapter are from that source. The two men met very occasionally in London, but otherwise kept up a regular correspondence, largely on professional matters, but coloured by the visible signs of ageing that afflicted them both. This exchange reveals much of Mahan's working methods, and the politics of both men. It was fitting that Mahan should, unknowingly, end his last letter to Laughton with a summation of his ideology [272]. In the event Laughton would live to draft an obituary for his friend [273], who died a year before him, although ten years younger. The obituary was a characteristically generous and vivid description of the impact Mahan's books had made on those that read them.

[1]Council Minute Book 22 May 1900 (NMM: NRS 1).

Nelson remained central to Laughton and Mahan's shared interests. The search for the truth about his conduct at Naples continued, with Laughton directing the Cambridge fellowship candidate H.G. Gutteridge in his work at Naples, supporting him with Record Society funds, and publishing his results by way of a summation of the debate [210, 215, 218–19, 237]. It was not surprising that Bridge, Mahan and Laughton were infuriated by the careless repetition of the old myths in the *Cambridge Modern History* [233–4]. No sooner was that task complete than the centenary of Trafalgar sparked a new debate on Nelson's tactics [238–9]. Once again Laughton kept himself on the sidelines; although avoiding any direct involvement, he supported Bridge and Mahan with his scholarship. Bridge gave a lecture on the subject at the 1905 Records Society Annual General Meeting [235]; however, the Council of the Record Society refused to circulate Philip Colomb's controversial paper, which Laughton had had printed for the occasion.

In 1904–5 Laughton and Mahan discussed the future of the British Empire and the United States. Both accepted Joseph Chamberlain's Imperial Preference and Tariff Reform Movement as inevitable [239–40]. They also considered the dangers of the new Liberal Government's position on belligerent rights at sea, which would have crippled British, and later American seapower [247–9]. By contrast both men opposed John Fisher's new all-big-gun battleship type, the *Dreadnought* [250–1].

Laughton's work at King's College developed as the College moved closer to the Federal University of London, and in 1912 he became a Professor of the University. A major theme he developed in his lectures was Imperial History, which he considered the true context for the study of naval affairs [221, 268]. In this way he laid the foundations of another branch of historical enquiry, one in which King's has retained a major interest to this day. As late as 1913 he was to be found at the London International Congress of Historical Sciences, lecturing on naval historiography[1] to an audience that included the First Sea Lord, Prince Louis of Battenberg, and colleagues two generations younger [265]. It reminded everyone that the navy and the historical profession recognised him as the most eminent figure in his field.

The award of a knighthood in 1907, from the new Liberal Imperialist dominated government, demonstrated his impact in a wider field. The award of the Chesney Gold Medal of the Royal United Services Institute, which also hosted his eightieth birthday celebration, enabled many

---

[1]JKL, 'Historians and Naval History', *The Cornhill Magazine* vol. 35, July 1913, pp. 33–43; reprinted in J.S. Corbett (ed.), *Naval and Military Essays* (Cambridge, 1914).

of his old pupils and followers, from the First Sea Lord, Sir Arthur Wilson (midshipman on board HMS *Calcutta* 1856–59) to Rudyard Kipling, to record their debt to Laughton.

In 1912, age, failing eyesight and the desire to complete his last great task led him to resign as Secretary of the Records Society, and from his Chair at King's [259, 260–7]. However, he continued to be involved in both institutions, particularly at King's, where he used his lectures to develop a book closely linking British history and naval history [270]. He hoped this book, provisionally titled 'The Interdependence of England's Naval and Political History' would provide a textbook for the Department of Naval History he hoped to establish at King's, within the Federal University. Tragically time ran out.[1] The outbreak of war in August 1914 added to the succession of problems that denied him the opportunity to complete his life's work. He had not achieved all the tasks he had set himself, and the prospect of doing so was no longer bright. He died on 14 September, 1915, loaded with years and honours.

The contents of this volume demonstrate the pioneering role that Laughton played in his subject, the breadth of his vision, and his astounding energy. He gave his subject form and purpose, secured the support of the Royal Navy, the English historical profession, the wider defence community and through such correspondents as James Thursfield of *The Times*, the major newspapers, all of which he used to develop naval history as the basis of naval thought, doctrine development, national policy and a major component in the teaching of statesmanship. His concept of naval history based on documentary evidence linked the current concerns of the navy with the standards demanded by the newly professional historical community. It was in Laughton's mind that these ideas took shape, and largely through his remarkable energy that they were given concrete form. His memorials were the Navy Records Society, and the enduring strength of naval history in Britain.

204.   *Bridge to Laughton*

4 February 1901

I hope earnestly that you have quite recovered your indisposition. If you are still feeling at all seedy, do not give yourself the trouble to answer this, as it is not of extreme importance.

---

[1]See Chapter 6 for the draft text [276].

Am I right in saying that no naval historian, English or French, records any instance of Frenchmen cutting out British merchant vessels lying under the protection of British batteries, at any rate since Tourville destroyed some dozen fishing boats in 1690, when he really commanded the sea? You examined the story of his destruction of shipping in an article in the *Edinburgh Review* in October 1890.[1]

There may have been some cutting out by the French of vessels under British protection at Capri and other Neapolitan Islands early in the XIXth Century, but I think that there was no real 'cutting out' by them.[2]

The process seems to have been commonly adopted by us, coast batteries of the enemy notwithstanding.

205a.   *Mouchez*[3] *to Laughton*

14 Rue de la Rampe, Brest, 27 February 1901

[*Lieutenant Mouchez requests permission to publish extracts from* Dispatches and Letters relating to the Blockade of Brest *edited by John Leyland for the Navy Records Society.*]

205b.   *H.R.F. Yorke*[4] *to Laughton*

1 March 1901

As regards the Frenchman I do not think we have taken any steps to protect our books from being translated and, if that is so, there is no reason why anyone who likes should not translate them. I fancy that to protect a book from translation you must deposit a copy in the original language in the Foreign Country, but I am unsure. Some of your publishers could tell you for certain. Anyhow I should be inclined to write a civil letter to the Gentleman & say the Society saw no objection etc, etc.

As to the Liverpool Public Library, I don't see that it is possible to differentiate between one subscription and another. The rule of the

---

[1]JKL, 'Mahan on Maritime Power', *Edinburgh Review*, **CLXXIV** (1890), pp. 420–53.

[2]Bridge is evidently examining the different ways in which Britain and France used the sea. With command of the sea, cutting out and other forms of coastal warfare become inevitable.

[3]C. Mouchez, Lieutenant de Vaisseau, French Navy.

[4]Sir Henry Francis Redhead Yorke KCB (1842–1914); Treasurer of the Navy Records Society.

Society is that Volumes are not issued until subscriptions are paid and we have no right to depart from this rule. Solvency has no more to do with the question than it would have in taking a ticket on the railway; the Rule is that you don't get a ticket until you have paid. A solvent man who is elected a member of a Club is like an insolvent man, not entitled to use the Club until his entrance dues are paid. I should answer _____ in the terms of the enclosed.

205c.   *Yorke's draft reply to Mouchez*

6 March 1901

Sir, in reply to yours of the 27th Ultimo I am instructed to say that the Council has much pleasure in complying with your request, & in giving you permission to publish a translation of the *Dispatches and Letters etc*, edited for the Society by Mr Leyland.

They must – however stipulate that in the translation – as published – due acknowledgement be made of the Society & to Mr Leyland.

206.   *Mrs. Jodrell to Laughton*

Merchistoun Hall,[1] 9 March 1901

So many statements in your article on my father Sir C. Napier in the Biographical Dictionary are either incorrect or exaggerated that I deem it necessary (having all his correspondence both public and private in my possession) to make public the misstatements, some I presume furnished by his enemies.

   I regret you did not apply to me in the first instance as being his only child I was of course the proper person, and truth and not embellishment, enhances a book that is supposed to prove one of reference.

Fanny Jodrell

It is my intention to publish all Sir Charles's Correspondence and then the present and future ages will judge for themselves whether he had a desire for 'theatrical effects and unpleasant exaggerated actions, naval or military – civil and diplomatic.'

[*Endorsement by JKL*] answ'd civilly 12.iii 01

[1]Horndean, Hampshire.

glad to hear of the proposed publication – the historians business is to hold the balance [between] friends and enemies, sometimes to the annoyance of both.

207. *Laughton to Lee*

15 March 1901

I dare say you will hear it from other quarters, but it is as well to let you know that Southeran in the Strand had a first folio[1] in his window this afternoon; priced 300 guineas – also a second folio, at 40 odd.

I had a letter from Mrs Jodrell a few days ago. I sent her a soft answer which ought, if she has any sense of religion – to turn away her wrath.

208. *Laughton to Browning*

9 April 1901

Dear Sir,[2]

Several of our fellow contributors to the *Dictionary of National Biography* desire to pay a last tribute of respect to the late Mr George Smith, the projector and proprietor of the undertaking.

We learn that the funeral will take place at Byfleet Church on Thursday afternoon at 3.15, and that the train leaves Waterloo Station at 1.40 for Weybridge, whence carriages will convey those attending to Byfleet. The return train to London leaves Weybridge at 4.52.

We propose forwarding a wreath on behalf of the contributors and we shall be glad if those wishing to contribute for this purpose would forward 2/6d to Mr H.E. Murray at 15 Waterloo Place S.W.

209. *Mr. S. Parry to Laughton*

10, Downing Street, Whitehall SW, 5 May 1901

Mr O'Byrne[3] had received two Royal Bounty grants, so far as I can trace them – one of £100 from Mr Gladstone in September 1884, and one of £125 from Mr Balfour in July 1896.[4]

---

[1]Of Shakespeare, Lee's particular interest. Southeran was a noted London bookseller.
[2]The formal style of address reflects JKL's opinion of Browning after the *Rooke* affair; until that time he had been accorded a more friendly greeting.
[3]William R. O'Byrne, compiler of the *Naval Biographical Dictionary* of 1849.
[4]JKL was researching another *DNB* note.

On the second occasion, which is the one to which you refer, the Admiralty appears to have lent my predecessor their file of papers on the subject, and it may be these that you have in your mind.

I send you all the papers preserved here with references to the two grants, and would only ask you to let me have them back at your convenience, and not to utilise anything of a private or confidential nature.

210. *Gutteridge to Laughton*

16 Vico Monteroduni, Ponte di Chiaga, Naples, 22 May 1901

I have been at work in the Archives here, so far unfortunately without success. I have drawn a blank as far as any new matter is concerned, but I [am] hoping to be able to make a new collation of the MSS printed in Dumas vols. 4 & 5.

I have come to the conclusion that Dumas has been guilty of pillaging. The lacunae in the MSS ranging over a period from 1799 to 1815 coincide so very remarkably with the documents he has printed in his work, I trust I shall shortly be able to trace the missing papers (amongst which I may perhaps find some new matter) or else definitely to establish the above theory.

From here I am going on to Palermo, to see if anything can be found there.

Would it be of any use, do you think, for me to endeavour to get an introduction to Maresca?[1] The documents here are all in various sections, diplomatic, military, naval, judicial, etc, & one might spend a lifetime in foraging amongst them all. The officials are also, I fear, a little suspicious & inclined to resent the competition of the *uitlander*.[2] At first they made such regulations, that I & another foreigner working in the diplomatic section struck. We have now got these set aside & I think the obstacles are gradually vanishing.

Badham says in the *Historical Review* that he verified Dumas's letters, I wonder if this is really so? He returns thanks to a certain Signor Capasso whom I am diligently searching for at present.

I shall be very glad of any suggestions you could make as to the best course to pursue.

---

[1]Benedetto Maresca, historian and archivist at Naples; see [197].
[2]Boer word for 'outsider' then much in use due to the Second Boer War, 1899–1902.

211. *Mahan to Laughton*

University Club, Fifth Avenue & 54th Street [New York],
31 May 1901

Yours of the 19th was received only this morning. I have written to my Boston publisher, to see if he, who is a very old resident there, can procure me the loan of the De Lage MS., if they will let it go to me.[1] I will examine and report at once. I send this to catch tomorrow's steamer.

I am inexpressibly grieved at what you tell me about your eyes. To a man with your habitual interests and occupations a threatened privation of this kind must be peculiarly distressing; and I assure you I feel for you most sensibly, but trust that with economy in the use of it, and careful attention to symptoms, the other eye may be maintained in good working order. A slight cessation in the high pressure at which you have worked may perhaps benefit you otherwise. That is the only consolation that occurs to me.

I had seen mention of Gardiner's illness but did not know it was so extreme.[2] It will be deplorable to everyone, and tragic for himself if he falls before touching his goal, when so near it. It is in any event a great life's work, if it stop short here; but the desire to see it finished is too natural for disappointment not to be most keenly felt. I do hope he can fetch clearly to the Restoration. My Boston publisher, who was also Parkman's,[3] once told me that the latter's last years were harassed by the fear that he would not live to finish his series, but he did.

My address till October will be Quogue, N.Y.

212. *Mahan to Laughton*

Slumberside, Quogue, Long Island, 18 June 1901

The delay in hearing from Boston proves to have been due to Brown's absence, as I fancied, I regret to say that the reply of the *Athenaeum* is unfavourable, the rule is 'invariable' not to allow MS. to be taken out. They don't doubt my care, but who can assure safety in transit. I am not

---

[1] 'The Journal of M. De Lage de Cueilly, Captain in the Spanish Navy', printed in J.K. Laughton (ed.), *The Naval Miscellany* II (NRS, London, 1910), pp. 207–88.

[2] Gardiner appears to have had a stroke in March 1901, and never recovered. He died on 23 February 1902. He did not reach the Restoration, his last volume ending in 1656. His friend and pupil Charles Firth completed the task.

[3] Francis Parkman (1823–93), American historian of the Anglo-French wars for North America. See H. Doughty, *Francis Parkman* (New York, 1962).

sure that this is wholly unreasonable, for loss would, of course be irreparable. Now, if you like and can wait, I can go on to Boston in time, but I don't like to promise before the fall; and I certainly cannot before August. From New York one goes in a night, and returns the following, losing only a day; but from here the trip to N.Y. spoils a day each way making a total loss of three, which just now I can't at all afford. Six hours in the library might not improbably allow me to read the whole, and in any case certainly enough to be able to estimate its value for the NRS.

I am extremely glad to see mentioned among your forthcoming issues the MSS. connected with Nelson at Naples under Gutteridge's editing. I trust his work will be expansive and settle the matter for ever. It is a singular instance of the effect of mud-throwing, in getting some to stick, that even I, after all my examination and with the bias inevitable with one who has taken part in the arguments, cannot free myself of the apprehension that there may yet be something wrong; and that despite the fact that every argument on the other side has, in my opinion, been overthrown, not by force of argumentation, but by sheer incontrovertible fact or inevitable inference.

Pray make what use you can of me for the NRS without hesitation. I shall still remain a debtor to it, and especially to you personally.

I sincerely hope your eyes may be giving you some encouragement.

213. *Mahan to Laughton*

12 July 1901

Thank you for the enclosed [*JKL* Ham. Cf.27] which I have read with much interest. You do not say explicitly, but I infer we have here Hamilton's own English, and I congratulate you upon the soundness of your judgement, which I well remember surmised the mistake in tense made by the Italian translator.

Considered simply as an historical study Gutteridge has here a very fine field, and further the noble possibility of so eliciting and marshalling the evidence as to put Nelson's fame beyond future challenge. It is vain to ignore the continuing force of the ancient slander – as we believe it to be. As a matter or argument I thought my demonstration inference better than Badham's; but the occasional press notices I saw seemed unable to shake themselves clear of the ancient bias for which Southey[1] is the great culprit.

---

[1]Robert Southey, English poet and author. His biography of Nelson was the most successful work in the field between 1815 and 1895. It takes an inaccurate and hostile view of the Naples issue.

I am at work at present on some sketches which I call *Types of Naval Officers, drawn from the British Navy*.[1] They have taken their rise from some Magazine Articles written in 1893. I take Hawke, Rodney, Howe, St. Vincent, Saumarez & Pellew. The two former I regard as typifying the advance of the 18th Century, the others as types that occur in all ages of naval – or land – warfare. I hope to publish in the autumn. After that I shall probably undertake a Text Book of U.S. History, which I have been strongly urged to attempt.[2]

I will bear in mind De Lage's MS, and intend to communicate with the librarian, as to its length etc.

214. *Troubridge*[3] *to Laughton*

HMS *Pelorus*[4] at Torbay, 8 August 1901

Thank you very much for your kind congratulation. I feel it also an honour to bear the name of Captain Troubridge[5] and I hope when my time comes to be able to live, or die, up to it.

With regard to the letters I must tell you in confidence that, years ago, when I was far away at sea my brother, to my infinite regret, sold those letters. I would have starved for a year, sooner, had I only known it. My Aunt Mrs H. Jones since dead, also without my knowledge, published that ridiculous article in the *Century*.[6] She is as I said deceased and my brother has no interest or rights whatever in the letters, so if [you] have the permission of the *Century* you can use them and nothing would give me greater pleasure. I agree to a certain extent about Lady N[elson] and Josiah[7] being the cause of the rupture. Troubridge could have told us a lot about it. My grandmother, the wife of the second Sir Thomas, was another religious creature, who disapproved so violently of Lady Hamilton that her name was never allowed to be mentioned in my grandfather's house, and she actually <u>destroyed</u> everything connected with her in Sir T. T's correspondence. These two signatures to letters written to him were given to me by my late aunt Miss Troubridge, the letters themselves having been destroyed, but I

---

[1] Published under that title, Boston 1901.

[2] A constant, but unfulfilled theme in correspondence towards the end of Mahan's life.

[3] Admiral Sir Ernest Thomas Troubridge (1862–1926), great grandson of Nelson's friend Admiral Sir Thomas Troubridge.

[4] Third-class cruiser, 2,100 tons.

[5] Ironically, in view of this letter, he would fail his only big test and was court martialled for refusing action with the German battlecruiser SMS *Goeben* in 1914.

[6] JKL had corresponded with Mrs Jones about this in 1886.

[7] Captain Josiah Nisbett, Lady Nelson's son.

send them to you to return at your leisure as I think the writing and expression is such an indication of the character of the two women. I often read the letters my brother sold in old days, at home, and remember one about Josiah. I was obliged to write to Mr Hannay the other day, to reprove him for quoting Ralfe's story about Troubridge, Sir C. Saunders &c &c as at the time Sir C. S. was at the Admiralty Mr Troubridge had been 5 years in his grave, having died when his son was 2 years old, in 1760. I wonder if in the course of your investigation of affairs in Naples, you ever came across anything referring to all the most valuable works of art in the Vatican which Napoleon was sending to France and which were intercepted at Civita Vecchia by Troubridge and sent back by him, and for purposes of prize money sold to King Ferdinand[1] for £30,000, a sum stated to be not one tenth of their value, but of which that astute monarch never paid a farthing. My grandfather 20 years after tried to get the money out of him as also the arrears of Troubridge's pension, £3,000 but failed to get anything.

215.   *Gutteridge to Laughton*

Royal Societies Club, St. James' Street SW, 11 September 1901

I have just returned from Ireland & have received your letter addressed to me here.

I left Naples at the beginning of August, feeling that it would be of very little use for me to stay there any longer. I ran up to Rome & saw Mr George Buchanan, who received me very kindly, but advised me not to delay my departure. Shortly after my return I received from him a copy of a letter from Ponzo-Vagla; which . . . shows is that there is nothing in the Palace at Naples, but no mention is made of any search in the Casa Reale papers at Rome, a point which I laid some stress on in my application. Unfortunately, as Mr Buchanan said, I was entirely in their hands & it was useless to press the matter any further. The fact still remains that there are documents missing from the Archives de Stato at Naples. Either Dumas commandeered these, under the *aegis* of Garibaldi, or else the Italian Government sequestered them. I am bitterly disappointed at not having been able to trace them, & I hope that some day I may lay my hands on them. The Italian Government is clearly reluctant to assist in their discovery. I was also foiled in my endeavours to get at the papers of the Ruffo family; the Neapolitans are intensely suspicious of the outlander & regarded me as a poacher in their preserves.

[1]Of Naples.

Maresca was a brilliant exception & I am greatly indebted to him. He remarked to me that no period of Neapolitan history is so obscure owing to lacunae in the documentary evidence, & suggested that an order had been given to destroy all papers connected with this matter, which had only been partially carried out owing to the incompetence of the official entrusted with the task. I got hold of an old priest eighty years of age, the last survivor of the Bourbon archivists, who stuck to his post all through the dictatorship of Garibaldi, but he either could or would not tell me anything.

For the present the matter rests there: I fear it will be some time before any further progress can be made. However I have a good deal of new material, 42 unpublished Nelson letters & the whole of the Hamilton–Acton correspondence in June 1799. If you think it advisable I will at once set about the compilation of my report for the Council of the Society. The 42 letters I speak of above are from January to July 1799 & are, I think, interesting. I suppose there would be no objection to my using them for the purpose of a fellowship thesis.[1]

I have a new theory as to Sacchinelli's facsimiles which I suggested to Maresca, & which he admitted shook his confidence in the views he expressed as to the identity of Micheroux's 'due documents' in the Archives Storica. I thought as you were away from town, I would not trouble you with this matter till your return.

I hope Dr Gardiner is better.

216.   *Mahan to Laughton*

160 West Eighty Sixth Street, 7 October 1901

As I see no probable occasion for having to go to Boston, I made an occasion last week and took a more than cursory glance at De Lage's MS. As you perhaps know, it is about 13,000 words in length. I had expected therefore to read the whole in the nearly three hours I allowed for the work; but, though in no sense illegible, it is a little difficult to get on with from antiquated spelling and other peculiarities, so that I did not accomplish more than ¾. This, however, is quite enough for your satisfaction.

There are three principal divisions. First, a title page such as gives a first impression of a <u>publication</u>; for it bears at the bottom the words 'A Amsterdam Chez Francois Girardi, MDCCXLVI'. Stupidly enough I

---

[1]See [218–19].

have not noted whether this page is in printed character, but my recollection is pretty distinct that the words quoted are.

Upon this follows (2) an 'Avis de L'imprimeur', the opening paragraph of which, after extolling the interest of the narrative, ends with 'J'ay cru faire plaisir au publicq de le luy priseuter'. These words tend to confirm the impression of a publication. The Avis is in written character, resembling lithographic productions with which I was familiar in boyhood. A principal feature is a certificate of good service, in lengthy detail, given by Don Navarro to De Lage, dated Oct 26 1743, after the destruction of his late command, the *San Isidor*.

After this comes (3) the Journal proper. The greater part of this is in a fair, current, clerkly writing, resembling that of the Avis, and like it suggestive of lithography; but along with it occur passages, neither interpolated nor interlined, in a different, and hand writing. In these I think to distinguish two hands, but it may be the impression is casual and mistaken. Upon the whole, I incline to think that the work is a true MS, not a publication, but that in form it was prepared for the printer, & then dropped. My opinion, however, is not that of an expert in such judgements.

The journal begins on his return to Toulon from a visit to Paris, between Oct. 1743, and January 1744. It is less a journal than a narrative. On Feb 13 he went on board the *Real Felipe*, . . . I must mention that his dates are New Style. The diary ends with the ship anchoring at Cartagena, March 10. The great interest is of course the account of Feb. 22. This is an inside view of the happenings in an enemy's vessel on that day. As regards the incidents of the action, it is in the main very confirmatory of the British accounts; the variations are less than one would anticipate from Spanish witnesses. The principal difference I noted was a more important part played by the second astern of the flagship, (Burrish in the *Devonshire*); but De Lage may have mistaken the ship whose fire-effect he distinguishes. The most interesting feature is connected with the approach and destruction of the fireship. He places her closer to the *Real* than I had inferred. I forget the distance he names, but within a length of the Spanish ship; and he devotes several lines to extolling the heroic bearing of the English officers as they drew near. If you are willing to believe him, I should think the recovering, for these obscure men, the credit due them would be worthy of the NRS.

After the 22nd the vivid interest of course decreases. Without particularising, I should say that the value there lay wholly, as on the 22nd partly, in incidental mentions, from which an instructed reader gleans knowledge. eg. the hammock nettings, or upper works, of Spanish ships are so high, in order to protect against musketry, that in order to see outside one must clamber on to something. One comical detail is a long statement, signed by three surgeons and an apothecary, of the order in which wounded Spanish officers were brought down, and the degree of their injury. This was a net set to catch Navarro, who is said to have come down third, with trivial hurts, particularised, and to have refused to return to the deck. He preferred to stay below, says De Lage, telling his rosary.[1]

I think this gives you a sufficient insight. As regards my own opinion, if I had a voice I should vote for printing, but you know better whether this fits in with the NRS objects. To copy would require a very careful man, exceptionally competent in French as the spelling tends to be both archaic and phonetic. I asked the librarian if he would at his leisure inquire if a fit man could be found, and what would have to be paid. I presume what you would wish would be an exact copy, translated neither into English nor correcter French.

Friday, Oct. 11

I want this to catch to-morrows steamer. I enclose a note from the librarian which explains itself. Of course, when the NRS decides, if it does, to have a copy, further inquiry as to price can be made. My own experience fails here. I had Matthew's action well in mind, for it enters at large into an introductory chapter I have written, for a book I am shortly to bring out, under the title of *Types of Naval Officers* Hawke, Rodney, Howe, Jervis, Saumarez, Pellew. The theme of the Introductory Chapter is 'Naval Warfare at the Beginning of the Eighteenth Century' as furnishing the starting point from which to measure the progress of the Century. Matthews and Byng I conceive to have furnished illustration of the ideas of the early century and I accordingly have analysed their proceedings, and given pretty full accounts of the two actions, dwelling upon their typical side. The book took its origin in some articles I published as far back as 1893; but in deciding to republish I had to steer clear of your *Howard to Nelson*, and of *Our Naval Heroes*, so that professional character, regarded from the point of view of type, forms the burden of my treatment.

I hope the summer has treated you well, and that you continue to have no trouble from your valid eye. With much regard.

---

[1]For this battle, see H.W. Richmond, *The Navy in the War of 1739–48* (3 vols, Cambridge, 1920), vol. II, pp. 1–57.

217.   *Laughton to Lee*

10 November 1901

In connection with the Tracts of Sir W. Monson Oppenheim asks 'if his belief that there is no reference to the navy in Elizabethan drama & poetry' is correct?

I take it there is no-one better able than you to answer his query, so if you will do so, we shall be greatly obliged. If he is wrong, please give some references.

I have been away for the last five weeks & have just returned. I don't know whether you also are not out of town. With kind regards.

218.   *Laughton to Austen-Leigh*[1]

18 December 1901

I am quite willing to read Mr. Gutteridge's essay: but I ought to let you know that I have been for some time back in correspondence with him on the subject of it, & have followed his researches at Naples with much interest. He has, in fact, undertaken to edit all the original papers bearing on this for the Navy Records Society, and thus I know in advance what material he has been working with & what line he has taken. Of the essay itself I know nothing, though your letter reminds me that he did once ask if there was any reason he should not base it on these researches. Clearly there was not, more especially as all that he has done so far has been at his own expense.

It seems right to tell you this, but I don't see that it in any way disqualifies me for giving an opinion on his present work; & if you care to send it to me, I shall be happy to undertake the job.

219.   *Laughton to Austen-Leigh*

28 December 1901

Herewith I enclose a report on Mr Gutteridge's dissertation, which I hope may be of use to you.

I am returning the volume by parcel post & shall be obliged by your acknowledging its receipt.

Nelson and the Neapolitan Revolution of 1799. By H. G. Gutteridge.

[1]The Revd A. Austen-Leigh, Provost of King's College, Cambridge.

Mr. Gutteridge appears to have digested all that has been published on this vexed question, bringing to the task his unusual familiarity with Italian, as well as a competent knowledge of French and German. He has also studied the MSS in the British Museum & especially those recently purchased from Lord Bridport, which include the letters of Troubridge & others to Nelson. Above all, by his researches at Naples, he has succeeded in bringing together a quantity of new material, some of which is of the highest importance, I may particularly mention the letter from Hamilton to Acton of 27 June (p.211), hitherto only known by the inaccurate translation made for Dumas, whose confused grammar has been insisted on as proving an altogether erroneous sequence of events.

I agree with Mr. Gutteridge that absolute certainty cannot be obtained until we can have accurate knowledge of the documents enclosed by Micheroux to Acton (pp.153–5) though differing from him, I have a provisional opinion that they were copies of Hamilton's letter to Ruffo of 26 June and Sacchinelli's so-called fac-similie of Troubridge's declaration: Hamilton to Acton of 27 June seems to indicate the first of these. Captain Mahan, on the other hand, inclines to the opinion that no reliance can be placed on Micheroux's story in the *Compendio*: it is, he thinks, incredible that, in a matter of life and death, the garrisons accepted his bare word in contradiction of Nelson's former written message; and did not trouble themselves to see the paper on which their lives depended. However that may be, these enclosures, as well as the perfect-copy of the *Compendio* have not yet been found; but Mr. Gutteridge has undertaken to renew the search, supported by such interest as the Navy Records Society may be able to give him (p. xvii).[1]

Meantime, from the material which he has Mr. Gutteridge has drawn out an exceedingly interesting narrative of the course of events on those days 24–30 June, which appears to me as satisfactory as may be in the present state of the evidence, and he has very ably marshalled the arguments in support of his own conclusions, or in contradiction of those of his opponents.

I am thus inclined to estimate Mr. Gutteridge's work at a very high value; and not the less so because in the collateral narrative of purely naval affairs he has fallen into some inaccuracies. It is, for instance, misleading to say (p. x) that Nelson 'placed himself at the beck and call etc'; when, in fact he was so placed by very positive instructions from England. It is incorrect to speak (p.16) of 'Great Britain's preponderating naval strength in the Mediterranean' in 1797 and the beginning of

---

[1]References are to the text of Gutteridge's paper.

1798. Great Britain's fleet had somewhat ignominiously evacuated the Mediterranean in 1796. The mention of 'Earl St. Vincent' (p.16, line 5 from the bottom) is a slip of the pen; so also 'Admiral' Mahan (p.152) 'Lady Emma' (p.23, & freq.) is probably the result of a partially foreign education. I would only add that, personally, I do not agree with the extreme condemnation (pp.149–9) of the execution of the traitors; but that is a side issue, irrelevant to the main subject, as the others are trifles which cannot be held to detract from the very great merit of the dissertation.[1]

220. *Mahan to Laughton*

160 West Eighty Sixth Street, 21 January 1902

I am sending you today under another cover the copy of the De Lage MS. The copyist has been paid by me, and I have received from Stevens notification that the NRS has deposited £5 with him to my account. I enclose a note from Bolton, that you may see just where the matter of proof comparing rests. I have asked him if he could give me the price for your information.

I have delayed sending as soon as I received the MS., because I had hazarded the query whether you wished to print here or in England. I afterwards regretted making it; but having done so, thought best to wait. From your not writing I infer that you prefer first to see the paper.

A few days before sending Bolton wrote me that he had 'compared a few paragraphs of copy with the original, and it was carefully and accurately done; but I do not wish in any way to hold myself responsible for the accuracy'. I have also looked over a few portions, to judge of its conformity with my recollections of the general character. It is so far satisfactory to me, but of course that goes for little with no original before me. The comparison of the proof should however remove all errors.

I think I have not written since yours of Dec. 19. The Cleopatra cap of liberty was of course beyond my cognisance, but I am a little vexed with myself not sooner to have thought of the habit of dubbing naval and military men 'Esquire'. I have among my earliest recollections one of a ship's log, headed 'U.S.S. *Preble* commanded by John B. Marchand Esq.' The Washington and Howe story however has had currency with

---

[1]The other two reports on this fellowship examination were provided by A.W. Ward and Oscar Browning. They were exactly as would be expected from two such different scholars. Ward's was long and positive, but only in qualified agreement with the analysis. Browning was brief and gushing.

us always, and I presume there is no doubt as to the misunderstanding on Washington's part; or perhaps, even understanding, he thought expedient for diplomatic reason to extol the General, if he could, as an acknowledgement of the authority whence he received it.[1]

I deeply grieve at what you tell me of Gardiner's state. Our acquaintance was only one of correspondence; I never met him but once. But in addition to the interest of such association, and to common human commiseration, the loss to history of his completion of his own work is greatly to be deplored.

221. *Laughton Lecture Notes*

LECTURE SERIES LENT 1902
Thursday 11 am beginning Jan. 23rd.

'The Unity of the British Empire'

1. Growth of our Colonies based on our Maritime power.
2. The disaffection and revolt of our North American Colonies.
3. The Settlement of Canada.
4. The Government of India.
5. The Federation of Australia.
6. Imperialism in the present and the future.

1. Seeley: History 'should not merely gratify curiosity about the past, but give a clearer picture of the present, or forecast of the future.' *Expansion of England* p.1

So considered, in speaking of the history of England, the point which we have to keep specially in view is whither are we tending? What is the destiny in store for us?

Some such question often asked, often answered Liberties, Democracy, – a republic.

Liberty there is in fact no tendency that way – we have it, have had it for a couple of centuries.

Democracy – no doubt there has been a vast stride toward it – will it continue? So the term + Liberty is it not just the tyranny of the lawless crowd (Tennyson *Collected Works* p. 576) that we have been taught to abhor, of which <u>freedom</u> loathes, even as she does the lawless crowd. And onto the Republic. Are we tending towards one? I think not: I see no signs of it – I saw the late Queen's Jubilee 14 years ago, her

---

[1] As JKL's letter to Mahan does not survive, the meaning is unclear.

Diamond Jubilee 4 years ago – only 7 days ago I saw the crowds that assembled to see our King go to open Parliament and properly uncovered to the music of God Save the King. No – it did not seem to me like the prelude to a republic.

However there can be no question but that there has been a tendency to <u>democracy</u> during all the last century, 1830, 1867, 1885. I fancy it has reached its' height.

But there is a modern tendency in our national life, a tendency which has been completely unmarked and certainly, in my opinion, unwished for. The tendency to Extension – to Expansion. If you deliberately consider the way in which during the last 300 years, from very small beginnings, the English nation and the English tongue has spread over the world 'till now it covers all (or almost all) North America, South Africa, Australia to say nothing of the countless islands which are English, or of India which our influence and our power dominates. This is a _____ such as the world has never seen before or elsewhere.

Ancient Rome, Persia, Assyria,
Modern Russia
contrast

England has spread by colonisation. It is the legitimate spread of her people. The unfortunate war which broke the American Colonies off [from the] mother country must not be allowed to blind us to the great fact that colony or independent State, that now is greater than us as a nation, as a race belong to us.

Now what are our colonies. Every body thinks he knows and would answer as children so often do, I know but can't say. Let us try. It may perhaps be defined as a settlement made in a more or less distant country, with the intention of remaining, whilst preserving the allegiance to and the protection of the sovereign power of the country left. It assumes that the new country is either wild, uninhabited, or inhabited only by savages, whose rights (according to the Christian Code of Ethics) need not be respected. The new settlers must be the dominant power in the new country: thus then a colony (properly so called) cannot be established in China or Japan. India is not properly called a colony, partly because no-one goes there intending to stay there, with his family, for all future generations, but – on the contrary – to get out of it again as soon as possible, but also the settlers find themselves among a people advanced to a conspicuous state of civilisation – different indeed from our own – but still so well marked that it has never entered the head of the most brutal in-comer that they ought to be or indeed could be wiped out – as the red indian of America or the black fellows of Australia or the Hottentots of South Africa. The Kaffirs open out a new and difficult problem which we may pass over for the present. Well, accepting such a definition and looking at the map, we find that the only really great colonising powers of modern times are Spain and England. Spain began 100 years before we did, and established herself in positions where her descendants remain to this day. But France; – we know when she began; that she has made many attempts at establishing colonies; but has failed, and now, the map speaks for itself. Why?

I suppose you have often heard that the fact is that we English have a superior genius for colonization – an instinctive knack of governing and organising them: of keeping friendly relations with the natives and so on.

Friendly relations with the natives!

In our wars with France in North America which side was most favoured by the Indians? I beg you recollect Fenimore Cooper's novels, if nothing better, will tell you. I have read of quieting red indians, by letting them loot a wagon crossing the prairie loaded with blankets that had been gathered out of a small-pox hospital: this was not by the French, but by the people who are said to have a better knack of getting on with the savages. I have heard of shooting down blackfellows at sight, as if they were wolves or wild cats: this was in Tasmania, and Australia. I believe any comparative examination would tell greatly in favour of the French. Try again. Superior organisation and administration. Well, the French colonies did not revolt and throw off their allegiance to the mother country; ours did, and ever since we have tried to persuade ourselves that this was the natural course of things, just as a ripe plum or pear separates itself from the parent tree when it is fully ripe. Of this separation I shall have to speak next week; here I will only point out that the Spanish colonies – the faults of whose governments we could always see, or think we saw, came into being long before ours and continued in their allegiance for long after.

I will not lay more stress on facts which may perhaps be accounted for by the more robust nature, character, of the men of our race. The determination that if a thing is to be done the sooner it's done the better: the objection to the Spanish maxim, 'never do today &c' manana, but as a matter of fact, I think the systems pursued by the 2 governments was very much alike. No, the all important difference between our colonies, and I will say more specifically the French, was our maritime power:– sea power.

Canada, Jamaica
Cuba, Martinique, Guadeloupe
Mauritius
  Dwell on these

I have often read and heard say that the history of the 18th century is dull, stupid. It is that many historians and many readers take as their one ideal of history the doings of the vestry of their parish, or the parliament of their one little island, and do not take into account, at all how Britain changed into <u>Greater Britain</u>, the beginning of which growth was in the 18th century, in that period of 'abominable dullness'.

I think – nay I am sure that it is within the last thirty years, almost within the last twenty, that people have generally begun to realize that we are a vast Empire. Thirty-five years since Dilke's *Greater Britain*, five and twenty years since Empress of India, barely twenty since *Expansion of England*. These are the steps in the awakening of the people. For long a people used to talking a sort of patronising way of the Queen on whose dominions the sun never set, or as I once heard a bull-headed Irishman give it <u>never shone</u>. One had as much meaning for him as the other.[1]

222.   *Longman, Co. to Laughton*

39 Paternoster Row, London E.C., 24 February 1902

I am in receipt of your letter of yesterday and am much obliged to you for your communication. I have the pleasure of informing you that we are willing to publish your proposed work on the war of the Austrian Succession at our expense and risk. On receipt of the MS.[2] we will make a calculation and communicate with you further as to terms, etc. Hoping you have been keeping well this winter and with kindest regards.

T. North Longman

---

[1]This lecture lays the foundation of the study of Imperial, or Commonwealth history at King's College; it was followed by others, and the appointment of A.P. Newton to develop this area. The main influences are clearly Seeley and Mahan, but there were others, including Dilke.

[2]JKL did not complete this task. However, it appears that he passed it on to Herbert Richmond, than a promising young naval officer/historian, whose *The Navy in the War of 1739–48* (Cambridge, 1920), was effectively complete by 1914.

223.   *Bridge to Laughton*

HMS *Alacrity*[1] Nanking, 15 June 1902

I wrote some time ago to Prince Louis of Battenberg on the subject of his notice of Suffren in his little book *Man of War Names*.[2]

He communicated with a friend of his, the Marquis de Balincourt, who induced his family – which is connected with the Suffren's – to undertake researches. Count Edgard de Balincourt has published a pamphlet and has sent me a copy. It is called *La mort du Baillie de Suffren d'apres ses historiens et d'apres sa famille*. Nimes Gervais-Bedot, 21 Rue de la Madelene 1902.

He disposes of the story of the duel and makes out that Suffren died from over-bleeding by the surgeons treating him for an illness. The Suffren de St. Tropez who accompanied Hompesch in his retirement from Malta was a younger brother of the great Admiral.

I hope you are all well

224.   *Mahan to Laughton*

Slumberside, 8 August 1902

I am shockingly behind hand with a letter long owing to you, my only excuse being an unusual amount of writing which, as I have perhaps pleaded before, is substantially the same sort of thing as correspond-ence, which therefore presents none of the relief which a change of occupation sometimes affords. I am more ashamed in alleging this reason to you than I am to most, for I confess to being astounded at times at the amount of work you turn out, being also, as you have told me, some seven or eight years older than myself at a time of life when increase of years does not mean increase of working power. My last occasion for this reflection is very recent, upon the receipt of the *Naval Miscellany* of the N.R.S., under your editing, and containing a most tempting bill of fare when I shall be able to get at it. I am glad that we are in this way realising very substantially upon your stores of naval knowledge, which you have not found time to elaborate into a formal history of your navy. The lack of this is continually a regret to me; but at least when your time arrives you will not depart like Lord Acton without having realised to the world any thing out of a vast store of erudition.

[1]Despatch vessel, 1,600 tons, used by the C-in-C, China Station.
[2]Published at Portsmouth, 1900.

I am also glad to see that Gutteridge has been able to make some advance in his mission in Naples, for I presume the contribution promised from him will contain something more than an arrangement of that which we have already known. It is true, undoubtedly, that this known material is scattered, and only needs systematisation and massing; but I fancy the N.R.S. might hesitate to do that alone for writers who might be expected to do it for themselves. Still, the reputation of Nelson is a very worthy object by itself alone.

I have not yet made time to read Rose's *Napoleon*,[1] though I turned over the pages for a while, and looked up the passage about the galleons – or rather frigates – to which you referred me. The mistake was somewhat singular; but I notice, as you doubtless have, that the moment shore historians touch salt water a mist comes over them, a mist and a haze which prevents their comprehending things which they see. This quite independent of the liability all of us sadly experience of barking our shins against fact in any historical field. I have been struck by this in Fiske's *American Revolution*,[2] a book of undoubted ability; though a little vulgarised by failure to correct the offhand clap-trap of a lecture series. When he gets on the water, he ceases to be a historian and becomes a parrot; what he has heard right he repeats right, but he evidently don't fully know about what he talks.

The copy of your review of *Types* reached me duly. I had already seen it at the Club and attributed it to you, but I was glad to have a copy for home. It was a satisfaction that you could give it a general good approval, & particularly to find that you agreed with me on this steady increase in the size of battleships, which is due, not to any unified conception of what they ought to be, but a number of separate demands of separate interests – represented with us by Bureaus – all of which cannot be met except by increase of size in each new batch.[3] L'appetit vient en mangeant [the appetite grows with eating]; the next batch sees each demand larger and a fresh concession to size. Four years ago I wrote a remonstrance to the Secretary [of the U.S. Navy] on this matter, saying that as things were going, and for the same reasons, there was no reason why we should not go to 20,000 tons and beyond. His reply virtually was that it was in the hands of his professional advisers, but he thought there was no prospect of 20,000. We are now at over 16,000. As I understand, we have a board of Bureau

---

[1] J.H. Rose, *Life of Napoleon* (2 vols, London, 1901).
[2] J. Fiske, *The American Revolution* (2 vols, Boston, 1891).
[3] JKL, Bridge and Mahan were the leaders of the school of thinking that opposed big battleships.

Chiefs who discuss these matters, and their joint recommendations go to the Secretary. Now, I know nothing of their proceedings, but I fancy one says I must have more room for machinery, another the armour must be heavier, another she must carry more coal than the last, and the only solution to the wrangle is to have a bigger ship like the great bill for 'Giving Everybody Everything'. I don't believe the tactical demands are ever considered, nor yet again the strategic question of available numbers. At all events I know of no appointed provision to insure that these purely military requirements should receive due attention. You may remember I gave a concrete illustration of the need of numbers from our recent experiences in my *Lessons of the War with Spain*, p.37–8.[1] I return to the charge, incidentally, whenever opportunity offers, as I do to another illusion of my countrymen's on the immunity of national commerce in war – but I have not the inside track.

This letter is at least so far an amends for its predecessors which were not written – like David Copperfield's disappointing sister – that it is long enough for two. May it either not reach you in a busy season, or be laid aside till you have time for trifles! One thing at least, it will be easier for you to read a long letter than for me to write it in this weather, hot even here within 500 yards of the sea. Farewell.

225.   *Mahan to Laughton*

160 West Eighty Sixth Street, 10 December 1902

While staying with friends near Philadelphia a few weeks ago, I came across the enclosed extracts. While you are familiar with the general condition of things which they illustrate, I think it probable you will not have seen the incidents themselves; for while the narrator, Mr Samuel Breck, was a cultivated and notable member of Society in Philadelphia the first half of the past century, it is not likely that his memoirs had other than local interest. Making every allowance for writing nearly fifty years after the events – in 1830 – the incidents are of the sort a lad remembers. I may add that the name Linzee still holds in Boston. I myself know some members of the family and there is among our officers a Linzee Amory – now retired – whom I know very well.

---

[1]Boston, 1898. A copy in the Library of King's College, London is signed by Mahan to Laughton.

I was in Washington when my latest book, *Retrospect and Prospect*,[1] came out; and being much preoccupied with overhauling musty documents concerning the 1812 period, forgot to send you a copy. With the exception of one article – 'Disposition of Navies' – there is in it nothing very strictly professional and you probably may have seen most of the book, if you cared to read it, when it appeared as articles in the *National*. However, I send you a copy to complete your file of my works, and at the same time testify my best wishes for you and yours at the Christmas and New Year season.

For myself, I am niggering along as usual, my more immediate task, as I think I told you, being the war of 1812.[2]

226. *Bridge to Laughton*

Commander in Chief, China Station, 16 February 1903

It was most thoughtful and kind of you to send me the Reeve–Krasinski[3] correspondence. Luckily the book came just as I was going to sea so that I have been able to read a good deal of it. It has interested me much. It has enabled me to see what a really distinguished man Reeve was.

As a rule I have not time for reading. The necessary work out here is very heavy and it is made very much heavier by the large amount of quite unnecessary, but quite compulsory, labour on paper. The way in which paper-work has increased of late in the Navy is truly astounding. It will break us down, if we do not mind it seriously. The worst of it is that the excessive scribbling is much less due to clerks in the public offices than to my own officers. The rage for returns and written reports prevails amongst certain large classes of officers like a plague. On the whole I am – after a life of optimistic feeling – becoming a pessimist as regards the navy. There is no doubt whatever that we are growing less and less naval and more and more shore-going. As the Americans said, 'In these days everything naval has a tendency towards the beach'. A perception of this fact justifies gloomy forebodings.

I wish you and yours all happiness and prosperity and am,

---

[1]Boston, 1902.

[2]*Sea Power in its Relation to the War of 1812*, published in 1905.

[3]Count Sigismund Krasinski and his family had been long-term correspondents of Reeve, and this new material had just appeared.

227.   *Corbett to Laughton*

7 May 1903

We shall have a very good report to present to the meeting – things are really well in hand now thanks to your labour.[1]

But it distresses me that you should have all this piled on to you. I know what a trouble it must have been. I have had to re-do work like that myself. The Council ought to know what they owe to you, but it is difficult to make it known without hurting the Admiral's feelings. I went to see Prothero[2] this afternoon but missed him. I found Newbolt however and told him something – knowing I might safely do so. He quite feels with me that it is very hard on you to have had all this work without any recognition. You have done quite enough for the Society without that, and I am sure you can ill afford the time. If I can help you, let me know. I shall be going fairly light for the next three months while my proofs are coming in and might be able to save you a bit. I will tell Prothero about it – judiciously I mean – but no-one else without your authorisation.

I have found one or two useful things in the Pepys calendar and have sent Tanner[3] a note or two which he may find helpful.

228.   *Mahan to Laughton*

Slumberside, 25 September 1903

Can you give me any information of a general kind as to the sources upon which James[4] drew for his *Naval History*? I am disposed to credit him with entire honesty and more than usual care – for those days – in

---

[1]This would appear to refer to the inadequate editing carried out by Vesey-Hamilton on his edition of *The Letters of Admiral Sir Thomas Byam Martin* (NRS, London, 1903); vol. I was published out of sequence and a year after vol. III. There were no other admirals at work on Record Society projects. See [125], [136] and [137] for Vesey-Hamilton's problems with the *Blockade of Brest* volume and the *Howard to Nelson* project.

[2]G.W. Prothero, Vice-President of the NRS 1901–04.

[3]J.R. Tanner; Councillor 1893–96, 1902–7, 1913–16; the leading authority on Pepys; edited six volumes for the Society. After Tanner's death his life's work appeared as Arthur Bryant's three-volume study. Bryant's failure to complete the project revealed all to clearly that the original scholarship on show was not his own. See A. Roberts, *Eminent Churchillians* (London, 1994).

[4]William James (d. 1827). His researches included spending 1813 and 1814 in American harbours, personal inspection of the ships, and two years at Halifax, Nova Scotia. These were developed through extensive private correspondence with those involved, and considerable, if undeclared, official help.

research, and to trust implicitly any statement of fact; though I think him constitutionally unable to make fair inferences where his prejudices enter.

The particular occasion of my question is the *Shannon* and *Chesapeake* fight;[1] and in that the statement that the *Chesapeake* squared her mainyard as she ranged up. This does not appear in James's first edition; it does in the later. In a print of the action by Capt. King RN, dedicated to Broke,[2] [produced in] 1830 the yard is not square. The usual resource of Court Martial evidence is wanting, for every spar deck officer of the *Chesapeake* was killed, except midshipmen, and the whole record lacks completeness, from this cause mainly. Admiral Luce of our navy, always held among our best seamen, doubts whether Lawrence,[3] a first rate deck officer, would do anything so unseamanlike; but it seems to me beyond question that Lawrence was in nervous haste that day, or rather his action shows precipitancy throughout; and that the *Chesapeake* had more way than she should is beyond dispute. James diagram shows the yard square in the first positions, up in the fourth, and in the fifth both main and mizzen topsails square aback; which by the way agrees with the evidence of the only midshipman of the *Chesapeake* who speaks to that point.

I have been inclined to think that James 'interviewed' Broke and that his minute statement of times, and especially of what the *Chesapeake's* manouvres indicated at a particular moment, reproduced Broke's impressions, possibly noted at the time.

You will infer that I at last have in hand my long intended War of 1812. A great part is done, and will appear serially, though in places much condensed, in *Scribner's Magazine*, beginning next January. It will scarcely appear in book form before the spring of 1905; for ere committing myself to the permanent form I must spend some time in Canada overhauling records, and possibly in England also, where I may be next summer.[4] I wanted to omit the single ship actions, but found it

[1]On 1 June 1813, HMS *Shannon* captured the USS *Chesapeake* off Boston in a brilliant action lasting only 11 minutes. The action was fought at close quarters, and the casualties were very heavy. Mahan's insight is interesting, and is supported by modern authors. Lawrence came alongside the *Shannon* with too much way on, and luffed up to reduce his speed, and keep his guns bearing. Mahan's account is in his *War of 1812* (London and Boston, 1905), vol. II, pp. 131–48.

[2]Captain Sir Philip Bowes Vere Broke Bt, Captain of HMS *Shannon*, and the father of modern naval gunnery. For the battle, and the pictures, see P. Padfield, *Broke and the Shannon* (London, 1968).

[3]Captain James Lawrence USN; successful sloop commander, he died of his wounds after the capture of the *Chesapeake*.

[4]This shows that Mahan had developed a more sophisticated approach to the magazine serial publication for his major works.

impossible; and it is true that our successes in them, exaggerated as they were in popular appreciation, gave the navy its first lift to fame. I doubt if you know that four months before we declared war, Congress refused to appropriate for any additional ship.

I received your postal [card] about Caracciolo, but as nothing more has come I shall wait for the full publication of Gutteridge's results. I know nothing on the [peasant?][1] matter, beyond that Caracciolo was out of the castles by June 23. Last winter I gave everything I had collected on the subject to the New York Public Library, asking it might be bound and kept together, with Badham's papers, and my own in the *EHR*. This will be done. Poor Gardiner, before his break down, wrote me that he thought I need not trouble about anything further that B. might write. This was after his pamphlet, published by Nutt.[2] You doubtless know Gardiner refused to publish in the *EHR* after the first exposure of Badham's methods.

P.S. The *Shannon's* log, as usual, sheds little light. I have not yet the Captain's Journal.

229. *Laughton to Mahan*

12 October 1903

As I told you by a hurried post-card, I was sending your letter to Sir Lambton Loraine,[3] who married one of Broke's Grand-daughters: the other married Lord de Saumarez,[4] & to this last – being the elder – the relics etc. of the family belong. But Lorraine & Saumarez are on perfectly friendly terms and both are members of the N. R. Society. Lorraine is an old messmate of mine, which will explain why I referred to him rather than to the husband of the elder sister. I now enclose you Lorraine's reply; which – with its references to Brighton's[5] book, is probably all that can now be got. As Broke was for long after the action, incapable of giving any exact account of what happened, Wallis must be considered the best available English authority: and he, being very young at the time, & no longer young when Brighton examined

---

[1]Caracciolo disguised himself as a peasant after fleeing from Republican service.
[2]F. Badham, *Nelson at Naples* (London, 1900), printed by Nutt.
[3]Rear-Admiral Sir Lambton Loraine, 11th Baronet (1838–1917).
[4]James St. Vincent, 4th Baron de Saumarez (1848–1934); Captain, Grenadier Guards.
[5]The Revd J.G. Brighton; biographer of Broke and Sir Provo William Wallis, the senior surviving Lieutenant of the *Shannon*.

him, with the additional complications that he was rather a duffer[1] and Brighton a clergyman – altogether makes it difficult to be sure of minute accuracy . . .

I am truly glad to hear that you are working at the war of 1812: but I greatly wish you would arrange to have your most valuable contribution to Clowes's big work reprinted as a separate volume.[2] It would be a classic. As it is, it can only be a work of reference. Roosevelt's[3] chapter is also very good; but his decisions are those of a scholar, not of a master; so that I shall be very glad to see your work on the same period.

Gutteridge's vol. will be out very shortly, and will I hope settle the controversy. At any rate, I do believe that embodies all the evidence which is at present available. Whether some still hidden may hereafter be brought to light, we cannot say: but until it is, it must be a very wrong-headed man (of course Badham is) who will contravene G's deductions on any important point.

230.   Mahan to Laughton

160 West Eighty Sixth Street, 28 October 1903

It is very kind of you and Loraine to take the trouble you have, and I am not the less indebted that so little is obtainable. Few single ship actions can have been so ill off for competent observation and report; every spar deck officer of the *Chesapeake* killed, Broke knocked on the head, his first killed, as also his clerk, who I believe was supposed to note times etc. We have on this side a Court of Inquiry held eight months after the action, and subsequent Courts Martial on officers accused of misconduct. I have read all the testimony, which tends necessarily to elucidate some points, but gives little information about the manoeuvres. I have also had Schetky's[4] drawings before me, but

[1]Admiral of the Fleet Sir Provo Wallis (1791–1892). As the senior surviving Lieutenant of the *Shannon* he brought the *Chesapeake* into Halifax harbour after the battle, Broke having been critically wounded. Wallis lived to become Admiral of the Fleet in the 1890s; Laughton's assessment of him is fair. J.G. Brighton, *Admiral of the Fleet Sir Provo William Wallis* (London, 1892).

[2]*The Major Operations of the Navies in the War of American Independence* (Boston, 1913).

[3]Theodore Roosevelt; one-time lecturer in history at the Naval War College, then President of the United States. His first book was *The Naval War of 1812* (New York, 1882), and he wrote on the same subject for Laird Clowes's *The Royal Navy*.

[4]John Christian Schetky (1778–1874); Scottish marine painter, later drawing master at the Royal Naval College. His 'A Series of Four Views . . .' published in 1830 were based on drawings by Captain Richard King. See R. Gardiner (ed.), *The Naval War of 1812* (London, 1999), pp. 58–60 for all four views.

King[1] was not present himself and the publication is 1830 – 18 years after the fight. I have also the log of the *Shannon*, having had it copied for several days after the battle. You know better than I how bare logbooks of this time were. This seems no exception. It does not, however, mention the *Chesapeake* heaving-too at any time, as Wallis said she did. The omission proves nothing, but the general impression, derivable from the entries is that she came down unhesitatingly.

My expression concerning Lawrence's nervous haste, which Lorraine queries, should perhaps be better expressed by precipitancy. I infer it from the general accounts. Lawrence appears to have acted against his better judgement, under the influence of feeling; and my experience is that men thus moved are liable to eagerness to get the doubtful action over and done with. The hour also was late, even for June. The *Shannon's* log notes that, short as the action was, there was not time to ascertain loss and get things at all to rights before dark. Nothing seems to me more matter of course than that a ship ranging up, as the *Chesapeake* did, should not overshoot; better be a little abaft the beam than at all forward of it. Lawrence overshot badly, though an excellent seaman. That he luffed to deaden his way all agree, and probably that luffing, co-operating with the accident to the tiller ropes,[2] got the ship aback. All, I fancy, the result of hurry.

Upon the whole I incline still to trust myself to James, though I should much like to know where he got those curiously minute times. I don't understand the gunner being where Wallis was, when the action was about to begin, or his taking times. With us, in all my time, the gunner in action has been in the main magazine.[3] I suppose I must send for a copy of Broke's official journal.

Thank you for your suggestion about the separate publication of my part of the *Naval History*. Marston at one time contemplated it, but I presume would not carry out the purpose until the bloom is off the sales of the *History* proper. I intend to bring the matter before him ere long, now that the publication is complete.

---

[1]Captain Richard King (d. 1862) entered the Navy under Broke, a near neighbour of his father, and served continuously with him until 8 March 1813, missing the famous battle by a few months, but rejoined the *Shannon* shortly afterwards as a Lieutenant.

[2]It was no accident. Broke placed a gun to shoot away the American ship's wheel.

[3]The gunner was in the magazine; Broke had given him his watch to time the action. James was in correspondence with Broke. Therefore it can be assumed that the information came from Broke.

231. *Mahan to Laughton*

Bad Nauheim, 9 June 1904

I received here today your invitation to be present at the Annual Meeting of the NRS. I should much have liked to be present, though I will not pretend to like making speeches; but in fact we left London for this May 31, having been in town only three days. Had there been a possibility of meeting you – that is with any possibility of keeping an appointment, I would have let you know; but we came to London from France merely to consult Sir Hermann Webb about my wife; who has been ill all spring after an attack of influenza. He ordered us here as soon as possible, and we accordingly came without delay. He is to remain six weeks – till about July 20. I may come to London for a fortnight about July 1, for I want to look over some papers in the Record Office, if I can get permission, with reference to 1812.

We had intended in any event to come across this year; but all our projects as to the direction of our travels have been upset by Mrs Mahan's indisposition. Notably, we expected to give six weeks to the British islands, and I now doubt whether we shall get there at all – that is, as a party.

I wrote a brief review of Gutteridge's work for the *Bookman*,[1] in which incidentally I tried to give the N.R.S. some of the credit it deserves. I corrected the proof somewhere, since arriving, but have not seen the publication.

232. *Mahan to Laughton*

Dom Hotel, Koln, 25 June 1904

Your postal, with kindly offer of help in the Records matter was duly received, but it was not till my arrival here last evening that I received the information as to other people's movements which I needed to formulate my own. I now expect to arrive in London the evening of July 1, and after about the 4th will probably be the guest of Sir Francis and Lady Jeune until my departure about the 15th. (79 Harley St W.) A letter to B.F. Stevens will always reach me, and I intend to make that my address for usual correspondence. It has been my expectation to avail myself of that firm's familiarity with the Record Office to start me on my way; but it is very probable that your own personal acquaintance

---

[1]Not noted in Hattendorf and Hattendorf.

with Admiralty files may supply a gap, the more so as the Navy is usually the neglected sphere of historical enquiry.

My particular object at present is to ascertain the purpose and orders of the British Government for the American War, after Napoleon's overthrow in 1814. To some extent they are shown in already published correspondence (Castlereagh[1] and Wellington[2]); but I want to see the intimate correspondence, of Bathurst[3] Minister of War & Colonies, with Prevost[4] and Castlereagh; and also that between Warren's[5] successor, Cochrane,[6] and the Admiralty, particularly the instructions of the latter. The period to be covered would be from April 1 to Oct 1 1814.

I have copies of a good deal of Warren's correspondence, and the Admiralty replies, also of the Courts Martial on the Lake Erie and Champlain squadron fights, the only really decisive battles, land or sea, in my judgement, of that little war. I likewise got copies of the *Guerriere* and *Macedonian* Courts, the latter of which is really very interesting; but I have not thought it essential to waste minute research on the other naval duels, except the *Chesapeake* and *Shannon*, concerning which I have got together all I could find. The newspapers of the day tell the true 'innards' of the war, as regards military events, much better than do gazettes.

I am here on my way back to Nauheim, 'convoying' one daughter, and bring back another who is to join friends in London. Please excuse stationery.

I am glad to say that Mrs. Mahan is deriving great good from the baths.

---

[1]Robert Stewart, Viscount Castlereagh (1769–1822); Foreign Secretary 1812–22. Marquess of Londonderry (ed.), *Memoirs and Correspondence of Viscount Castlereagh* (12 vols, London, 1848–53).

[2]Arthur Wellesley, 1st Duke of Wellington (1769–1852) in 1814 commanding the British Army in France. See H. Gurwood (ed.), *The Dispatches of Field Marshal the Duke of Wellington, 1799–1815* (12 vols, London, 1837–38).

[3]Henry, 3rd Earl Bathurst (1762–1834); Secretary of State for War and the Colonies 1812–1827. See F. Bickley (ed.), *Manuscripts of Earl Bathurst* (London, 1923). At this date the MSS. were at Cirencester Park, in private hands.

[4]General Sir George Prevost (1767–1816); Governor General of British North America 1812–15, recalled in disgrace, but died before he could be tried.

[5]Admiral Sir John Borlase Warren (1753–1822); C-in-C of the North American Station 1812–13.

[6]Admiral Sir Alexander Forrester Inglis Cochrane (1758–1832), C-in-C of the North American Station 1814–15; uncle of the more famous Lord Cochrane.

233.   *Bridge to Laughton*

1 Eaton Terrace S.W., 10 October 1904

Is any notice going to be taken of the outrageous statements on pages 631–2 of the newly published volume (VIII)[1] concerning Nelson's action at Naples in 1799? Your own publications, as well as Mahan's on the subject are completely ignored by this new 'historian' and to aggravate the case he actually puts Gutteridge (NRS XXV)[2] amongst his authorities.

You must feel ashamed of your old University that it could stoop so low as to lend the sanction of its venerable name to 'history' of this kind. I expect to see you tomorrow afternoon.

234.   *A.W. Ward[3] to Laughton*

The Cambridge Modern History, 18 October 1904

I should have sooner acknowledged your letter of the 10th, enclosing a letter from Sir Cyprian Bridge; but I wished to confer with one of my colleagues. I am sorry that you have so poor an opinion of Mr Wilson.[4] Mr Rose,[5] who as you may perhaps have noticed, puts the view to which objection is taken more strongly than Mr Wilson; like him trusts to Mr. Gutteridge's evidence. I am very sorry that their estimates of it should differ from that taken by an authority like yourself.

I have assumed that in your chapter on the Elizabethan Naval war you have used Old Style[6] throughout. Pray do not trouble to reply, if this is the case.

---

[1]Of the *Cambridge Modern History*, begun by Lord Acton, but completed by A.W. Ward. Laughton had contributed to Vol. III.

[2]H.G. Gutteridge (ed.), *Nelson and the Neapolitan Jacobins* (NRS, London, 1902).

[3]Adolphus William Ward (1837–1924), historian.

[4]H.W. Wilson, who wrote the offending chapter. See [158].

[5]John Holland Rose (1855–1942); a pupil of Ward's and the scholarly biographer of Napoleon and Pitt the Younger; Vere-Harmsworth Professor of Naval History at Cambridge 1919–34.

[6]Calendar. In the reign of Elizabeth I England was still using the Julian calendar, while the Catholic world had adopted the Gregorian.

235. *W. Graham Greene[1] to Laughton*

18 December 1904

I have reported to Lord Spencer the proposal which was discussed at the last meeting of the Navy Records Society [Council][2] and shortly his opinion is as follows:–

Lord Spencer quite approves of the proposal that the annual meeting of the Society in 1905 should be distinguished by associating with the usual business to be transacted an address by an authority on Naval History on some incident in Naval History, preferably those connected with Lord Nelson's life – and looking to the fact that the Society includes among its members many foreigners and foreign institutions, he does not think it would be inappropriate to invite a foreigner (say Admiral Mahan) if it be the opinion of the Council that an address by a foreigner would be more popular and attract more notice than one by an English Naval Officer or writer. He thinks it, however, important that, whatever may be the decision, the address should not include anything which might wound the susceptibilities of France or of any other foreign nation.[3]

Lord Spencer further thinks that it would be desirable for him to ascertain on behalf of the Council the views of the King on the proposal, and that he might then suggest that the Prince of Wales[4] should be invited to attend the meeting. He thought it was possible that His Majesty himself might take an interest in the proceedings of the Society.

On the question of having an annual address Lord Spencer was inclined to think it would be a mistake, but that possibly once every three years (or thereabouts) it might be an advantage to repeat the proposed special meeting, if subsequently thought desirable.

---

[1]Sir William Graham Greene (1857–1950), Secretary to the Admiralty; here acting as Treasurer of the NRS (1904–48).

[2]The approach to Lord Spencer followed a motion by J.R. Thursfield (the naval correspondent of *The Times*) at Council on 11 October 1904 that something should be done to make the AGM more popular. Mahan was unable to accept and in the event Bridge gave the address. The apparent sensitivity of the subject, and the high level of notice taken of the Society's work is remarkable.

[3]This sensitivity followed the Anglo-French Entente of 1904.

[4]Later King George V (1910–36); he had been a naval officer.

236. *Fremantle[1] to Laughton*

4 March 1905

Thank you for calling my attention to the *Athenaeum* review.

It is certainly the best I have seen. Of course I like the friendly and appreciative tone, but your ample knowledge of naval history and of the service has enabled you to do full justice to the alteration and improvements which have made our naval personnel what it is, without underrating the Old Navy.

You have touched on the point of most importance I think, and your notice is the most complete I have seen.

I suspect the story pp.20–21 you mentioned did refer to Sir Wm. Hoste,[2] he is so accurately described. In the book it is a mix up of Hoste, the *Samarang*, and Belcher[3] and the *Spartan*. I never heard Hoste's name in connection with the hen coop story, but I have some idea that I have heard the cabin yarn as applicable to him, though I am pretty sure it did not occur in the *Spartan*.

237. *Gutteridge to Laughton*

10 October 1905

I have delayed answering your letter until I feel I had time to look into the matter, and I hope I have not inconvenienced you thereby.

The Neapolitans of the 18th century computed time from sunset to sunset numbering the hours from one to twenty four. Thus the compiler of the *Diario Napoletano* (see *Nelson and the Neapolitan Jacobins* page 184) has 'vente treemezzo' 23 ½ O'clock. This in June would roughly speaking [be] 7–7.30 p.m. The use of this computation was not universal e.g. Micheroux in his '*Compendio*' sometimes uses the ordinary present day method of reckoning time. Ruffo used Italian time (see *NRS* vol. xxv p.236) &, so far as I can judge, the usual method of reckoning was from sunset to sunset. Where Italian time was used it was customary to add the abbreviation 'Ital'. Thus '23 ½ Ital' I can only speak from Neapolitan documents but I think the usage would be the same elsewhere in Italy. I have met old people in Naples who still

---

[1]Admiral Sir Edmund Robert Fremantle (1836–1929), grandson of Nelson's companion. He had just published his memoirs: *The Navy as I Have Known It* (London, 1904).

[2]Rear Admiral Sir William Legge George Hoste (1819–68), son of Nelson's protegé Captain Sir William Hoste.

[3]Admiral Sir Edward Belcher (1799–1877); surveyor and explorer; noted for his foul temper and the low morale among his officers.

clung to this old fashioned computation, but it is never met with in practice now.

To distinguish the European computation it was not uncommon in the 18th cent. to add the words 'nella mattina' [*from the morning*] or 'dopo pranzo' [*after lunch*] to show that Italian time was not being used. If I found time mentioned in a Neapolitan 18th C. document without any such qualification I should assume in the absence of evidence to the contrary that Italian time was meant. But it is sometimes difficult to say which is meant by persons at the close of the century. Thus Micheroux uses both computations (see pp 117 & 121 NRS vol. xxv). I hope this will give you the information you require.

238. *Mahan to Laughton*

Grand Hotel de la Paix, Madrid, 31 December 1905

Your letter of Nov. 22 reached me here, soon after my arrival. The apparent contradiction between the address given, and my going to Gibraltar, was due to the fact that we took a tour through Spain, from South to north, as our method of reaching Pau. We should have been there over a fortnight ago; but five days after reaching here my younger daughter came down with scarlatina. Fortunately, there is a reasonably comfortable hospital, which was willing to receive her, and she is to-day pronounced not only well, but uninfectious. This contretemps has caused us four weeks delay over the time scheduled for our trip; during which period I have myself been the victim of an extremely violent catarrh, which after causing ten days of misery in the nasal passages, made its way to the bowels causing an upset unparalleled in my experience. I am now well, but have not regained fully either weight or strength. On Tuesday we leave here for San Sebastian, hoping to arrive in Pau about Jan. 12.

As regards the Trafalgar[1] matter, Bridge sent me a copy of his address – type written – and I read the *Times* articles, 'The Nelson Touch'. All can now say is that when preparing my book on the *French Revolution*, and *Nelson*, I read all the then current narratives known to me, and never conceived the slightest suspicion that the attack was made other than in two irregular 'columns' using the term in its' natural sense. Neither Bridge nor 'the Nelson Touch' seemed to me convinc-

---

[1]The centenary was the occasion for a wide-ranging, if unrewarding, debate on the tactics of the battle. The discussion was concluded by the Admiralty Committee of 1911, and the work of Corbett.

ing. The diagram in one of the closing papers of the latter seemed to me open to the objection that, as the two columns were drawn (as shown there), the wings of the allies so far from 'being both abaft the beam', as Collingwood mentions, were one of them well forward of the beam, the other alone abaft. True, when Collingwood turned towards the enemy, the phrase would be justified; but then, by this new construction, he would no longer be '<u>leading</u> down', to use his own words, but taking part in a line abeam, simultaneous, bearing down of his division. Again, in the diagram, the wind is so far forward of the beam that the incident of the lower stunsail becomes impossible. With the wind as shown the mainsail would of course be set, and a lee lower stunsail preposterous. Fortified by your opinion I shall not enter the lists, or trouble myself further, I don't think the case, as stated needs further reply; and my experience with Badham makes me rather hopeless of convincing a public. To think that Wilson should again give currency to the condemnation of Nelson in that matter.[1] I do not indeed regret the trouble taken to refute Badham. I could scarcely have done otherwise under the conditions, but I have been unable to trace any reversal of the verdict obtained by Southey's misstatement. By the way, do I understand Thursfield[2] wrote the Nelson Touch, or only the *Times* leader on the matter?[3]

Passing through Spain I have seen two things that may interest you. One, of which you probably were aware, is a likeness of Sir W. Hamilton in the Prado Gallery here by Battoni. He appears as a full, round-faced, blooming young man, of not over 35. The other can scarcely have come to your knowledge. At Rouda [Rota?] there is an old house known as the Casa del Rey Moro, from the rear of which one gets an excellent view of one part of the great chasm which rends the town in twain. In the patio of the house were some half a dozen old engravings, giving the Spanish version of Matthew's action off Toulon. I had no time to examine them, and it may be you know the engraving, though in your sea-going days Rouda was not as accessible as now from Gibraltar.

My newspaper mail is held up in Pau for my arrival there, so I have not yet seen your article in the *Quarterly*.[4] And, by the way, if you saw an article I gave the *Graphic*;[5] Oct 21, the text only was mine. The

[1]See [233–4] above.

[2]Sir James Richard Thursfield (1840–1923); naval leader writer for *The Times*; a founder member of the NRS.

[3]Thursfield wrote both: see his *Nelson and Other Naval Studies* (London, 1909); Chapter 1 consists of the 'Nelson Touch' articles.

[4]'The Centenary of Trafalgar', *Quarterly Review*, CCXIV (1905), pp. 611–30.

[5]'The Consistency of Nelson as a Tactician', *The Graphic*, LXXII (21 October, 1905), p. 514.

diagram associated to it was their devising, and did not represent me, nor my text.

239.   *Mahan to Laughton*

4, Rue D'Orleans, Pau, 20 January 1906

Here we are at last; but I regret to say that we are not yet out of all tribulations, for my daughter, as a sequel to scarlatina, developed acute rheumatism, from which she is now suffering.

Can you point me to any published papers, in which either Togo or Rozhdestvensky make full report of their several operations?[1] When leaving home, I brought with me all I could glean from the *Weekly Times*, and I have read the subsequent issues with sufficient care; but I find little light additional to the early reports. Wilson had an article in the *National Review*; but it does not seem to me to rest upon anything more authoritative. In the *Times* excerpt from Togo's official report, – the whole was not given – there are apparent inaccuracies, due doubtless to transmission by cable. If either of the immediate question above, or by communication of any other source of information, you can help me to further knowledge, I shall be greatly obliged; as I have promised an article to the *National*, conditionally. As you may be over busy for a letter to me, I have requested B.F. Stevens & Brown to obtain for me anything you may indicate to them.

Since my arrival here I have read, somewhat hastily, Colomb's article[2] which you sent me, and more carefully your reply. There was in Colomb's a lack of lucidity which somewhat tried my patience; and when, upon turning to yours, I found he had omitted to give Majendie's[3] endorsement of the *Naval Chronicle's* diagram, and had overlooked the evident connection and mutual relation and effect of signals 72 and 76, I wanted nothing more to satisfy me that he had jumped at conclusions without adequate verification of his data. Collingwood's despatch, with which he opens his attack, so far from bearing the construction he forces upon it, appears to me absolutely confirmatory of the received tradition, and is unshaken by anything he adduces. My own opinion has always been that the essence of the Nelson Touch was the attack in two (or three) columns on the centre and rear; that that was what the Captains understood, as well as that, so delivered, the allied van could

---

[1] The Japanese and Russian Admirals in the Tsushima Campaign. Mahan was writing on current affairs, and his 1906 output was dominated by this campaign.
[2] On Trafalgar.
[3] French captain at Trafalgar.

not come to aid in time. Column or line is a detail. The latter, as by the memorandum far from windward, would be better; but I was glad to see how forcibly you drew attention to the very decisive fact that from leeward Nelson intended just the kind of assault (& so instructed the Captains) which he in the event adopted from the windward. I had said the same in my article for the *Graphic*, but I am glad to have your endorsement independently, for your article appeared before mine. I don't know whether I mentioned in my last that the diagram with which the *Graphic* saw fit to accompany my article was none of mine. It contradicts my text, but I never saw it till I received the number.

Our plans are all disarranged by my daughter's illness. I am confident that we shall be delayed here by her convalescence till mid February at least, and probably longer; though it may be that we may be advised to seek other air to hasten the process. We had intended to sail for home probably from Naples, the end of April, but here again a course of baths may be ordered for her or for my wife, who has derived immeasurable benefit from two seasons at Nauheim.

I see the astounding results of your elections. Personally, I am certain that either other countries will modify their protection policies, or Great Britain must come down into the arena and hit out.[1] The former I do not expect; the latter I believe will come with the next bad times.

240.   *Mahan to Laughton*

28 January 1906

I am much indebted for your letter and for Bridge's article. I will look out for the latter carefully and return it as soon as I shall have mastered the contents sufficiently for my purpose.[2] It came in good order. Today I have also your postal that you had written Stevens and Brown to send me the *Blackwood*; for which also many thanks. I feel a particular interest in knowing how Togo stationed his fleet during the siege of Port Arthur; and how far he was successful, or attempted, to keep out supplies; but from Bridge's letter I fear these data are not easily to be ascertained.

I am glad to see that your diagnosis of the dispositions indicated by the general election agrees mainly with my own; though I would have

[1] The reference is to the 1906 General Election in which the Liberals secured power, and the Conservative vote was divided by the Tariff Reform Movement of Joseph Chamberlain. Both Mahan and JKL were in sympathy with Chamberlain, and his leading theorist, Halford Mackinder.

[2] Probably Bridge's article on the Russo-Japanese War, published in the *Edinburgh Review*, **CCXIV** (1905).

been disposed to attach more weight to a popular conservative prepossession in favour of trade. I am, with you, distinctly of the opinion that Chamberlain's[1] general views will be adopted at no distant period. I mean that democracies are Imperialistic in tendency; and that for imperialism to become a concrete, operative, fact, some method analogous to his own in general plan must be adopted.

241. *Mahan to Laughton*

31 January 1906

Almost immediately after last writing you, I received a copy of the *Edinburgh Review*,[2] and the packet of newspaper cuttings kindly presented me by Bridge. I take the former to have been sent by you, although in my unmethodical way of handling my correspondence, under present conditions, I do not find mention of it in your letter. Thursfield, to whom I had also written for such information as he might possess, wrote me he had asked the *Review* editor to send me a copy. Possibly this may be from him, although its arrival seemed to me over early. In any event, it has given me the opportunity of reading the article on Naples in 1806,[3] which from a remark in Bridge's letter I inferred was by you. The period after 1805 is unfamiliar to me, and I have read this with much appreciation and instruction, as well as interest. Now that I have the *Review*, in whole, I will endeavour to get your pamphlet copy of Bridge's article off by the mail that takes this.

I am sorry Bridge did not send me the *Japan Times* he destroyed. The effect upon Japanese commerce and shipping receives some incidental mention in the parts sent. I am particularly interested in the effect of commerce destruction, direct or indirect, regarded as contributive to the determination of war. Of course, the few brief raids of the Vladivostock squadron could not produce much effect; but it is about all we have since our Civil War. You probably know that our Government has proposed for the next Hague Conference (as it did at the last) the freedom from capture of 'private property', so called, at sea. I believe that to do this would be to surrender much of that control in which Sea Power consists, and that the phrase 'private property' is a misnomer. This thesis I developed pretty fully in *1812* (Vol. 1 pp.144–8) and I

---

[1] Joseph Chamberlain (1836–1914), British politician; he had just split the Conservative Party with his movement for Imperial preference.

[2] The October 1905 issue of the *Edinburgh Review* contained Bridge's article on the Russo-Japanese war; see fn. 2 on p.233 above.

[3] JKL, 'Naples and Napoleon', *Edinburgh Review*, **CCXIV** (1905).

think it will be worth while for those of us, who study these questions carefully, to prepare our minds as to whether the decision is to be taken like that of the Treaty of Paris, by snap judgement. I have seen that your new Lord Chancellor[1] has pronounced in favour of it, I sent a proof copy of the above pages to President Roosevelt, but he is too busy to digest such a matter; and Hay's successor[2] probably has not even given thought to a matter which under wholly differing circumstances was a natural object of American policy, and so remains by prepossession while circumstances are wholly changed.

I see, on re-reading that I have omitted to say thank-you for Bridge's papers, and letter sent with your notes; but you know the thanks are there, all the same.

242. *Mahan to Laughton*

Bad Nauheim, 22 May 1906

Although I have not had the pleasure of seeing you during this visit abroad, I am yet writing by way of saying good bye, as we are sailing on Saturday, in the *Barbarossa* from Bremen. Since I last wrote you, from Pau, we have come here by way of the south of France, Italy, and the St. Gotthard arriving here April 15. My wife has undergone treatment here the last two season, with extraordinary benefit; and from that, and the reassurances of the physician, I venture to hope the same for my daughter after the rheumatic attack. That left the heart much involved, but not in such a way as to preclude hope of restoration to almost, if not quite, the previous strength. But we go home baffled; with the exception of the trip through Spain, which resulted so disastrously to my daughter, we have in our seven months fulfilled scarcely a single object we had proposed.

While in Pau I received from my London publisher a copy of the *Athenaeum*, with a review of my *1812*, in which I think I recognised your work; both because I know you review for it, and by 'internal evidence', as the modern phrase runs. Whoever the writer it was very gratifying to me, because evidencing the appreciation of a person who from knowledge of the subject in general could discriminate. There is nothing one misses more in reviewers than the faculty to note decisive points; and this is necessarily specially so of naval matters.

---

[1]Robert Threshie Reid (1846–1923), Lord Loreburn; Lord Chancellor 1906–14; favoured the London Convention on Neutral Rights at Sea.
[2]As United States Secretary of State.

We are passing through an interesting stage of naval development. Custance writes me that general opinion in the British Navy is tending against the excessive size and speed, which receive increment in each new ship.[1] I am satisfied a stop must come soon, but am not able to see any weight of opinion to pull up, and rather fear that when it comes it will be disastrously revolutionary, particularly in view of the general character of your present ministry. For this reason, in the interests of both peoples, while I regret the vote for our new monster ship, I am not sorry to recognise a retort to the *Dreadnought*, and trust it may suggest to both the query 'What's the use?' I am continually reminded of the race between Chauncey and Yeo on Ontario,[2] which ended in nothing, scarcely even smoke.

My home address, should you have occasion to write me, will be Quogue, N.Y. meanwhile, wishing you every happiness for the coming years, believe me.

In packing, I came across your photograph and wondered if I had ever thanked you for it. It is an excellent likeness, and I am very glad to have it, though it seems to me exaggeratedly sedate. Otherwise it is very good.

243.   *Mahan to Laughton*

Slumberside, 20 July 1906

Your letter of July 1 was received a few days ago. I should have been interested to take up the lectures you suggest, for although I have not taken myself very seriously as a historian, judged by the modern standards – with which I do not wholly agree – I have formed some views of my own during my period of writing. As I have sent you pretty generally whatever I have written, I suppose I did not omit an address before the Historical Society,[3] of which I was temporary president, on Subordination in Historical Treatment.[4] It indicates my general point of view, which I would probably have taken, and from it followed up, could I accept.

---

[1]Custance shared the perspective of Mahan, Bridge and JKL in favour of the smallest effective battleship. In 1930 Herbert Richmond would end his naval career by writing to the press on the same issue.

[2]In the War of 1812 both commanders kept building ever larger ships, rather than fighting for command of the Lake.

[3]The American Historical Association.

[4]His Presidential Address, given on 26 December 1902: 'Subordination in Historical Treatment' in *The American Historical Association Annual Report*, I (Washington, 1903), pp. 47–63; reprinted in *Naval Administration and Warfare* (Boston, 1910).

Unhappily I cannot, though I should have enjoyed the opportunity to formulate my views, and still more would have appreciated the distinction. Everyone needs occasionally to be buttressed, and I should have so estimated this. But as far as I can foresee now, family considerations will compel my remaining on this side next year; the more so that my wife and daughter may – probably will – have to return to Nauheim for a course. I have to remain to keep the family constitution together. Please express to the authorities of the university my regrets and my appreciation.

I am as yet, since my return, doing miscellaneous work – at this moment an appreciation of the submarine's future. I am also writing my service Recollections, a thing which would never have entered my head to do, but for a request by a periodical that pays well.[1] Admiral Luce has been urging me to take up my old lectures at the War College on Naval Strategy – revise (from 20 years ago) and bring up to date.[2] I incline to do this, if the Government, in addition to putting me on duty, which gives an increase of pay, will allow me to publish. The two together would probably make it worth while. I cherish besides a plan of writing a history of the U.S., primarily for the ages of 16–20. There are already more than a million [such text books], as the boys say; but I gather that the readable one is yet to come. I certainly think so, from my reading of existing books with a view to this. I am not talking of this, because it is in the air still; but of course success will depend purely on the personal factor, the ability to present with clearness and interest a story not replete with striking incident. In the distance lies the Navy's effect upon our Civil War which some of our historians want me to take up. So you see I have no period of idleness before me.

I presume you have seen Jane's *Heresies of Sea Power*.[3] By dint of misinterpreting, and worse, he manages to set up a target, but his own shooting, even at that, is so bad that I shall pay no attention. The book may be left to find its own level; but what a droll thing to imagine that 'Fitness to Win', personnel being superior to materiel, is a new discovery.

---

[1] *From Sail to Steam: Recollections of a Naval Life* (New York, 1907).

[2] *Naval Strategy Compared and Contrasted with the Principles and Practice of Military Operations on Land* (Boston, 1911).

[3] Fred T. Jane, *Heresies of Sea Power* (London, 1906); the book was an attack on simplistic extreme blue-water thinking, rather than Mahan's more sophisticated ideas.

244.   *Smith, Elder & Co. to Laughton*

15, Waterloo Place, London S.W., 18 March 1907

The subject of your letter of the 14th, for which we thank you, has been kept constantly before us since we wrote to you in its regard on the 28th November 1904, and the consideration of your advancing years which you mention is not forgotten. The question is a large one, in view of the further categories which would stand to be made were the Sailors of the *Dictionary of National Biography* reproduced in any substantive form as an independent publication.[1] And we fear that we cannot say more today in favour of the adoption of your proposal than we said two years ago. We will however bear the matter carefully in mind.

245.   *Laughton to Browning*

29 June 1907

Many thanks for your kind congratulations.[2] I just write a line – though doubtful if you will get it before you leave – to say that I have written to Mr Johnstone in answer to his letter & telling him to apply to me if he wants further information on the subject.

246.   *Laughton to Corbett*

27 July 1907

It is really most kind of you to send these two lovely birds which have arrived this morning.[3] We will eat them to your health and good sport following successful work.

I see the *Seven Years War*[4] is to come out today. I have been looking forward to it, and it comes at a happy time, when I have just got rid of the London Exams, which have been a bugbear and nightmare for the last month. Our final meeting is tomorrow.

As I have not got your country address, I am obliged to send this to Hans Crescent.

---

[1]The failure of this proposal denied JKL the merit of standing alone as the author of what might have been the most significant work on naval history hitherto written.

[2]On his knighthood.

[3]From the date these would have been grouse.

[4]J.S. Corbett, *England in the Seven Years' War* (2 vols, London, 1907). Corbett's Naval War Course lectures developed for a wider public, noted for their use of Clausewitz, and the masterly, if slightly forced, symmetry they imposed on the British war effort.

Make Colomb[1] join [the] NRS. He can take up his father's sub[scription]. and have the back vols at subs price, if he likes.

247. *Mahan to Laughton*

Slumberside, 6 September 1907

Your letter of June 17 came in due course of mail, and not long afterwards I saw your promotion to knighthood, with, I assure you, much personal satisfaction. I have felt that I ought to begin this with 'Dear Sir John', on the same ground that O'Brien desired Peter Simple to touch his cap to him, just once, when he heard of his promotion to lieutenant in a French prison.[2] You will, however, have had plenty of that, ere now, and will have found, I am sure, that the pleasure of the recognition itself will have been doubled to you by the satisfaction it has given your friends.

The foretaste you sent me of the coming volume of the Navy Records Society does excite my interest. The period is one with which I still feel myself unfamiliar, much as I have written about it. I have never had with it the *connaissance intire* that I have seemed to realise in the later days of the Nile and Trafalgar. In fact, Nelson seems to draw a broad line between the days before and after him. Just to what this is due, I have not analysed.

I am glad to know that you liked the article on the capture of 'Private Property'.[3] I have decided to collect four articles, of which this is one, and have obtained permission from Corbett and a gentleman named Pritchett, an American, to reproduce one of each, under the title *Some Neglected Aspects of War*. The above sentence is awkward, but you will gather that there will be six papers. My object in this is to give a mild start to something like a forward opposition to the extravaganzas of the Arbitration propaganda. If discussion be provoked, the common people, who are accepting Arbitration at its face value, will soon realise its limitations. I will send you a copy.

Beyond this my summer has been occupied chiefly in completing for the press my naval recollections, which are to come out this autumn under the title, chosen by the publishers *From Sail to Steam*. You will

[1]Admiral Philip Colomb (1867–1958); son of Admiral Philip Howard Colomb (d. 1899), JKL's correspondent in this volume.

[2]From Frederick Marryat's novel *Peter Simple* (London, 1833).

[3]'The Hague Conference: the Question of Immunity of Belligerent Merchant Shipping', *National Review*, **XLIX** (1907), pp. 521–37; reprinted in A.T. Mahan, *Some Neglected Aspects of War* (Boston, 1907).

find in it little but one phase of the life you knew in your active service days. I have written, purposely, with my eye on the public, and popularly, as far as I could. The work has been a pot-boiler, and not much to my taste. I have aimed chiefly to make it readable. The firm, Harper's, have brought out some extracts in their Magazine, but have used it in that way but little, considering the price they paid for serial rights.

I am sorry to hear of your gout. I can sympathise somewhat, though not fully; for the disease leaves me alone for the most part. I have had occasional twinges in the tendon Achilles. Old age makes us all pay; this last year it has taken a more evident grasp upon me. I have been surprised to see, by *Who's Who*, that you have ten years disadvantage of me; for such at our age a decade must be considered. However, when our times come to go men must admit of us both, that we do not leave the record of idle lives.

The Hague Conference seems likely to adjourn having done less harm than might have been feared. The number of its propositions defeated one another, like the programme of your Liberal Party. I incline to think that a permanent Court may be a real gain; for, after all, War is an evil that we must desire to soften, though it never can be accomplished without disaster by shriekers like Stead and Carnegie.[1]

248.   *Mahan to Laughton*

Lawrence L.I., 1 November 1907

I sent you by book post a few days ago a copy of my reminiscences to which the publishers, not I, gave the title *From Sail to Steam*. I could not write the same day because I am a bit of an invalid, having to undergo some five weeks ago a severe surgical operation, from which I am not yet fully restored. Indeed, I am only a week out of hospital, and you may possibly see something of the tremulousness I still feel in my hand.

You will not find much in the book, except the kind of thing current in all naval services. As I had nothing important to communicate, I aimed chiefly to entertain, with some eye to right doctrine for non-naval readers.

We have nearly ready for issue a volume called *Some Neglected Aspects of War* chiefly my own articles, but one by another American. I will send you a copy when out. We had hoped to include Corbett's on

[1] William Thomas Stead (1849–1912), English journalist, drowned on the *Titanic*; and Andrew Carnegie (1835–1908), Scots-American steel magnate and philanthropist.

the capture of private property; but our request was addressed to him, with the request that he would obtain the consent of the magazine. Knowles took offence at our not addressing him personally, and has refused his permission, and as we do not know where the property right lies, we of course do not print, although having Corbett's consent the matter has been put in type. I am very sorry for I think the article good, and especially calculated to open the eyes of our people to the continental attempt by diplomatic indirection [*Mahan means 'dishonesty'*] to neutralise the maritime power of Great Britain.

The one thing the Hague Conference really demonstrated is that War is still a potent factor, the power to use which no great nation will abandon.

249. *Mahan to Laughton*

21 February 1908

I am greatly indented to you for the cuttings. I had seen in one of our papers that there had been a discussion in [the] House [of] Commons the first week in February, and charged my memory to look it up in the *Times* when I could get to my club; but it is very convenient to have been able to read it here, while still confined, practically, to the house.

The fundamental mistake – and this is a pre military question – made by your advocates of immunity, is well nigh universal here, and I presume with you too, among non-military men. It is the assuming defence a paramount consideration relating to offence. As towards Germany and France they do not see the power to injure the hostile trade is a sure guarantee of peace and shortness of war than any amount of mere protection to British trade.

If my memory serves me I have not written you since November. At the end of that month it became evident that my first operation was having consequences which rendered a second necessary on Dec. 2. For three weeks after I was scarcely myself owing I suppose to the double shock, and since then I have been undergoing continuous treatment, all for the sake of getting the urinary canal properly and permanently, clear. I was nine weeks confined to the house, and since then get out only for a few minutes shamble about the country lanes here. The doctors assure me of a full recovery, but I am still a semi-invalid.

I grieve to hear that you are feeling old, but at least you can look back on much accomplished. I can sympathise a little, for weakness and years combined have made me too feel full of years and disability.

I hope I may resume; but it is a curious fact that, busy as I have been, there is nothing that calls me decisively; no unfinished work; a full new start upon something wholly new will be necessary. You will appreciate that this tends to postponement, and may drift into entire non-action. There are several things that might and do interest me; but to get a new one on, at my age, a trifle daunts me.

Wishing you still a long period of happy repose, should happy activity have to be in measure curtailed, believe me.

250.   *Mahan to Laughton*

6 March 1908

It was very nice of you to let me know of the Editor's modification. It so happened that the day before your postal came I got over to New York, for the first time in three months, and at the club saw your review. The concluding sentence made rather an abrupt break from the tone of what preceded; but you can believe that, kind as most reviewers have been to me, I am not by this resistive to honest criticism; so had I been you I should have relented. Badham is the very man who has thrown me off my balance; and in his case I believe I was, at first, as much annoyed by the feeling that I ought to have consulted the Italian writers, as I afterwards became by his own purblind 'cussedness'. I suppose that when articles are unsigned, something still survives of the tradition I associate with the name of Giffard.[1]

We are having a bit of a tempest in our naval tea-pot just now, mainly with reference to the proper position of the water line armour belt; also as to the safety of the ammunition hoists. I was particularly struck with the statement of Admiral Converse[2] that he considered our *South Carolina*,[3] the most perfect type of what a battleship should be. To the natural question 'Why then build bigger?' he replied 'Only because other nations are doing so'. Converse is one of the few really all-round men, who also have very superior qualities, alike afloat or in council, or in administration. I think your Admiralty have made the mistake which St. Vincent pointed out as regards Fulton's[4] proposals for torpedoes. 'We lead the world as it is, why foster what may take the lead from us'.

---

[1]He means William Gifford (1756–1826); first editor of the *Quarterly Review* 1809–23.

[2]Rear Admiral George A. Converse USN, Chief of the Bureau of Navigation 1904.

[3]The first American Dreadnought, completed 1908, 16,000 tons, 8 × 12-inch guns.

[4]Robert Fulton (1765–1815); American submarine, mine and steamship pioneer; sold his devices to the British in 1804–05.

You led, and still lead in shipbuilding power. Why then start this insane competition for size of ship and consequent awful cost? My lot have waited at least till some one else was foolish enough to begin. You could always lead; now you have started a competition which can be followed, though at a distance and which at least diminishes the value of your fleet before existing.[1]

I am glad I am retired for present proceedings tire me, even to read about.

251. *Mahan to Laughton*

5 December 1908

I have mailed you today a copy of my last book *Naval Administration etc.* You will easily recognise the pot-boiler in the scratch collection of articles, most of which also you may have seen. Pray accept it as a testimony of my regard rather than as itself valuable.

I have made two or three attempts to get from Sampson, Low – and from the successors of the [old?] firm the consent to publish separately the chapters I contributed to Clowes's *History of The Royal Navy*; a course you may remember you suggested to me. All has been in vain. The present incumbents seem to cherish a sense of injury in the price paid me at the time, and to wish to recoup by making me pay now for the privilege. As a matter of fact I did the work at much less than the prices I was commanding at the time, out of regard to Marston. I don't propose to be done in any such way, and must leave them under their impression that they were done – which they were not. I believe their policy is mistaken, and that the separate publication – after ten years – would rather fillip the sale of the *History*. But as it is the matter is held up by their attitude.

I trust this may find you well and happy, looking forward to a Merry Christmas. I have continued to improve slowly, and am now in pretty good shape; but more nervous and fussy than I like, due to years; so at least I flatter myself. I am now engaged in revising some lectures on Naval Strategy[2] which I wrote for our War College over twenty years ago; before any of my Sea Power books saw the light. The lectures have never been published but have continued ever since as part of the course. Possibly, after revision, publication may follow; but that will depend on the Government, which is employing me for this work.

---

[1]Mahan was wrong on this issue – and was soundly defeated in print by William Sowden Sims USN. See R. Seager, *Alfred Thayer Mahan; The Man and his Letters* (Annapolis, 1977), pp. 525–6.

[2]A.T. Mahan, *Naval Strategy* (Boston, 1911).

252.   *S.R. Scargill-Bird[1] to Laughton*

Public Record Office, 27 May 1910

My attention has been called to your letter in *The Times* of the 17th instant, in which you make the assertion that all the Pay Books of the Royal Navy hitherto preserved in the Public Record Office have been recently destroyed. I enclose for your information a copy of the 12th Schedule of Admiralty Documents the destruction of which was proposed in 1908, from which you will perceive that it was decided to preserve <u>one complete set</u> of the Ships Pay Books, taking the 'Treasurer's Series' as a nucleus and filling up any gaps therein from the other series.

Duplicate copies only have been destroyed.

253.   *Sir Frederick Kenyon[2] to Laughton*

British Museum, 24 June 1910

I am very grateful to the Navy Records Society for the honour they have done me in electing me as Vice-President. It is an honour to which I have no claim beyond a very real and long standing interest in naval history and naval matters, and I owe it, no doubt, mainly to my present position at the head of one of the great depositories of naval records; but however it be come by, it is very pleasant to be associated with so many distinguished officers and historians, and my expression of gratitude is something more than a mere formality.

254.   *Laughton to Sir John Scott Keltie[3]*

16 October 1910

Can you put me in the way of answering this question which has been sent me from Sydney NSW.

When and why was Cook's *Point Hicks* (near the S.E. corner of NSW) changed to Cape Everard?[4]

The first step towards answering seemed to be to establish the truth of the assertion; and it does not seem to me at all certain that Cape

[1]Deputy Keeper at the Public Record Office.
[2]Sir Frederick George Kenyon (1863–1952); Director of the British Library 1909–30; he would serve the Society as President between 1925 and 1947.
[3]Keltie (1840–1927), Secretary and Editor for the Royal Geographical Society.
[4]J.C. Beaglehole, *The Life of Captain James Cook* (London, 1974), p.227.

Everard is identical with Point Hicks. A comparison of the modern chart with the reduction of Cook's Chart (I fancy out of Wharton's *First Voyage*) seems to show Cape Everard as a projection about half way between Pt. Hicks and Rame Head, but this is doubtful. Can you help me to a decision?

Anyway, who was Everard and why does he give his name to a Cape? My correspondent suggests Sir Everard Home, which is perhaps fanciful.

Perhaps you can turn this over to one of the young men in the Map Room, but I could not make much of it when I spent ½ an hour there today.

255.   *Mahan to Laughton*

Quogue, 15 November 1910

I send you today, what I had meant to send a fortnight ago, a copy of a small book I have just published. You will find in it little to interest you, or any European; it being written for our own people expressly, who also probably will not read it, one in a million. Talk about insularity, your silver streak isn't in it with our three thousand miles of sea.[1]

We have not exchanged letters since your eightieth birthday, the observance of which I noted with much pleasure, meaning also myself to write you a letter of congratulation; but the thief of time robbed me of the opportunity. I myself turned seventy on Sept. 27, on which occasion, to my unbounded amazement, I received a very flattering cable message from the Dutch Minister of Marine. Subsequently one also from a German officer, head of their Naval College at Kiel, so they at least bear me no grudge for my articles in the *Daily Mail*.[2]

I was glad to infer from the notices that you bear your years well. I have myself no cause for complaint on the score of health, having continued well and active since my operations of three years ago. We have fine sea bathing here, and I was childishly desirous that on my 70th birthday the sea should favour me with just such roughness as would entitle me to say 'I knew I could'. And it did behave just that way; enough surf for headers, not enough to exhaust.

I am occupied now in preparing for press some lectures on Naval Strategy which I wrote twenty odd years ago, and have revised within the last two. The job sought me, the prime mover being Admiral Luce.

---

[1]*The Interest of America in International Conditions* (Boston, 1910).
[2]A.T. Mahan, 'The International Significance of German Naval Development', *Daily Mail*, 4 and 6 July 1910.

It has put me on duty since this time two years ago, and in that way has been very opportune, helping me to carry my son through the beginning years of a young lawyer who hung out his shingle[1] in New York at the same moment. The fixed increase of income was very *apropos*; but for that I might have hesitated to consent to what I never should myself have undertaken. Luce affirms they will add to my reputation. I rather fear the reverse, but as I really don't much care it don't much matter. But I hate old lectures.

But for this occupation we would probably have come abroad this winter. My family are so wedded to our new home here that I fancy we shall never be absent from it willingly in summer; but once abroad (by Southern route) we – or at least I – may get over to England for a few days in spring to see old friends again. At our age there are uncertainties; but one thing is certain – never in my life have I been continuously more happy than now in age.

256. *Admiral Sir E. H. Seymour[2] to Laughton*

Queen Anne's Mansions, St. James' Park S.W., 23 January 1911

Many thanks for your kind and interesting letter in reply to mine.

You ask about my commission as 'Admiral of the Fleet'. It calls me 'Admiral and Commander in Chief of His Majesty's Fleet'. That is in keeping with there only being one such official; as you tell me was the case 'till the close of the 18th century. My friend Dewey was promoted to be 'Admiral of the Navy' in the U.S. Fleet, but he is the only one so called.

I did not know what you tell me about the 'Red' not having existed till 1805, as a Full Admiral's rank, as I understood you, but that in the centre or Commander in Chief's Squadron the Vice and Rear Admiral's hoisted Red Flags. This seems to explain why the Union Jack was hoisted by the Admiral of the Fleet; but still I object to it because it is a national flag, and also is used for other things.

I would give him a special flag, & I did design one 6 years ago, and put it before King Edward, but the Admiralty did not agree about it.

When I went to New York in 1909 in the *Inflexible*,[3] we flew going out of and into Portsmouth Harbour 2 Union Jacks, one at the fore, for a pilot, and mine at the main. If we had had only one mast, as some

---

[1]Advertising board, from the wooden tile.

[2]Admiral of the Fleet Sir Edward Hobart Seymour (1840–1929); taught by JKL on board the *Calcutta* 1856–59; wrote *My Naval Career and Travels* (London, 1911).

[3]Battlecruiser, completed 1907, 17,900 tons, 8 × 12-inch guns, 25 knots.

ships have, 2 jacks must have flown together. The jack is also flown singly for 3 other purposes.

'Marshal Admiral' might do. The Germans use 'Gross Admiral' we might have Grand, or High. But I say Admiral must not be the first, as no one goes further than to use <u>it</u>. Once more many thanks & I am

257.   *Mahan to Laughton*

45 West 35th Street, University Club, Fifth Avenue & 54th Street,
17 November 1911

I have been meaning to write you for a fortnight past, to let you know I had ordered and sent you a copy of my last work, *Naval Strategy*; my last in more meanings than one, I fancy, for I do not contemplate writing any more books on Sea Power or naval matters specially. As my own copies of the work have not yet reached me, this letter will probably anticipate the arrival of it with you.

I wonder if you have been following actively the discussion of the past few years, in which Thursfield, Bridge and others have been combating the tradition as to Nelson's form of attack at Trafalgar. Captain Kerr[1] kindly sent me a copy of the *19th Century* containing his paper in the same sense. I have not had time to read it critically, indeed only to read half of it at all; but I wrote Kerr that there were certain incidental mentions, eg. Nicolas's narrative in the appendix to Hargood's (of the *Belleisle*, I think) life of the conversation between him and the captain of the *Tonnant* as the ships passed which seemed to me difficult to reconcile with the bow and quarter line (as I was taught to call it) in which the new advocates maintain that Collingwood's division bore down. I also pointed out to him that his own diagram seemed to show that Nelson's column actually was nearly in column and bows on to the part of the allied order which he attacked.[2]

I hope this will find you still in good shape, with your four score and one on your head. With ten years less, I am happy in excellent health having apparently fully recovered from my prolonged severe experience of four years ago. I surf-bathed nearly every day last summer, often at a temperature which a few years ago I thought too cool, walk four or five miles a day at nearly four miles the hour, and do my day's stint of writing. All this does not alter the fact that I am over seventy

---

[1]Admiral Mark Edward Frederic Kerr (1864–1944), protégé of Prince Louis; contributor to the Trafalgar debate; hostile to Corbett's work.
[2]The two columns had different roles, and approached the enemy in different formations.

one, and that I have tokens enough of the limitations which the years put on my powers. But I am very happy in all my surroundings & have nothing of which to complain.

We are spending this winter in New York, in an apartment; the first time in five years that we have lived in town. We had thought of going abroad, but I am in government employment momentarily, and the increase of income is acceptable under certain increased expenses, so we gave it up. I don't think we shall ever again be willing to spend a summer away from our own home, which is now settled at Quogue, where we have built up those interests of gardens etc., etc., which are particularly dear to ladies, very pleasant to myself, and with the concomitants of climate, bathing etc., endear the place to us.

258.   *Mahan to Laughton*

Quogue, 17 June 1912

Messrs. Sampson Low have at last consented to the separate publication of the paper contributed by me to their History of the Royal Navy, on the subject of the major operations, 1774–1782. I intend of course to re-read carefully, and in a sense to revise; but of alteration I expect there will be little, except where facts newly brought to light since 1897, my date of writing, may require.

The object of this letter is to ask whether you have any suggestions to make as to new sources likely to modify materially my presentation as it now stands. I have a recollection that you sent me once some data relative (I think) to Howe's preparation for defence in New York lower bay in 1778. It is a memorandum I could not have destroyed, but a pretty careful search this morning fails [to] reveal it. In this, or in any other respect, I shall be very glad of suggestions from you, as the most comprehensive source of information known to me.[1]

I trust your years are treating you well, though by your last you were finding age cutting you short in enjoyments, as it does us all. I am down to almost nothing in coffee, my greatest table delight, and have to look at the abundance of strawberries our vines are bearing now, but which I cannot eat. In most respects, however, I am up to what I have to do, and fairly vigorous.

[1]See [186].

259.   *Mahan to Laughton*

23 July 1912

I have received your kind reply, together with the book by book post; for which, and for the references to Duncan's Journal in the *Miscellany*,[1] I am much indebted. As regards the other books of notes which you offer me, you probably have forgotten that you did me the kindness to lend me several of them many years ago; my impression is for the very work which I am now about to revise. My recollection is very clear, as is my association of them with Rodney's actions in the West Indies.

I did the work so thoroughly at the time that I propose revision to extend no further than careful reading, and correction or addition by any really new accessible material, such as Duncan.

I read with sympathy and interest your retirement from active occupations.[2] That from the Records Society I saw appreciatively noticed in the last annual report which reached me lately. Well, you have the satisfaction of looking back upon an unusual amount of solid work accomplished, and of knowing that the enforced cessation is simply showing the lot common to all, though not all can feel the same self-approval of well-spent time. I trust you may yet have many happy years to enjoy conditions to which, as to all changes, some time is needed to adapt oneself and to find pleasure in them. If as was suggested and I hope will take place your son succeed you in the Navy Records it must be a great satisfaction.[3]

P. S. I am a titular admiral, promoted after retirement, but have consistently kept Captain as the *nom de plume* under which I became known.

260.   *Laughton to Charles Napier Robinson*

10 September 1912

I am greatly indebted to you for your letter, which I am sending off, with the miniature, to my Yankee correspondent – who mentioned Mahan as having told him to apply to me; so I have advised him to write direct to you if he wishes to take advantage of your offer to make further enquiries.

[1] 'Journals of Henry Duncan, Captain, Royal Navy', in J.K. Laughton (ed.), *The Naval Miscellany* I (NRS, London, 1901), pp. 105–220.
[2] JKL had resigned as Secretary of the Navy Records Society, and as Professor at King's College; he remained a Professor of the University of London, and still taught.
[3] Leonard would succeed, but would not give 'satisfaction'; see [267].

Many thanks for your kind enquiry. I fancy the time has come for me to pipe down. I have resigned from King's College also, but they are keeping me on there for some months longer, perhaps the year, till my successor can take on, but any thing like regular work becomes a 'grind', otherwise, I am in fair health, & work in my own way comfortably enough.

261.   *Mahan to Laughton*

24 October 1912

I return by this mail the note-book you kindly sent me, with thanks for the use of it. The material has now all gone to the printer, so that the revision on my part is concluded; and I promise myself never again to undertake revision of work some years old. A more tedious and uninspiring task to myself I have never undergone.

I write in haste, closing up a number of matters, expecting to sail for England Nov. 9. We will not give London more than a week at this time of year, and intend to strike promptly for Pau where Mrs Mahan has a sister married, but I trust I may find an opportunity of seeing you.

262.   *Mahan to Laughton*

Fleming's Hotel, Clarges Street, Mayfair W., 20 November 1912

We are here for a week, having arrived night before last. Can we arrange a meeting some time during it? Thursday I have a matinee, and on Friday a lunch engagement, but otherwise my days are unoccupied. I saw a notice in yesterday's paper that you were making an after dinner speech. Hurrah for you! I have plead [*sic*] disability to that for some years back.

263.   *Mahan to Laughton*

21 November 1912

Unfortunately, we have an engagement to lunch already on Sunday which makes that impracticable. I am very sorry but entirely appreciate your feelings about London streets. Even with my large practice as a New Yorker I find myself, with excellent eyesight, somewhat perplexed at the strife of motors; much increased by the English passing to the left which causes me always to turn my head in the wrong direction to look for danger. The going down to Wimbledon offers no difficulty except that of time, which is exiguous, as we leave on the 27th or 28th and engagements have piled up on us. If I can manage a chance I will run down in any event to see you but I can't be certain.

In any event all good wishes to you, and many thanks from us both to Lady Laughton for our kind invitation, which we very much appreciate.

264. *Mahan to Laughton*

23 November 1912

I will be at King's College at 3.10 on Tuesday, unless something now unforseen should present, and shall look forward with pleasure to seeing you there for a half hour.

265. *Harold W. V. Temperley[1] to Laughton*

Peterhouse, Cambridge, 15 March 1913

Hubert Hall has passed me on your letter about Chatham.[2] The point that the laying down of a single line of battleship by the House of Bourbon (beyond an ordered number) should be a <u>casus belli</u> – is interesting. I don't recollect any specific saying but it is quite in harmony with some of his ideas. I don't think it is sufficiently understood that his policy against France was primarily naval or anti-naval and that he went to great lengths in this way e.g. he wished to retain Guadeloupe not so much because its commerce would benefit England and increase her navy, as the lack of it to France would destroy a naval nursery. For the same reason he wished to exclude France altogether from Newfoundland. The nearest he comes to formulating a limit to the ship building policy of the House of Bourbon is in 1770 – when he wished to fight Spain over the Falkland Isles. I think there were two points clear (1) the F.I. were a nursery for English smugglers and a possible strategic base (2) to abandon them might give a chance to French smugglers – and, anyhow, the Fleet of the 2 Bourbon powers was now so strong that, either we must increase our fleet largely, or fight at once (the latter idea – the preventive war). I have very little doubt that the real key to his opposition over Falkland Isles is to be found here c.p. *Parliamentary History* XVI pp.1101–4.

---

[1]Harold Temperley (1879–1939), historian.
[2]William Pitt (1708–78), 1st Earl of Chatham; also known as 'Pitt the Elder'.

Thus though I cannot recollect that he ever formulated his policy in a phrase of this kind, it is in substance true that he was ready to act upon it. He even went further in some ways, as in 1762–3, when he appears to have wished to deprive France of all hope of ever again getting a Navy.

I am very glad that you are going to help us at Section IV of the Congress[1] (of which I am Secretary). [It] was fortunate in being able to secure you – and I hope we shall have a good attendance at the U.S.I.[2]

266. Mahan to Laughton

Hotel Panormus. Palermo, 24 March [1913][3]

Have you any clue as to where Nelson resided during his stay in this city in 1799, and I believe also in 1800? being here for the first and probably only time in my life, I have thought I would like to identify the house whence 'he never put his foot to the ground'. When writing the *Life*, the locale never struck me as one of interest, but when here I should like to realise the position. I have 'slummed' through a large part of the old city of his time, now full of smells, wash [*sic*] clothes out of windows, dirt and garbage of every kind; but, as in all old Italian towns I have seen, big substantial palaces occur every few hundred feet, now robbed of their glory and diverted to base uses but still in architecture and decoration testifying to former glories.

I should assume that he and the Hamiltons would have been assigned a house of that description, preferably near the old port, in easy communication with ships that came in. But this is pure surmise on my part.

Since I saw you in London we have been leisurely enjoying ourselves. A month in Pau where Mrs Mahan has a sister married; three weeks in San Remo where one of my daughters has a childhood friend; a fortnight in Florence, and now doing a month in Italy, Palermo is our final stop. We expect to sail from here for home on April 16. The city not only has a good many points of interest itself but is a centre for seeing others; and my wife demanded besides that she should have a fortnight of quiet before sailing.

---

[1]The International History Congress. JKL delivered his paper 'Historians and Naval History' at this session. See also the Introduction to this chapter, and fn. 1 on p.196.

[2]In the event Prince Louis came down from the Admiralty to chair the session.

[3]R. Seager and D.D. Maguire (eds), *Letters and Papers of Alfred Thayer Mahan* (3 vols, Annapolis, 1975), vol. III, pp. 491–2, Mahan to Captain Bouverie Clark RN, 24 March 1913, containing some of the same points, confirms the date.

I don't know whether you were here while afloat,[1] or otherwise, and in any event should not attempt description. Its general history you know, and probably its association with Nelson is for you the chief interest, as it is to me. Although I have been very well I do not find the warm climates suit me as well as our bleak but invigorating northwest and northeast winds. Sicily has wonderful scenery but also extraordinary dust. The trees in the parks here look as though they had been powdered for a fancy dress ball, and both here and else whirlwinds of dust, rising to the second and third stories, salute the unhappy wayfarer. The streets are not generally paved but macadamised with a rather soft friable stone which quickly yields an abundance of light white detritus.

It is a great pleasure to look back upon our brief meeting in London, and I trust you have found occupation upon your final retirement from work. I find myself already chafing under my mental inactivity and I have no such record of steady work behind me as you have. As an old friend of mine, whose death is just reported, used to say, 'The exercise habit is like the cocktail habit, not to be shaken off'; and it is much the same with hard work.

267. *Laughton to Graham Greene*

20 July 1913

I am greatly distressed about all this. I forwarded your letter to me to my son, with a very strong one from me, but have had no answer. Either the boy[2] is from home, which is very probable, or is off his head, which also seems probable. I can only hope that to morrow's post will bring some reply.

I am myself far from well and very shaky, or I would go over and see – if there was anything to see – which very possibly there is not.

[1] He was, in 1861; see *Foundations*, p. 21.

[2] Leonard Carr-Laughton had taken over from Sir John as Secretary in 1912, but signally failed to carry out the duties of the post. At the AGM of 30 June 1913 he had resigned on grounds of 'ill-health'. In the months preceding the appointment as Secretary of W.G. Perrin, the Admiralty Librarian, Cyprian Bridge, Graham Greene, Albert Gray and Erskine Childers had all helped out with the secretarial side of Society business.

268.   *Lecture Notes: 1913*

8 October 1913

I

I propose in these lectures to call your attention to the influence which the English Navy has had on the development of the Kingdom, and the Expansion of the Empire. I believe that many of you have not considered English history from the point of view that it is really based on the Navy. Some of you, I don't know that I can say all of you – have read that – According to Act of Parliament it is on the Navy etc 'the Good providence of God the wealth, safety and strength of the Kingdom chiefly depend', but to most, that is I fancy, merely a form of words, very few understand it or believe it.

If more did, we should not hear so much about the necessity for enlarged military defence. The first lesson that a boy (or girl) is taught of the geography of Great Britain is that it is an island, but all his historical teaching is – in effect – that it is a continental state. Books and lectures alike assume it; that it is subject to the same dangers as other continental states, to be guarded against in the same way. It is only a few days ago that I read, in the *Times* I think, an interesting account of the system of military service in Switzerland, with the very evident inference that this was the solution of the problem of National Defence. Well, this problem is no new danger. It has faced the country for many centuries, and it must have been solved in a fairly satisfactory way before and during the era of <u>Expansion</u>. It is worth enquiring what that way was, how far it was effective, and when and how or why it has not been effective. The answer, as it seems to me is that through the centuries, the country rested on the navy. This idea is, I'm sure <u>really</u> new to you. If you think I'm wrong, examine yourselves. You will find that in your heart of hearts you believe, and have always believed that the greatness of the country, not merely its glory, but its substantial greatness, safety and strength have rested on its military prowess, on Cressy, on Agincourt, Blenheim, Waterloo. I want to show you an alternative way of estimating it, that the glory, strength and the rest are <u>based</u> on the navy.

I think in [the] first place – that one source of confusion is a general belief that the navy is quite a modern institution. In Gardiner & Mullinger's excellent introduction to English History,[1] it is said, in so

---

[1] S.R. Gardiner and J.B. Mullinger, *English History for Students* (London, 1881).

many words that for the study of English Naval History <u>James</u> will be sufficient. Now James begins with the Wars of the French Revolution, 'though he has two or three pages touching of previous events. As he knew nothing of the early history he very properly did not write about it. Our naval history then – according to these distinguished writers began at the French Revolution. Gardiner, of course, knew much better, and lived to write and edit a good deal of detail concerning a much earlier period. Sir John Seeley wrote that our Naval History begins with Elizabeth, we had no navy before her time; and Lord Acton, in his delightful essay on Wolsey,[1] has put this prominently as <u>one</u> of the marks of Wolsey's greatness. He is indeed referring to Brewer,[2] a still greater authority, but the two are agreed. Acton's words are in effect, that when England was <u>small, poor</u> 'without dependencies and <u>without a fleet</u>' Wolsey, by the force of his solitary genius, raised the Kingdom to a position among the European nations not inferior to that which it now enjoys.

When this was the belief of the distinguished men that I have named, we cannot be surprised that smaller men and the writers of text-books have followed suit. And yet some of them must have seen the older maxim, dating back to the times of the Plantagenets that the navy was the wall and fence of the country, and you would have thought had asked How So! if there was no navy. The belief perhaps arose in an idea that the <u>navy</u> must be fully and exactly organised, that a body of ships not organised on something like modern lines, is not a navy. That I think is wrong. The navy, I take it, is the shipping of the country, capable of being arrested for aggression or defence, and that shipping is necessarily the shipping of the age. It is not to be compared or contrasted with the shipping of other ages. As well might we say that there was no navy before the reign of Edward VII because all the ships that fought at Trafalgar could not stand against one of King Edward's ironclads, as say we had no navy in the time of Elizabeth before the Armada, or in the time of Edward III for Sluys. The ships at Sluys, Gravelines or Trafalgar fought against ships of their own age, as the ships of George V will have to do, should occasion arise – that they will do their duty as well let us be assured.

[1] Cardinal Wolsey, Chief Minister of Henry VIII. See Acton's 'Wolsey and the Divorce of Henry VIII' in *Quarterly Review* (1877); reprinted in *Historical Essays and Studies* (London, 1907), pp. 1–64.

[2] John Sherren Brewer, editor of the *State Papers during the Reign of Henry VIII* (11 vols, Historical Manuscripts Commission, London, 1830–52).

269. *Mahan to Laughton*

Quogue, 14 May 1914

Your letter of April 24 arrived while we were in the midst of breaking up in New York, to return to our home here. Consequently, I did not attempt to reply at the time, nor even took the book out of its wrap until after my arrival here four days ago.[1] I am much obliged for it, and from title, and authors, not least your own, anticipate reading with pleasure.

I share the growing indisposition to work of which you speak; but as you are at an additional disadvantage – for such it is at our time of life – of being ten years older than I, probably I feel it as yet less. When stirred up to interest, I have little difficulty in undertaking and writing; but in default of this I tend to procrastinate. My mind now is pretty well made up to do no more distinctly naval writing. I cherish a project of a History of the United States from the point of view of national expansion – imperialism it is called here, in disparagement; but whether I can complete the undertaking is to me doubtful. I don't care as to that, provided it provides me with interested occupation for my remaining days. It is arranged that I am to spend next winter in Washington, at the request of the Carnegie Institute, to do research work in co-operation with it; and I propose to use the occasion for the above subject, as I am to have full discretion as to my work.

You will have seen that we have in part realized your wish for our intervention in Mexico, tho' I must regret that it was too late to hinder the severe affliction you here suffered, and for which I express my sympathy.[2] What will come of it all, I fail to foresee. The course of our government, so far as I can see, represents merely a curious idiosyncrasy of one exceptionally obstinate man, the President.[3] His obstinacy seems now, to me as an outside observer, to have been transmuted, by a not unnatural mental process, to violent personal obstinacy against Huerta[4] for having so long stood out against him. From the outside, judging by avowed motives, and external actions, it is to me a most curious instance of personal diplomacy as distinguished from national; the diplomacy of what the first Napoleon used to call an ideologist. The country is largely indifferent, supports the president as head of the nation, but I don't think there is real hearty confidence in his judgement in external relations.

---

[1] See fn. 1, p. 196.
[2] British lives were lost, and interests damaged during the civil unrest in Mexico.
[3] Woodrow Wilson (1856–1924); 24th President of the USA 1913–21.
[4] Victoriano Huerta (1854–1916); President of Mexico 1913–14.

270. *Draft Memorandum*[1]

2 June 1914

As I am asked to lecture next session on the 18th C. I am leaving a big gap and going to write up that as the basis of my lectures. If therefore, as is very possible and probable, I should never get back to the 16th C., Leo,[2] or whoever it may fall to to make this MS into publishing form must boil down and assimilate my several writings on the 16 and 17th C. As far as I can remember he may take.

> 16th C Royal Inst. Lecture 1888
> 'A Tercentenary Retrospect'
> (Essays II)[3]
> Introd. to *Defeat of Armada*
> Drake &c (Essays II)
> Chapt. in Vol.III of *Cambridge History*
> 'Howard' in *From Howard to Nelson*
> Arts. in *DNB*
> 17th C 'Sovereignty of the Sea' *E. R.* (Essays III)
> 'Last Years of the Protectorate' *E. R.* (Essays III)
> 'Pepys' – 'Jean de Witt' *E. R.* (Essays I)
> 'E. of Sandwich' *E .R.* Oct [19]12
> The proof slips are fuller.[4]
> 16 Chs. av. 4,500 – 5,000.

[*Various titles were projected*]

> 'The Navy's Place in the History of England' or
> 'The Interdependence of England's Naval and Political History'
> and 'The Dominance of the Navy in the History of England'

It is not the mere fact of England's being an island that has permitted our constitution to develop itself on purely national lines, and has enabled our rulers at all times to frame our policy in accordance with the national will. Easy access by water has more commonly had rather the opposite tendency, and has seemed to invite foreign interference or

---

[1]Note left with the manuscript of JKL's draft book.

[2]Leonard Carr-Laughton, his eldest son.

[3]These references are to the three volumes of bound-up essays that JKL prepared in the last decade of his life, as the basis for this project. They are now in the library of the Royal Military College, Kingston, Ontario, having been purchased by Professor Schurman.

[4]After publication JKL had amended the proof copies of these papers, and he advised Leonard to use them.

foreign aggression. What distinguishes the history of England from that of every other country with an extended seaboard is the action of our navy, intensified both by the geographical situation of the island, and by the absolute negation of access to it by land. It is the navy, in its weakness as in its strength, which has always been the determining factor in our domestic revolutions, and in our foreign relations, whether for peace or war.[1]

271.   *Bridge to Laughton*

6 July 1914

Several months ago I was informed that Colonel Desbrière[2] expected from the British authorities some recognition of his considerable services to our naval history. I at once brought this to the notice of the Admiralty and was told in reply, courteously but decidedly, that nothing could be done to meet the Colonel's wishes.

As far as my personal view goes I feel that Col. Desbrière has done very exceptional work in elucidating questions relating to the history of the British Navy and that recognition by authority of his work would be not only a graceful act, but also the payment of a debt due to him.

I will see if anything more can be done: but the former refusal to do anything was so decided that I do not look for a favourable result from an application.

I am delighted to hear that you are well: Ditto me.

272.   *Mahan[3] to Laughton.*

24 August 1914[4]

My reply of yours of the 5th has been delayed by the number of letters I have had pressing upon me. The report in *The Times* was of an interview; but, as this was by pre-arrangement, I prepared for it by writing out and having type-written my diagnosis of the political situation and of the series of immediate causes. Some conversation followed which the re-

---

[1]See Chapter 6 [276] for the draft, as it stood when JKL wrote this note, and for Leonard's attempt to follow his father's directions.

[2]Éduoard Desbrière, editor of two major texts: *Projets et tentatives de débarquement aux îles Britanniques 1793–1805* (5 vols, Paris, 1902) and *La Campagne Maritime de 1805: Trafalgar* (5 vols, Paris, 1907).

[3]This would be Mahan's last letter to JKL.

[4]War had broken out.

porter for the most part of got down rightly enough. I was non-committal on submarines and aero-planes, not because I have not opinions, but because after all only the test of war, which is now on, can give any reliable bases for estimate. It is to my mind very significant, that in the past moonless week no attempt by the Germans to torpedo has been reported. I can conceive no cause for delay, and it is to me imperative that they get rid of some of your best ships by these means. Otherwise, they can hope nothing from an open battle, because your superiority is too great; and, most important, even if they have success by land, it can scarcely be so decisive as to enable Germany to bear the wasting disorder of your blockade of the Elbe and the Weser. Sea Power I think will vindicate itself again, and exhaustion effect what possibly the Entente armies cannot. I am fairly puzzled for the German torpedo inaction, and have been inclined to ascribe [it] to the great superiority in torpedo vessels you and France can mass, with other cruisers, against all their exits, including Heligoland. In short, I attribute the immunity of your fleet to judicious scouting; both of the enemy's shores, and by outpost work around the battle-fleet. In case you are victorious, the re-cession of Heligoland should be a *sine qua non*. It has only military value, the loss cannot injure Germany financially and, despite the way Germany has behaved, I don't think it would be wise policy for Great Britain or France to weaken her permanently. The Slav peril would at once loom up.[1]

You will easily believe that my full sympathy goes with Great Britain. One of our papers has published in full Sir E. Grey's correspondence as given to Parliament; also the equivalent German account. But, besides kindred speech, I know G.B. stands essentially for freedom and for right, and that in so far (and further) our interests now are the same as yours.[2]

273. *Draft Obituary*[3]

Rear Admiral Mahan USN.

Amid the engrossing interest in and anxieties about the war every incident that does not relate to it, however serious in itself is dwarfed

[1]See Mahan's *The Problem of Asia* (Boston, 1900) for his thinking on race.

[2]It is almost uncanny that Mahan should, unknowingly, end his last letter to JKL with a summation of his ideology.

[3]This is a draft, compiled on the day JKL heard of Mahan's death, written on the back of a page from the MS of his unfinished book, and so closely written and full of abbreviations as to require editorial latitude. Those passages within square brackets are conjectures, based on a close reading of the text, attempts to unravel the characters and familiarity with the author's hand. The remainder is a fair transcript.

[by] the terrible losses recorded every day. The peaceful death of even personal friends is apt to escape notice; but whatever [the events] the sudden and unexpected death of Admiral Mahan[1] cannot be so passed over. For [as well as] a personal friend of the writer, for the last twenty years, he was a very great deal more; a man whose writings have had a most powerful effect on the policy of his own country, and on that of many others; so noted in the case of Germany, that it may be said, without pardon, that they are among the primary causes of the present war. Certainly Mahan when he first spoke, as lectures, and published in book form his *Influence of Sea Power Upon History* (1890) and a few years later his *Influence of Sea Power Upon the French Revolution and Empire* (1893) he had no thought of Germany, whose navy [those who wrote then] described as contemptible; he spoke and wrote for his own classes as a Professor at the United States Naval War College, and published for his own people, to convince them of their foolish error in turning their backs on the sea as they had done since the confirmation of the Union by the victory over the seceding states. Mahan adduced the evidence and the subject of History on the Influence of Sea Power [*sic*]. He and his publishers indeed calculated on the volumes attracting notice here in England, as indeed they did, though not at first, to the extent which he and they had hoped. Some few years later, I was told by Mahan himself that the first sale of *The Influence of Sea power Upon History* was disappointing; though well made up afterwards: in professional circles, the reception even from the first was enthusiastic. I remember one day, shortly after its appearance, [meeting] my old messmate Sir Vesey-Hamilton, the First Sea Lord of the Admiralty, in St. James' Park, and his stopping me, busy man as First Sea Lords must be, for a good quarter of an hour to talk over this interesting book. Its matter was not new: the historical details were often faulty, those of the battles inexact, but the picture of the influence, of the importance, of the effect of sea power was worked up [with] a vividness and power of language, [and] a wealth of illustration which was bound to carry conviction to any understanding mind. That was the discussion of we two, that day in St. James' Park, and that apparently was the decision of the Kaiser and such of his advisers as were competent to have an opinion. It is of course possible that they had had some such opinion before them, but if so, here it was confirmed with hitherto unknown power, and without any political intention, as far as Germans were concerned. The effect will be realised by a comparison of dates.

---

[1]Mahan had died in Washington on 1 December 1914. The sense of impending mortality that his death impressed upon JKL is all too obvious from this draft.

Mahan wrote many other books, a list of which would fill at least a column, but though they fully supported his reputation and perhaps made it more widely and popularly known, they have not really increased it. His last public utterance; as far as I know – was the report in the *Times* [5th of August last] of an interview on the 3rd. I wrote to Mahan, congratulating him upon it and discussing slightly some of the points in it. His reply – a letter dated 24th August is now before me. In it he says that the interview was pre-arranged and that he had his 'diagnosis' of the political situation and of the series of immediate causes 'written out' and typed. The report may properly be called a publication. The news of his death came to me this morning as a painful surprise. He was not to be called old, as men go now a days, and even for 74 he was slim and vigorous. In one of his recent letters, he spoke of walking, and swimming in the sea as a daily exercise and delight and spoke, in some detail, of certain literary projects, now also dead with their illustrious author.

One word in conclusion. Many years ago I was personally instructed by himself in the pronunciation of his name, which is not Mààn, or Màhãn – like the bleating of an anxious ewe, but Má hãn.

274. *Laughton to Walter Smith*[1]

7 February 1915

The Income Tax paper which came in yesterday from the College at £256.10.0d., for the year from April to April, that is ⅔ £250 & ½ £150. If it is calculated really from April to April, this is not correct (unfortunately for me) it should be ⅓ £250 & ⅔ £150 = but perhaps your calendar is to count from January to January which would make the count right. Will you pardon the ramblings of a doddering old man, & let me know if it is right.[2]

275. *Laughton to Walter Smith*

16 June 1915

The Navy Records Society is in difficulty about a room for its annual meeting, sometime about the end of the month, the United Services

---

[1]Walter Smith, Secretary of King's College (1895–1919).
[2]This, the last letter found in Laughton's own hand, is written in a tiny, cramped version of his original hand.

Institution which it usually has being occupied by the Government. Would it be possible for it to have its meeting in our Theatre.[1] I should be glad if you could let me have an answer at once, as we have a Council Meeting on next Monday to decide what is to be done.[2] Our meeting would only last about 40 minutes and would consist of perhaps not more than thirty or forty members.

p. G. E. L.[3]

replied 17 June.

[1]Meaning King's College's Theatre.
[2]The reply would appear to have been unfavourable; the Council Meeting on the 21st decided to hold the Annual Meeting at the home of John Murray, a Councillor.
[3]JKL's daughter, Grace E. Laughton, actually wrote the letter.

6

SIR JOHN KNOX LAUGHTON'S
UNFINISHED NAVAL HISTORY OF ENGLAND

Although he taught at King's College from 1885 to 1914, Laughton spent very little time actually teaching naval history; his work at the College was primarily of a general nature. The formation of the Federal University of London and the development of University-wide history teaching encouraged Professor Albert Pollard[1] of University College, who had worked with Laughton on the *Dictionary of National Biography*, to use his inaugural lecture to call for a post-graduate school. Among the subjects for study he placed naval history 'first and foremost'; Laughton was the expert to provide the teaching.[2] Although the amount of specialist and post-graduate teaching he was able to provide remained small, by 1910 Laughton believed the moment was right to establish naval history at King's College, within the University of London. He wanted to create a department that would prepare naval historians for an educational role in an expanding navy. Although he officially retired from his post at King's College in 1912, he remained a Professor of the University of London, and in 1913 and 1914 he gave, in line with college policy, public lecture courses, the first on 'English Naval History', 'Seapower and the Empire' and 'The Influence of the English Navy in the Eighteenth Century'. These were in addition to his regular teaching.[3] His theme was constant: because Britain was an island, unlike the continental states of Europe, the navy was central to the history of the nation, and explained the unique political and military institutions of the country. Furthermore, the navy was far older and far more important than was generally recognised.[4] Despite resigning his chair in 1912, at the same time that he resigned as Secretary of the Navy Records Society, he had been

---

[1]Albert Pollard (1869–1943) later founded the Institute of Historical Research where the 'Naval and Military Room', both in itself, and in the order in which the names were given, marked his sense of the importance of Laughton's subject.

[2]For Pollard's original lecture see: *Foundations*, 212–13.

[3]College Calendar, King's College, London: 1913–14 and 1914–15. F.J. Hearnshaw, *The Centenary History of King's College, London* (London, 1929), p. 459. Cuttings from *The Times*, LGH 41.

[4]Lecture Notes, 8 October 1913 [268].

pressed to continue lecturing.[1] He agreed, and did so until Christmas 1914. He struggled on in the gathering gloom of failing eyesight, finding the London traffic impossible after dark. His principal reason for continuing was to secure the establishment of the Department of Naval History. In 1913 he produced a significant historiographical paper for the International History Congress in London. It dealt with the period down to the mid-nineteenth century, and was designed to warn future scholars against ignoring the role of the navy in history.[2] When he composed this paper Laughton was also writing a textbook, 'The Navy's Place in the History of England', but he was hampered by age, infirmity and the continued demand for lectures. Reflecting a lifetime's learning and insight, the book was based on his articles, reviews and *DNB* entries, which he collected, catalogued and bound into three stout volumes.[3] Aware that time was running out, Laughton prepared his manuscript and notes in June 1914 so that the book could be completed by his son Leonard, who was directed to use specific papers from the bound collection.[4]

Sadly, Laughton only completed two draft chapters, and the fragment of a third. They covered the period from 1066 to the death of Henry VIII, a total of 15,000 words. The manuscript is far from being a simple history of the navy. Here it stands in marked contrast to any extant work, including Clowes's seven heavy volumes, because it has a clear theme, and links naval activity to the wider context rather than descending into the details. It is the work of a fine historian. Unlike other scholars in the field, Laughton had mastered the wider context of his subject, and consciously pushed naval history into the academic mainstream, emphasising the significance of naval success, and naval failure, in the history of England. The major theme was naval defence against invasion, which was still being debated as he wrote,[5] and Laughton took care to explain the link between naval success, as opposed to mere stress of weather, and the failure of hostile efforts. The manuscript is peppered with Laughton's characteristic insight and humour, along with his prejudices and moral judgements. It still reads well and would, if completed, have made a major contribution to the

[1]Laughton to Charles Napier Robinson, 10 December 1912 (NMM: Napier Robinson MS).

[2]Temperley to Laughton, 15 March 1913 [265]. JKL, 'Historians and Naval History' in J.S. Corbett (ed.), *Naval and Military Essays* (Cambridge, 1913).

[3]These are now in the Library of the Royal Military College, Kingston, Ontario, having been purchased in London in the 1960s by Professor Schurman.

[4]MS Note of 2 June 1914 with the manuscript chapters of the projected book [270].

[5]A.J. Marder, *From the Dreadnought to Scapa Flow* (5 vols, Oxford, 1961–70), vol. I, pp. 344–57.

promotion of naval history in the university sector. The best work being published at the turn of the twenty-first century shares the same ambition, and not infrequently some of the insights, that Laughton first deployed. No other document so clearly demonstrates the scope of his ambition, or recaptures those ideas which he conveyed to his contemporaries.

As a life-long writer of textbooks Laughton believed he could achieve far more to promote the study of naval history with a good textbook than with narrow monographs which would be read only by those already interested. Despite his efforts, the College, which was expanding the range of its interests and departments throughout this period, did not create the department he sought.[1]

Leonard approached Oxford University Press in 1925,[2] and they expressed some interest in the manuscript, but aside from a few marginal notes, nothing more was done with the text. In this section all matter enclosed in square brackets, including footnotes, are editorial insertions. The remainder is original. Amendments by Leonard have been ignored.

276. *'The Interdependence of England's Naval and Political History'*

[Chapter] II: 1066–Edward 1[3]

The changes brought about in England by the forcible intrusion of the Normans were numerous, and to the former inhabitants – Saxons, Angles or Anglo-Danes – were exceedingly distasteful; but among them all, the one of most importance, the one whose advantages, as they appear to posterity, may be held to outweigh all the misery and suffering caused by the others, was the unification of the country. England was no longer a mere geographical expression including a number of independent political units, which in name acknowledged, but in effect denied the overlordship of the West Saxon King. The Norman king, with a powerful nucleus of Norman soldiers at his command, was able, in the course of a few years, to impress on the whole country, the acceptance of a real sovereignty in place of a barren suzerainty. His methods might be brutal; from the point of view of eleventh century Englishmen, they undoubtedly were so; but they made England one in a sense that no English or West Saxon king had been able to approach.

---

[1]Hearnshaw, p.469.
[2]Leonard Laughton to Humphrey Milford, publisher at the University Press, 29 May 1925 (NMM: LGH 37).
[3][JKL did not write Chapter I.]

The task, however, fully occupied him, & the threat of foreign inter-ference found him unprepared. It was quite out of his power to offer any opposition to an enemy by sea, and it is possible that he did not realise how absolute was the security which might be obtained in that way. Harold's attempt to get it had, indeed, delayed him for some weeks, but in the end, had so utterly broken down, that it may well have seemed to him a mere pious wish, good in theory but futile in practice, and in any case, calling for much longer and more costly preparation than he could give it.

Accordingly, in 1069, when Harold and Cnut, sons of the then King of Denmark, with a numerous fleet and a large force of adventurers from the Baltic, ranged along the coast of England, entered the Humber and called the Anglo-Danes of Yorkshire to arms, the revolt was crushed and the invaders driven back to their ships by the army which William brought up from the south. It was then that, at once to punish the rebels and to convince them of the inexpediency of supporting any similar invasion in the future, the king had Yorkshire laid waste with a persist-ent thoroughness whose marks remained for many decades as a terrible evidence of the Norman's fierce and unscrupulous determination.

So again in 1085, when the King of Denmark, in conjunction with the Count of Flanders, collected a fleet, with a view to reconquering England, the preparations to repel him were entirely on shore, and involved, on the one hand, the bringing over, at a vast expense, a large force of mercenaries – men of Brittany, Maine and other parts, and on the other, the laying waste a broad strip of the East Anglian coast, on which the enemy was expected to land. The Danish king, however, was assassinated, the coalition broke up and the invasion was not even attempted; but William had realised the danger of his position and being – it would seem – unable to provide any defence by sea, or very probably unwilling entirely to trust English sailors, his administrative measures, culminating in the compilation of Doomsday Book and in the Oath of Salisbury, rendered impossible the development in England of anything resembling the feudal system of France, which amid anar-chy and rapine was there met by the institution of the Peace of God, but was never known in England save in the wretched days of Stephen.

With this the Danish invasions came to an end; and so long as Normandy and Brittany were in the hands of English kings, with Flan-ders more or less a vassal state, there could be no apprehension of any dangerous attacks from beyond sea. Meantime, for occasional service – such as the suppression of piracy or the enforcement of trade restric-tions – and in addition to a few ships built expressly for such work, a small navy was organised out of the shipping along the south coasts of

Kent and Sussex clustering round what then became and have ever since been known as the Cinque Ports, five towns which were granted, in return, many and peculiar privileges. It was, indeed, then and always claimed that every ship in the kingdom, as much as every able bodied man, was liable to be arrested for the king's service; but through several centuries the ships of the Cinque Ports were effectively the Royal Navy of England.

During this state of relative peace, maritime commerce increased enormously, and with it, the size of ships – ships built primarily for carrying merchandise, but converted into ships of war by the simple process of putting on board of them a body of soldiers and ample supply of stones. These last, thrown out of the tops on to the decks of an enemy's ship, and seconded by missiles discharged, at a lower level, from slings, cross bows or long bows, were very effective in clearing the way for the soldiers to pass on board and finish the matter off with sword or mace. But during the reign of Henry II and Richard I, when the coast of France as far as Bayonne was subject to the English King, there could be no war at sea. A threatening bond between the powers of the east coast of the North Sea was impossible, and the English Channel and the Bay of Biscay were English waters in the same sense that the Bristol Channel and the Irish Sea may be called so now; the English king might, with all propriety, claim them as part of his kingdom. A navy was wanted not for war against a foreign foe, but for occasional police duty and for the transport of troops to France or Ireland.

There are thus *prima facie* grounds for accepting the statement that in the very beginning of his reign, King John did actually, by proclamation, claim the Dominion, or, as it has been more commonly called, the Sovereignty of the Sea, although the text of the proclamation – if it ever existed – has been lost, and the territorial conditions which warranted it were almost immediately changed, so that for the next hundred years it remained a dead letter, whilst the necessity of naval defence was brought prominently to the front.

Within a couple of years, the opposite coast of the Channel fell into the hands of an enemy, and the same objection to an Angevin ruler which caused the Normans to yield a ready submission to a French invader, made them also active supporters of his further designs and eager to undertake another conquest of England.[1]

We are not here called on to consider whether John was that unadulterated monster of iniquity which the spite of monkish chroniclers has portrayed; it is at least certain that he was not that fatuous compound of

[1][The French conquest of Normandy.]

imbecility, cowardice and sloth which they have described, and that, whatever faults he may have had, he was able to understand, with remarkable clearness, the advantage he would derive from being powerful at sea.

It was thus that, from the very first, he paid great attention to providing a strong and effective fleet, so that in 1212 he was able to bring a cruel pressure on the Prince of North Wales, by what was, in modern language, a strict blockade, cutting off the assistance which he had hoped to derive from the Irish Danes; and when the King of France, acting on the Pope's suggestion, was preparing to invade England, he was able – in every sense of the word – to prevent the blow by sending over to the Norman coast a fleet which, at Barfleur, at Harfleur, at Fécamp, captured and burnt or brought away a considerable number of French ships and finished off by burning Dieppe. He may have judged that this turning of the tables would stimulate Philip – Philip Augustus the King of France – to greater exertions; to be beforehand with him, he ordered a general arrest of ships. This was the basis of his military preparation to meet the coming danger; his political [intention] was – as is familiarly known – to break up the overwhelming coalition against him by submitting to the Pope, who now, recognising John as a vassal, ordered Philip to desist from his hostile measures.

As Philip, with great trouble and at great expense, had got together a large fleet – to the number, it is said, of 1700 ships – he was unwilling to do this, and wished to go on with the undertaking. His vassals, however, were timorous about disobeying the Pope's order, but readily assented to a proposal to punish Ferdinand, the Count of Flanders, who, though a near connection of the French king, had not only refused to join the expedition, but had concluded a treaty of alliance with John. The French army accordingly marched into Flanders, and with little or no opposition, took and sacked Bruges – then the most wealthy town in Western Europe – and laid siege to Ghent.

The fleet, which had, in the first instance, been mustered in the *embouchure* of the Seine, went round to the Swyn, where, in the harbour of Damme – then the sea-port of Bruges – they seized and despoiled the merchant ships rich with the wares of the East; after which – no danger being expected – they landed the fighting men, who joined the army before Ghent.

Meanwhile Ferdinand had appealed to John, who got ready a fleet, not indeed of 1700 ships, but a more efficient one of – it is said – 500; probably of a much smaller number. As, however, they were got together to dispute Philip's passage and invasion, we may assume that – according to the standard of the age – they were on a war footing, and that the French ships, intended rather for mere transport service, were not altogether so. The English fleet, commanded by John's illegitimate brother the Earl of Salisbury, went over at once to the Flemish coast, and finding the French fleet deserted by its fighting men and crowding the harbour of and river approach of Damme, captured a large number of ships laden with their valuable plunder and burnt a great many of the rest.

Before the work was finished, the French army, hastily raising the siege of Ghent, came to defend their fleet. The English troops, insignificant in point of numbers, could offer no resistance on shore and did not attempt it; but the French were not able to prevent them getting on board their ships and leaving the river, which they did without material loss. With their prizes they went over to the opposite coast and lay at the Isle of Walcheren, waiting to attack the French fleet, still numerically formidable, when it put to sea. Philip, however, had – it has been said – lost the control of his temper, or else –which seems more probable – he judged that, with its reduced numbers and inferior equipment, the fleet would not be able to meet the English on equal terms and was afraid of its falling into their hands. He ordered it to be burnt, and the whole armament was thus destroyed – with the exception that is, of those ships which had been taken out by the English and were actually brought to England, greatly, it would appear, to the benefit of John's exchequer. 'Never' says a contemporary poet, 'came such wealth into England since King Arthur came to conquer it'.

For the time, the project of invasion was completely stopped, and if the coalition which John had formed had had the good success which, not without warrant – he had hoped, the story of his reign would have been very different. As it was, the French victory at Bouvines (July, 1214) falsified his expectations, and left him, a defeated soldier and discredited politician, to make what terms he could with his domestic enemies. The result was Magna Carta, June 15, 1215.

It may be conceded that, in a false and unscrupulous age, John was false and unscrupulous, but above all, he was resourceful. The greater number of the barons were quite as false, quite as unscrupulous, but had neither the king's ready wit nor his resourceful ability. The more honest of their body separated from the others, and the remnant, insolent in their triumph and greedy in their use of it, almost forced a renewal of the struggle upon the king who was now better prepared for it. The Pope annulled the charter and absolved the king from his oath, and he, by bringing over some thousands of Flemish mercenaries was able to meet his enemies with a force which threatened their speedy subjection to his will.

In this extremity they applied to France for assistance. They believed they could count on Philip; but to make sure, they offered the crown – of which John was to be deprived – to Louis the Dauphin, whose marriage to Blanche of Castile – daughter of John's sister Eleanor – gave him, according to feudal ideas, a sort of claim to be John's successor; or at least, permitted the barons to speak of him, for the occasion, as one of the royal family. Philip would not put himself in open opposition to the Pope; but privately he approved of the Dauphin's acceptance of the offer, and permitted him to levy troops for the new conquest of England. As the attempt proved altogether futile, many of our historians have passed it over as a mere incident of the civil war, in itself of little importance, and which could not have had any other result than failure. French writers have attached more serious value to it; and indeed it seems quite certain that Louis and his father fully intended it as a conquest of England, which was to be reduced to a province of France.

Following the precedent set by William the Conqueror, whose pretended claim bore some resemblance to that now put forward, Louis, whilst calling on the service of his own vassals, the barons of Artois, promised lands in England to such other French barons as should accompany him. There were plenty of adventurers ready to stake life against a fortune, and Louis had at his command an army which, if landed in England in its entirety, might have turned the war altogether in favour of the rebellious nobles. But Louis was not William, and John was a very different man from Harold. By means of castles scattered broadcast over the country, he held England with a grip such as Harold could scarcely have conceived: he maintained a large force of mercenaries – professional soldiers; and – what was still more to the purpose – he could assemble a large fleet organised in a manner infinitely superior to that of the crowd of ships which Harold got together in the summer of 1066. It was not, indeed, able to prevent the landing of detachments of French soldiers sent in advance to relieve the pressing need of the barons, but it sufficed to cause the utter failure of the main attempt – a failure which, like many others, has been frequently attributed to a mere accident of the weather.

Louis had collected his transports – to the number of, as stated, about 800 – at Calais, under the command of a notorious pirate, Eustace an unfrocked monk, who, after the French conquest of Normandy, had for some time adhered to the party of John, but afterwards, making his peace with Philip, had rendered his name terrible to the English by his savage raids on the south coast. His daring and success pointed him out to Louis for the command of his expedition, but as an admiral his good fortune forsook him. It might, perhaps, be said that he was wanting in the qualities that make for a good commander in chief. Through the earlier weeks of May, 1216, the transports assembled at Calais, were unable to put to sea on account of the presence or immediate neighbourhood of the English fleet, which had its headquarters at Dover and Sandwich. On the 19th this was compelled by a strong northerly wind, to raise the blockade and draw back to Dover or other ports to the westward. Eustace, apparently did not understand the meaning of this; it was sufficient for him that the passage was clear, and he seized the chance.

On the evening of the 20th the French fleet put to sea and almost immediately found itself in the clutches of a violent gale from the north, which sent many of the transports, with all on board, to the bottom, hurled others on the coast of France, drove most of them back to Calais, and barely permitted the Dauphin, with seven of his ships to make Stonar in the Isle of Thanet – a very different arrival from what might have been if the English fleet had allowed Eustace to put to sea in fine weather. The rest is familiar history. It is not for me to follow the various incidents of the war which was continued after the death of John, until the defeat of the Dauphin at Lincoln, May 20th, 1217 rendered it necessary for him to procure immediately reinforcements both of men and more especially of military stores. His wife, Blanche, persuaded her not unwilling father in law to provide these, and they were put on board a fleet of some 80 or 100 ships which sailed from Calais, again under the command of Eustace the Monk, on August 24, 1217.

It was fine summer weather, and with a fresh southerly wind the fleet made for the North Foreland, intending – as Sandwich was held in force by the royal troops – to go up the Thames and join Louis at London. But as they passed to the north of the South Foreland, Hubert de Burgh, the Warden of the Cinque Ports, put to sea from Dover with a hastily raised fleet of 30 or 40 ships, armed only for the occasion, many of them very small – and, with the advantage of the wind, fell on the French rear. The ships in the French van, being dead to leeward, could offer no assistance, and the whole fleet was destroyed piece-meal; some half a dozen ships only escaped. Eustace, as a pirate, renegade and traitor, was summarily beheaded; the nobles and knights were reserved for ransom, and the rest, who had no money value, were thrown overboard, according to the custom of the age, the ships and the inanimate part of their cargo remaining the prize of the victors.

This was the decisive battle of the war and virtually put an end to it. It not only destroyed the reinforcements, which Louis was sorely in need of and which it might be difficult or even impossible to replace, but it also brought home to him the fact, not yet fully understood, that it was a most foolhardy thing to attempt to carry troops over the sea, unless the military command of the route had been secured. And this the French were not able to secure. There were plenty of ships in France, plenty also of capable sailors, but organisation and leaders seem to have been wanting, and Eustace, unfrocked monk and cruel pirate as he was, was quite incompetent as an admiral.

There has been a certain unwillingness to admit the decisive nature of this battle off Sandwich, as if it was unreasonable to believe that the fighting of a parcel of cock-boats could really have any serious significance. But as I have already pointed out, the ships of any age are the ships of that age only, and cannot be valued in comparison with ships of a later century; and in this instance the decisive nature of the battle is clearly shown by tabulating the dates, thus:–

The Fair of Lincoln	May 20, 1217
The Battle of Sandwich	August 24, 1217
Louis, in London, receives the news	August 26
Louis opens negotiations	August 28
Treaty signed at Lambeth	September 11

It is evident that the battle of Sandwich was the determining cause of the treaty.

For the next hundred and twenty years there was no overt thought of another French conquest of England. Occasional disputes there were, such as were bound to come so long as the English king held some of France's richest provinces, but they were fought out on French soil, their sphere of the disputes being practically limited to the disputed territory; but on the whole Henry III and Louis IX (Saint Louis) were fairly good friends, and when the civil war in England broke out, Louis was quite willing to allow his wife to assist her sister – the wife of Henry – in collecting French mercenary soldiers and French ships for the service of Henry in England. But for some reason – it would be difficult to say why – the Cinque ports were altogether opposed to the royalist faction; and in face of their opposition, Queen Eleanor and her ships and the troops which she had engaged, remained at Calais. Time slipped away: the Queen's money was exhausted; the troops disbanded, and the English dispute – as to the merits of which we are not here concerned – was decided chiefly by the English to whom it belonged.

The respective sons of Henry and Louis – Edward I and Philip III (le Hardi) – continued in amity; but it seems to have been quite well understood that this was always uncertain, that the equilibrium, so to speak, was unstable, and it gave way in the reign of Philip IV (le Bel), when a bitter quarrel sprang up between the two kings which may properly be called the immediate herald of the Hundred Years' War. The direct occasion of it was rather trade rivalry than national jealousy, though both were involved; between the ships of the Cinque Ports, the Norman Ports and Bordeaux there were many skirmishes, which culminated in a fierce fight off St Mahé in Brittany (May 15, 1293) between an Anglo-Gascon fleet on the one hand and a Norman fleet on the other; the Normans were completely defeated and the Anglo-Gascons came back to Portsmouth with their prizes and much booty.

Naturally each king laid the blame of this aggravated breach of the peace on the subjects of the other, and Philip, as Edward's lord in France, summoned him to appear before him, and answer for the piracy and misdeeds of the Gascons. The negotiation that followed, the trickery and wiles of Philip, the blind credulity of Edward's brother who represented him in Paris are fully described in all our histories; it is unnecessary to speak of them here or to say more than that the whole business emphasises the real ineffectiveness of any claim to the Sovereignty of even the English Channel, when the king's police were quite unequal to hinder rival traders from openly flying at each other's throats.

And yet Edward had at his disposal a small navy which elsewhere was rendering him excellent service, as, first, in the celebrated Welsh War of 1277. Every one knows that Wales was first brought into real subjection by Edward I, and the details of his conquest have been excellently worked out by Dr J.E. Morris;[1] but so inveterate is the habit of the average man to find in a book only what he looks for, that comparatively few of his readers have realised how entirely the result was brought about by the skilful use which Edward made of his little navy. The difficulty of a hostile advance into Snowdonia had been manifested over and over again; twice had Henry II been repulsed from the mountains; John had tried it and failed; and had then devised a method which he had been other ways prevented from giving full effect to; now, improving on it, Edward practically invented a plan which can properly be described as the dawn of new possibilities in the art of war.

The failures of his ancestors and his own experiences as Earl of Chester, in 1256–7, had taught him the danger of plunging blindly into the entanglements of forests and hills, from which the Welsh – avoiding battle – would swoop down on the flanks or rear of a baggage-encumbered line of march. He resolved therefore, to march by the coast without a baggage train, resting for his supplies on the ships which

[1][J.E. Morris (ed.), *The Welsh Wars of Edward I* (Oxford, 1901).]

were to accompany him. And so, having ordered a number of the ships of the Cinque Ports, with others from Southampton and Bayonne, to go round to the Dee, he started from Chester as his base, August 1277, moved slowly and steadily – securing his way as he went – to Flint, to Rhuddlan, to Conway. At each of these places he constructed strong fortifications, mostly of timber brought by the ships, and from them dominated the neighbouring country. Llewellyn retired to the mountains; but when Edward, by the aid of his ships occupied Anglesey, cut the hay and corn – which Llewellyn had meant for his own people and their cattle – and employed them for the sustenance of the English army, the game was up. By the end of August Llewellyn offered to surrender; and though the negotiations were drawn out for a couple of months, in the hope of some happy change of fortune, the Welsh were at length forced by lack of food to come down from their hills, and the treaty of Conway was signed on November 9.

It was not to be of long duration. Within five years (1282), the Welsh prince was again in arms, but was subdued by a repetition of the strategy of 1277, the ships of the Cinque Ports, assisted, apparently, by a number of coasting vessels, very useful for transport being brought round as a floating and moveable base. The death of Llewellyn in the following year, at the battle of Orewyn Bridge put the seal on the conquest; although again in 1294–5, there was a dangerous outbreak, in the course of which the king was shut up in the castle of Conway, suffering much hardship, till relieved by ships from Bristol and Dublin. It was not of course by the navy that Wales was directly subdued, but it was only the action of the navy that made the work of the army possible, and it is just this which the casual reader is so apt to overlook.

What Edward had done in Wales he repeated in Scotland, when called, by the rising in 1296, to lead an army north of the Tweed. A fleet, collected in the first instance in the Tyne, moved north and co-operated in the siege and capture of Berwick, and accompanying the army in its march, was with it at Dunbar, in the Forth, at Aberdeen, Banff and Elgin. The ease with which the march was carried out without exciting the active hostility of the Scots, has often been commented on. The absence of this hostility has been taken as the cause instead of the effect; for the army being amply supplied with provisions had no necessity to plunder and, by Edward's care, was kept well in hand. Far from giving him no opportunity of showing his generalship, the bloodless conquest was the result of generalship of a high order and of a strategy of which he may be called the inventor.

In his later campaigns against Scotland he was again supported by a numerous fleet, and thus operations and marches were rendered possible which could otherwise not have been attempted, or only with heavy loss. It was a strategy which he had in view up to the last, and whether his final advance into Scotland was on the east side or the west; he had prepared a fleet to attend his march. He died before the advance, which was not made.

[Chapter] III: 1307–1485

Edward I is frequently called the Greatest of the Plantagenets; sometimes even the greatest of English kings. His son and successor might properly be called the least; Edward II must be the despair of apostles of heredity and professors of eugenics. We have fortunately nothing to do here with his general worthlessness and incompetence; we are concerned only with the strength of his government at home and the strength of his kingdom abroad. From the point of view so taken, Edward II appears as one of the most incompetent of our kings; and as such he righteously suffered the fate of other incompetents; which is not saying that in each and every case the regicides were actuated by righteous motives. That is quite another question.

Every child has read of the terrible mess which the political methods of Edward II got him into; he has also read of the disgraceful end of his one great military enterprise, without perhaps seeing that it was disgraceful, that it was not due entirely to the surpassing genius of Robert Bruce, but very largely and indeed principally to Edward's neglect of his father's methods, alike in politics and in war, and especially, so far as we are here concerned, to his neglect to use his navy in the way his father had shown him. With an army wanting consolidation, organisation and discipline; with an enormously exaggerated baggage train and with the time limit perilously shortened, he plunged into the enemy's country, with the result that forced marches exhausted the strength of his troops and they arrived in front of the enemy, beaten almost before the battle began. The neglect of every reasonable precaution by Edward; the experience and able tactics of Bruce did the rest, and the English army was quickly in headlong and panic stricken flight.

It was well for the Scots that they won that great battle; it was perhaps still better for the English that they lost it, and lost it in a manner so disgraceful that the memory of it must have clung to them through the rest of their lives, an effectual check on any undue self confidence, a perpetual reminder of the need of care, order and discipline. Many of the men who fled from Bannockburn may, thirty years later, have seen the French similarly flying from Cressy; and would be able, and we may be sure, willing to impress the double lesson – more specially the latter – on their sons or their sons sons. At the date of Bannockburn (June 24, 1314) Edward III (b. Nov. 13, 1312) was an infant; but as he grew into boyhood and adolescence, he must have heard tales of the glories of his grandfather, which his eager young mind would contrast with the silence as to the deeds of his own father, of which – not impossibly – he heard something from his mother.

This, however, is presumption. What is certain is that he, as if by instinct, waged war in the manner pointed out by his grandsire; that the English army which fought at Duppelin Moor (August 12, 1332) was carried by ship from the Humber to Kinghorn on the coast of Fife; that the army which was besieging Berwick in the early summer of 1333 was resting on and supported by the fleet; and that both Duppelin Moor and Halidon Hill (July 19, 1333) were fought and won on the tactics which Edward I had brought into play at Falkirk and which were to be still further developed at Cressy and in other battles in France.

On shore, active war with Scotland was ended by the battle of Halidon Hill; but at sea, it continued with much vigour, nor had the English by any means all their own way. French ships and Flemish ships, in very considerable numbers, joined the Scotch; and destructive raids on the coast of England, leading again to bloody retaliation on the coasts of France or Flanders – a state of things which we are too much accustomed to ignore when discussing the causes of the Hundred Years' War.

There is of course much to consider as to questions of Flemish trade and the danger of allowing France to establish her sovereignty in the Low Countries: much, very much, as to lands held in France by the English king; and there can be no doubt that these had great weight in bringing French and Flemish ships to support the quarrel of the Scots; but it is quite certain that the direct war with France beginning in 1337 grew out of the indirect war, waged in gradually increasing bitterness during the previous four years. It is too, very commonly forgotten that, though, after 1337, the war with France fills the stage, the war with Scotland still went on, and Scottish ships in alliance with French, gave the English as much as they could do. The struggle, which had seemed to our historians as waiting on Flemish, German and papal negotiations and on Edward's poverty or ineptitude, was – in fact – being ruthlessly waged at sea; the Channel Islands and the South coast of England were being cruelly raided by French ships or squadrons; England was being taught what might be the lot of a country in which the enemy was dominant. The counter raids of the English were no doubt as cruel, though no towns at all equal to Portsmouth or Southampton fell to them, and the French believed that the advantage of this cross raiding was entirely with them.

I am not here examining the policy or diplomacy of the contending governments, but I may say, as a matter of familiarly known fact, that both of them sought the aid of the Italian maritime powers – Genoa and Venice, and that a considerable Genoese contingent joined the French, bringing to them not only the increased numerical strength but – what might have been much more important – some insight into the old discipline and tactics which had never wholly died out in the Mediterranean.

By the end of 1338, the French king, Philip VI (of Valois) conceived that the time had come for striking a decisive blow, and he suggested to the Normans – who formed the great bulk of his navy – that they should attempt the invasion and conquest of England. The Normans were as ready to try this now as they had been under Philip II; it was no fault of theirs that it had not been done then; it should be done now as it had been under the Conqueror. In spirit, though not in actual words, they were singing –

'Où le père a passé passera bien l'enfant'
[where the father went, so too the son].

What was more to the immediate purpose, they collected ships and stores and prepared a mighty armament, intended to be under the immediate command of John, the king's son, at that time Duke of Normandy.

Throughout the year 1339 the cross raiding continued as before, and there were many little fights, of the details of which we know next to nothing. And on shore Edward's main work was cultivating the alliance of Ghent and the personal friendship of Jacob van Artevelde, to whose suggestion is attributed his formal assumption of the title and arms of the King of France, on January 25th, 1340. He then went back to England, promising to return by midsummer; and to prevent this, Philip sent the fleet which was preparing for the invasion of England, with a Genoese and – apparently – a Spanish contingent added, to waylay the English arrival at Sluys. Edward had timely information of this, and also mustered a considerable fleet, with which he arrived off Sluys on the morning of Midsummer day, Feast of St. John the Baptist; and there and then was fought this great battle – by far the most important for England in the five centuries following the Norman conquest.

But we can say little more; the details are hopelessly confused, and the chroniclers have been guilty of every conceivable sin both of omission and commission. We are sure, for instance, that cannon were present in both fleets, and presumably employed; but they are not mentioned by a single writer of the age – as if they were held to be black magic, altogether too shameful to be spoken of by a God fearing Christian. On the other hand, we know that the English attacked from the north, between eleven o'clock and noon; but every chronicler describes them as having waited till that time so as to have the advantage of the sun – which did not consist of having a noon-day June sun in the faces of the archers and slingers.

Everything else is equally vague or equally incorrect; the numbers are only to be guessed at; but we are perhaps not very far wrong if we say that the French had about 250 ships, more rather than less, and the English about 200, less rather than more; that the average number of men in each was about 100, and that the armament was roughly equal, though the force, the skill and the rapid shooting of the long bow told in favour of the English. Of the part played by the cannon we are quite in the dark; all that we are absolutely certain of is that after fighting till nightfall, the English won a complete victory; the French fleet was almost entirely destroyed, some 30 ships only making their escape, and these almost entirely Genoese; the English being too weary to pursue. The rest were all captured or sunk; their crews held to ransom, put to the sword or thrown overboard, to the number of not fewer than 20,000 – possibly more. Of the loss of the English it is impossible to speak. French writers have put it at 10,000; but there is really no authority for the statement and it should remembered that in medieval as in ancient battles, the carnage that now seems so shocking, fell mostly on the defeated, after the fighting was over.

It is not, however, the arithmetic, one way or another, that gives the battle its extreme importance. That comes from its effect on the destinies of the two nations; and primarily from the fact that it gave the keynote to the whole war. It put into the hands of the English king power to take the military command of the narrow seas; and this he did steadily, if slowly, during the years immediately following.

The truces which our histories record, had little effect at sea; there fighting went on almost continuously, and – though the story of it is lost in obscure and contradictory tales of impossible victories or equally impossible defeats – the result shows that it confirmed the decision given at Sluys; for the time being the French naval force was utterly destroyed; and then – that is, after ten years hard fighting – the war had liberty to develop on the lines with which we are all so familiar; that is, it was waged in France, not, as Philip and the Normans had intended, in England; they were French homesteads that were burnt, not English; French cattle that were slaughtered, French crops that were trodden down, French women and children on whom the horrors of war fell; the English armies were composed of trained soldiers commanded by skilled officers, whilst the French were composed of raw, half-armed peasants, officered by men who had no quality of the soldier but his personal courage; and the results, primarily due to the victory Sluys, are written large in the annals of both nations. Cressy is a mere corollary of Sluys.

It has been said that Edward never understood this; that to him, Sluys was a mere display of chivalry; the scouring of the seas were as courses in a tournament. Such an idea is quite contradicted by Edward's own letters at the time and his achievement in the years that followed. What he caused to be written is of greater authority, what he did is better evidence than the mere hearsay of any chronicle; and no record can possibly be equal to the official one which remains to this day and can be seen by anyone at the British Museum – among other places – the gold noble of 1344, showing the King, with crown, sword and shield, standing in a ship; the armed majesty of the country resting on its navy.[1]

On the other hand we are permitted to believe that from the battle of Sluys and the course of the war thereby ordered, came the troubles of France, not only then but through many centuries – the despotic character of the monarchy, the privileges of the nobles, the oppressive incidence of taxation, the Revolution, the Reign of Terror. It is not for me here to trace this result in detail; it is enough if I indicate the line of thought.

The map will show those who do not know the locality that Calais, as a sea-port, offered exceptional facilities to the English, either in peace or war, for landing merchandise or landing troops, and that it was therefore very desirable for the English to possess it. This had been generally accepted as the reason for Edward laying siege to it, as soon as the victory at Cressy permitted him to do so – It has been ignored or forgotten that Calais, far from being the innocent, harmless trading post that it is sometimes represented, had been for many years an insolent and noxious nest of pirates; and that, only eight years before, several English fishermen, taken prisoners and brought there, had been most brutally mutilated, marched through the town as a public exhibition and then put to death. There is no difficulty in believing that there was much righteous indignation or vengeance in Edward's determination to take the place, as there was of warlike or commercial expedience.

At that date it was almost impossible to take a well-fortified, well-guarded town except by blockade and Edward was not long in realising that the blockade of Calais by land only would be utterly useless. His command of the sea enabled him to make the blockade effective, and

---

[1] [This was the emblem JKL selected for the NRS in 1893. It appears on the cover of this volume.]

for this purpose an enormous fleet was mustered from all the ports of England, to the number of 700 ships, manned by 14,000 sailors, exclusive of such soldiers as it was expedient to put on board when hand fighting was to be expected. During the first months of the siege a few victuallers from time to time succeeded in bringing in a little relief to the imprisoned garrison, but when the ships were gathered, when the blockade was fairly closed, the fate of the town was sealed. After enduring the horrors of war, famine and pestilence for nearly twelve months, it surrendered in the early days of August 1347, and remained in English hands for 200 years, an unbearable danger to France in time of war, a cause of extreme fiscal embarrassment or commercial loss in time of peace.

The conquest of Normandy took away from the French king all immediate possibility of restoring his power at sea and drove him to seek for help in other countries. Castile, as a government, was in amity with both belligerents; and being moreover, busy with intestine troubles, was in no condition to give help to either; but there were rejected offshoots of the royal family ready for any adventure that promised fame and booty. One of these, Don Luis de la Cerda, had commanded French squadrons in the years after Sluys, and had won distinction by his attacks on the English coast; and now, his brother, Don Carlos de la Cerda, got together a goodly number of ships which sailed in the autumn of 1349, nominally on a trading voyage to Flanders.

It would seem to have been altogether a private venture, and the Spanish historians know nothing about it; but neither then, nor at any other time, was it the custom for Spanish princes to command fleets of mere merchant ships; and though it is not improbable that many of these ships were intent on trade, it is quite certain that they were larger, stronger and carried more men than was usual. It seems equally certain that on their way, whether across the Bay of Biscay or in the Channel, they seized many English, Gascon or Bayonne merchant ships – ships laden with wine are especially named – and threw their crews overboard. It was the custom of the age and, to a great extent explains the want of evidence as to the exact facts.

In Flanders, la Cerda was warned that an English fleet, fitted for war, would meet him on his return voyage, and he is reported to have prepared for it by taking on board an extra quantity of missiles – including bars of iron – and an extra number of men – French or Flemings; possibly also he got some additional ships; but all are spoken of as of the largest size. Off Winchelsea, on August 29, 1350, he was met by the English fleet under the personal command of the king and of his eldest son, the Black Prince, a fact which gives the battle a higher repute in history than it is perhaps entitled to; for though it was stoutly fought by the Spaniards, and gallantly won by the English, who captured or sank almost half the Spanish ships, it merely confirmed, for the present, the decision of Sluys and would seem to have convinced the Spaniards of the impolicy or imprudence of interfering in quarrels which were no concern of theirs.[1] For more than twenty years there was no serious attempt to dispute the English command of the sea; there was uninterrupted commerce between England and its French dependencies, which now included the whole coast of France, and – which, with regard to the war, was of more importance, there was not, there could not be any hindrance to military transport. This was the secret of the hold on Bordeaux, on Acquitaine. Grand achievement as it was, Poitiers was but a corollary to Winchelsea, or as it was popularly called 'Les Espagnols sur mer'.

After Sluys, Calais and Winchelsea, we held the sea, practically undisputed for more than 20 years. During that time our passage to France was never seriously interfered with, and we landed our men when and where and as we liked. On shore the war lulled for a few years after 1360 and the so called treaty of Bretigny, which was, in reality, no treaty at all; what fighting there was was in Spain. But when the Black Prince returned thence, ruined in health and in temper; when Charles le Sage was king in France, and – by his refusal to pay his father's ransom – found himself in funds; when, too, he had formed the nucleus of a regular army, with capable officers, the war broke out again in 1369. Failing health compelled the Black Prince to retire to England early in 1371, leaving the government of Acquitaine to his brother, the Duke of Lancaster, who thought he saw his advantage in marrying Constance, daughter of the murdered Pedro, King of Castile, and proclaiming himself, by right of his wife, Pedro's successor. This threw Pedro's murderer, the reigning king, Henry, commonly called 'of Trastamara', into closer alliance with Charles, at whose suggestion it presumably was that he sent a large and powerful fleet to co-operate with the French Army then besieging Rochelle and especially to prevent the arrival of a number of English ships reported on their way with reinforcements and stores. These were under the command of the Earl of Pembroke, an inexperienced youth of 25, but son in law of the king, and now appointed Lieutenant of Acquitaine, Lancaster having returned

[1]In *La Marina de Castile* [Madrid, 1894] p.99 [et.] sq. Fernandez Duro gives an account of this battle, but only from English and French chroniclers. His Spanish authorities know nothing of it. It would seem fairly certain that the ships were Biscayan; in part, merchant ships; in part pirates, and in part paid by the King of France, but the Spanish evidence is wanting.

to England with his bride, apparently with the design of pushing his pretensions to the throne of Castile.

We cannot say that Pembroke had certain intelligence of the presence of a hostile fleet off Rochelle, but he had every reason to expect it and yet acted as if he had none. It was known that the King of Castile had at his disposal large and powerful ships, which would too be fitted for war, and that only; but the English ships attempting to relieve Rochelle were few in number compared with the Spaniards, and were transports rather than men of war. On every point they were inferior to the Spaniards – in size, in number and in equipment – strong only in the prestige of having been masters of the sea for the last 30 years. It was not enough; and when, on June 23, 1372, they encountered the Castilians they were defeated and driven on shore. The next day the ships were all either burnt or taken possession of, the men killed or made prisoners; it does not appear that one escaped; Pembroke himself died three years later as he was on the point of being released. The consequences of this defeat were most serious. Rochelle fell almost at once; and the Constable of France, taking advantage of the panic which spread among the English, advanced in force into Poitou and captured – almost on his march – Moncontour, Saint Sévere, Poitiers and Thouards; and the Duke of Lancaster, hastily ordered to Guyenne with reinforcements, was unable to sail, possibly by reason of continued bad weather, probably because a fleet able to cope with the Spaniards could not be provided. The French rose to the occasion; by the spring they had assembled a large number of ships, which, in conjunction with the Spaniards, held not only the Bay of Biscay, but the French coasts of the Channel, a force before which the English had to retire, and the Duke of Lancaster instead of carrying his army to Bordeaux by sea, as had been intended, was compelled to cross over at the Narrows, to land at Calais and to undertake that disastrous march through France in the summer and autumn of 1373, the result of which, more perhaps than any single episode of the war, sealed the fate of the English provinces.

Through the coming years, French squadrons, stiffened by Spanish, held the Channel and scourged the coast of England almost at will. The evils of war, from which the English had been secured for more than thirty years by the victory of Sluys were now brought home to them. From Penzance in the far west to Scarborough in the north, there was scarcely a town or village within reach of the coast but what was plundered and burnt – several of them twice over. Folkestone, Rye, Winchelsea, Lewes, Hastings, Portsmouth, Poole, Dartmouth, Plymouth and Fowey are all specially named, Gravesend was burnt in 1380, and it is more than a little suggestive to note that it was among the fishermen of Fobbing – a village on the north side of the Thames, nearly opposite to Gravesend – that the Peasant's Rising of 1381 first broke out. It is conceivable that whilst, in accordance with human nature, these men objected to taxation of any kind, they more especially objected to it when it took the form of payment for seeing an enemy's fleet come up an English river and make a bonfire of an English town, and the suggestion is strengthened by the fact that the revolt extended along the coast as far as Scarborough and not beyond – that is, it adopted the same limits as the French raids had done.

During this time, the English government was powerless. The navy of England, which, forty years before had sufficed to exterminate that of France, which, thirty years before had crushed that of Spain, had now almost ceased to exist. The causes of this were numerous, but – bearing in mind that an English fleet was composed mainly of merchant ships levied for the king's service – they may be stated briefly as: firstly, the frequency of these levies during the thirty or forty years that the war had lasted, and the custom – careless or dishonest – of enforcing the levies, often several months before the ships were wanted, during which time they were kept up at their owners' cost; and secondly, the granting to foreigners, in return for heavy loans or payments, such privileges and monopolies as virtually put into their hands the whole export trade.[1] By the action of these, it had come about that the merchants were impoverished, the seaport towns fallen into decay, their walls in ruins, the shipping not kept up, and the sailors, unable to find employment, had taken to other means of earning a livelihood.

The evils were repeatedly stated in detail, both in petitions to parliament and by parliament to the king; but it was not till 1381 that the government devised a measure, at once simple and effective for putting new life into the shipping interest and the Navy. This was the first Navigation Act, and ordered 'that none of the king's liege people do from henceforth ship any merchandise in going out or coming within the realm of England in any port, but only in ships of the king's liegeance' under penalty of forfeiture. This at once led to reform in the necessary direction, but it was some time before the lost strength could be restored, and the French Admiral, Jean de Vienne, a really capable man, was urgent in his endeavours to persuade his king to invade England in force. 'What an indignity is it' he is reported as saying, 'to see everlastingly at our gates these English who, after all, are but few;

---

[1]Trevelyan, *England in the Age of Wycliffe 2nd edn.* [(London, 1904), JKL had reviewed the first edition in the *Edinburgh* in 1900] p. 223 map at p. 254. [Charles] Petit-Dutalis, [*Etude sur la vie et le régne de Louis VIII, 1187–1226* (Paris, 1894)] pp. cii, ciii.

to nurture them in our bosom and to provide them with weapons to use against ourselves! Can we not, in our turn go and destroy their homes, so that in their distress they may leave us masters of Guyenne, of Normandy, and of Flanders? The Saxons conquered England with but a handful of men far from their own country; William the Bastard, with nothing but his sword. Is it to be doubted that you – with a kingdom full of men, of provisions and of money – would attain the desired end?' He himself, in the summer of 1385, sure that the English could offer no opposition by sea, went to Scotland, hoping to give the English king such distraction as would render it as impossible for him to oppose a French invasion on land. Richard did, in fact, lead the strength of his army as far north as Aberdeen; and if the French had been ready – as, under energetic command, they might have been – there could have no opposition to them either at sea or on shore. But they were not ready [and it] is not absolutely impossible, before he started on his northern march, Richard had clear intelligence that they were not and could not be ready. At any rate, nothing was done that year.

Jean de Vienne returned from Scotland not pleased with his entertainment there (Lang I 278 sq.)[1] and even less pleased with the neglect to push forward the invasion for which he had prepared the way. The French and their king hoped that the next year – 1386 – would be more propitious to them. At a lavish expense they assembled an enormous fleet – numbering, it is said, 1200 ships – at Sluys; but though it effected nothing and was broken up piece-meal, this was the result of Charles's youth, of the incompetence of his trusted advisers, and – to some considerable extent – of bad weather, but not at all, of English enterprise. That had practically no weight, the strength of the kingdom – such as it was – having been largely led astray in the expedition of the Duke of Lancaster to Spain and in the attempt of his brother, the Duke of Gloucester, to . . . the throne. It is certain that in 1386 England had not the ships to attack and destroy the armament at Sluys, which was assuredly very large; as also that this diminution of naval power was due to the mal-administration of faulty methods during a long period and to the feeble government during the king's minority, but aggravated at this time by the king's not unnatural desire to escape from Lancaster's control by getting him out of the country and still more by the treason of Gloucester, whose influence with parliament was sufficient to prevent it from voting supplies, and with the public, to make it believe that the evident weaknesses and consequent danger of the kingdom was entirely the fault of the king and his ministers. An adequate

[1]Lang [*Continuation of the History of Great Britain* (London, 1795)].

sketch of the political position is given by Professor Oman.[1] The panic in London was extreme and Gloucester possibly thought that he exercised a praiseworthy restraint in having only ministers put to death; for there can be no doubt that he and his party carefully nursed this panic to bring about the inversion of government which is known in history as the Administration of the Lords Appellant.

Those who can call to mind some of the nameless panics that have swept the country during the last 50 years in consequence of statements – true or false – as to the weakness of the navy, and especially that in the spring of '09 when we were almost deafened by excited cries for 8 Dreadnoughts, will have no difficulty in understanding how easily, in modern times the mob might be excited to deeds of violence. Mr. Trevelyan has well said that at that time a mob riot was the equivalent of a modern mass meeting; a civil war, or a ministerial crisis.[2]

By 1387 the shipping had been sensibly restored and was able to contend with that collected by France on fairly equal terms; but from that time on for many hundred years, it could never establish a decisive superiority; the English could never regain that practically perfect command of the sea which they had held during a great part of the reign of Edward III. Cross raiding went on as in the early years of the war. Scotch and French landed, plundered and burnt in England; Englishmen did the same in Scotland or in France; each accused the other of being the aggressor, demanded compensation and made reprisals. Pirates – and every ship not in the king's commission was a pirate when opportunity served – fought with pirates; the Hansa took advantage of the confusion and added effective piracy to their normal trade. There was no power that could prevent it, no power that could enforce the observance of the truce between France and England of 1390, or of the more definite peace which followed Richard's marriage with the infant daughter of the French king, in 1396.

Richard's endeavours to preserve it were neither understood nor admired. Gloucester headed the war-party which, even after their chief's irregular but not unwarranted removal, could represent itself as 'national' against a king described as subservient to France and careless of the disgrace and loss caused by French attacks. This feeling must be considered as contributing to the extreme unpopularity of Richard and to the wholesale desertion not only by the nobles who were directly affected by the allegations of intended tyranny and of encroachments

---

[1][C. Oman] *The Political History of England 1377–1485*, London: Longmans, 1905, Vol. IV, pp. 99–101.

[2]*England in the Age of Wycliffe* 1904 p. 47 'a riot, in the days before mass meetings and resolutions, was a useful, almost a legitimate mode of expressing public feeling'.

on their rights and privileges, but also of the common people who were little likely to be offended by an attack on the powers of the barons, and yet were very ready to assist in deposing the king and in murdering his adherents.

Henry IV had a clearer perception of the danger and encouraged the building of ships both as men of war and for commerce; but as opposed to Scotland, Flanders, the Hansa and more especially France with a hired contingent of Spaniards and of Genoese, the finances of Henry, controlled in a parsimonious spirit by the House of Commons, were with difficulty equal to the bare defence of the kingdom's interests. Our popular histories have thrown a veil over this. They ignore or minimise the naval war which, on a large or small scale, went on all the while; they speak of the capture of the Scottish prince – afterwards James I – as an act of piracy, and the English king's detention of him as – politic perhaps, but – unscrupulous. They have almost entirely omitted the share of the French in the rising of Owen Glendower; the arrival of French soldiers in Wales has seemed to them so much a matter of course as not to call for special notice or explanation; and they speak of the 'unauthorised' siege of Bourg – which may be described as an outwork of Bordeaux – by the Duke of Orleans, without referring to the share taken in it by a French fleet, and to the collapse of the siege when that fleet was signally defeated by an English one in the mouth of the Gironde. In reality, during the whole reign of Henry IV the naval war went on, mostly, indeed, but by no means always to the advantage of England.

From his accession Henry V paid the closest attention to this element of his country's strength, so much so that he has been called the Founder of the Navy. This, of course, is nonsense; but he did see to it that several ships of the largest size were built, with all possible speed, for his service. His army which, on 13 August 1415, landed him on the *Chef de Caur*, the ground afterwards covered by Havre de Grâce, was carried over and escorted by a large fleet – said to have consisted of 1400 ships; many of which remained to take an effective part in the siege of Harfleur; and in the following year, when the Count of Armagnac endeavoured to recapture it, supporting the attempt by a large fleet – French, Spanish and Genoese – this was signally defeated in the mouth of the Seine by an English fleet led by the King's brother, the Duke of Bedford (15 August, 1416). The victory, however, though effective for the immediate purpose of relieving Harfleur, was far from decisive, and the French were still able to interfere with English transports or trade and to render special precautions necessary, as in the summer of 1417, when Henry was preparing to invade Normandy in force.

This led to the battle off the mouth of the Seine on the 29th June, and the decisive defeat of the French fleet by the king's cousin, the Earl of Huntingdon, which was the prelude of the conquest of Normandy. This put an end to the naval war, so far as France was directly concerned, though Spanish, Scotch and Flemish ships or small squadrons continued to give a good deal of trouble and annoyance, and were able in the end of 1420 or the beginning of 1421 to carry over from Scotland a number of men, amounting in the aggregate to perhaps 6000, who joined the French army and actively assisted in the defeat of the English at Baugé (22nd March 1421). So also they were able in the beginning of 1424 to take over a considerable number of Scots, under the command of the Earl of Douglas, who, with the greater part of his men, was killed at Verneuil (17th August 1424). Douglas's official interviews with the English were not happy. He had met them at Halidon Hill in 1402, when he lost an eye and his liberty; again at Shrewsbury in 1403, to be again made prisoner after being seriously wounded; and now, for the last time at Verneuil in 1424, when he, his son James, and his son-in-law the earl of Buchan, were slain. The liberation of the Scottish king about this time, after marrying an English princess, secured peace with Scotland; the internal affairs of Castile did not favour interference in foreign wars, and the whole French coast was controlled by the English; and though piracy and piratical raids were still frequent, notably by Flemings in the North Sea, the Council may perhaps be excused for thinking that these might be restrained by a cheaper method than by keeping a navy afloat for the purpose. They were, in fact, in serious trouble for want of money. The late king had died deep in debt; and though this had been mostly contracted in the public service, he was held to be responsible. By his will, his personal property was to be sold and the proceeds used for settlement, and the ships of the Navy Royal were held to belong, literally, to the king. The greater part of them were accordingly sold, but how far the price went to pay the debts is doubtful. The police duty was done by hired ships or by contract: certain merchants, that is, contracted to clear the sea of pirates, received the money and left the pirates severely alone.

As far, however, as the war was concerned, there was an effective command of the sea. There was no possibility of the enemy opposing, or even interfering with the transport of troops or stores; and even when, in 1436, after the change in his policy, the Duke of Burgundy laid siege to Calais, there was no difficulty in bringing to nought all his attempts at blockade. So too, as late as 1449, when a large Hanseatic fleet tried to pass down the Channel without acknowledging the Sovereignty of the English king, it was forcibly brought in as forfeit to the crown. But smaller offences went unpunished, and piratical raids were not uncommon. Readers of the Paston Letters[1] will remember the state of alarm in which, during this time, the Flemish raids kept the coast of Norfolk; and Norfolk was perhaps the quietest county in England. It seems certain that the want of Governance on the sea, the absurd discrepancy between the claimed Sovereignty and the actual anarchy of the sea had much to do with the disrepute into which the king's government fell. And as the state of things ashore got worse and people began to long for a strong government, so also afloat, they began to think that the appointment of York as minister was the only cure for the prevailing evils. It is to this that we must attribute the fact that from the very beginning of the disturbances, the seamen of the kingdom as a body were the Duke's declared partisans. He was not personally connected with them, but they knew and had suffered from the mal-administration of Suffolk, and their affection for York was so well known that, in 1450, when the captain and crew of the *Nicholas of the Tower* executed on Suffolk the sentence which the sense of the nation had passed on him, it was commonly believed that they were acting in the interest of, if not under orders from, the Duke of York. The name of the ship has seemed to give form to the notion, for *of the Tower* was the 15th century equivalent of the modern H.M.S., and in 1450 the Admiral of England, Captain of the Sea and Constable of the Tower was the Duke of Exeter, York's son-in-law and then a very young man. There is not a vestige of proof that Exeter was in any way connected with the affair, and the suggestion falls to the ground when we know that in this case *of the Tower* had once been of the Tower; the ship was one of the king's ships sold in 1423–4 to merchants of Dartmouth, the chosen home of pirates and freebooters from the days of Chaucer and before.

Such as it was, and however imperfectly, the hired navy did police the seas, but as an instrument of war it was powerless, unable to defend the English interests, unable to control the enemy's attacks. It cannot, of course, be said that our naval weakness was responsible for the loss of French provinces; that must have come from the union of France with Burgundy, under an able government, and from the relative inferiority of the English population; but it was the gross mismanagement of affairs in England, more even than in France, that – at the time – sealed the fate of English domination. Still, the catastrophe was hastened by the utter want of power on the sea. The final capture of Bordeaux after

---

[1][J. Gardiner (ed.), *The Paston Letters* (London, 1904). Reviewed by JKL in the *Edinburgh* in 1908.]

the battle of Chatillon was directly due to this, to the inability of the naval force which was sent to the Gironde to keep open the communications.

The force – from Rochelle and largely from Spain – which Charles assembled at the mouth of the river, blocked the English ships as well as the town, and capitulation was the necessary result (19th October 1453). This for the moment, ended the war on land. (Beaucourt V 278 sq.).[1] Calais was the only remaining territory in France held by the English, and before Charles was in a position to attack it, the defence of it had passed into more competent hands than those of the Duke of Somerset. Following his [Somerset's] death in the first battle of St. Albans (22nd May 1455) the earl of Warwick had been appointed Captain of the town. He was quite equal to its defence by land, and afloat he proved himself singularly active and more directly won the hearts of the seamen. When the Duke of Exeter showed his incompetence to restrain or prevent the French raids on the south and Kentish coast, the public indignation forced the queen to deprive him of his office of Captain of the Sea and to confer it on Warwick. There would seem to have been already a personal quarrel between the two young men, and this may very well have embittered it. Whether it was altogether this, or in great part the difference with his wife – the particulars of which are not known – that completely alienated Exeter from his father-in-law cannot be determined. Probably both had their effect, but it remains certain that up to the death of Henry VI he was an active opponent of the house of York. To Warwick, however, the twofold appointment was of enormous political advantage. It gave him the opportunity of winning golden opinions from the seamen by his success in checking the piratical raids of French or Spaniards and the insolence of Hanseatic merchants, whom he forced to salute the flag. This, which was simply his prescribed duty, appeared to the sufferers as a wanton attack on a friendly power, and Warwick was summoned to London to meet their complaint. To the queen this seemed a chance to get rid of him, but he was happily able to escape the snare, and Calais afforded him a secure refuge while he studied how to even matters between himself and his murderous enemies. He had there a safe place in which to conduct his intrigue and lay his plans; from which he could go, to which he could come as his will directed. The control of the Narrow Sea permitted him, in January 1460, to send over to Sandwich and seize Lord Rivers, whom the queen had nominated to supersede him as Governor of Calais; in

[1]G. du Fresne de Beaucourt [*Histoire de Charles VII* (6 vols, Paris, 1881–91)].

May, it permitted him to go to Ireland to consult with the Duke of York, and to return, in defiance of the attempt of the Earl of Exeter to intercept him. In June it permitted him again to send over to Sandwich and seize Mundeford, Warden of the Cinque Ports, and afterwards enabled him to land, with such forces as he could dispose of, in Kent and to begin that march inland which culminated in the battle of Northampton (1460). And so, for the time, ended the direct share of the navy in the Civil War, though not its influence.

Queen Margaret was willing to go to great lengths to re-establish her own power and to secure the inheritance of her son. Her ambitions were purely personal – she had not, she could not have, any English sympathies. For a promise, or perhaps rather a suggestion of assistance, she sold Berwick to the Scots; she offered the Channel Islands to the Grand seneschal of Normandy, Pierre de Brézé, an old retainer of the House of Anjou, who, she supposed, might now have some sea-force at his disposal; and she gave Charles to understand that Calais was in the market and might be his. Charles, the husband of her mother's sister, was of friendly disposition, but was unwilling to waste the forces of his kingdom in a quarrel in which neither his personal interests not the interests of France were involved. The offer of Calais was a bribe not to be resisted, and he had mustered a considerable fleet in the hope of securing it, when the news of Towton stayed the expedition. He then appears to have meditated landing in force in Wales, and is said to have actually done so in Cornwall, but his sudden death (1461) put an end to these fruitless attempts.

Less even than Charles was his son and successor, Louis XI, a likely man to give anything for nothing, and when Queen Margaret, driven out of England and paid to quit Scotland, succeeded in getting to Brittany and pleading her cause in person, he exacted a precise promise of the cession of Calais for a loan of 20,000 livres – about 2000 pounds English. Edward, on his side, or Warwick for him, was quick to meet the French threat, and a savage raid in force down the west coast of France – the Isle Ré is mentioned as a particular sufferer – seems to have convinced the French king of the inadvisability of meddling in English affairs just then. The 20,000 livres, however, and the gift of the Channel Islands, equipped a Norman fleet and persuaded Brézé to undertake command of an expedition intending to land some 2000 men in Northumberland. That it reached the coast was probably owing to the absence of the main part to the English fleet in the Bay of Biscay; but enough remained to prove that aggressive action against the land cannot be carried out by one fleet in presence of another.

It is commonly said that Brézé's force was broken up and dispersed by a storm. That is possible, though the details of the story are sadly wanting. What seems certain is that the English fleet was not, and that it completed the destruction of the French. Instead of a substantial reinforcement of 2000 trained soldiers, the Queen brought to her northern partisans only a few stragglers who could not affect the course of the struggle. Utterly defeated after two months, she considered herself fortunate in again reaching Bamborough, protected and guided – if there is any truth in the legend – by a sentimental brigand. Thence, in company with Brézé; she escaped to Flanders, and for the time the war was ended. Margaret, indeed, endeavoured to incite Louis to further attempts in her behalf; but, recognising that – for the present at least – the Lancastrian cause was dead, he rightly judged that, in the then divided state of France, it would be impolitic to add to the number of his enemies a united England, fired by recollections of a loss as yet only ten years old. Henry V had renewed the war after a longer pause.

Now, in the twentieth century, some effort is needed to realise that in 1463, all the fighting men of England had been nurtured in tales of Agincourt and the conquest of France; that a large proportion of them had actively served in France, and still smarted under the shameful memories of Somerset's misgovernment and defeat. There can be little doubt that; at the time of the 'League of the Public Good', an English invasion of Guienne led by a brilliant soldier, such as Edward IV certainly was, would have been most inconvenient for Louis and possibly a serious danger for France. That it did not take place was largely due to Edward's sloth and sensuality; but it was clearly also the aim of Louis to secure his good will, and the extreme favour which he showed to Warwick, in the first instance, may be attributed to that end alone, though he readily grasped at the opportunity given by the rift in the friendship of the two, and there can be little doubt that he was, to some unknown extent, a factor in the quarrel.

The sympathies of the English king were Burgundian; those of the French king were Lancastrian; it was therefore clearly his wish as well as his policy to unite the two parties hostile to his Yorkist opponents, and this, as is familiarly known, he succeeded in doing. When Warwick broke out in open rebellion, it would appear – there is no positive evidence – that the shipping interest of the country, as a body, adhered to him, as it had done all along. In April 1470, when he had to fly, he found ships and ready transport at Dartmouth, which carried him over to the Seine, and brought him back in the following September. On the other hand, when Edward had to fly, he had to trust himself and his small following to chance ships – not improbably alien – at Lynn. Certainly when he returned, five months later, it was in Flemish and Hanseatic ships supplied by the Duke of Burgundy. To us, at the present moment, the point of interest is: why was he allowed to land in England? It cannot be supposed that Warwick was not alive to the danger of Edward's return with a strong force of exiles and Burgundian allies and mercenaries. He had a certain amount of naval experience and must have known that such attempt might – and ought – to be met at sea. The only explanation of the fact that it was not, is, that in the circumstances, it was not possible for him so to meet it; that he had not the ships capable of keeping the sea for an indefinite time and engaging an unknown number of men of war and large merchant men. He had, indeed, stationed his cousin, the Bastard of Fauconberg, with a squadron of uncertain strength in the Narrow Sea, at Calais or Sandwich; and this, at the critical moment, had gone into the Channel, to examine, possibly to plunder some Portuguese merchantmen, which were certainly in the interest of Burgundy; but, as far as we know, the Bastard had no instructions to watch Flushing, nor was his station at all adapted for such a duty. Everything would imply that, wanting ships, Warwick had made his preparations for repelling his enemy from the shore. It is, at any rate, clear that Edward met with no opposition at sea; that, sailing from Flushing, with somewhere about 20 ships, on the 11th March, 1471, he made the coast of Norfolk on the evening of the 12th, and would have landed there, but found the county too strongly held by Warwick's friends; that he went north and on the evening of the 14th and through the 15th, landed at the mouth of the Humber and at different points along the Yorkshire coast, without opposition. But this county was held for Warwick by his brother, the marquis of Montagu; and the only explanation of the certain fact are that Montagu was unfaithful to his trust, or was unequal to it – it is impossible to say which: he may have been a traitor; it would not have been for the first time; he may have been a fool; but he was Warwick's brother, and stupidity did not run in the family: he may have been held by some feudal enemy, but it has not been recorded. All that can be said is that the land defence, which was there, was no better than the sea defence, which was not.

The battles of Barnet and Tewkesbury followed; and with the death of Warwick, of Henry, of Henry's reputed son, and with the imprisonment of Margaret, the civil war came to an end; though the Earl of Oxford and other irreconcilables, who, sooner than acknowledge the House of York, elected as the Lancastrian representative the twice-laid bastard of the House of Tudor, then only a boy of 14, and kept the Channel and the North Sea alive with piracies which Edward was never able to quell.[1] The weakness of the Yorkist kings at sea is, in fact, a salient feature of their reigns. When Edward at last, in alliance with his brother in law, undertook to wage war in France, vast as were the pretensions he put forward, he was quite unable to carry his army to Guienne, where he would have been welcomed by the Gascon nobles; unable to carry it to Normandy, where he would have joined hands with the Duke of Bretagne; unable to ferry it to Calais, only twenty miles off, without the assistance of the Duke of Burgundy who supplied 500 flat-bottomed boats, and even with these, the transport took three weeks. Nothing had been done to render the sea secure; to clear it of pirates, or to make it dangerous for them to approach the army in its passage; and a French chronicler has put it on record that the French king had the power, if he had known how to use it, to have destroyed the whole.[2] As the army only stayed in France for three months and was then returned from Calais in the same dilatory fashion, we must suppose – for none of the chroniclers has told us – that the Burgundian boats waited to bring them back.[3]

[1]Everyone knows that Henry of Richmond was, on the mother's side, the representative of the legitimatised line of the Beauforts; but there are probably many who do not know that his father was the legitimatised offspring of the illicit union of Owen Tudor and Catherine, widow of Henry V. It is scarcely to be doubted that it was the fact of Edmund Tudor's being recognised as a half-brother of Henry VI that was the real basis of the claim of Edmund Tudor's son. Foreigners could not see that this, or even his mother's descent was any claim at all, and some fifty years later, Chapuys, the Imperial Ambassador, wrote to the Emperor that there were many in England who thought that he – the Emperor – had 'a better title than the present King [Henry VIII], who only claims by his mother, who was declared by sentence of the Bishop of Bath a bastard, because Edward had espoused another wife before he married the mother of Elizabeth of York.' *Letters and Papers, Henry VIII* vol. vi No. 1528; vol. vii No.1368. Chapuys, of course, could not understand Henry VII's parliamentary title, by virtue of which he and his descendants reigned.

[2]Comines. His account was thus told in English *Tudor Translation* 1897 vol. I p.243: 'When King Edward came to Dover, the Duke of Burgundy, to further his passage, sent 500 boats of Holland and Zealand, called Scuts, which are flat and low, built very commodiously for transporting of horses. But notwithstanding all this help they had from the Duke, and all the King of England could command himself, he was above three weeks in passing between Calais and Dover; yet are they but seven leagues distant; whereby you may perceive with how great difficulty a king of England invadeth France. And if the king, our master, had been as well acquainted with the wars by sea as by land, King Edward had never passed over, or at least not that summer. But the king understood them not, and those that had charge of them much less.'

[3]The story of this expedition offers a marked instance of the neglect or misrepresentation of naval affairs, even by modern historians of repute. Here are a few examples. C. Oman (*Political History of England* Vol. IV) p.456, Charles of Burgundy's 'whole field army was far away on the Rhine when the English king landed at Calais on July 4.'; p.459 'Having thus secured peace . . . the king returned to England and disbanded his army.' Ramsay (*Lancaster and York* vol. II) p.407 20th June 'On that day . . . The shipment to Calais began' and note 'The shipment was said to have taken three weeks'; p.410 'The descent at Calais was contrary to his [Charles's] advice, which was in favour

Richard, a more able man than his brother, might probably have done something to strengthen the sea defences of the country, had time and opportunity been allowed him. As it was, he was impotent; and though, warned of the approaching danger, he raised a small force to guard the south coast, which the attempt of 1484 seemed to indicate as the enemy's aim, it could only do so by neglecting the west, where the threatened attack fell, as a prelude to the battle of Bosworth (22nd August 1485) and the change of dynasty.

Chapter IV

The invasion of England by the Earl of Richmond, who was presently to become King Henry VII, is one of many incidents in our history which have been referred to as proofs of the fallacy lurking in the statement that the navy is a sure defence of England's coasts. How can it be a sure defence, it is asked, when time and again the country has been invaded? In reality the several invasions are so many confirmations or corroborations of the proposition. No one has ever suggested that a non-existent navy can be any obstacle to invasion; or yet a navy whose force, by carelessness, incompetence or incapacity, is stationed in a wrong place. But the fleet, which might have been an obstacle in the way of William the Conqueror, was in good time removed from its proper sphere of action: the difficulties which a fleet even imperfectly organised, could offer to Louis the Dauphin have been discussed; the weakness of the navy under Richard II, and the consequent injury sustained by the kingdom, both in its foreign and domestic affairs, have been illustrated; and if no attempt was made to stay the landing of Henry of Bolingbroke in 1399, or of Edward IV in 1471, it merely denotes that the government had ignored or unduly minimised the danger, or had not a sufficient sea force at command, or did not understand the use of what it had. The naval force which Richard III could dispose was certainly very small, though it could have interfered in Henry's voyage, with disastrous effect, if only it could have met it; but it was not sufficient to guard both the south and west coasts. Henry's

---

of a landing at the mouth of the Seine for an advance on Paris, in which the Duke of Brittany could co-operate'; p.413 'By the 4th September the whole host had returned to Calais and the reshipment followed at once.' And, though not modern, curious as a writer professedly naval, Campbell (*Lives of the Admirals* vol. I) p.227 'to the assistance of [Charles] he [the king] passed over with a mighty army, attended by a fleet of 500 sail with which . . . he entered the road of Calais where he debarked his force. This sufficiently shows the great maritime strength of England in these times; when the king, after such an unsettled state and so many revolutions . . . was able in a year's space to undertake such an expedition as this, and that too with so great a force.'

attempt in 1484 and possibly some old woman's prophecy led Richard to suppose that the south coast would be his objective, and in fact he was in such a position that he might direct the blow to which ever coast was not guarded. It fell on Milford in Wales because Milford in Hampshire was carefully secured, and Richard had not the force necessary to secure both.

Henry VII was quite capable of understanding where his first advantage had lain, and scarcely needed the landing of Schwartz in 1487 and of Perkin Warbeck in 1495 to convince him of the necessity of strengthening the navy. More distinctly than any of our early kings he seems to have taken the lesson to heart and to have devoted pains and time and money to forming and developing a true naval organisation. That it was worked and grew together with trade, commerce and voyages of discovery is merely a proof that he could and did realise the interdependence of sea-power and sea-riches. When we find his son from his accession in early youth carrying on the same policy and developing the same ideas with a persistence not to be expected from a boy of 18, we are warranted in attributing this to the father's teaching and example.

Henry VII passed on to Henry VIII his conception of the importance of the navy; and thus from the beginning of Henry VIII's reign we find the development and increase of the navy holding a high position among objects aimed at. To the ordinary reader Henry VIII is mainly the man who occupied himself with divorcing or murdering his wives when he was not busy murdering harmless women or holy men – the Countess of Salisbury, the Nun of Kent, More, Fisher, the Carthusians, for instance. The careful student of history knows him also as the man who developed and organised the navy on modern lines; who gave an enormous and immediate increase to the very small navy left by Henry VII. Within the first four years of his reign – what by building, by buying or by taking from the enemy – he had added to it some 26 ships, of sizes varying from 100 to 1000 tons, rough measurement; and of them something like 15 were, according to the standards of the day, what would now be called 'battle-ships'. By 1525, there were 18 more, of which about half might be called ships of the second class; and before the end of the reign, upwards of 50 more, of which about half were 1st or 2nd class battle ships, and the rest, smaller vessels. Of these last 50, all, or nearly all were built subsequent to 1539 and thus mainly by the money arising out of the dissolution of the monasteries. We are to some extent accustomed to the general statement that Henry VIII enlarged the navy. Figures such as those just quoted show a more distinct and definite enlargement than any mere general statement; but I would more especially call attention to the important points that these ships, so enumerated, were ships actually belonging to the crown, ships primarily built and maintained for purposes of war; and that then, as always, the crown was entitled to call on – to 'arrest' – every ship in the kingdom; that during the reigns of these two Henrys, sea-borne commerce increased enormously, and with it, also, the number and size of merchant ships, which were available, when wanted, as ships of war, not indeed of the 1st class, but useful; and that there were always in the southern ports – London and Southampton especially – considerable numbers of foreign ships still large – Venetians, say and Hansa – which could be hired, or, if need was, bought for the king's service. I am dwelling on these figures to show you that even by 1525, when the great break in Henry's policy followed the Emperor's victory at Pavia, he had at his disposal a very substantial force of ships of war, which might be strengthened at will into a very large one.

It is in this that we have the explanation of the political status of our country at this time, which some painstaking historians have seemed unable to appreciate, and have described England as powerless, because it had no standing army. It is thus that Henry has been represented as at this time swayed alternately by lust and fear; now by his passion for Mistress Anne and anon by his abject dread of the wrath of the mighty emperor for whom, if war broke out, a Dutch fleet would land a body of Spanish and German veterans on the east coast; whilst Henry had no force capable of opposing them. It is interesting to note the casual way in which a 'Dutch fleet' is introduced – one out of many – without evidence that there was one or part of one, or any consideration of the number of ships necessary to bring over an army. That the Dutch ports had numerous ships is, of course, admitted, but it no where appears that they were or would have been at the disposal of the Emperor, if he had wanted them; and, in any case, he had too keen an insight into the realities of war to suppose that he could ferry his legions across a contested sea. But this is the very point which landmen apparently find it so difficult to understand. In the whole story of Charles, it no where appears that he ever gave a serious thought to the possibility of invading England. None, indeed; although Henry's action in respect of the divorce must have been galling in the extreme, Charles's demeanour towards him was always conciliatory, with the exception, possibly, of the months immediately following Pavia, when it can be understood that the young victor, barely 25, was suffering from a swelled head and believing that he could now stand alone. A very short time convinced him that he could not; that without at least the neutrality of England, his relation to a hostile France would be most disadvantageous; that England's army had nothing to do with it, that England's navy had a great deal, and its location almost still more. The way in which England's shipping could be stationed so as to command the Channel, from Penzance to Dover was not a consideration which lessened the value of England's friendship to a government whose aim it must be, in peace or war, to keep open the communication between Spain and the Low Countries. To France, on the other hand, as the enemy of Spain, it was almost as important to have England an ally. Even if her navy had been as strong as England's – and just at that time, in Western seas it was not – its Channel stations were geographically inferior, and English protection would go far to bear Spanish convoys unharmed. Hence there was, of necessity, a keen competition for that English alliance which had been scouted at as a thing ludicrously worthless – because the English king would have had difficulty in mustering even a few thousand soldiers with which to make a show on the Continent, and those men who at the moment were wanting in the practice and discipline of war.

APPENDICES

APPENDIX 1

LIST OF DOCUMENTS USED IN THIS VOLUME

No.	Description	Date	Reference

1 'THE SCIENTIFIC STUDY OF NAVAL HISTORY', 1875–85

No.	Description	Date	Reference
1	Laughton to Luce	9 July 1875	LoC: Luce Mss. Cont. 7
2	Luce to Laughton	26 July 1875	LGH 12/1–2
3	Laughton to Luce	10 August 1875	LoC: Luce Mss. Cont. 7
4	Laughton to Fanshawe	13 March 1876	PRO: ADM 203/1
5	Allan to Laughton	21 December 1876	LGH 1/12
6	Bridge to Laughton	1 February 1877	LGH 7/1–6
7	Warre to Laughton	3 August 1877	LGH 55
8	Warre to Laughton	18 August 1877	LGH 55
9	Warre to Laughton	18 November 1877	LGH 55
10	Laughton to Luce	6 January 1878	LoC: Luce Mss. Cont. 7
11	Tuxen to Laughton	4 May 1878	LGH 1/14
12	White to Laughton	8 May 1878	LGH 1/15
13	White to Laughton	16 May 1878	LGH 1/16
14	Domvile to Laughton	8 December [1878(?)]	LGH 6
15	Laughton to the Secretary, RGS	3 March 1880	RGS: Laughton Mss.
16	Laughton to Markham	28 April 1880	RGS: Laughton Mss.
17	Bridge to Laughton	26 July 1880	LGH 7/7–8
18	Bridge to Laughton	23 October 1881	LGH 7/9–13
19	Laughton to Stephen	10 November 1882	Bod: Lee Mss. Dom e 121, f. 77
20	Laughton to Stephen	24 December 1882	Bod: Lee Mss. Dom, e 121, f. 79

2 PROFESSOR OF MODERN HISTORY, 1885–90

No.	Description	Date	Reference
21a	Laughton to King's College	6 July 1885	KCL: KA/1C/L60
21b	Admiral Luard to Laughton	27 December 1884	Ibid.
21c	Reeve to King's College	3 July 1885	Ibid.
21d	Lambert to King's College	1 July 1885	Ibid.
21e	Main to King's College	3 July 1885	Ibid
21f	Archer Hirst to Laughton	1 July 1885	Ibid.

21g	Fanshawe to King's College	n.d.	Ibid.
21h	Sturges Jackson to King's College	30 June 1885	Ibid.
21i	Key to King's College	6 July 1885	Ibid.
22	Laughton to Cunningham	6 July 1885	KCL: KA/IC/L59
23	Laughton to Cunningham	8 July 1885	KCL: KA/IC/L59
24	Laughton to Cunningham	11 July 1885	KCL: KA/IC/L59
25	Laughton to Cunningham	17 July 1885	KCL: KA/IC/L59
26	Longman Contract	21 August 1885	RUL: Longman Archive II 233/104
27	Laughton to Cunningham	24 September 1885	KCL: KA/IC/L59
28	Laughton to Cunningham	10 October 1885	KCL: KA/IC/L59
29	Laughton's Service Record	n.d.	PRO: ADM 6/446
30	Laughton to Browning	28 May 1886	KCC: Browning Mss.
31	Gardiner to Laughton	10 October 1886	LGH 9/1
32	Alcester to Laughton	4 November 1886	LGH 4
33	Alcester to Laughton	8 November 1886	LGH 4
34	Laughton to Cunningham	9 November 1886	KCL: KA/IC/L62
35	Laughton to Cunningham	27 November 1886	KCL: KA/IC/L62
36	Yonge to Laughton	7 December 1886	LGH 31/5–6
37	Yonge to Laughton	12 December 1886	LGH 1/22
38	Bridge to Laughton	20 December 1886	LGH 7/14–15
39	Nesham to Laughton	6 February 1887	LGH 1/24–5
40	Bridge to Laughton	8 February 1887	LGH 7/16–17
41	McClintock to Laughton	9 February 1887	LGH 6
42	Church to Laughton	15 June 1887	LGH 54
43	Church to Laughton	30 June 1887	LGH 54
44	Bridge to Laughton	5 October 1887	LGH 7/18–19
45	Hall to Laughton	10 December 1887	LGH 31/17–18
46	Luce to Laughton	22 December 1887	LGH 12/3–4
47	Laughton to Browning	6 April 1888	KCC: Browning Mss.
48	Hull to Laughton	11 June 1888	LGH 4
49	Laughton to Cunningham	24 June 1888	KCL: KA/IC/L65
50	Kerr to Laughton	28 March 1889	LGH 1/29
51	MacGregor to Laughton	4 May 1889	LGH 31/23–4
52	Laughton to Luce	11 August 1889	LoC: Luce Mss. Cont 8
53	Bridge to Laughton	23 August 1889	LGH 7/20–1
54	Firth to Laughton	26 October [1889?]	LGH 31
55	Warre to Laughton	3 April 1890	LGH 31/39–40
56	Laughton to Seeley	8 June 1890	UoL: Seeley Mss.
57	Seeley to Laughton	10 June 1890	LGH 18/23–4
58	Hornby to Laughton	12 June 1890	LGH 31/41
59	Laughton to Cunningham	29 June 1890	KCL: KA/IC/L66
60	Laughton to Luce	3 August 1890	USNWC: Luce Mss. Coll. 10 folder 2

61	Laughton to Luce	12 August 1890	USNWC: Luce Mss. Coll. 10 folder 2
62	Luce to Laughton	10 November 1890	LGH 16/5–7
63	Laughton to Luce	7 December 1890	LoC: Luce Mss. Cont. 8

3   THE NAVY RECORDS SOCIETY, 1891–95

64	Wheatley to Laughton	29 May 1891	LGH 4
65	Morgan to Laughton	22 June 1891	LGH 4
66	Laughton to Cunningham	7 October 1891	KCL: KA/IC/L70
67	Phillimore to Laughton	28 October 1891	LGH 24/8–11
68	Bridge to Laughton	21 December 1891	LGH 7/22–24
69	Firth to Laughton	9 January 1892	LGH 19/9–10
70	Oliver to Laughton	30 March 1892	LGH 31/61–2
71	Jodrell to Laughton	4 April 1892	LGH 31/64–5
72	Hall to Laughton	3 May 1892	LGH 31/68–9
73	Colomb to Laughton	26 July 1892	LGH 31/86–9
74	Sulivan to Laughton	21 November 1892	LGH 22
75	Laughton to Mahan	11 March 1893	LoC: Mahan Mss. Microfilm Reel 2
76	Bridge to Laughton	14 March 1893	LGH 7/27–30
77	Bridge to Laughton	15 March 1893	LGH 7/31–4
78	Mahan to Laughton	21 March 1893	LGH 13/1–4
79	Laughton to Earl Spencer	13 June 1893	BL: Althorp Mss. K342
80	Froude to Laughton	12 June 1893	LGH 17/27
81	Laughton to Spencer	21 June 1893	BL: Althorp Mss. K342
82	Laughton to Spencer	15 July 1893	BL: Althorp Mss. K342
83	Froude to Laughton	23 July 1893	LGH 17/28
84	Oppenheim to Laughton	24 July 1893	LGH 4/1–2
85	Froude to Laughton	29 July 1893	LGH 17/29
86	Laughton to Corbett	8 August 1893	NMM: Corbett Mss. Box 14
87	Mahan to Laughton	16 August 1893	LGH 13/5–6
88	Laughton to Corbett	28 September 1893	NMM: Corbett Mss. Box 14
89	Bridge to Laughton	30 October 1893	LGH 7/35–6
90	Laughton to Lee	23 November 1893	Bod: Lee Mss. f. 246
91	Amos to Laughton	28 November 1893	LGH 3
92	Mahan to Laughton	1 December 1893	LGH 13/7–9
93	Hornby to Laughton	29 December 1893	LGH 3
94	Laughton to Hornby	31 December 1893	NMM: Hornby Mss. PHI/120d
95	Hornby to Laughton	4 January 1894	LGH 3
96	Hamilton to Laughton	14 January 1894	LGH 3

97	Mahan to Laughton	31 January 1894	LGH 13/10–11
98	Mahan to Laughton	18 February 1894	LGH 13/12–13
99	Laughton to Hornby	3 April 1894	NMM: Hornby Mss. PHI/120d
100	Mahan to Laughton	22 May 1894	LGH 15/121–2
101	Mahan to Laughton	13 June 1894	LGH 13/14–15
102	Lee to Laughton	13 June 1894	LGH 31/125–6
103	Hornby to Laughton	16 June 1894	LGH 3
104	Laughton to Corbett	3 January 1895	NMM: Corbett Mss. Box 14
105	Laughton to Corbett	5 January 1895	NMM: Corbett Mss. Box 14
106	Laughton to Corbett	1 February 1895	NMM: Corbett Mss. Box 14
107	Bell & Sons to Laughton	23 February 1895	LGH 5
108	Gardiner to Laughton	11 April 1895	LGH 9/5–6
109	Gardiner to Laughton	14 April 1895	LGH 9/7–8
110	MacMillan & Co. to Laughton	15 April 1895	LGH 5
111	Laughton to Corbett	8 May 1895	NMM: Corbett Mss. Box 14
112	Laughton to Corbett	20 May 1895	NMM: Corbett Mss. Box 14
113	Gardiner to Laughton	28 June 1895	LGH 9/9–10
114	Gardiner to Laughton	1 July 1895	LGH 9/11–12
115	Oppenheim to Laughton	26 July 1895	LGH 4/7–8
116	Mahan to Laughton	14 August 1895	LGH 13/16–18
117	Mahan to Laughton	28 August 1895	LGH 13/19–21
118	Mahan to Laughton	2 September 1895	LGH 13/22–3
119	Bridge to Laughton	23 September 1895	LGH 7/37–40
120	Corbett to Laughton	4 October 1895	LGH 32/14–15
121	Laughton to the Librarian, Gonville and Caius College	21 October 1895	College Library
122	Laughton to Browning	16 November 1895	KCC: Browning Mss.
123	Gardiner to Laughton	17 December 1895	LGH 2

4   FIGHTING FOR NELSON, 1896–1900

124	Laughton to Browning	24 January 1896	KCC: Browning Mss.
125	Laughton to Lee	26 February 1896	Bod: Lee Mss. Eng. Misc. d. 178 f.248
126	Mahan to Laughton	20 March 1896	LGH 13/24–7
127	Laughton to Laird Clowes	31 March 1896	NMM: Laird-Clowes Mss. Naval History File
128	Bridge to Laughton	21 April 1896	LGH 7/41–3
129	Mahan to Laughton	1 May 1896	LGH 13/28–9

130	Chevalier to Laughton	17 May 1896	LGH 3
131	Colomb to Laughton	7 September 1896	LGH 1/74–5
132	Burrows to Laughton	26 September 1896	LGH 32/42
133	Fitzgerald to Laughton	28 September 1896	LGH 4
134	Mahan to Laughton	6 November 1896	LGH 13/30–33
135	Lyall to Laughton	18 November 1896	LGH 17/4
136	Hamilton to Laughton	15 December 1896	LGH 14/30–1
137	Hamilton to Laughton	18 December 1896	LGH 19/32–3
138	Laughton to Browning	31 January 1897	KCC: Browning Mss.
139	Laughton to Browning	2 February 1897	KCC: Browning Mss.
140	Laughton to Browning	18 February 1897	KCC: Browning Mss.
141	Mahan to Laughton	23 February 1897	LGH 13/34–6
142	Laughton to Browning	28 February 1897	KCC: Browning Mss.
143	Laughton to Mahan	21 April 1897	LoC: Mahan Mss.
144	Mahan to Laughton	29 April 1897	LGH 13/37–9
145	Laughton to Browning	5 May 1897	KCC: Browning Mss.
146	Laughton to Browning	6 May 1897	KCC: Browning Mss.
147	Laughton to Browning	8 May 1897	KCC: Browning Mss.
148	Mahan to Laughton	21 May 1897	LGH 13/40–3
149	Mahan to Laughton	24 June 1897	LGH 13/44–5
150	Mahan to Laughton	28 June 1897	LGH 13/46–7
151	Mahan to Laughton	3 August 1897	LGH 13/48–52
152	Hall to Laughton	4 August 1897	LGH 2
153	Laughton to Browning	6 August 1897	KCC: Browning Mss.
154	Clarke to Laughton	8 August 1897	LGH 4
155	Clarke to Laughton	9 August 1897	LGH 2
156	Mahan to Laughton	16 August 1897	LGH 13/53–4
157	Gardiner to Laughton	10 September 1897	LGH 9/47–50
158	Wilson to Laughton	17 October 1897	LGH 24/26–7
159	Wilson to Laughton	27 October 1897	LGH 24/28
160	Oppenheim to Laughton	5 November 1897	LGH 4/21–2
161	Gardiner to Laughton	19 November 1897	LGH 2
162	Mahan to Laughton	29 November 1897	LGH 13/55–8
163	Laughton to Browning	1 December 1897	KCC: Browning Mss.
164	Laughton Errata note	n.d.	KCC: Browning Mss.
165	Laughton to Browning	5 December 1897	KCC: Browning Mss.
166	Gardiner to Laughton	11 December 1897	LGH 9/60–1
167	Laughton to Carr-Laughton	12 December 1897	LGH 26/1–4
168	Gardiner to Laughton	13 December 1897	LGH 9/62–3

169	Gardiner to Laughton	14 December 1897	LGH 10/1–2
170	Gardiner to Laughton	15 December 1897	LGH 10/3–4
171	Gardiner to Laughton	19 December 1897	LGH 10/5–6
172	Gardiner to Laughton	21 December 1897	LGH 10/7–10
173	Laughton to Browning	18 January 1898	KCC: Browning Mss.
174	Mahan to Laughton	11 February 1898	LGH 14/59–60
175	Gardiner to Laughton	28 June 1898	LGH 10/42–3
176	Oppenheim to Laughton	15 July 1898	LGH 4/35
177	Marquess of Bath to Laughton	22 September 1898	LGH 19
178	Bridge to Laughton	13 October 1898	LGH 7/44–8
179	Mahan to Laughton	4 November 1898	LGH 14/61–3
180	Gunton to Laughton	16 November 1898	LGH 19
181	Sturges Jackson to Laughton	25 November 1898	LGH 54
182	Bridge to Laughton	30 November 1898	LGH 7/53–4
183	Colomb to Laughton	19 December 1898	LGH 19/1–4
184	Markham to Laughton	4 January 1899	LGH 19/34–5
185	Mahan to Laughton	9 January 1899	LGH 14/64–7
186	Laughton to Mahan	23 January 1899	LoC: Mahan Mss.
187	Colomb to Laughton	11 March 1899	LGH 2
188	Murray to Laughton	11 May 1899	LGH 2
189	Mahan to Laughton	18 May 1899	LGH 14/68
190	Mahan to Laughton	23 May 1899	LGH 14/69–70
191	Mahan to Laughton	17 June 1899	LGH 14/71–2
192	Mahan to Laughton	21 June 1899	LGH 14/73–5
193	Mahan to Laughton	4 July 1899	LGH 14/76–7
194	Laughton to Newbolt	19 July 1899	Bod: Eng. Lett. C302 Edward Bridges Mss. f.15
195	Colomb to Laughton	21 August 1899	LGH 19/5–6
196	Mahan to Laughton	23 November 1899	LGH 14/81–3
197	Mahan to Laughton	19 December 1899	LGH 14/84–5
198	Laughton to Dilke	28 March 1900	BL: Add. Mss. 43,916, f.203
199	Gutteridge to Laughton	28 April 1900	LGH 19/18–19
200	Gutteridge to Laughton	30 May 1900	LGH 19/16–7
201	Mahan to Laughton	28 August 1900	LGH 14/86–7
202	Laughton to Corbett	11 November 1900	NMM: Corbett Mss. Box 14
203	Mahan to Laughton	25 December 1900	LGH 14/91–2

5   WORKING TO THE END, 1901–15

204	Bridge to Laughton	4 February 1901	LGH 7/55–6
205a	Mouchez to Laughton	27 February 1901	LGH 17/14–17
205b	Yorke to Laughton	1 March 1901	Ibid.
205c	Yorke to Mouchez	6 March 1901	Ibid.
206	Jodrell to Laughton	9 March 1901	LGH 31/66–7

207	Laughton to Lee	15 March 1901	Bod: Lee Mss. Eng. Misc. d. 178, f.250
208	Laughton to Browning	9 April 1901	KCC: Browning Mss.
209	Parry to Laughton	5 May 1901	LGH 2
210	Gutteridge to Laughton	22 May 1901	LGH 19/19–20
211	Mahan to Laughton	31 May 1901	LGH 14/94–5
212	Mahan to Laughton	18 June 1901	LGH 14/96–7
213	Mahan to Laughton	12 July 1901	LGH 14/98–9
214	Troubridge to Laughton	8 August 1901	LGH 24/31–4
215	Gutteridge to Laughton	11 September 1901	LGH 9/21–6
216	Mahan to Laughton	7 October 1901	LGH 14/100–104
217	Laughton to Lee	10 November 1901	Bod: Lee Mss. Eng. Misc. d. 178, f.252
218	Laughton to Austen-Leigh	18 December 1901	KCC 42
219	Laughton to Austen-Leigh	28 December 1901	KCC 42
220	Mahan to Laughton	21 January 1902	LGH 15/105–7
221	Laughton Lecture Notes	January 1902	LGH 41
222	Longmans to Laughton	24 February 1902	LGH 5
223	Bridge to Laughton	15 June 1902	LGH 7/59–60
224	Mahan to Laughton	8 August 1902	LGH 15/108–11
225	Mahan to Laughton	10 December 1902	LGH 15/112–13
226	Bridge to Laughton	16 February 1903	LGH 7
227	Corbett to Laughton	7 May 1903	LGH 19/7–8
228	Mahan to Laughton	25 September 1903	LGH 15/114–17
229	Laughton to Mahan	12 October 1903	LoC: Mahan Mss.
230	Mahan to Laughton	28 October 1903	LGH 15/118–20
231	Mahan to Laughton	9 June 1904	LGH 15/123–4
232	Mahan to Laughton	25 June 1904	LGH 15/125–6
233	Bridge to Laughton	10 October 1904	LGH 7/61–2
234	Ward to Laughton	18 October 1904	LGH 4
235	Greene to Laughton	18 December 1904	NMM: NRS/2
236	Freemantle to Laughton	4 March 1905	LGH 18/9–10
237	Gutteridge to Laughton	10 October 1905	LGH 19/27–9
238	Mahan to Laughton	31 December 1905	LGH 15/27–8
239	Mahan to Laughton	20 January 1906	LGH 15/129–32
240	Mahan to Laughton	28 January 1906	LGH 15/133–4
241	Mahan to Laughton	31 January 1906	LGH 15/135–7
242	Mahan to Laughton	22 May 1906	LGH 15/139–41
243	Mahan to Laughton	20 July 1906	LGH 15/142–4
244	Smith, Elder & Co. to Laughton	18 March 1907	LGH 32/91
245	Laughton to Browning	29 June 1907	KCC: Browning Mss.
246	Laughton to Corbett	27 July 1907	NMM: Corbett Mss. Box 14
247	Mahan to Laughton	6 September 1907	LGH 15/145–7
248	Mahan to Laughton	1 November 1907	LGH 15/148–9

249	Mahan to Laughton	21 February 1908	LGH 15/150–2
250	Mahan to Laughton	6 March 1908	LGH 15/153–4
251	Mahan to Laughton	5 December 1908	LGH 15/155–6
252	Scargill-Bird to Laughton	27 May 1910	LGH 4
253	Kenyon to Laughton	24 June 1910	NMM: NRS/1
254	Laughton to Keltie	16 September 1910	RGS: Laughton File
255	Mahan to Laughton	15 November 1910	LGH 15/157–8
256	Seymour to Laughton	23 January 1911	LGH 54
257	Mahan to Laughton	17 November 1911	LGH 16/159–61
258	Mahan to Laughton	17 June 1912	LGH 16/162–3
259	Mahan to Laughton	23 July 1912	LGH 16/164–5
260	Laughton to Napier Robinson	10 September 1912	NMM: Napier Robinson Mss.
261	Mahan to Laughton	24 October 1912	LGH 16/166
262	Mahan to Laughton	20 November 1912	LGH 16/168
263	Mahan to Laughton	21 November 1912	LGH 16/169
264	Mahan to Laughton	23 November 1912	LGH 16/170
265	Temperley to Laughton	15 March 1913	LGH 2
266	Mahan to Laughton	24 March 1913	LGH 15/138
267	Laughton to Greene	20 July 1913	NMM: NRS/3
268	Laughton Lecture Notes	8 October 1913	LGH 37
269	Mahan to Laughton	14 May 1914	LGH 16/171–3
270	Laughton Notes on Draft Manuscript	2 June 1914	LGH 44
271	Bridge to Laughton	6 July 1914	LGH 7/66–7
272	Mahan to Laughton	24 August 1914	LGH 16/174–5
273	Laughton, Draft Obituary of Mahan	December 1914	LGH 16/177–9
274	Laughton to Smith	7 February 1915	KCL: KA/IC/L77
275	Laughton to Smith	16 June 1915	KCL: KA/IC/L77

6 SIR JOHN KNOX LAUGHTON'S UNFINISHED NAVAL HISTORY OF ENGLAND

| 276 | 'The Interdependence of England's Naval and Political History' | n.d. | LGH 44 |

APPENDIX 2

LIST OF ARCHIVES FROM WHICH DOCUMENTS ARE DERIVED

Public Record Office, Kew, England

Admiralty Papers (ADM):

ADM 53   Ship's Logs, various
ADM 196/81 Laughton's Service Record
ADM 203   The Royal Naval College at Greenwich

National Maritime Museum, Greenwich, England

Laughton MS. Laughton's papers were deposited in 1979 by his grandson. They have just been catalogued as LGH in 57 numbered sections. The full list is available from the Museum.
There are also some notebooks, that were deposited by Leonard Carr Laughton, who had used them extensively.

Other collections in the NMM that were used:

Cyprian A.G. Bridge
William Laird Clowes Ms.93/001
Julian S. Corbett
Geoffrey T. P. Hornby
Charles N. Robinson

The Archive of the Navy Records Society is held on deposit at the Museum. The early minute books contain much information on the nature and composition of the navalist movement before the First World War.

The Archives of King's College, London

Laughton files, concerning his appointment and correspondence during his time at King's College

Naval Historical Branch, Whitehall, London

The John Laughton Pamphlet Collection: bound up by W.G. Perrin in 1916

King's College, Cambridge

Oscar Browning Mss.
King's College Mss.

The Bodleian Library, Oxford

Sidney Lee Mss. (including material belonging to Leslie Stephen concerning the *DNB*)
Bridges Mss.

The University of London Palaeography Room Senate House

Sir John Seeley Mss.

The British Library, Manuscript Division

Althorp MS. Papers of the 5th Earl Spencer
Sir Charles Dilke Mss.

The Royal Geographical Society, London

Society Archives, Minute Books, etc.
Papers and ms. Journal of Sir Clements Markham

Library of the Royal Military College, Kingston, Ontario

Sir John Laughton's personal bound collection of his articles, 3 volumes

Library of Congress, Washington DC

Papers of Alfred Thayer Mahan
Papers of Stephen Bleecker Luce

APPENDIX 3

THE PUBLISHED WORKS OF
SIR JOHN KNOX LAUGHTON

Physical Geography in its Relation to the Prevailing Winds and Currents (J.D. Potter, London, 1870; 2nd edition, 1873).

An Introduction to the Practical and Theoretical Study of Nautical Surveying (Longman, Green & Co., London, 1872; 2nd edition London, 1882).

Essay on Naval Tactics (Griffin & Co., Portsmouth, 1873). Commonly bound with Commander Gerard U. Noel, *The Gun, Ram, and Torpedo* (2nd edition, 1885).

At Home and Abroad; or First Lessons in Geography (London, 1878).

Studies in Naval History (Longmans, London, 1887; 2nd edition, J.J. Keliher, London 1896; reprinted by Conway Maritime Press, London 1970).

Nelson (MacMillan, London and New York, 1889, reprinted 1904; part of the 'English Men of Action' Series, illustrated edition 1900; reprinted 1905).

The Story of Trafalgar (Griffin & Co., Portsmouth, 1891).

The Story of the Sea, with W.L. Clowes, A. Quiller-Couch, H.O. Arnold-Forster and H.W. Wilson (Cassell, London 1895–96; 2nd edition 1897–98).

The Nelson Memorial: Nelson and his Companions in Arms (George Allen, London, 1896; 2nd edition 1899).

Nelson and his Companions in Arms, pocket format edition (George Allen, London, 1905). Omits the critical bibliography of 1896 edition.

Memoirs of the Life and Correspondence of Henry Reeve (Longmans, Green, and Co., London, 1898, 2 volumes; 2nd edition, 1898).

From Howard to Nelson: Twelve Sailors (London, William Heinemann, 1899; 2nd edition, London, 1907; 3rd edition, as *British Sailor Heroes*, adapted from the original edition, with 48 illustrations and maps, London, 1913; 4th edition, as *England's Sailor Heroes*, London, 1922, without attributions of the other authors, and with the editor now identified the sole author and named as T. Knox Laughton).

Sea Fights and Adventures (London, 1901, in 'The Young England Library'; 2nd edition, 1907).

The Pocket Life of Nelson, reprinted from the *Dictionary of National Biography* (The 1805 Club, London, 1993).

CONTRIBUTIONS TO BOOKS WRITTEN BY OTHER AUTHORS

'Introduction' to R. Southey, *The Life of Lord Nelson* (Cassell & Co., London, 1891).

'On Convoy', in *Brassey's Naval Annual 1894* (Brassey, London, 1894), pp. 225–41.

'The National Study of Naval History', in *Transactions of the Royal Historical Society*, XII (London, 1898), pp. 81–93.

'Britain's Naval Policy', in *Lectures on History in the Nineteenth Century*, ed. F.A. Kirkpatrick (Cambridge University Press, 1903), pp.59–78.

'The Elizabethan Naval War with Spain', in *The Cambridge Modern History III*, ed. A.W. Ward, G.W. Prothero and S. Leathes (Cambridge University Press, 1907), pp. 294–327.

'Historians and Naval History', *The Cornhill Magazine*, New Series XXXV (1913), pp. 33–43. Reprinted in *Naval and Military Essays*, ed. Julian S. Corbett (Cambridge University Press, 1914), pp. 3–22.

EDITED HISTORICAL DOCUMENTS

Letters and Despatches of Horatio, Viscount Nelson (Longman, Green & Co., London, 1886).

Memoirs relating to the Lord Torrington (Publications of the Camden Society, Vol. XLVI, London, 1889).

State Papers Relating to the Defeat of the Spanish Armada, 2 volumes (NRS, London, 1894; 2nd edition 1895; 3rd edition, Kenneth Mason, Portsmouth, 1981; 4th edition, in one volume, Temple Smith, Aldershot, 1987).

Journal of Rear Admiral Bartholomew James, 1752–1828, with J.Y.F. Sullivan (NRS, London, 1896).

The Naval Miscellany Volume One (NRS, London, 1902; reprinted Temple Smith, Aldershot, 1982).

Report on the Manuscripts of Florence Victoria, Lady Du Cane (HMC, London, 1906).

The Recollections of Commander James Anthony Gardner, 1775–1814, with Admiral Sir Richard Vesey-Hamilton (NRS, London, 1906).

Letters and Papers of Charles, Lord Barham, 3 volumes (NRS,

London, 1907, 1910, 1912; all 3 reprinted Temple Smith, Aldershot, 1984).

The Naval Miscellany Volume Two (NRS, London, 1912; reprinted Temple Smith, Aldershot, 1982).

Manuscripts of and relating to Admiral Lord Nelson (London, 1913).

CONTRIBUTIONS TO PERIODICALS

ST = reprinted in *Studies in Naval History*.

'The Sovereignty of the Sea', *The Fortnightly Review*, **V** (August, 1866), pp. 718–33.

'Le Bailli de Suffren', *United Service Magazine* (May and June, 1867). ST.

'An Inquiry into the Evidence on which the Theory of the Circulation of the Atmosphere is based', *Philosophical Magazine*, **XXXIV** (November, 1867), pp. 359–65.

'On the Natural Forces that produce the Permanent and Periodical Winds', *Philosophical Magazine*, **XXXIV** (December, 1867), pp. 443–9.

'Colbert: The birth of a Navy', *St Paul's Magazine* (December, 1868), pp. 342–57. ST.

'On Atmospheric Currents', *Symonds Meteorological Magazine*, **V** (1870), pp. 158–60.

'On the Great Currents of the Atmosphere', *British Association Report*, **XL** (1870), p. 170.

'Sketches in Naval History', *St Paul's Magazine* (October, 1870), pp. 51–65.

'Ocean Currents', *JRUSI*, **XV** (1871).

'Barometric Differences and Fluctuations', *Philosophical Magazine* (May 1871), pp. 325–63.

'Land and Sea Breezes', *The Proceedings of the Junior Naval Professional Association*, Part II (Portsmouth, 1873), pp. 75–90.

'Land and Sea Breezes', *Quarterly Journal of Meteorology*, **I** (1873), p. 203.

'Nautical Meteorology, Parts I, II, and III', *Naval Science* (1874 and 1875).

'Nautical Meteorology, Part IV', *Van Nostrand's Engineering Magazine*, **XII** (1875), pp. 72–80.

'On Diurnal Variations of the Barometer', *Quarterly Journal of Meteorology*, **II** (1874), pp. 155–64.

'The Scientific Study of Naval History', *JRUSI*, **XVIII** (1874), pp. 508–27.

'Du Quesne: The French Navy in the Seventeenth Century', *Fraser's Magazine* (November, 1874), pp. 638–53. ST.

'Scientific Instruction in the Royal Navy', *JRUSI*, **XIX** (1875), pp. 217–41.

'The Venetian Navy in the Sixteenth Century', *Fraser's Magazine* (October 1875), pp. 483–500.

'Changes of Climate', *British Quarterly Review* (1 October, 1876).

'The French Privateers: III Thurot', *Fraser's Magazine* (January, 1878), pp. 71–88. ST.

'Paul Jones. "The Pirate"', *Fraser's Magazine* (April, 1878), pp. 501–22. ST.

'Tegetthoff: Experiences of Steam and Armour', *Fraser's Magazine* (June, 1878), pp. 671–92. ST.

'Weather Forecasting', *Fraser's Magazine* (August, 1879), pp. 242–54.

'The Heraldry of the Sea:– Ensigns, Colours and Flags', *JRUSI*, **XXIV** (1880), pp. 116–48.

'Naval Promotion, Arithmetically and Historically Considered', *JRUSI*, **XXIV** (1880), pp.535–60.

'On the Several Systems of European Naval Education', *JRUSI*, **XXIV** (1880), pp. 108–29.

'Law of Storms and Heaving-to Tack', *Nautical Magazine* (September, 1880).

'Jean de Vienne: A Chapter from the Naval History of the Fourteenth Century', *United Service Magazine* (October, 1880). ST.

'Henry John Codrington, Admiral of the Fleet', *Fraser's Magazine* (January, 1881), pp. 73–86.

'Our Winter Storms', *Fraser's Magazine* (June, 1881), pp.758–70.

'Privateers and Privateering: I Fortunatus Wright', *Fraser's Magazine* (October, 1881), pp. 462–78. ST.

'Privateers and Privateering: II George Walker', *Fraser's Magazine* (November, 1881), pp. 589–623. ST.

'The French Privateers: I Jean Bart', *Fraser's Magazine* (March, 1882), pp. 343–60. ST.

'Naval Education', *JRUSI*, **XXVI** (1882), pp. 339–68.

'The French Privateers: II Du Guay-Trouin', *Fraser's Magazine* (April, 1882), pp. 498–518. ST.

'The French Privateers: IV Robert Surcouf', *United Service Magazine* (February/March, 1883). ST.

'Historical Sketch of Anemometry and Anemometers', *Quarterly Journal of the Royal Meteorological Society*, **VIII** (July, 1882), pp. 161–89.

'Presidential Address', *Quarterly Journal of the Meteorological Society*, **IX** (January, 1883), pp. 71–83.

'Wind Force and how it is measured', *Longman's Magazine*, **I** (April, 1883), pp. 615–27.

'Presidential Address', *Quarterly Journal of the Royal Meteorological Society*, **X** (April, 1884), pp. 77–87.

'Notes on the Last Great Naval War', *JRUSI*, **XXIX** (1885), pp. 909–33.

'The Invincible Armada', Lecture to the Royal Institution 1888.

'Nelson's last Codicil', *Colburn's United Service Magazine*, **II**: Part 1 'The Spanish War' (November, 1888–April, 1889), pp. 647–62; **III**, Part 2 'The Watering the Fleet' (May, 1889–Oct, 1889), pp. 10–23.

'The Captains of the Nightingale', *EHR*, **IV** (January, 1889), pp. 65–80.

'Jenkins's Ear', *EHR*, **IV** (October, 1889), pp. 741–9.

'The Early Development of Naval War', *Colburn's United Service Magazine*: Part 1 (September, 1889), pp. 523–37; Part 2 (October 1889), pp. 683–99.

'Beachy Head', *Army and Navy Gazette* (1890).

'Our Naval Literature', 12 parts, *The Army and Navy Gazette* (1892–3), pp. 70, 119, 198, 275, 291–2, 459, 479, 679, 732, 840, 986, 1131. Part two entitled 'New Lights on the Old Navy'.

'Barfleur and la Hogue', *The Army and Navy Gazette* (19 May, 1892), pp. 437–8.

'Recent Naval Literature', *JRUSI*, **XXXVII** (November, 1893), pp. 1161–82.

'Thirty Years Since', *St Andrews Magazine*: 'Beyrout' (April, 1894), pp. 82–7; 'Naples' (May, 1894), pp. 98–102; 'Corfu' (June, 1894), pp. 128–36. Taken from Laughton's notebooks of 1861–62.

'Sir George Rooke', *JRUSI*, **XXXIX** (April, 1895), pp. 328–32.

'The Battle of the Nile: an Anniversary Study', *Cornhill Magazine*, **LXXIV** (1896), pp. 147–58.

'The Study of Naval History', *JRUSI*, **XXXX** (1896), pp. 795–820.

'Our Navy Records', *Navy and Army Illustrated* (29 May, 1896).

'Nelson at Naples', *The Athenaeum*, no. 3748 (26 August, 1899).

'The Naval Exhibition at the Hague', *The Monthly Review* (November, 1900), pp. 67–82.

'Nelson's Home at Merton', *Wimbledon and Merton Annual* (1903), pp. 32–44.

Introductory Notice for the Society for Nautical Research, *USNIP* (1910, part 2), p. 636.

'Historians and Naval History', *Cornhill Magazine*, New Series XXXV (1913), pp. 33–43.

BOOK REVIEWS

Almost all of Laughtons' major book reviews were written for the *Edinburgh Review* (*ER*), with three in the *Quarterly Review* (*QR*). These took the form of long, usually multi-volume, notices, with a significant contribution by the reviewer, including source references and substantial argument. The following are Laughton's own short titles, written out in his own hand in the volumes held by the Royal Military Academy, Kingston, Ontario.

Arctic Exploration	*ER*, April 1875
Lindsay's 'Merchant Shipping'	*ER*, April 1876
New Arctic Lands	*ER*, January 1877
Charles Kingsley	*ER*, April 1877
Low's 'Indian Navy'	*ER*, October 1878
The King's Secret	*ER*, April 1879
Reign of Queen Anne	*ER*, April 1880
Pepys Diary	*ER*, July 1880
Trevelyan's Charles James Fox	*ER*, October 1880
Gustavus III	*ER*, July 1881
The Bonapartes	*ER*, January 1882
Brassey on the British Navy	*ER*, April 1882
Baron de Stael	*ER*, January 1883
Frederic II & Maria Theresa	*ER*, April 1883
Vicksburg & Gettysburg (Mahan)	*ER*, October 1883
John de Witt	*ER*, October 1884
The State of the Navy	*ER*, April 1885
Naval Warfare	*ER*, July 1885
Frederic II & Louis XV	*ER*, October 1885
Hobart Pasha	*Longman's Magazine*, **IX**, (November 1886).
A French Corsair	*ER*, April 1888
Stratford de Redcliffe	*ER*, January 1889
Maria Theresa	*ER*, July 1889
Naval Supremacy & Naval Tactics	*ER*, January 1890
Mahan on Maritime Power	*ER*, October 1890
Forts and Fleets	*QR*, April 1891
Austria in 1848–9	*ER*, October 1891
Rodney & the 18th Century Navy	*ER*, January 1892

Baron de Marbot	*QR*, January 1892
Marshal de Saxe	*ER*, October 1892
Mahan on Maritime Power	*ER*, April 1893
Battle of La Hogue and Maritime War	*QR*, April 1893
Sir Richard Burton	*ER*, October 1893
Naval Armaments	*ER*, April 1894
Naval War in the East	*ER*, October 1894
Weather Prevision	*ER*, April 1895
History of Spain	*ER*, October 1895
House of Conde	*ER*, January 1896
Emma, Lady Hamilton	*ER*, April 1896
Gunpowder Plot	*ER*, January 1897
Mahan's Nelson	*ER*, July 1897
Duke of Grafton	*ER*, April 1899
Peasants' Rising	*ER*, January 1900
Goldwin Smith's United Kingdom	*ER*, July 1900
Corbett's 'Drake'	*ER*, July 1901
The French in Egypt	*ER*, October 1901
Holland-Rose's Napoleon	*ER*, April 1902
Mastery of the Pacific	*ER*, July 1902
Blockade of Brest/Desbriere	*ER*, January 1903
Charles V	*ER*, April 1903
Siege of Quebec	*ER*, July 1903
John Moore	*ER*, July 1904
'The American Revolution'	*The National Review*, March 1904
Corbett's 'England and the Mediterranean'	*ER*, July 1904
Typhoons & Cyclones	*ER*, January 1905
Naples and Napoleon	*ER*, October 1905
Centenary of Trafalgar	*QR*, October 1905
Holland's Whig Party	*ER*, July 1906
Acton's Lectures	*ER*, April 1907
Desbriere's 1805	*ER*, October 1907
The French in Egypt II	*ER*, July 1908
Paston Letters	*ER*, October 1908
Firth's Protectorate	*ER*, April 1910
Malta	*ER*, July 1910
Tudor King's	*ER*, January 1911
Sovereignty of the Seas	*ER*, October 1911
Holland Rose's Pitt	*ER*, January 1912
Sandwich	*ER*, October 1912

Readers requiring further bibliographical information should consult: A.D. Lambert, *The Foundations of Naval History: Sir John Laughton, the Royal Navy and the English Historical Profession* (Chatham Publishing, London, 1998).

INDEX

NAVY RECORDS SOCIETY
(FOUNDED 1893)

The Navy Records Society was established for the purpose of printing unpublished manuscripts and rare works of naval interest. Membership of the Society is open to all who are interested in naval history, and any person wishing to become a member should apply to the Hon. Secretary, Professor A. D. Lambert, Department of War Studies, King's College London, Strand, London WC2R 2LS, United Kingdom. The annual subscription is £30, which entitles the member to receive one free copy of each work issued by the Society in that year, and to buy earlier issues at reduced prices.

A list of works, available to members only, is shown below; very few copies are left of those marked with an asterisk. Volumes out of print are indicated by **OP**. Prices for works in print are available on application to Mrs Annette Gould, 5 Goodwood Close, Midhurst, West Sussex GU29 9JG, United Kingdom, to whom all enquiries concerning works in print should be sent. Those marked 'TS', 'SP' and 'A' are published for the Society by Temple Smith, Scolar Press and Ashgate, and are available to non-members from the Ashgate Publishing Group, Gower House, Croft Road, Aldershot, Hampshire GU11 3HR. Those marked 'A & U' are published by George Allen & Unwin, and are available to non-members only through bookshops.

Vol. 8. *Naval Accounts and Inventories in the Reign of Henry VII*, ed. M. Oppenheim. **OP**.

Vol. 9. *Journal of Sir George Rooke*, ed. O. Browning. **OP**.

Vol. 10. *Letters and Papers relating to the War with France 1512–1513*, ed. M. Alfred Spont. **OP**.

Vol. 11. *Papers relating to the Spanish War 1585–1587*, ed. Julian S. Corbett. TS.

Vol. 12. *Journals and Letters of Admiral of the Fleet Sir Thomas Byam Martin, 1773–1854*, Vol. II (see No. 24), ed. Admiral Sir R. Vesey Hamilton. **OP**.

Vol. 13. *Papers relating to the First Dutch War, 1652–1654*, Vol. I, ed. Dr S. R. Gardiner. **OP**.

Vol. 14. *Papers relating to the Blockade of Brest, 1803–1805*, Vol. I, ed. J. Leyland. **OP**.

Vol. 15. *History of the Russian Fleet during the Reign of Peter the Great, by a Contemporary Englishman*, ed. Admiral Sir Cyprian Bridge. **OP**.

*Vol. 16. *Logs of the Great Sea Fights, 1794–1805*, Vol. I, ed. Vice Admiral Sir T. Sturges Jackson.

Vol. 17. *Papers relating to the First Dutch War, 1652–1654*, ed. Dr S. R. Gardiner. **OP**.

*Vol. 18. *Logs of the Great Sea Fights*, Vol. II, ed. Vice Admiral Sir T. Sturges Jackson.

Vol. 19. *Journals and Letters of Admiral of the Fleet Sir Thomas Byam Martin*, Vol. II (see No. 24), ed. Admiral Sir R. Vesey Hamilton. **OP**.

Vol. 20. *The Naval Miscellany*, Vol. I, ed. Professor J. K. Laughton.

Vol. 21. *Papers relating to the Blockade of Brest, 1803–1805*, Vol. II, ed. J. Leyland. **OP**.

Vol. 22. *The Naval Tracts of Sir William Monson*, Vol. I, ed. M. Oppenheim. **OP**.

Vol. 23. *The Naval Tracts of Sir William Monson*, Vol. II, ed. M. Oppenheim. **OP**.

Vol. 24. *The Journals and Letters of Admiral of the Fleet Sir Thomas Byam Martin*, Vol. I, ed. Admiral Sir R. Vesey Hamilton. **OP**.

Vol. 25. *Nelson and the Neapolitan Jacobins*, ed. H. C. Gutteridge. **OP**.

Vol. 26. *A Descriptive Catalogue of the Naval MSS in the Pepysian Library*, Vol. I, ed. J. R. Tanner. **OP**.

Vol. 27. *A Descriptive Catalogue of the Naval MSS in the Pepysian Library*, Vol. II, ed. J. R. Tanner. **OP**.

Vol. 28. *The Correspondence of Admiral John Markham, 1801–1807*, ed. Sir Clements R. Markham. **OP**.

Vol. 29. *Fighting Instructions, 1530–1816*, ed. Julian S. Corbett. **OP**.

Vol. 30. *Papers relating to the First Dutch War, 1652–1654*, Vol. III, ed. Dr S. R. Gardiner & C. T. Atkinson. **OP**.

Vol. 31. *The Recollections of Commander James Anthony Gardner, 1775–1814*, ed. Admiral Sir R. Vesey Hamilton & Professor J. K. Laughton.

Vol. 32. *Letters and Papers of Charles, Lord Barham, 1758–1813*, ed. Professor Sir John Laughton.

Vol. 33. *Naval Songs and Ballads*, ed. Professor C. H. Firth. **OP**.

Vol. 34. *Views of the Battles of the Third Dutch War*, ed. by Julian S. Corbett. **OP**.

Vol. 35. *Signals and Instructions, 1776–1794*, ed. Julian S. Corbett **OP**.

Vol. 36. *A Descriptive Catalogue of the Naval MSS in the Pepysian Library*, Vol III, ed. J. R. Tanner. **OP**.

Vol. 37. *Papers relating to the First Dutch War, 1652–1654*, Vol. IV, ed. C. T. Atkinson. **OP**.

Vol. 38. *Letters and Papers of Charles, Lord Barham, 1758–1813*, Vol. II, ed. Professor Sir John Laughton.

Vol. 39. *Letters and Papers of Charles, Lord Barham, 1758–1813*, Vol. III, ed. Professor Sir John Laughton.

Vol. 40. *The Naval Miscellany*, Vol. II, ed. Professor Sir John Laughton.

*Vol. 41. *Papers relating to the First Dutch War, 1652–1654*, Vol. V, ed. C. T. Atkinson.

*Vol. 42. *Papers relating to the Loss of Minorca in 1756*, ed. Captain H. W. Richmond, R.N.

*Vol. 43. *The Naval Tracts of Sir William Monson*, Vol. III, ed. M. Oppenheim.

Vol. 44. *The Old Scots Navy 1689–1710*, ed. James Grant. **OP**.

Vol. 45. *The Naval Tracts of Sir William Monson*, Vol. IV, ed. M. Oppenheim.

*Vol. 46. *The Private Papers of George, 2nd Earl Spencer*, Vol. I, ed. Julian S. Corbett.

Vol. 47. *The Naval Tracts of Sir William Monson*, Vol. V, ed. M. Oppenheim.

Vol. 48. *The Private Papers of George, 2nd Earl Spencer*, Vol. II, ed. Julian S. Corbett. **OP**.

*Vol. 49. *Documents relating to Law and Custom of the Sea*, Vol. II, ed. R. G. Marsden.

*Vol. 50. *Documents relating to Law and Custom of the Sea*, Vol. II, ed. R. G. Marsden.

Vol. 51. *Autobiography of Phineas Pett*, ed. W. G. Perrin. **OP**.

Vol. 52. *The Life of Admiral Sir John Leake*, Vol. I, ed. Geoffrey Callender.

Vol. 53. *The Life of Admiral Sir John Leake*, Vol. II, ed. Geoffrey Callender.

Vol. 54. *The Life and Works of Sir Henry Mainwaring*, Vol. I, ed. G. E. Manwaring.

Vol. 55. *The Letters of Lord St Vincent, 1801–1804*, Vol. I, ed. D. B. Smith. **OP**.

Vol. 56. *The Life and Works of Sir Henry Mainwaring*, Vol. II, ed. G. E. Manwaring & W. G. Perrin. **OP**.

Vol. 57. *A Descriptive Catalogue of the Naval MSS in the Pepysian Library*, Vol. IV, ed. Dr J. R. Tanner. **OP**.

Vol. 58. *The Private Papers of George, 2nd Earl Spencer*, Vol. III, ed. Rear Admiral H. W. Richmond. **OP**.

Vol. 59. *The Private Papers of George, 2nd Earl Spencer*, Vol. IV, ed. Rear Admiral H. W. Richmond. **OP**.

Vol. 60. *Samuel Pepys's Naval Minutes*, ed. Dr J. R. Tanner.

Vol. 61. *The Letters of Lord St Vincent, 1801–1804*, Vol. II, ed. D. B. Smith. **OP**.

Vol. 62. *Letters and Papers of Admiral Viscount Keith*, Vol. I, ed. W. G. Perrin. **OP**.

Vol. 63. *The Naval Miscellany*, Vol. III, ed. W. G. Perrin. **OP**.

Vol. 64. *The Journal of the 1st Earl of Sandwich*, ed. R. C. Anderson. **OP**.

*Vol. 65. *Boteler's Dialogues*, ed. W. G. Perrin.

Vol. 66. *Papers relating to the First Dutch War, 1652–1654*, Vol. VI (with index), ed. C. T. Atkinson.

*Vol. 67. *The Byng Papers*, Vol. I, ed. W. C. B. Tunstall.

*Vol. 68. *The Byng Papers*, Vol. II, ed. W. C. B. Tunstall.

*Vol. 69. *The Private Papers of John, Earl of Sandwich*, Vol. I, ed. G. R. Barnes & Lt. Cdr. J. H. Owen, R.N. **OP**. Corrigenda to *Papers relating to the First Dutch War, 1652–1654, Vols I–VI*, ed. Captain A. C. Dewar, R.N.

Vol. 70. *The Byng Papers*, Vol. III, ed. W. C. B. Tunstall.

Vol. 71. *The Private Papers of John, Earl of Sandwich*, Vol. II, ed. G. R. Barnes & Lt. Cdr. J. H. Owen, R.N. **OP**.

Vol. 72. *Piracy in the Levant, 1827–1828*, ed. Lt. Cdr. C. G. Pitcairn Jones, R.N. **OP**.

Vol. 73. *The Tangier Papers of Samuel Pepys*, ed. Edwin Chappell.

*Vol. 74. *The Tomlinson Papers*, ed. J. G. Bullocke.

Vol. 75. *The Private Papers of John, Earl of Sandwich*, Vol. III, ed. G. R. Barnes & Cdr. J. H. Owen, R.N. **OP**.

Vol. 76. *The Letters of Robert Blake*, ed. the Rev. J. R. Powell. **OP**.

*Vol. 77. *Letters and Papers of Admiral the Hon. Samuel Barrington*, Vol. I, ed. D. Bonner-Smith.

Vol. 78. *The Private Papers of John, Earl of Sandwich*, Vol. IV, ed. G. R. Barnes & Cdr. J. H. Owen, R.N. **OP**.

*Vol. 79. *The Journals of Sir Thomas Allin, 1660–1678*, Vol. I (1660–1666), ed. R. C. Anderson.

Vol. 80. *The Journals of Sir Thomas Allin, 1660–1678*, Vol. II (1667–1678), ed. R. C. Anderson.

Vol. 81. *Letters and Papers of Admiral the Hon. Samuel Barrington*, Vol. II, ed. D. Bonner-Smith. **OP**.

Vol. 82. *Captain Boteler's Recollections, 1808–1830*, ed. D. Bonner-Smith. **OP**.

Vol. 83. *Russian War, 1854. Baltic and Black Sea: Official Correspondence*, ed. D. Bonner-Smith & Captain A. C. Dewar, R.N. **OP**.

Vol. 84. *Russian War, 1855. Baltic: Official Correspondence*, ed. D. Bonner-Smith. **OP**.

Vol. 85. *Russian War, 1855. Black Sea: Official Correspondence*, ed. Captain A.C. Dewar, R.N. **OP**.

Vol. 86. *Journals and Narratives of the Third Dutch War*, ed. R. C. Anderson. **OP**.

Vol. 87. *The Naval Brigades in the Indian Mutiny, 1857–1858*, ed. Cdr. W. B. Rowbotham, R.N. **OP**.

Vol. 88. *Patee Byng's Journal*, ed. J. L. Cranmer-Byng. **OP**.

*Vol. 89. *The Sergison Papers, 1688–1702*, ed. Cdr. R. D. Merriman, R.I.N.

Vol. 90. *The Keith Papers*, Vol. II, ed. Christopher Lloyd. **OP**.

Vol. 91. *Five Naval Journals, 1789–1817*, ed. Rear Admiral H. G. Thursfield. **OP**.

Vol. 92. *The Naval Miscellany*, Vol. IV, ed. Christopher Lloyd. **OP**.

Vol. 93. *Sir William Dillon's Narrative of Professional Adventures, 1790–1839*, Vol. I (1790–1802), ed. Professor Michael Lewis. **OP**.

Vol. 94. *The Walker Expedition to Quebec, 1711*, ed. Professor Gerald S. Graham. **OP**.

Vol. 95. *The Second China War, 1856–1860*, ed. D. Bonner-Smith & E. W. R. Lumby. **OP**.

Vol. 96. *The Keith Papers, 1803–1815*, Vol. III, ed. Professor Christopher Lloyd.

Vol. 97. *Sir William Dillon's Narrative of Professional Adventures, 1790–1839*, Vol. II (1802–1839), ed. Professor Michael Lewis. **OP**.

Vol. 98. *The Private Correspondence of Admiral Lord Collingwood*, ed. Professor Edward Hughes. **OP**.

Vol. 99. *The Vernon Papers, 1739–1745*, ed. B. McL. Ranft. **OP**.

Vol. 100. *Nelson's Letters to his Wife and Other Documents*, ed. Lt. Cdr. G. P. B. Naish, R.N.V.R. **OP**.

Vol. 101. *A Memoir of James Trevenen, 1760–1790*, ed. Professor Christopher Lloyd & R. C. Anderson. **OP**.

Vol. 102. *The Papers of Admiral Sir John Fisher*, Vol. I, ed. Lt. Cdr. P. K. Kemp, R.N. **OP**.

Vol. 103. *Queen Anne's Navy*, ed. Cdr. R. D. Merriman, R.I.N. **OP**.

Vol. 104. *The Navy and South America, 1807–1823*, ed. Professor Gerald S. Graham & Professor R. A. Humphreys.

Vol. 105. *Documents relating to the Civil War, 1642–1648*, ed. The Rev. J. R. Powell & E. K. Timings. **OP**.

Vol. 106. *The Papers of Admiral Sir John Fisher*, Vol. II, ed. Lt. Cdr. P. K. Kemp, R.N. **OP**.

*Vol. 107. *The Health of Seamen*, ed. Professor Christopher Lloyd.

Vol. 108. *The Jellicoe Papers*, Vol. I (1893–1916), ed. A. Temple Patterson.

Vol. 109. *Documents relating to Anson's Voyage round the World, 1740–1744*, ed. Dr Glyndwr Williams. **OP**.

Vol. 110. *The Saumarez Papers: The Baltic, 1808–1812*, ed. A. N. Ryan. **OP**.

Vol. 111. *The Jellicoe Papers*, Vol. II (1916–1935), ed. Professor A. Temple Patterson.

Vol. 112. *The Rupert and Monck Letterbook, 1666*, ed. The Rev. J. R. Powell & E. K. Timings.

Vol. 113. *Documents relating to the Royal Naval Air Service*, Vol. I (1908–1918), ed. Captain S. W. Roskill, R.N.

*Vol. 114. *The Siege and Capture of Havana, 1762*, ed. Professor David Syrett.

Vol. 115. *Policy and Operations in the Mediterranean, 1912–1914*, ed. E. W. R. Lumby. **OP**.

Vol. 116. *The Jacobean Commissions of Enquiry, 1608 and 1618*, ed. Dr A. P. McGowan.

Vol. 117. *The Keyes Papers*, Vol. I (1914–1918), ed. Professor Paul Halpern.

Vol. 118. *The Royal Navy and North America: The Warren Papers, 1736–1752*, ed. Dr Julian Gwyn. **OP**.

Vol. 119. *The Manning of the Royal Navy: Selected Public Pamphlets, 1693–1873*, ed. Professor John Bromley.

Vol. 120. *Naval Administration, 1715–1750*, ed. Professor D. A. Baugh.

Vol. 121. *The Keyes Papers*, Vol. II (1919–1938), ed. Professor Paul Halpern.

Vol. 122. *The Keyes Papers*, Vol. III (1939–1945), ed. Professor Paul Halpern.

Vol. 123. *The Navy of the Lancastrian Kings: Accounts and Inventories of William Soper, Keeper of the King's Ships, 1422–1427*, ed. Dr Susan Rose.

Vol. 124. *The Pollen Papers: the Privately Circulated Printed Works of Arthur Hungerford Pollen, 1901–1916*, ed. Professor Jon T. Sumida. A. & U.

Vol. 125. *The Naval Miscellany*, Vol. V. ed. Dr N. A. M. Rodger. A & U.

Vol. 126. *The Royal Navy in the Mediterranean, 1915–1918*, ed. Professor Paul Halpern. TS.

Vol. 127. *The Expedition of Sir John Norris and Sir Francis Drake to Spain and Portugal, 1589*, ed. Professor R. B. Wernham. TS.

Vol. 128. *The Beatty Papers*, Vol. I (1902–1918), ed. Professor B. McL. Ranft. SP.

Vol. 129. *The Hawke Papers: A Selection, 1743–1771*, ed. Dr R. F. Mackay. SP.

Vol. 130. *Anglo-American Naval Relations, 1917–1919*, ed. Michael Simpson. SP.

Vol. 131. *British Naval Documents, 1204–1960*, ed. Professor John B. Hattendorf, Dr Roger Knight, Alan Pearsall, Dr Nicholas Rodger & Professor Geoffrey Till. SP.

Vol. 132. *The Beatty Papers*, Vol. II (1916–1927), ed. Professor B. McL. Ranft. SP

Vol. 133. *Samuel Pepys and the Second Dutch War*, transcribed by Professor William Matthews & Dr Charles Knighton; ed. Robert Latham. SP.

Vol. 134. *The Somerville Papers*, ed. Michael Simpson, with the assistance of John Somerville. SP.

Vol. 135. *The Royal Navy in the River Plate, 1806–1807*, ed. John D. Grainger. SP.

Vol. 136. *The Collective Naval Defence of the Empire, 1900–1940*, ed. Nicholas Tracy. A.

Vol. 137. *The Defeat of the Enemy Attack on Shipping, 1939–1945*, ed. Eric Grove. A.

Vol. 138. *Shipboard Life and Organisation, 1731–1815*, ed. Brian Lavery. A.

Vol. 139. *The Battle of the Atlantic and Signals Intelligence: U-boat Situations and Trends, 1941–1945*, ed. Professor David Syrett. A.

Vol. 140. *The Cunningham Papers*, Vol. I, *The Mediterranean Fleet, 1939–1942*, ed. Michael Simpson. A.

Vol. 141. *The Channel Fleet and the Blockade of Brest, 1793–1801*, ed. Roger Morriss. A.

Vol. 142. *The Submarine Service, 1900–1918*, ed. Nicholas Lambert. A.

Occasional Publications:

Vol. 1. *The Commissioned Sea Officers of the Royal Navy, 1660–1815*, ed. Professor David Syrett & Professor R. L. DiNardo. SP.

Vol. 2. *The Anthony Roll of Henry VIII's Navy*, ed. C. S. Knighton and D. M. Loades. A.